Sophia Studies in Cross-cultural Philosophy of Traditions and Cultures

Volume 30

The Sophia Studies in Cross-cultural Philosophy of Traditions and Cultures focuses on the broader aspects of philosophy and traditional intellectual patterns of religion and cultures. The series encompasses global traditions, and critical treatments that draw from cognate disciplines, inclusive of feminist, postmodern, and postcolonial approaches. By global traditions we mean religions and cultures that go from Asia to the Middle East to Africa and the Americas, including indigenous traditions in places such as Oceania. Of course this does not leave out good and suitable work in Western traditions where the analytical or conceptual treatment engages Continental (European) or Cross-cultural traditions in addition to the Judeo-Christian tradition. The book series invites innovative scholarship that takes up newer challenges and makes original contributions to the field of knowledge in areas that have hitherto not received such dedicated treatment. For example, rather than rehearsing the same old Ontological Argument in the conventional way, the series would be interested in innovative ways of conceiving the erstwhile concerns while also bringing new sets of questions and responses, methodologically also from more imaginative and critical sources of thinking. Work going on in the forefront of the frontiers of science and religion beaconing a well-nuanced philosophical response that may even extend its boundaries beyond the confines of this debate in the West – e.g. from the perspective of the 'Third World' and the impact of this interface (or clash) on other cultures, their economy, sociality, and ecological challenges facing them – will be highly valued by readers of this series. All books to be published in this Series will be fully peer-reviewed before final acceptance.

More information about this series at http://www.springer.com/series/8880

Peter Wong • Sherah Bloor
Patrick Hutchings • Purushottama Bilimoria
Editors

Considering Religions, Rights and Bioethics: For Max Charlesworth

Springer

Editors
Peter Wong
China Studies Research Centre
Latrobe University
Melbourne, VIC, Australia

Patrick Hutchings
SHAPS
The University of Melbourne
Melbourne, VIC, Australia

Sherah Bloor
Committee on the Study of Religion
Harvard University
Cambridge, MA, USA

Purushottama Bilimoria
School of Historical and Philosophical
Studies
University of Melbourne
Melbourne, Australia

Graduate Theological Union and
University of California
Berkeley, CA, USA

ISSN 2211-1107 ISSN 2211-1115 (electronic)
Sophia Studies in Cross-cultural Philosophy of Traditions and Cultures
ISBN 978-3-030-18147-5 ISBN 978-3-030-18148-2 (eBook)
https://doi.org/10.1007/978-3-030-18148-2

This Springer imprint is published by the registered company Springer Nature Switzerland AG.
The registered company address is: Gewerbestrasse 11, 6330 Cham, Switzerland

Max Charlesworth by Lewis Miller (courtesy of the Charlesworth family)

Introduction: Maxwell John Charlesworth AO FAHA, 1925–2014

Max Charlesworth, co-founder of *Sophia* with Graeme E. de Graaff in 1962, was Foundation Dean of Humanities at Deakin University from 1975 until 1980, when Weston Bate took over. Max was then Professor of Philosophy, Chair of the Professorial Board, and from time to time Acting Vice-Chancellor. He retired in 1990. Deakin in some ways resembled the Open University (OU) in the United Kingdom, being both a distance education and an open access institution. Like the OU, it had course teams writing the textbooks. This was managed without too much friction. Less than at the OU I gather. Max himself could sum up complex issues and write them up, plainly. Someone whom I know was on the Secretariat assisting Parliamentary Committees which sat to discuss various pressing issues. Max sent an invited submission to the committee on *Dying with Dignity*. The memorandum was clear, exhaustive, and elegantly concise: 'even the pollies could understand it!' The matter was controversial: Max's paper was at once incisive and so neatly put as not to offend persons unlikely to be of his opinion.

In controversy, Max was always polite, never at all shrill, but often ironic.

Max Charlesworth was a public intellectual, widely – and deeply – read, and a prolific author. He gave the Australian Broadcasting Corporation's Boyer Lectures – very prestigious – in 1989 on *Life, Death, Genes and Ethics*. Max was constantly being called on to give lectures: many of which were published, sometimes in pamphlet form, and sometimes in collections of essays. The public intellectual life was mirrored in the courses which Max devised for Deakin.

Charlesworth became interested in problems in Medical Ethics, 'getting up' a lot of technical information. There was no Deakin course on this. No doubt there would have been, but Deakin had no Medical School at that stage.

How Did Deakin Get to Be and to Be so Deakin?

Deakin was founded, in response to a local demand for a regional university, by the amalgamation of two already existing institutions: the Gordon Institute of Technology in downtown Geelong and a Teachers' Training College. 'The Gordon' had a small Humanities Department which merged into Humanities Deakin. I was delighted on first arriving in 1978 at the Waurn Ponds Campus – tiresomely inaccessible – to find that Deakin had an elegant necktie, blue (somewhere between Oxford and Cambridge blue) with little shields each with a Greek capital *delta* on it, in gold. I congratulated Max on this, but he said that the credit was due to Francis West, Dean of the *School of Social Sciences* and a classical scholar. The Gordon and the Training College came to be Deakin at the sharp point of the aspiring, Δ. The lecturers at Deakin, newcomers and the people from the older institutions, aspired too. We got on remarkably well, all in all, though the Education people tended rather to go on as before. The – new – Δ style was interdisciplinary, and this was not quite suitable for them.

Why Interdisciplinary?

The old boundaries between the 'subjects' to which people of Charlesworth's – and my – generation were accustomed were often there simply because they were convenient. By the end of the twentieth century, some of the fences were falling down. In the 'Information Age', there are flows and countercurrents of ideas: 'things fall apart', but *pace* Yeats, in a benign way, at least sometimes.

The key to the choice of mildly melding courses at Deakin lies in the width of Max's own interests. In addition, his PhD was from Louvain – as Gilbert Ryle once remarked to me – 'always a crossroads for ideas' – and Max was accustomed to the French *genre* of *haute vulgarisation*, defined in the *Micro Robert* dictionary as *le fait d'adapter un ensemble de connaissances … de manière à les render accessibles à un lecteur non spécialiste*. In Deakin English something like, 'give them an introduction from which they can go on to the harder stuff'. What was needed in the special circumstances of Deakin – its open access – was (a) neat introductions to topics and (b) good 'maps' forward. Everything we wrote courses on had somehow to start from (a) and encourage the going forward from (a). By and large we managed this. Deakin had a ration of very able undergraduates. Some students who looked unpromising turned out to be outstanding. Even the less able came away with widened horizons. And Deakin graduates found employment rather easily, despite coming from a very new university.

In the Beginning

Not being a foundation appointment myself, I do not know how the key topics for the first 'subjects' were negotiated. I moved from a 'Sandstone' to a very experimental Deakin in 1978, attracted by its novelty and promised excitement. By the time I got there, the course books – many of them – had already been written and published by the Deakin University Press. I recall Max was driving me somewhere soon after I joined Deakin. He was going to address some important meeting or others for an hour, leaving me in his car with *Images of Man*. This proved to involve existentialism and the notion of alienation, seen from both a Marxist viewpoint and from an Existentialist one. 'All', as Max used to say, '...sound of wind and limb'. It was very like a course on Sartre and Camus that I had taught elsewhere.

I was delighted to find that there was a course, led by Professor Weston Bate and Renata Howe, on *Australian Studies*. This was historical and geographical – 'Regionalism' – and involved some urbanology. As a 'foreigner' (born in New Zealand), I found this interesting and illuminating. I eventually contributed something on Australian Art, and from the undergraduate essays, of which I graded some, it was obvious that 'OzStuds' was very much to the taste of the students and of real use. With 1988 on its way, Australian nationalism needed to be addressed. And that without jingoism. Aboriginal religion was written into another course, so the invaders of the continent were not left entirely in spiritual possession of it.

This other course was something called *Religious Experience*. It was one on which, although I had never had such an experience, I taught. It raised such questions as: 'If I had a religious experience, would this be empirical proof of the existence of God?'; 'If I had such an experience, would it come in a culturally-determined form?'; 'Christ for Christians, Shiva or Kali for Hindus?'; and so on. Otto's *The Idea of the Holy*, William James' *Varieties of Religious* experience and the *Bhagavad Gītā* were on the reading list. And in Purushottama Bilimoria, we had someone who could read and explain Sanskrit texts. Nevertheless the introduction to the *Gītā* came in the form of an Indian comic book written for Indian children. The study guide and essays were not comic book responses. Max had a serious interest in Aboriginal Studies and much on Aboriginal Religions featured in the course. Doctrinal controversies were left to one side, prudently. If someone had claimed to have a religious experience, Thomas Merton or Carlos Casteñeda, they were on the same *empirical* footing. And so treated. There was another course based on a thesis that the *content*, not just the financing etc of science was socially constructed. With this, I agreed to differ.

In addition to lectures, for those on campus, course books, and essays, we had, especially for off-campus students, weekend schools which were usually with important speakers from outside Deakin. I remember some Buddhist priests, a Rabbi, and the Catholic mystic Brother David Steindl-Rast. Purushottama introduced some Hindu luminaries and notably Dom Bede Griffiths, a celebrated expert on Indian religion and culture, of whom a good story is told. In Rome as a tourist, he was summoned to an audience with the Pope: 'What do you do in India?' 'Oh, study Sanskrit, chant a bit with locals in temples; have *agapaic* meals with religious chaps, and so on.' 'But what about the Conversion of the heathen?' 'Oh, my dear, it goes on all the time, to and fro y'know, back and forth.' The reply of His Holiness nobody knows. Dom Bede was a very posh Englishman, the last man I heard pronounce the name of the subcontinent, 'Iṅjā'. The 'to and fro, back and forth' Max would have found most congenial as we all found Dom Bede.

Deakin was a 'continuous assessment' place, and one read rather a lot of essays. The policy was right: with open access, one needed to teach, in one's comments on the essays, both the subject and how to do an essay. Some students already wrote well, many needed help and some quite a lot.

Max Charlesworth and Religion

In 1936 *The Catholic Worker* had been founded by Kevin Kelly, Frank Maher and Bob Santamaria. Santamaria was eventually to become Max's *bête noir.* Max became involved in the paper in the 1940s and in the 1950s contributed from overseas. In the 1960s–1970s, he began attending editorial meetings to uphold the views of the left. Tony Coady joined Max on *The Catholic Worker* in 1971 and stayed until the paper folded in 1975. Santamaria – something of a zealot – gained the ear of the formidable Archbishop Daniel Mannix (1864–1963). Santamaria had not ill-founded fears that the communists were set to take over certain trade unions. He played very successfully on these fears with unfortunate consequences.

Santamaria was also something of a social conservative. The Labour Party split into the old Labour and the new Democratic Labour Party (DLP). This was a *retardataire* institution which kept Labour, the traditional party of Irish – and other – Catholics, out of office for a long time. Coming from a working social democratic country, New Zealand, I smelt mothballs each time I met a member of the DLP.

Max was a man of the – moderate – left in matters of religion and of politics, as his list of publications (see Appendix) testifies. A late book, *A Democratic Church: Reforming the Values and Institutions of the Catholic Church* (2008), addresses the role of Catholicism in an open and largely secular, multicultural society. And it reminds bureaucrats of the Catholic Church of the spirit of the Second Vatican Council (1962–1965) whose reforms and findings they had tended to wrap piously in pure linen napkins and religiously conserve in the cedar drawers of their sacristies.

In *The Catholic Worker* days, Max had been bidden to the palace of Archbishop Mannix. What transpired, Max didn't say, but he said that he still remembered faded wallpaper and the smell of dust and old men. Max did recall one of Mannix's *apparatchiks* telling him, 'What is in *The Worker* is not always in accord with the Mind of His Grace'. Max wondered, 'Is this Mind a separate or separable entity from the Archbishop?' But he told me that, at the time, he forbore to voice the point.

In 1970 Max was appointed to the Secretariat for Dialogue with Non-Believers, directly by the Vatican: this partly through the good offices of Don Miano who had a post there and had been one of Max's PhD supervisors at Louvain. Max had the tact, knowledge and empathy for such a job. Nevertheless, the local DLP-slanted hierarchy was scandalised at this endorsement of Max by the Vatican.

Though a left-of-centre thinker, Max was no pious follower of the then current ideology, 'the opium of the intelligentsia'. He recalled that he had friends in Paris who were Maoists and who drove Jaguar motorcars. I recall the irony in his voice and on his face as he told me this. When amused he had an oddly shark-like grin.

In hospital with TB, 1950–1952, Max did not re-read *The Magic Mountain*, instead a many-volumed history – in French – of the Catholic Church. He remarked, 'A very demystifying exercise indeed'.

I recall an Australian broadcasting service programme on which notable persons were asked about their favourite poets. Max's choice was wide. And I remember his reading Virgil, in Latin, in a very stylish way.

Max Charlesworth was very much a man of parts. In his retirement he told me that he had given away all of his books on Sanskrit. 'I think I'm too old to learn it now, but it has always been one of my projects.' When the ANU – or perhaps Canberra University – lost its lecturer in Ancient Philosophy, they flew him up from Melbourne twice a week to fill in. If – though busy – he could take this on, then why not Sanskrit?

The End of an Era for Deakin

Max and I co-wrote the course *Understanding Art*: two approaches ending up in an Aristotelian middle way – the way of virtue itself. In my time at Deakin, more courses were written, but the funding promised by the federal government to enable us to rewrite every 5 years never came through. The so-called university reforms blocked it. I stuck pins in a doll representing the then Minister for Education. It did not work.

Max and I in our retirements were supposed to write together a book on aesthetics. Like lots of good things, it didn't happen.

As an experiment, Deakin Humanities worked, and like any university in the late twentieth century and early twenty-first century, Deakin has now changed. New knowledge and new trends have to be caught before they whizz on by. Deakin is now much larger, and I suspect more like a standard Australian university than it was in my time there. But it was exciting to be there at the Big Bang!

When Max retired from Deakin in 1990, it felt as though some *petit fonctionnaire* had come in and switched off the lights. We had lost a man of *la plus grande distinction*.

***

I owe Max and his wife Stephanie a deep debt of gratitude for the forbearance and support which they gave me in an existential crisis in my own life.

***

Sophia, one of Max's best ideas, was originally run from the boot of his car and set up by a local printer. Max was the sole referee. It still flourishes, very much an international journal, published by Springer, Dordrecht, the house which issues the present volume. *Sophia* gets lots of interesting submissions, many canvassed by Purushottama Bilimoria, Sophia's indefatigable Editor-at-large, now at two universities in California: University of California (UC), Berkeley, and Graduate Theological Union. He is also an inveterate conference goer. All papers sent in to *Sophia* are duly refereed. Max would be pleased at the mix of philosophical, theological and religious dispositions of the people involved in getting the regular and the special issues of *Sophia* up and running. Of the current editorial team, two are from the Indian traditions, one is a Vatican II Catholic, and one is a student of contemporary religions and of medieval mysticism, and there is a Confucian-Zen practitioner: very 'Catholic', in the original, non-sectarian sense as it should be. Max himself was too Catholic for 'the Mind of the Archbishop'.

Two issues of *Sophia* have already honoured Max Charlesworth, the 1995 100th – Max having handed over his editorship to new incumbents; the second tribute issue was published in 2012. A few chapters of the present volume are drawn from the 2012 *Sophia*.

Preparation of this memorial volume began in early 2017. A few of us from *Sophia*, Purushottama Bilimoria, Patrick Hutchings, Peter Wong and Sherah Bloor, met in a Melbourne café, and the idea of putting together a collection of papers in memory of Max was raised. A list of possible persons to approach were drawn up – mostly those who have had association with Max or have written on topics to do with Max's various interests and involvements. Later, the Charlesworth family were also consulted about the project and their resounding support received.

Although Max Charlesworth was an influential writer – and person – there was no 'School of Max': he ran no line that people would inherit, stick to and propagate, no *école Max*. The essays in this volume are various – as various as the points of view of their authors. If any reader is looking for a unity – even a thematic one – hir expectations shall not be met. That is just the way it falls out. We remember Max but in different ways.

The volume is divided into four parts that are broadly to do with different aspects of Max's life and thought. Part I of this volume consists of contributions from those who have had a close personal association with Max. **Doug Kirsner**, who is a former student and colleague of Max, provides a comprehensive review of Max's intellectual contributions across a number of areas that reflect his involvement in academia, the Roman Catholic Church and significant public debates, especially in the field of bioethics. Kirsner offers insights into Max's intellectual life through exploring Max's publications, interviews and an unpublished memoir by Max.

Hilary Charlesworth recounts the experience of living with her father, the philosopher, which includes a richly detailed and intimate description of Max's earlier life that complements Kirsner's account. It both pays tribute to Max the father and provides personal context to Max the intellectual. **Alexander Linger** honours Max, his grandfather, by reflecting upon the nature of memory amidst his reminiscence of Max. Linger challenges certain accounts of memory understood as strictly personal, which he finds to be inadequate to describing his memory of Max, memory formed as a result of belonging to a family which include the memories of other members of the family. Linger posits his memory of Max is broader and richer than that conceived as episodic and direct. And finally, there are some remarks by the Reverend **Michael Elligate** on Max from his perspective as the Parish Priest of St Carthage's, Melbourne. St Carthage's is the home of Melbourne University's Catholic Chaplaincy. While pithy, this contribution reminds the reader to consider the extent to which Max's interests were motivated by his religious faith.

The chapters in Part II reflect Max's intellectual engagement to do with ethical issues within the liberal society, particularly in the field of bioethics. **Loane Skene** begins with an examination of the legacy of Max's book, *Bioethics in a Liberal Society,* in the area of human cloning and embryo research. More specifically, Skene is interested in exploring Max's contribution to decision-making in a liberal society in cases of controversial issues with divergent opinions within the community: How can public policies be formulated when there is no consensus in the community about what constitute its core values? The subsequent piece by **Jeff Malpas** acknowledges and critically reflects upon Max's development of contemporary bioethical thinking particularly to do with dying. Malpas questions whether the principle of autonomy and the notion of asserting control over one's life are adequate in addressing the issues which one faces at the end of life. For Malpas, the distinction of autonomy as a procedural principle renders it in effect an extreme expression of liberalism. **Tony Coady**'s article on the ethical thoughts of Bonhoeffer pays tribute to Max's significant contribution to the relations between religion, morality and politics. Coady focuses on Bonhoeffer's book *Ethics* and considers how the work raises question about the nature and significance of ethics. Moreover, it has implications for the notion of a Christian ethic. Crucially for Coady, doubts about an ethics that is uniquely Christian have to do with understanding the difference between morality and moralism, a distinction that finds support in Bonhoeffer's writings. This is followed by **Morny Joy**'s paper, delivered in 2015 at the Inaugural Max Charlesworth Memorial Lecture, at the Burwood campus of Deakin University. Her reflections on Paul Ricoeur and Hannah Arendt, whose writings emphasise the significance of paying attention to the world and the need to engage with it, reflect well Max's own concerns. Joy's paper covers many aspects of the continuity and discontinuity between the thoughts of Arendt and Ricoeur; discussions include Arendt's 'natality' and Ricoeur 'narrative self' and 'dialogical construction of the self'.

Part III celebrates the life of Max the philosopher. The first chapter reprints an article by **Max Charlesworth** that was published in *Sophia* in 1962. In this paper Max defends the cogency of Anselm's ontological argument and argues that it is deserving of attention. We note that this was subsequently followed by the publication of Max's translation of Anselm's *Proslogion* 3 years later. The next chapter is by **Richard Campbell** who writes on further developments of studies in Anselm's ontological argument and offers an innovative reading of the *Proslogion*, one which requires a re-evaluation of the logic of Anselm's argument. For Campbell, this involves, among other things, clarifying the premise to his so-called ontological argument. In the final analysis, Campbell concludes that Anselm's proof of the existence of God is not an ontological argument but in fact a cosmological argument. **Maurita Harney**'s contribution on the concept of "intentionality" highlights a theme that recalls Max's interest in continental and medieval philosophy. Harney defends a view of intentionality as embodied and rejects Cartesian dualism which renders intentionality purely subjective. This understanding of intentionality is articulated in the early philosophy of Merleau-Ponty. The paper further maintains that even in Merleau-Ponty's later development on the ontology of the flesh, the notion of intentionality can be retained; this view Harney sought to justify by tracing the history of the notion of intention from Aristotle to Ibn Sīnā (Avicenna) and Ibn Rushd (Averroës). Intentionality thus understood restores the idea of nature as living, creative and evolving. **Patrick Hutchings** in his chapter argues that David Hume's idea that one cannot deduce an 'ought' from an 'is' is mistaken. Contrary to Hume's idea that morality is purely a matter of sentiment, Hutchings insists that reason is needed to articulate the many and particular premises that allow one to deduce particular values from particular facts. The heroine of Samuel Richardson's novel *Pamela* (1740) acts on *principle*: principles equal the *maxims* which Kant's categorical imperative censors. Kant's *Groundwork* of 1785 sinks Hume's insistence on the primacy of passion. If Hume in his essay of 1740 had read *Pamela* of 1740, he might have thought again. Pamela gets the point before Kant. Nevertheless, Kant's 'act only on that maxim that you could will to become a universal law' is complicated by different forms of life. Even the categorical imperative is not absolutely universal. Reason is needed all the more, but there is no easy solution. This section is rounded off by **Purushottama Bilimoria**, who highlights 'nothingness' as the preeminent notion in Eastern philosophical thought; it is celebrated by Buddhism, the instigating idea in the development of different branches of Indian philosophy, and a fundamental imagery in Chinese Daoism. Rather than Leibniz's question, 'Why is there something rather than nothing?', the Eastern tradition offers the reassurance that radical Nothingness ought not be feared: it may even have therapeutic value in the Wittgensteinian sense.

Part IV features papers on the topic of religion and religious diversity. **Constant Mews**' contribution on the songlines of Australian Aboriginals and medieval Ireland highlights a further theme that was an abiding interest of Max – religiousness in the Australian Aboriginal tradition(s). Mews sketches the phenomenon of songline in one section of Aboriginal Australia and provides a description of the use of chants and other oral traditions in medieval Ireland. While admitting that there are many points of difference between the two, Mews raises the possibility of similarity between the two through their respective commitments to the natural world and form records of a form of cultural code that is different from the written text. Next, **Graham Oppy** critically examines Max's account of the philosophy of religion in his work *Philosophy and Religion: From Plato to Postmodernism*. Oppy maintains that despite Max's attempt at a comprehensive account of how philosophy relates to religion, there are serious drawbacks to his descriptions of the different relationships between philosophy, religion and philosophy of religion. For Oppy, given the diversity of religious worldviews, the philosophy of religion is concerned with borderline questions for which there are no agreed-upon methods of solution, so the project of philosophy of religion needs to include articulation, comparison and assessment of worldviews both religious and non-religious; it cannot confine itself to the concerns of the Abrahamic faiths. **Paul Rule** is concerned with the difference and tension between 'religion' as a universal truth and the pluralism of 'religions' as a modern human condition and how it might be reconciled. Rule begins his paper by considering Max's claim that the problem of religious diversity remains unsolved and his assertion that dialogue between believers of different religious traditions are absolutely necessary. In exploring Max's work *Religious Inventions: Four Essays*, Rule highlights and discusses the viability of Max's proposal of a credo for the religious believer as a way of promoting inter-religious dialogue. Finally, **Peter Wong** examines the viability of Max's strategy to enable 'ecumenism' among the various religious traditions of the world. For mutual acceptance or appreciation to be possible, could religious values be recognised across different religions? How can the adherent of a tradition come to appreciate another tradition as valuable? Furthermore, how can adherent of a theistic tradition come to accept the religious nature of another tradition that is not expressed in terms of belief or faith? Wong offers a description of the non-theistic Confucian tradition as a case study. He then concludes the paper by considering how someone from within a Confucian tradition could come to terms with other different and incompatible religious systems in the world.

Patrick Hutchings
(Presently an Editor of *Sophia*
and
Sometime Reader in Humanities,
at Deakin University)

Appendix Timeline of Max Charlesworth's life and a list of his most important publications from the Order of Service at his Requiem Mass at Newman College Chapel, Melbourne, 9 June 2014. So large was Max's circle of friends and colleagues that there was – in the very large chapel – standing room only for latecomers.

Max Charlesworth: A Brief Timeline

30 December 1925	Born in Numurkah in Victoria, younger son of William and Mabel Charlesworth.
1943	Law at the University of Melbourne. Transfer to BA.
1948	MA in Philosophy, the University of Melbourne.

1950	Marriage to Stephanie Armstrong.
1950–1952	In Gresswell T.B. Sanatorium.
1953–1955	Studied at the University of Louvain, Belgium.
1955	Awarded PhD (*avec la plus grande distinction*).
1956	Lecturership in Philosophy, at the University of Auckland.
1959	Appointed lecturer in the Philosophy Department, the University of Melbourne.
1948–1965	Played a major role in the publication *The Catholic Worker*.
1962	Co-established with Graeme de Graaff *Sophia: A Journal for Discussion in Philosophical Theology* (later to be variously known as *Sophia: A Journal for Philosophical Theology and Cross-cultural Philosophy of Religion; Sophia: International Journal for Philosophy of Religion, Metaphysical Theology and Ethics;* and currently, *Sophia: International Journal of Philosophy and Traditions*).
1963–1964	Nuffield Fellow, Courtauld Institute.
1968–1969	Visiting Professor, University of Notre Dame, Indiana, USA.
1970	Appointed to Secretariat for Non-Believers, following Vatican II.
1972	Visiting Professor, Katholieke Universiteit Leuven, Belgium.
1974–1975	Chairman, Department of Philosophy, the University of Melbourne.
1975	Founding Dean of Humanities, Deakin University.
1980	Visiting Professor, *Maison des Sciences de L'Homme*, Paris.
1987–1980	Chairperson, Advisory Committee, Centre of Human Bioethics.
1991	Awarded the medal of an Officer of the Order of Australia.
1992–1994	Director, National Institute for Law, Ethics and Public Affairs, Griffith University.
2006	Visiting Professor Bioethics, Katholieke Universiteit, Leuven, Belgium.
2 June 2014	Died peacefully at home.

Significant Publications

Philosophy and Linguistic Analysis, Duquesne University Press, 1959.

St Anselm's 'Proslogion', Oxford, Clarendon Press, 1965.

Philosophy of Religion: The Historic Approaches, Herder and Herder, 1972.

Church, State and Conscience, University of Queensland Press, 1973.

The Problem of Religious Language, Prentice Hall, 1974.

The Existentialists and Jean Paul Sartre, University of Queensland Press, 1975.

Science, non-science and Pseudo science, ABC Science Show lectures, Deakin University Press, 1982.

The Aboriginal Land Rights Movement, Deakin University Press, 1983.

Religion in Aboriginal Australia: An Anthology, Charlesworth, M. Morphy, H. Bell, D. Maddox, K. (eds), University of Queensland Press, 1984.

Religious Worlds, Hill of Content Publishing, 1985.
Life Among the Scientists, Charlesworth, M. Farrell, L. Stokes, T. Turnbull, D., Oxford University Press, 1989.
Life, Death, Genes and Ethics (1989 Boyer Lectures), ABC Books, 1989.
Aristotle: The Etic of Happiness, Deakin University Press, 1991.
Bioethics in a Liberal Society, Cambridge University Press, 1993.
Religious Inventions: Four Essays, Cambridge University Press, 1997.
Religious Business: Essays on Australian Aboriginal Spirituality, Cambridge University Press, 1998.
Thinking about God: From Plato to Postmodernism, One World, 2002.
Aboriginal Religions in Australia: An Anthology of Recent Writings, Charlesworth, M. Dussart, F. Morphy, H. (eds) Ashgate, 2005.
Philosophy for Beginners, University of Queensland Press, 2007.
A Democratic Church: Reforming the Values and Institutions of the Catholic Church, John Garratt Publishing, 2008.

Note

Max Charlesworth's Grandson Alexander Linger has compiled an archive of Max's work which is available on the Deakin University online archives collection. This digital version is made possible through the work of Antony Catrice and his colleague David Tredinnick from Deakin's Information and Records Services. Max's archive can be accessed in https://www.deakin.edu.au/library/aotw. (Click 'Search Now' to go to a search page, and in the form displayed type in 'DUS1' in the box 'Series Number', then click 'Search' button on the bottom of the form. Locate 'Max Charlesworth papers 1957–2013' in the window below. To access individual boxes, click on the plus in the expand column. Click on the plus symbol to locate items within those boxes. Where items are digitised they can be accessed by clicking on the PDF or other file type in the Download column.)

University of Melbourne
Melbourne, Australia

Patrick Hutchings

Contents

Introduction: Maxwell John Charlesworth AO FAHA, 1925–2014 vii
which includes a brief timeline and significant publications, Patrick Hutchings

Part I Remembering Max

1 **Emeritus Professor Max Charlesworth AO (30 December, 1925–2 June, 2014): A Philosopher in the World** 3
Douglas Kirsner

2 **Living with a Philosopher** 13
Hilary Charlesworth

3 **Remembering Babo** 23
Alexander Linger

4 **Max Charlesworth: A Parish Priest Reflects** 37
Michael Elligate

Part II Love of the World

5 **Community Consultation in a Liberal Society** 41
Loane Skene

6 **Dying in a Liberal Society** 51
Jeff Malpas

7 **Moralism and Anti-moralism: Aspects of Bonhoeffer's Christian Ethic** 63
C. A. J. Coady

8 **Love and Affirmation of the World: Inaugural Max Charlesworth Memorial Lecture, Deakin University, Melbourne, 2015** 81
Morny Joy

Part III Life of the Mind

9 **St. Anselm's Argument** 105
M. J. Charlesworth

10 **That Anselm's God Exists and Gaunilo's Island Does Not** 115
Richard Campbell

11 **Intentionality – Evolution of a Concept** 139
Maurita Harney

12 **'Is and Ought': Yet Again** 155
Patrick Hutchings

13 **Why Is There Nothing Rather Than Something? An Essay in the Comparative Metaphysic of Nonbeing** 175
Purushottama Bilimoria

Part IV Between Religion and Religions

14 **Songlines, Sacred Texts and Cultural Code: Between Australia and Early Medieval Ireland** 201
Constant J. Mews

15 **Charlesworth on Philosophy and Religion** 219
Graham Oppy

16 **Religion and Religions** 233
Paul Rule

17 **A Perspective on Religious Diversity** 241
Peter Wong

Part I
Remembering Max

Chapter 1
Emeritus Professor Max Charlesworth AO (30 December, 1925–2 June, 2014): A Philosopher in the World

Douglas Kirsner

Born in 1925 Max Charlesworth spent his last seven decades in the fields of philosophy and religion in which he spanned an incredible variety of interests in both breadth and depth. These included philosophy of religion, bioethics, social studies in science, European philosophy, aboriginal religions, the role of the Church and the liberal democratic state, the structure of the Catholic Church. Max did not see philosophy so much as a technical pursuit as a way of being, ways to understand and communicate with the wider society about the 'big questions'. Education was a primary focus for Max, both in extending the roles of the university and going beyond it by reaching out both to other disciplines and to the general public. For Max philosophy was an activity at its best when applied in the world. The pluralist 'broad Church' approach to philosophy, religion and how we can best live together in a liberal democratic society represent some of his abiding concerns. His publications spanned a very wide spectrum. A random sample: *Life, Death, Genes and Ethics*; *Philosophy for Beginners*; *A Democratic Church*; *The Existentialists and Jean-Paul-Sartre*; *Life among the Scientists – an anthropology of science and scientists at the Walter and Eliza Hall.*

Max always appreciated, encouraged and implemented criticism in the context of his phlosophically liberal respect for different views as core values in the service of flourishing and well-being. Max saw it as a crucial part of the job of a philosopher to be out in the world using critique and reflection, understanding and welcoming a genuine diversity of points of view while at the same time evaluating and critiquing them in a sympathetic yet rigorous way. He had a special capacity for understanding and communicating the main thrusts of ideas empathically to 'cut to the chase',

An earlier version of this chapter appeared in 2012, the Special 50th Anniversary Issue Tribute to Max Charlesworth: "Max Charlesworth: a philosopher in the world", *Sophia 51*(4), 561–69.

D. Kirsner (✉)
Deakin University, Geelong, VIC, Australia
e-mail: douglas.kirsner@deakin.edu.au

P. Wong et al. (eds.), *Considering Religions, Rights and Bioethics: For Max Charlesworth*, Sophia Studies in Cross-cultural Philosophy of Traditions and Cultures 30, https://doi.org/10.1007/978-3-030-18148-2_1

expressing complex ideas in plain English. Max was simply excited by ideas, new and old. His approach was demonstrated not only in numerous wide-ranging publications but in action through contributions to higher education, especially the open campus program at Deakin University together with significant public roles over the decades. He regularly taught adult education classes and often lectured at seminaries for decades. I had the privilege and pleasure of being a student, colleague and friend of Max's since my undergraduate studies in philosophy at the University of Melbourne in the 1960s. I tutored in Max's course Contemporary European Philosophy in the 1970s, and in 1976 was appointed to Deakin University where I am now Emeritus. This chapter traces some significant aspects of Max's trajectory, approach and foci with the help of a document Max generously wrote for me, 'Some of my life and times' (Charlesworth 2012b).

1.1 University of Melbourne and the University of Louvain

Max was himself much as he described Professor Alexander Boyce Gibson, his professor in the Melbourne University Philosophy Department. Boyce Gibson was, according to Max, 'very much a pluralist in philosophy' and was interested in what Boyce Gibson termed the 'interfructification' of the two schools of positivism and metaphysics. Max often approvingly quoted Boyce Gibson describing the aim of philosophy as producing 'fruitful confusion'. Boyce Gibson's attitude to religion as involving what he saw as a 'fruitful tension' between doubt and belief became Max's too. In the now long gone age of the God-professor, Boyce Gibson could declare in 1949 that he had 'built the department out of their difference of opinion'. At the time, Boyce Gibson was contrasting pluralism with the monistic Andersonian philosophy department at Sydney University. Boyce Gibson, a Christian who was interested in existentialism, phenomenology and religion, retired in 1966 (see 1996). This is how Max described his mentor:

> Although a very shy man, Boyce Gibson showed great personal warmth and loyalty to those who knew him well. He also had a nice sense of humour. Again, despite his reserve, he loved academic life, and, as dean (1939–41) of the faculty of arts and chairman (1949–52) of the professorial board, he enjoyed the devious twists and turns of university politics. (Charlesworth 1996).

As a first year philosophy student in 1965, I was fortunate to audit Boyce-Gibson's most erudite, engaging and thought-provoking year-long set of lectures on Plato's *The Republic.* However, with the exception of some individuals like Max, by the 1970s Oxford philosophy monistically swept away virtually everything else in philosophy departments throughout Australia and New Zealand. European philosophy was often seen as 'bad poetry', guilty of Rudolf Carnap's criticism of Heidegger as making meaningless pseudo-claims such as 'the Nothing noths', which a sound training in Fregean logic would surely have sorted out. Max recalled his own eventful early days in the Philosophy Department at the University of Melbourne where he obtained his B.A (Hon.) in philosophy in 1946 and his M.A. in 1949.

> When I began philosophy at Melbourne the Department had just been converted to Wittgensteinian 'linguistic analysis'. "Converted' is an apposite word because the change from the earlier direction of the Department was so radical. Camo Jackson and Douglas Gasking had just returned from Cambridge where they had studied with Wittgenstein and later George Paul visited from Oxford. The Head of the Department was Sandy (Alexander) Boyce Gibson who was the son of W.R. Boyce Gibson, formerly professor of philosophy at Aix en Provence in France who was a close friend of Edmund Husserl, the founder of Phenomenology in Germany. Sandy Boyce Gibson was not himself attracted by the new Wittgensteinian approach, which he thought neglected ethics and political philosophy, but he certainly aided and abetted it by appointing a number of people – Camo Jackson, Douglas Gasking, Kurt Baier, Peter Herbst, Don Gunner – who were Wittgensteinians of different complexions (Charlesworth 2012b).

Boyce Gibson was clearly a significant mentor for Max (as Max was for many, including myself) in his open-minded pluralism, interest in the philosophy of religion and Continental philosophy, as well as his kind of proactive leadership in building the Department. Max made a very significant decision when in 1949 he was awarded the Mannix scholarship for post-graduate study overseas. It was customary for philosophers to go to Oxford or Cambridge in that period and for decades later; it was almost unheard of to go anywhere else. In the late 1970s some Australian philosophers went to study in Paris and the US but were far from assured of employment at universities in Australia upon their return, as were graduates of Oxford. By the 1970s there was a new widening in higher education in Australia with the creation of new universities, which provided the opportunities for different kinds of philosophy. From his appointment in 1967 as Foundation Professor of Philosophy at Macquarie University, Max Deutscher, together with his colleagues, led the way in phenomenology and the new Deakin University provided a major opportunity for European philosophy under Max Charlesworth. But while it may not have seemed a good career move for Australians in the 1970s to study European philosophy in Europe, it must have seemed sheer madness in Max's earlier days of doctoral studies. True, Louvain was a Catholic university, which fitted religious interests. But beyond that Max had become interested in French philosophy:

> I decided to go to the University of Louvain in Belgium, which was a centre for Husserlian phenomenology. During the Second World War Husserl was targeted by the Nazis because he was a Jew and after his death his formidable wife managed to move his huge personal library as well as his own unpublished works to the university in Louvain. This Husserl Archive attracted German and French philosophers (for example, Merleau-Ponty and Gabriel Marcel) and I thought that Louvain would be a good place to do my doctorate.
>
> I was, however, persuaded by my supervisor Georges Van Riet to do my thesis on linguistic analysis since most Europeans knew very little of the Wittgensteinian movement. The thesis was successful and was awarded 'avec la plus grande distinction'. It was later published as *Philosophy and Linguistic Analysis* (Duquesne University Press 1959).

After completing his doctorate, Max obtained a lectureship in philosophy at the University of Auckland in 1956 and in 1959 was appointed as Lecturer in Philosophy back at the University of Melbourne, Senior Lecturer in 1962 and Reader in 1968.

It was a tribute to Boyce Gibson's continuing pluralism that Max was appointed as a lecturer in philosophy. At the University of Melbourne, Max recounted, 'Among other things I set up a course in medieval philosophy and I translated for my students the celebrated work of the 11th century St Anselm of Bec, *The Proslogion*'. This was published as a book (Charlesworth 1965).

1.2 Philosophy of Religion

While at the University of Melbourne he also published *St Thomas Aquinas Summa Theologica, vol. 15* (1970), *Philosophy of Religion: The Historic Approaches* (1972), *Church, State and Conscience* (1973) and *The Problem of Religious Language* (1974). Max's interest in a critical approach to religion and understanding the social, historical and cultural contexts and applications of religion are evidenced by his founding co-editorship of *The Catholic Worker* in the early 1960s, which presented a critical counterpoint to B. A. Santamaria and the 'Movement'. He participated in the conference on Belief and Non-belief in Rome in October, 1970. Max recalled, 'Being a Christian I have always been interested in the relation between philosophy and the Christian religion in its various forms. In 1966 I was appointed by Pope Paul VI to be a consultant to the newly formed body The Secretariat for Non Believers, an international body of theological and philosophical scholars' (Charlesworth 2012b). This was under the presidency of Cardinal Koenig, and Max recalls an abiding memory of the meetings held in Rome at the Vatican in 1970 is being served black caviar at morning tea.

Max's time as a visiting professor at the Notre Dame University, a Catholic University with a critical approach to religion, in the US in 1968–69 at the height of the Vietnam War had a profound effect. It further galvanized Max's open and critical approach to Catholicism and its social place and role in society at large as well as democracy within the Church. In tandem with this he also spent 1972 as a Visiting Professor at the University of Louvain.

There is a clear and abiding line of focus on the philosophy of religion. Max was the Founder and Co-editor of the journal *Sophia* (1962–90). The first issue in 1962 published by the University of Melbourne, featured an article by Peter Geach, 'Causality and Creation' an article by Boyce Gibson, 'Credal Affirmations and Metaphysics' together with articles by Dom Illtyd Trothowan, Graham de Graaf and Ninian Smart. Max Charlesworth contributed an article, 'St Anselm's Argument' to the second issue (1, 2, 25–36). In a 2007 editorial, Max reflected on the origins and context of the journal:

> As a co-founder of the journal, I must say that I am immensely proud that my brain-child has been so successful. When I joined the Department of Philosophy at the University of Melbourne, it was largely dominated by colleagues who had been influenced by Oxford/Cambridge linguistic analysis of a partly Wittgensteinian and partly logical positivist kind. In this context, there was very little interest in the philosophy of religion, as religion was deemed to be in the sphere of 'that whereof one cannot speak.' There was also some

old-fashioned feeling within the University of Melbourne that, as it was a 'secular' body without any kind of religious affiliation, it was in some way prohibited from providing courses in religion! Those days are happily gone forever (2007, p. 109).

Understandably in this context, the first few years of *Sophia* focused on Anglo-American philosophical tradition. However, Max wanted to move the journal beyond this limited view of religion to encompass other philosophical approaches. As he stated, 'I had done some work on Australian Aboriginal religions (possibly the oldest forms of religion we know of), and I saw how irrelevant the standard analytical approaches were in this context' (p. 109). As ever, Max was following his own path as a critical pluralist and pioneering new ways of seeing and doing.

Max's longstanding interest in the philosophy of religion is reflected in his later work too: for example, *Philosophy and Religion: From Plato to Postmodernism* (One World, Oxford, 2002*), Religious Inventions: Four Essays* (Cambridge University Press *Religious Business: Essays on Australian Spirituality*, (Cambridge University Press, 1998). In addition he co-edited with Howard Morphy and Francoise Dussart, *Aboriginal Religions in Australia: An Anthology of Recent Writings* (Ashgate, 2005). Involved with this theme, Max's long 2008 essay, *A Democratic Church: Reforming the Values and Institutions of the Catholic Church,* (John Garratt Publishing, 2008). Max commented, 'In that essay I ask what are the characteristics of a new view of the Church which would allow it to speak to the peoples of the developed world who live in democratic societies and who subscribe to the values of liberal society'. He added,

Recently I have been interested in the question of the interpretation of religious texts and I have just published an essay on this difficult subject. (See 'The Translation of Religious Texts' (Charlesworth 2012a)). It is often said by theologians that religious faith is a God-given 'grace' quite independent of rational (philosophical) assent. But this cannot be true because a believer must have some idea that what is being proposed is possible and not self-contradictory. One cannot believe by faith something that is philosophically unbelievable (Charlesworth 2012b).

1.3 Contemporary European Philosophy

Contrary to the culture of the University of Melbourne Philosophy Department, which mostly focused upon technical issues, Max was intent in taking philosophy beyond the 'ivory tower' of the university into society at large. He was secretary of Melbourne University's Extension Committee and the Vice Chancellor's representative on the Victorian Council of Adult Education (1962–72). Max was always interested in bringing philosophy to the people outside the university and spent many years teaching Adult Education classes.

In the late 1960s Max established the course that he called 'Contemporary European Philosophy', which focused on Sartre and de Beauvoir, Merleau-Ponty and others. This course was very popular with students and even attracted a slew of psychiatrists who undertook the course as a single subject. Although it was by far the most popular course in the Philosophy Department, this was a different time from now: it was not at that time regarded by Max's colleagues to be much of a bonus!

Although the philosophy department at the University of Melbourne was diverse in its religious composition and attitudes to materialism, Wittgenstein and ethics, the approach to Contemporary European philosophy was not. Max Charlesworth was pretty much a 'one man band' (Max once quipped after one of Jan Srzednicki's eruptions about Contemporary European Philosophy that he was 'certainly a Contemporary European'!)

Max was invited by the Australian Broadcasting Commission (ABC) to write three one- hour programs on 'The Existentialists and Jean Paul Sartre', broadcast in 1975 and subsequently published as a book by University of Queensland Press in1980. These very popular programs spurred the ABC to invite Max's colleague and friend, Tony Coady, to present a fascinating seven hour series, somewhat as a counter, on British philosophy, titled 'The Fly and the Fly-bottle', which included interviews with Sir Isaiah Berlin, Bernard Williams and Tom Stoppard. There were valuable contributions on all sides. Max remembered:

> When I was writing the script of these programmes I was keen to get live interviews with Sartre and de Beauvoir. The ABC's reporter in Paris, Pierre Vicary, asked me to prepare a set of questions which would make clear that our programmes were serious and not just chit chat, and he was able to cajole both Sartre and de Beauvoir to participate. Vicary's interview with Sartre at the end of his incredible life was extraordinarily moving. (Charesworth 2012b).

Max was a major innovator in bringing contemporary European philosophy to its current importance in Australia.

1.4 Deakin University

Max was Head of the Department of Philosophy of the University of Melbourne in 1974–75. At the end of 1975, literally as he turned 50, Max was invited by Victoria's fourth and newly just established university, Deakin University, to become Planning Dean of the School of Humanities in Geelong. It was an existential decision: would he spend the next 15 years in a 'good' job as Reader in Philosophy at the University of Melbourne, or would he do something quite different and less comfortable? Max opted for the challenge to help create what he often called 'the Athens of the South' at Deakin and set up the School of Humanities as interdisciplinary areas involving Philosophical Studies, Australian Studies, Literary Studies and Performing Arts. As Deakin was set up so as not to duplicate other universities, there was a licence and expectation to be different from alma maters, particularly the University of Melbourne. Another essential social mission for Deakin that aligned closely with Max's values was the innovation of off campus education with open entry for mature age students. This meant that many people over the age of 21 from around Australia who had missed out on study or were interested in further study could undertake courses that engaged them. This was all part of Max's adventure of ideas and social contribution. The overall aim was not to train would-be professional philosophers, for example, but to bring philosophy to a wide range of people who often found it made quite a difference in their lives. The pedagogical mode was writing quite elaborate study guides with readers, taped interviews and discussions, and weekend schools. This was certainly a project of philosophy in the world. Max always insisted that philosophy was in its element when it was applied.

As Planning Dean, Max played a significant role in appointing staff, and he set up new areas of study. He loved and encouraged interdisciplinary, lateral thinking and creativity. Max was able to appoint a varied and exciting group of academics in a number of disciplines across humanities. Philosophical Studies encompassed not only philosophy proper, but the history of ideas, religious studies and social studies in science. As one of the first appointed to Deakin in 1976 as a lecturer in Philosophy and History of Ideas, I can testify to how exciting, vibrant and enthusiastic the academic culture was at Deakin. And as it eventually turned out, owing to the expansion of higher education in Australia including Deakin, it wasn't such a bad career move to undertake doctoral studies in Europe. Appointments included Jocelyn Dunphy who undertook her PhD with Paul Ricoeur, Li Veit-Brause who studied for her PhD in Germany, and Russell Grigg who undertook his PhD in Paris with Lacan's close collaborator and son-in-law, Jacques-Alain Miller.

In his role as Planning Dean of the School of Humanities, Max mandated that all units would have course teams, often interdisciplinary, on the basis that two academic heads were better than one. Despite the success of the heady days of this early team approach in units such as the interdisciplinary 'Images of Man' in philosophy and literature (Sartre, Camus, Freud, Kafka, Marx, Brecht), and 'The Australian City' in the new inter-discipline of Australian Studies at Deakin, Max later gave a paper to the School following Freud's lead titled 'The Psychopathology of Course Teams'. In academic matters, experience counted at least as much as reason did. Max was mostly infinitely patient with notoriously individualistic academic colleagues, but in the end Max himself collaborated and wrote many study guides across a range of disciplines. Max was Foundation Planning Dean of the School of Humanities from 1975 to 80 and remained Professor of Philosophy until his retirement in 1990, when he became Emeritus.

Max played a wide variety of significant roles in education, the community, and the Church. Some highlights from a long list provide a flavour: member of the Charles Strong Trust; Chairperson of the Advisory Committee of the Centre for Human Bioethics (1987–90), Member of the Victorian Government Standing Review and Advisory Committee on Infertility; member, National Bioethics Consultative Committee (1988–90).

In addition to his role as a national innovator in education, Max's contributions to bioethics were also recognized nationally when in 1990 he was appointed as an Officer of the Order of Australia (AO) for his contributions both to education and to bioethics.

1.5 Bioethics

The field of bioethics was a major focus and application of philosophy for Max, who summarised his contributions to this area in his own words:

> In 1980 I became involved in the debate about the ethical implications of the new reproductive technologies (in vitro fertilization etc.) Peter Singer and Helga Kuhse at Monash University had established a group that was concerned with these questions and they invited me to join them. The Federal Government's National Health and Medical Research Council, of which I was a member entered the debate, and the Victorian Government established a Standing Review and Advisory Committee on Infertility of which I was a member was also involved.
>
> Later I was invited by the ABC to deliver the 1989 Boyer Lectures and I used them to critically appraise the new technologies. These lectures were published as *Life, Death, Genes and Ethics* (Charlesworth 1989). Again, in 1990 I was invited to give a paper at an international conference on Human Genetic Information: Science and Law and Ethics arranged by the CIBA Foundation in Switzerland. It was published by Wiley, in Ciba Foundation Symposium 149, 1990 "Human genome analysis and the concept of human nature". A little later, I published a book called *Bioethics in a Liberal Society* (1993) in which I argued that the fact that we live in a society in which the freedom of individuals has important implications for how we view death and dying, birth and family formation; the just distribution of health resources, surrogacy; etc. I view this book as perhaps my best publication and I was pleased when Cambridge University Press arranged translations of the book into Spanish, German and Italian. I might mention that I was, in 1963 awarded a Nuffield Foundation Fellowship for study at the Warburg Institute, University of London. At the Institute I did research about the beginnings of science in the 16th and 17th centuries. Some years later I was able to use some of this research in a study with three other colleagues on 'the anthropology of science' which resulted in Charlesworth et al. 1989 (Charlesworth 2012b).

Max made major contributions throughout his life in many fields. He was always interested in the new, and with his remarkable generosity of spirit, he very much encouraged others, particularly academic colleagues and students, to explore what was new and different.

Max pioneered a broader approach to religions going well beyond traditional philosophy of religion and extending our understanding of the anthropology of religion. Moreover, as Father Paul Collins observes, Max is 'truly the doyen of religious scholars in Australia. He has written on a range of issues from philosophy and reproductive ethics to Aboriginal religion. A genuinely "Catholic" man in the deepest sense, he has contributed an enormous amount to the ministry of the Australian church' (Collins 2009, p. 91).

Max was also interested in existentialism, structuralism, hermeneutics well before they became academically acceptable and fashionable. In fact, he played a major role in introducing European philosophy into Australia. Max led the way in many of the issues that are now accepted, including in particular the emphasis on philosophy as being best when it is applied to other disciplines, such as bioethics. Max played a crucial part in setting up Deakin University where he was planning dean of humanities. He introduced many innovations in the new off campus teaching of which Deakin was the clear quality leader in Australia. He powerfully influenced many individual students, both at the University of Melbourne and at Deakin, and played a critical role as a mentor to many academic colleagues. To cite just one example, Dr. Helen Szoke, Chief Executive of Oxfam Australia and former Race Discrimination Commissioner recalled her honours year at Deakin: 'My supervisor was the pre-eminent academic Professor Max Charlesworth. It was a magnificent year and he made a great impression on me' ('Strategist privileged to fight racism', 2012).

Max continued to make significant contributions to his calling until his unexpected but peaceful death at home on 2 June, 2014, aged 88, 25 years past his formal retirement. Max continued to be fascinated by the world around him and never stopped writing or trying to make a difference. He was an inspiration for the life of the mind and for critical thinking. His gentle humour, generosity of spirit and love and care of both people and ideas influenced many lives as was evident from the obituaries together with the virtual avalanche of letters and messages following his death. A comprehensive Wikipedia site (which includes a select bibliography) has been constructed on Max's life and work (Wikipedia Contributors 2018) and annual and biennial lectures and scholarships in his honour have been established. Max retains a unique place in the hearts and minds of his numerous friends, students and colleagues in Australia and around the world. He leaves his large and loving family: his beloved wife Stephanie; children Sara, Hilary, Stephen, Lucy, Bruno, Anna and Esther, their partners, 11 grandchildren and three great grandchildren.

References

Charlesworth, M. (1965). *St. Anselm's proslogion.* Oxford: Clarendon Press.
Charlesworth, M. (1989). *Life, death, genes and ethics.* Sydney: ABC Books.
Charlesworth, M. (1993). *Bioethics in a liberal society.* Cambridge: Cambridge University Press.
Charlesworth, M. (1996). Gibson, Alexander Boyce (Sandy) (1900–1972). In *Australian dictionary of biography.* National Centre of Biography, Australian National University. http://adb.anu.edu.au/biography/gibson-alexander-boyce-sandy-10295/text18215. Accessed 8 Sept 2012.
Charlesworth, M. (2007). Editorial. *Sophia, 46*(1), 109–110.
Charlesworth, M. (2012a). Translating religious texts. *Sophia 51*(4), 423–448.
Charlesworth, M. (2012b). *Some of my life and times.* Unpublished.
Charlesworth, M., Farrell, L., Turnbull, D., & Stokes, T. (1989). *Life among the scientists: An anthropological study of an Australian scientific community.* Oxford: Oxford University Press.
Collins, P. (2009). Review of Max Charlesworth, 'a democratic church[:] reforming the values and institutions of the Catholic Church', [in] *Voices: quarterly essays on religion in Australia. Sophia, 48*(1), 91–92.
Strategist Privileged to Fight Racism. (2012). *The Sydney Morning Herald*, July 23, 2012.
Wikipedia Contributors. (2018, December 20). Max Charlesworth. In *Wikipedia, the free encyclopedia.* Retrieved 04:47, January 18, 2019, from https://en.wikipedia.org/w/index.php?title=Max_Charlesworth&oldid=874584813

Douglas Kirsner is Emeritus Professor at Deakin University where he previously held a Personal Chair in Philosophy and Psychoanalytic Studies. His publications include *Unfree Associations: Inside Psychoanalytic Institutes* (Rowman and Littlefield, 2009), *The Schizoid World of Jean-Paul Sartre and RD Laing* (Other Press 2003), numerous journal articles, book chapters and edited collections. He was elected an Honorary Member of the American Psychoanalytic Association in 2015. He is Associate Editor of the *International Journal of Applied Psychoanalytic Studies* and *Organisational and Social Dynamics* and Editorial Advisor to *Psychoanalysis and History.*

Chapter 2
Living with a Philosopher

Hilary Charlesworth

The popular image of philosophers is that they are perplexed by real life. Their minds are so caught up in arcane inquiries, they are unable to fend for themselves and have failed to acquire some basic skills of life. The families of philosophers, if they exist, look on curiously and indulgently from a distance; or, like Rousseau's children, sent off to a foundling hospital, they are discarded or sidelined to allow the great thinker resources and space to pursue his work. Philosophers' emotional and affective lives, then, do not appear to impinge on their scholarly pursuits.

Meghan K. Robert's book *Sentimental Savants: Philosophical Families in Enlightenment France* (2016) offers a nice counterpoint to this picture. She uncovers the central role of the families of French scientists and philosophers in the eighteenth century not only in supporting their research and writing through assuming responsibility for the domestic world, but also through direct engagement with the scholarly work. Families observed, illustrated and translated for the *philosophes*. Families were sometimes drawn into an 'intimate form of empiricism' (Roberts 2016, p. 3), becoming guinea pigs for experiments in activities such as smallpox inoculation and children's education.

While we were no means a philosophical family in Robert's sense, we were all affected by Dad's life as a philosopher. In this chapter I offer a family, or more accurately a child's, perspective on Dad's life and work. In the later years of Dad's life, we would encourage him to write down his memories of his childhood and early years as an academic, but he would firmly resist all such cajoling. Delving into the past held no interest for him, although he had a stock of possibly highly embellished anecdotes about his youth that he would often recount at family gatherings.

Dad had an unlikely background as a philosopher. He was born in a small country town, Numurkah, in northern Victoria in 1925. His father, William, was a Law

H. Charlesworth (✉)
University of Melbourne, Parkville, VIC, Australia
e-mail: h.charlesworth@unimelb.edu.au

P. Wong et al. (eds.), *Considering Religions, Rights and Bioethics: For Max Charlesworth*, Sophia Studies in Cross-cultural Philosophy of Traditions and Cultures 30, https://doi.org/10.1007/978-3-030-18148-2_2

Clerk in the local solicitor's office, never qualifying as a fully-fledged lawyer. Working during the Depression, William was sometimes paid for his services in eggs and rabbits, and money was scarce. Dad's mother, Mabel, devoted herself to the home, bringing up my uncle Ian, born in 1919, and Dad. My grandmother belonged to a large Italian-Irish family in Bendigo and Dad was very proud of his Italian heritage. He would recall his grandfather, Carlo Ferrari, a stonemason from Tirano in northern Italy, holding court on the verandah of the tiny Bendigo house, which somehow accommodated nine children. Dad had an intense childhood memory of being tickled on his cheek by Grandpa Ferrari's whiskers.

Dad's first school was the local Catholic primary school, St Joseph's, and he then attended Numurkah High School. Dad's parents recognised the limitations of the local education system and, after he had won a scholarship, sent Dad to board at Assumption College in Kilmore, run by the Marist Brothers.

Dad would entertain us by recalling the horrors of the food at boarding school, the tough conditions of the dormitories and the woes of having little aptitude for sport in a sports-mad environment, but his time at Assumption College was pivotal in his intellectual development. He had a number of brilliant teachers among the Marist Brothers who introduced him to the joys of the study of history, languages, philosophy and theology. At Assumption, Dad first encountered the work of the French philosophers Jacques Maritain, Léon Bloy and Gabriel Marcel. This experience opened up for Dad the possibility of university study, an adventure no one in his immediate or extended family had undertaken.

After Dad finished school, he moved to Melbourne in 1942 and took up a cadetship with the Victorian Attorney-General's Department, the first step to becoming a lawyer. In the evenings, he would take various professional legal courses. The next year, Dad moved to fulltime study at the University of Melbourne, becoming a resident at Newman College. Both institutions left a deep mark on Dad. The University provided many rich paths for academic exploration and Newman offered a sociable community of Catholic students, many slightly older than Dad, returning from the Second World War. Dad maintained some of these friendships throughout his life, particularly with John Mulvaney, who became an eminent archaeologist.

As his parents hoped and expected, Dad enrolled in a law degree. He would recall the aridity of his study of law, although, years later, he would offer to lend me his notes in contract law in which, he would remind me wryly, he had earned a third-class honour. William died after a long illness in 1944 and this seems to have liberated Dad to abandon the law and to take up an Arts degree full time. The decision devastated his mother. It took the intercession of Father Jeremiah Murphy, the Rector of Newman, to comfort Mabel and to reassure her about Dad's future. Newman also waived Dad's fees to allow him to stay in residence. My grandmother's disappointment in Dad's career choice would occasionally surface years later. She kept her husband's gold watch and fob chain secreted away and finally produced them as a gift for my younger brother, Bruno, when he was admitted as a lawyer, to celebrate the appearance of a Charlesworth lawyer at long last. (Mabel batted off protests that I had been admitted some years before Bruno by noting, presciently, that I was unlikely to turn out a real lawyer).

From our perspective, the most significant event in Dad's university years was meeting Stephanie Armstrong at a 21st birthday party late in 1944. He recalled a striking woman wearing a green dress appliqued with silver leather gum leaves. Dad thought that anyone wearing such an outrageous outfit must be worth getting to know. Mum was in the WRANS at that time, decoding Japanese military signals. Later she studied social work at the University and got to know Dad properly then. Indeed, he coached Mum and her friend Alison Affleck in Ethics. Mum took some time to agree to marry Dad, but their marriage in February 1950 became the bedrock of Dad's life.

Dad flourished in his Arts degree, becoming immersed in the study of philosophy. He proceeded directly from his BA honours course to an MA in Philosophy, with a thesis on 'The Notion of Democracy in the Thomistic Tradition of Political Philosophy'. Professor Alexander (Sandy) Boyce Gibson, the head of the Philosophy Department, then encouraged Dad to do a PhD overseas. The Melbourne Philosophy Department was then a centre for linguistic analysis, strongly influenced by Ludwig Wittgenstein and his followers at Cambridge, and the United Kingdom seemed the obvious destination for graduate study for a young Australian philosopher. Dad, however, had grown increasingly dissatisfied with what he saw as the narrowness of the analytic approach and he had developed an interest in contemporary European philosophy. Boyce Gibson encouraged Dad in this direction, particularly towards the study of Phenomenology (Boyce Gibson's father, his predecessor as Chair in Philosophy, William Boyce Gibson, had studied philosophy in Germany and France, and had translated Edmund Husserl's work into English). Husserl's papers had been sent to the Catholic University in Leuven (Louvain) in Belgium, to escape the Nazi purge of Jewish intellectuals. Herman Van Breda established the Husserl Archive there and Leuven quickly became a centre of studies in Phenomenology. Dad therefore decided to head for Leuven to undertake a PhD in this area. The travel plans were interrupted when Dad was diagnosed with tuberculosis. Shortly after his marriage, he was sent to Gresswell Sanatorium in Mont Park. From here Dad would write almost daily to my mother. While this was a difficult time for him, Dad delighted in recounting stories about some of the extraordinary characters he encountered there, including his neighbour in the ward who would eat 17 fried eggs for breakfast each morning. Dad became very friendly with another Gresswell patient, Peter Wertheim, who later became a philosopher. Peter was kind, gregarious and full of humour and brought out Dad's playful side. As young children we saw a lot of the Wertheim family, and remain close today.

Overseas study would not have been possible without a scholarship. By great fortune, encouraged by Father Murphy at Newman, Archbishop Mannix had decided to establish a travelling scholarship for post-graduate Catholic students to study overseas. The terms of the scholarship gave preference to unmarried students who intended to remain unmarried during their studies abroad. Dad tackled this obstacle head on by visiting the Archbishop to argue that marriage should be seen as conducive to scholarship, rather than a hindrance. Dad was eventually awarded the inaugural Mannix Travelling Scholarship in 1951, but had to postpone taking it up until his discharge after 2 years at Gresswell.

Mum and Dad left for Europe in 1953. They spent a few months in the United Kingdom, where Dad got work digging on a Roman archaeological site. My sister Sara, my parent's first child, was born at this time in Kent. Dad started his doctoral studies at the Université Catholique de Louvain later that year (at that time the town was officially bilingual and hosted both Dutch and French-speaking faculties). His plans to write on Phenomenology were quickly derailed because his supervisor, Professor Georges van Riet, was much more interested in Dad undertaking a critical study of the English school of linguistic analysis. Dad recalled that, at that time, most Francophone philosophers considered linguistic analysis to be a joke, so he embarked on the task of presenting it in a positive light. During his time in England, Dad had attended some conferences at Spode House where he had encountered two leading Wittgensteinians, Elizabeth Anscombe and her husband Peter Geach. They were both were very helpful to Dad while he wrote his thesis, later published in English as *Philosophy and Linguistic Analysis* (1961).

When much later some of his children went through the slog of writing PhDs, Dad would regale us with his story of the agony of PhD examinations in Leuven, as if to cheer us up. As in most European universities, there was a public hearing or defence of the doctoral thesis before a jury of professors. The jury would retire to consider their verdict after the candidate had presented, and then return either to dismiss the PhD or to present one of three grades: 'avec distinction', 'avec grande distinction', or 'avec la plus grande distinction'. The candidate would be expected to have prepared a grand supper for the jury and supporters, whatever the outcome. Dad was proud that his thesis, written in French, was adjudged to have passed 'avec la plus grande distinction' and so his splendid supper could be thoroughly enjoyed!

My parents lived in a tiny apartment in Leuven, above a seedy cinema. They made lasting friendships with other international students there, and with Belgian families. Despite the cramped conditions, and the presence of two small children, Mum and Dad always recalled these days with great affection and they continued to visit Leuven throughout their lives. Dad never lost his capacity in French and was an expert tutor for all of us as we struggled with the language at school.

Like some of Robert's eighteenth century philosophical families, Dad had a large family of seven children, a potentially useful cohort for research support and investigation. But our lives could not have been more different to those of the French sentimental savants. While Dad was enthralled by his academic work, it remained somehow separate to life at home. There were times when he would bring his small typewriter to the kitchen table and tap away, oblivious to the chaos around him. If we demanded his intervention to resolve a dispute between us, he would offer a general remonstrance ('be kind', 'be generous') and quickly return to his manuscript. But overall, he was unusually engaged in domestic affairs for a man in the 1960s and 1970s. Dad was a keen ironer, especially when listening to a radio broadcast of his beloved Carlton Football team at play. He also enthusiastically wielded the vacuum cleaner, often as a way of encouraging our friends to depart: 'please don't feel you need to leave', he would say, 'but would you mind lifting your feet so that I can vacuum around you?'

We always felt that we were the centre of Dad's life. He had a very comforting and calm presence in a crisis and would pat us to sleep as small children if we were unhappy or wakeful, singing all the while. Dad would read and reread Hergé's Tintin books to us, and put on hilarious voices as Captain Haddock or the brothers Thompson. I remember particularly the wonderful stories he invented to tell us at bedtime. One was a series featuring Arabella, a feisty and intrepid girl detective. Dad was proud of most things we all did, always slightly overstating any success.

Our parents seemed to have both intense emotional and intellectual bonds, and it was difficult for us to play them off against each other. We were mortified when they jointly edited a book called *Large Families* (1968), which was placed on sale at our parish church. Although the chapters were written using pseudonyms, it seemed painfully clear which one described our family and our parents' marriage, giving what we thought was far too much detail about their relationship. Mum was the family disciplinarian, enabling Dad to avoid dealing with disputes or bad behaviour. Very occasionally, Mum would insist that Dad become involved in a disciplinary crisis and, when pushed to the end of his tether with us, he would threaten to 'spifflicate' us. We never discovered what this meant.

Dad's work gave us a chance for occasional travel. For us older children, his period of sabbatical leave as a Nuffield Fellow in London in 1963 was an exotic event. Dad spent his time at the British Library translating St Anselm's *Proslogion*. We lived in the stately but damp Nuffield Apartments in Prince Alfred Road, close to the Regent's Park Zoo. A highlight of this year was a camping tour in Europe, all of us squeezed into a little car, including a journey to St Anselm's Benedictine monastery at Bec-Hellouin in Normandy. My younger siblings went with my parents on Dad's 1968 sabbatical to Notre Dame University in Indiana, giving them a chance to observe the US Presidential primaries and election, a race between Richard Nixon and Hubert Humphrey, at close quarters. Dad had been impressed by Eugene McCarthy, Humphrey's challenger for the Democratic nomination, and brought back Sara and me, languishing in boarding school, lots of McCarthy's campaign material. Dad was also inspired by American Catholics who opposed the Vietnam war, and later helped organise visits of figures such as Daniel Berrigan to Australia. Other sabbaticals in the 1970s and 80s were spent in Leuven and Paris.

If the subtle shades of meaning in St Anselm's *Proslogion* did not impinge on our lives, Dad's willingness to engage in the political world did. I have early memories of helping Dad address and post copies of the newspaper, *The Catholic Worker*, out to subscribers, and of him marking up proofs and taking them to the printer. I did not understand much about the politics of *The Catholic Worker*, although we became aware, through comments at our local Church and at our schools, that it was regarded as a dubious, even subversive, publication in Catholic life. There was a regular trickle of abuse aimed at Dad. I recall once picking up the phone during Sunday lunch at home to receive a volley of invective against Dad, and anonymous letters denouncing him would sometimes arrive. Occasionally even teachers at our schools would inveigh against him. None of this seemed to trouble Dad, though it left us shaken and indignant.

As a child, I was always surprised that our gentle, temperate and rational father attracted so much criticism. It is easier to understand this now in light of his strong positions on matters of liberal values and social justice, and the threat that they posed to a generally conservative Australian Catholic hierarchy. The intensity of this perceived threat lingered; it was evident in the decision in the late 1990s by George Pell, as Archbishop of Melbourne, to withdraw an invitation to Dad, then in his seventies, to speak at a local seminary.

As we grew older, we would quiz Dad about his commitment to Catholicism. In the 1960s and 1970s, the official Melbourne manifestation of Catholicism was imbricated with the politics of the Catholic Social Studies Movement, the political organisation founded by the Catholic layman, B.S. Santamaria in 1941. The aim of the Movement was to combat the spread of Communism, particularly in Australian trade unions. The activities of the Movement precipitated a rift within the Australian Labor Party between anti-communist campaigners and more left wing Party members in 1955, known as 'the Split'. The Split had profound effects on Australian politics, splintering the ALP through the formation of the Democratic Labor Party by members of the Movement expelled from the ALP. Following Santamaria's lead, the Catholic Church supported Australia's involvement in the war in Vietnamin the 1960s and 1970s as a mechanism to curb the seepage of Communism into Australian life.

B.A. Santamaria had had some contact with Dad as a young man in university circles in the 1940s, and they seemed to have respect for each other. Dad had however published highly critical articles on the Movement in *The Auckland Advertiser* when he was lecturing at the University of Auckland between 1956 and 1958. When Dad returned in 1959 to become a lecturer at the University of Melbourne, Santamaria reached out to him, inviting Dad to meet him in an Irish pub in the city. But the doctrinaire views of the Movement had no appeal for Dad. Santamaria was understandably rather upset that the editorial line of *The Catholic Worker* had changed profoundly, as the paper had been founded by Santamaria in 1936 as a vehicle for the defence of Catholic doctrine in the face of both communism and capitalism. Santamaria indeed asked Archbishop Mannix to insist that the word 'Catholic' be removed from the title of the paper, but Mannix refused to intervene (Niall 2015, p. 280).

Considering the scepticism in which powerful sections of the Melbourne Catholic Church held Dad, we found it hard to understand why he remained such a devout Catholic. I remember at the height of Australia's involvement in the Vietnam War our parish priest warned his congregation about the pernicious influence on the young of 'so-called intellectuals' lurking in universities. This seemed clearly aimed at Dad, and we older children, eager to have an excuse to leave Sunday Mass early, whispered encouragement to him to lead a showy departure from the Church. To our chagrin, Dad insisted that we all remain, and he appeared quite unruffled by the attack.

Dad was outspoken about the fallibility and frailties of the institutional Church, arguing for a more democratic model of Church life. He distinguished this clearly however from the spiritual Church of the scriptures in which he found profound wisdom. One of his favourite passages from the New Testament was Luke's Parable of the Prodigal Son. We children had great sympathy for the complaints of the virtuous older son who did all the right things, and would struggle with the father's willingness to welcome back the dissolute son. Dad on the other hand was greatly moved by the power of forgiveness that the parable demonstrates. He loved the moody Rembrandt depiction of the parable on display in the Hermitage in St Petersburg.

Dad gained a lot from his participation in the Vatican's Secretariat for Non-Believers in the 1960s, becoming very interested in other religious traditions. Later in his life, he focussed particularly on Buddhism and Indigenous Australia. He made several trips to Indigenous communities with Deakin students and colleagues and was deeply affected by discussions about religion there. Dad's comparative approach is evident in *Religious Inventions*, published in 1997, in which he argues that religions are creative responses to the realities of human existence, rather than the product of divine revelation. Dad was enchanted at being able to collaborate with the brilliant artist Robert Ingpen on a children's book *Religious Worlds* (1985), which takes a similar view. He presented his grandchildren with lovingly inscribed copies.

Dad's personal faith was not at all showy, but it was steadfast and shaped his life profoundly. The extent of this influence only became clear to me after his death when I was sorting through some of his papers and found a few of his journals, full of his angular writing, with reflections on religious questions in his life, starting from his time in Gresswell Sanatorium. He calmly accepted that most of his children abandoned any religious observance once they left school, although this also saddened him. Dad once said that not having a religious faith seemed to him a great absence in life, much like having no appreciation of music.

While Dad appeared to us to be impervious to public criticism, I remember one incident where he responded in an uncharacteristically strong manner. In 1964 an article appeared in *Truth*, a weekly Melbourne newspaper specialising in the sensational. The article claimed that, although a Catholic, Dad supported the use of contraception in violation of Church doctrine. This claim had no basis and Dad was initially untroubled by the article. His lawyer friend from Newman days, Tony Harold, counselled Dad to bring proceedings for defamation against Southdown Press, the publisher of *Truth*, on the basis that the allegation suggested that Dad was hypocritical in his practice of Catholicism. Fellow members of *The Catholic Worker* editorial board were also concerned that the article undermined the legitimacy of their paper. Southdown Press quickly retracted the claim and offered a settlement of 600 pounds, an extraordinary windfall for my parents. The legacy of this unexpected bonus was a beautiful Persian tree of life carpet, still in my parents' home.

In 1975, Dad left the Philosophy Department at Melbourne University to become the Foundation Dean of Arts at the newly-established Deakin University. From our perspective, this mid-life change energised him to a striking degree and he became engrossed in the challenges of distance education. Dad was thrilled to be able to recruit a lively and talented group of academics to work with him (some of whom are contributors to this volume) and delighted in the gifted students he encountered in unlikely places, from the police force to prisons. He enjoyed working with scholars from other disciplines, savouring for example the ethnographic work at the Walter and Eliza Hall Institute on which *Life among the Scientists* (1989) was based.

During the Deakin years, Dad relished involvement in activities beyond the academic sphere and bringing philosophical insights to bear on practical problems. He chaired a Victorian government committee to organise activities to mark the International Year of Peace in 1986; and participated in national and state committees dealing with questions of ethics and bioethics. When he retired, Dad told me that his only regret about his career was that he had always remained within the university sector.

Dad operated a generous proof-reading and academic commentary service for his children, and later, grandchildren. I remember him patiently reading drafts of my doctoral thesis on bills of rights. I would post chapters to him from the United States, and they would return a few weeks later, heavily annotated with suggestions for improvement, ranging from correcting grammatical errors to increasing references to John Stuart Mill. Dad performed a similar service for my sister Esther's PhD in architecture, and many of his family's school and university essays. His last email, written hours before his death, was a suggested list of readings for a grandson embarking on a philosophy essay.

Roberts reports that French Enlightenment philosophers would use their families to cultivate their own reputation as moral and intellectual leaders. Family life was a vehicle both to test and promote ideas; it allowed the savants to 'unite the language of feeling with a rhetoric of empiricism' (Roberts 2016, p. 5). Our family life however did little to promote Dad's career as a philosopher. Dad liked to remark that parents' influence on their children was much less significant than children's influence on parents. In this spirit, he would take up our separate interests and concerns, from labour relations, Spanish literature and Pacific history to Indian studies and rock music, and engage with them enthusiastically, becoming knowledgeable about the major currents in the field. But, of course, he shaped us much more than we ever affected him, demonstrating the power of ideas and the importance of speaking out, not as a campaigner or advocate, but as a testament to rational thought and debate. Dad's commitment to liberalism was thoroughgoing. He modelled tolerance of other perspectives, a capacity for reflection and an openness to new approaches and ideas in both his private and public life.

We feel fortunate that Dad wrote so much. His handwritten journals, annotated typescripts, lectures, articles, books and even the draft of a novel have been a great comfort to us since his death. In them Dad's calm, mellifluous voice reappears, with his clarity of expression, his joy in ideas, his sense of purpose, his humour and his civility.

References

Charlesworth, M. J. (1961). *Philosophy and linguistic analysis*. Pittsburgh: Dusquesne University Press.

Charlesworth, M., & Charlesworth, S. (Eds.). (1968). *Large families*. Melbourne: Spectrum.

Charlesworth, M. (1997). *Religious inventions: Four essays*. Cambridge: Cambridge University Press.

Charlesworth, M., & Ingpen, R. (1985). *Religious worlds*. Melbourne: Hill of Content.

Charlesworth, M., Farrall, L., Stokes, T., & Turnbull, D. (1989). *Life among the scientists: An anthropological study of an Australian scientific community*. Melbourne: Oxford University Press.

Niall, B. (2015). *Mannix*. Melbourne: Text Publishing.

Roberts, M. K. (2016). *Sentimental savants: Philosophical families in enlightenment France*. Chicago: University of Chicago Press.

Hilary Charlesworth is a Laureate Professor at Melbourne Law School and a Distinguished Professor at the Australian National University. Her research and teaching are in the field of international law. She has held both an ARC Federation Fellowship and an ARC Laureate Fellowship. She served as Judge ad hoc in the Whaling in the Antarctic Case (Australia v Japan) in the International Court of Justice.

Chapter 3
Remembering Babo

Alexander Linger

Maxwell John Charlesworth is my grandfather. To me however, along with the rest of my cousins, he is known simply as *Babo*.

My memory of Max is then, not at all surprisingly, first and foremost as my grandfather; a kind, calm and witty old man who seemed to emanate a sense of wisdom with each of his frail movements. Someone who looked directly into your eyes with a genuine interest and respect, always with open ears and the time to listen, and, if you stuck around long enough, to teach you one or two invaluable lessons. He was Babo, and as a child this is all I knew.

As I entered my last years of high school, however, I slowly began to form a great love for philosophy and the insatiable curiosity and wonder that surrounds it. One day in year-11 my philosophy teacher asked Max to come in and speak to our class about his life, his works and what it means to be a philosopher. It was around this time that I began to realise that there was a whole life beyond this idea of Babo the grandfather; years and decades of so much thought, discovery, and action that despite so many people alluding to it, I had never thought to discover myself. I became curious: who was Babo before he was a grandfather? Before he was a father? Who was he as a young man, as a philosopher, as an educator, as a passionate and outspoken advocate for each of his many beliefs?

Over the next years as I delved further into the philosophical world at university, Babo and I began to have many more general and intensely philosophical discussions in person, or when I was overseas, via email, which he was known to print out in order to first scribble his reply with the more tangible pen and paper.

My personal memory of Babo, of Max, started to grow as I began to learn and understand more about his life and times. However, at the moment of his death, while I was on university exchange in Paris, I realised just how much there was to discover about this Max Charlesworth, my grandfather. Up until this point, my

A. Linger (✉)
Melbourne, Victoria, Australia

P. Wong et al. (eds.), *Considering Religions, Rights and Bioethics: For Max Charlesworth*, Sophia Studies in Cross-cultural Philosophy of Traditions and Cultures 30, https://doi.org/10.1007/978-3-030-18148-2_3

memory of this time was still very much an assortment of intimate and visceral recollections of Babo with only some vague ideas of who he was as a public intellectual and philosopher. I needed to discover more.

3.1 Retrospective Remembering

After I had returned to Melbourne, I had the perfect opportunity to do just that. Max had left many delightfully unorganised boxes in storage that contained valuable insights into his academic and intellectual life. The pungent smell of the oxidising paper when opening these long undisturbed boxes was a memorable and welcoming sign. Strewn about in no apparent order were typed articles, drafts, handwritten research notes, correspondence with friends, colleagues, and publishers, autobiographical sketches, as well as photos, recordings, even video footage of ABC debates with BA Santamaria, right down to the plethora of illegible scribbles on the back of any piece of parchment or pamphlet he could find when that one thought, be it of the sublime or the ridiculous, had struck.

My task was to collate and organise these storage boxes, and I realised quickly that this offered me the rare opportunity to learn about my grandfather's academic life *retrospectively*. I took plenty of time sticky-beaking into what Max was thinking at different times, while also doing my own research – gleefully diving down the rabbit holes that his words had opened up for me.

Sitting in my grandparent's study, I read closely through the piles of documents. I studied the words Max had chosen and typed out, often only to be later crossed out with a confident strike of his pen, a neat hand in black ink above it suggesting a more succinct description. I became very familiar with his slanted handwriting that seemed never quite to keep up with the thought that was flowing through him at the time. Via the recordings I became accustomed to the commanding and respectful voice of a Max Charlesworth at the peak of his powers, a strikingly different voice from the older and more frail Babo that I knew. With my grandma, my Nonna, I was lucky enough to have endless conversations. She would reminisce and regale me with stories of their travels, their work, and of decades-old academic gossip. With close colleagues and friends of Max, such as Tony Coady and Val Noone, I was able to pick their brains about what my grandfather meant to them and to the wider philosophical and religious communities. I watched them wistfully describe Max's omnipresent combination of calmness and determination in battles with certain individuals. And when I would head back home, my Mum would tell me stories about what it was like to grow up and live with someone so outspoken, her pride and affection at the tip of her tongue as she repeatedly told me of being singled out in church services during Max's anti-Vietnam war period.

It was thanks to these opportunities that I began to create a much larger and more comprehensive picture of Babo; I now knew more about who Max was, what he was thinking and feeling at different points of his life, what he had discovered, fought against and fought for. And *now*, when I think about Max, it is not just the damp handkerchief angling in to wipe my face, or the rough feel of his cheek against mine as we kissed hello or goodbye, nor the sound of his shoes, always a size too big, shuffling down the hall. Now these direct memories are intimately coupled with the posthumous retrospective discoveries of his life.

Throughout this process of sorting and reading through his archives, I began to wonder if this new information indeed contributed to my *memory* of Max.

Does this more comprehensive image that comes to mind when I think of my grandfather strictly count as memory? Can I say that I have a memory of something that I did not directly experience, and that even predated my birth? Moreover, does this more familial, personal memory, the image of a loved one's whole life, act differently to other forms of memory? And what criteria determine whether something is indeed a memory or not: is it the *means* by which it enters into the brain, mind, or soul, or the *end* itself, the memory-image and belief-feeling that is produced through the act of recollection?

3.2 What Is Memory?

The best place to begin, Babo once said to me with a wry smile, is of course at the beginning. So what is memory exactly and how does it work?

One of the first pieces that I plucked out amongst the plethora of pages in the Babo's storage boxes was one of his early writings on Aristotle's *De Anima*. Somewhere in one of these pages of draft notes, the slanted hand of a young Max mentions Aristotle's *Parva Naturalia*, and specifically one of the short treatises, entitled *On Memory and Reminiscence*.

Aristotle initially identifies memory in relation and in opposition to imagination and perception; it is of course not possible to remember the future, nor have memory of the present (Bloch 2007, p. 25).[1] Memory instead relates to the past. After all it is, according to Aristotle, the same organ whereby one perceives time that facilitates this act of remembering (Bloch 2007, p. 29). Focusing exclusively on propositions or sensory experience of events, Aristotle argues that one can only be said to truly remember when one has scientific knowledge, or former perception of events, that *is apart* from current actualisations or future expectations (Bloch 2007, p. 27). Included and annexed to these representations of propositions or events is always the consciousness of a 'formerly'; that inner voice suggesting and insinuating 'I *formerly* heard, perceived or had this thought' (Bloch 2007, p. 27).

Aristotle sees memory as an impression, like a seal impressed into the wax tablet of our brain or soul leaving an impression of the original experience (Bloch 2007, p. 31). This seal-like representation requires *direct* sensory experience to be transferred into memory. I must be *there*, at the source, in order to have a sensory

[1] References to Bloch is of his translation of Aristotle's *De memoria et reminiscentia*. The material herein from Bloch refers to *De memoria* 449b4–450a; 451b.

experience that can be successfully stamped into my mind's wax tablet as a potential memory to be retrieved at a later date.

What is important according to Aristotle is the *means* of a memory; what the source is and how it is implanted into the wax tablet of the time-perceiving organ. He would surely accept that I can remember a young Max Charlesworth travelling to the *Université Catholique de Louvain* hoping to explore the Husserl Archives for his doctoral thesis, but only as a statement of fact, as a proposition. However, Aristotle would be completely unwilling to accept that I could remember this as a memory of the event itself. Put simply, I could not have had direct experience of this event in 1953 to impress into my personal wax tablet, my own mother having only just been born. Similar to Aristotle, most of us would want to say that to have a memory of something one must first have *experience* of its source. Without directly experiencing an event it would simply not be possible to produce a memory. However, what exactly the requirements of this 'experience criterion' are is far less obvious.

At first blush it seems that for Aristotle what is most important in determining what is and is not memory comes down to the means of its implanting. Importantly, however, he also concedes that memory can only be said truly to exist in the very moment of recollection (Bloch 2007, p. 39). Therefore, when determining what counts as memory, the means of impression is not the only or most important issue. What is produced, how it appears and feels, must also be analysed and appreciated when discussing memory.

Bertrand Russell's *The Analysis of Mind* does just this, focusing on what exactly a memory-image is and specifically how it *feels* during moments of recollection. Rummaging around in Max's storage boxes, I came across a darkened manila folder, chocked to the brim with oxidising sheets of foolscap paper. These held various academic reviews that Max had once thought and typed up. Two of these focused on Russell's *Cambridge Essays: 1888-1889*, and *Authority and the Individual*. Max's descriptions and analysis immediately piqued my interest and I promptly began to look further into Russell's ideas. Fortuitously, I stumbled upon his *The Analysis of Mind*. The ninth lecture of this book, *Memory*, presents a highly intuitive and unsettlingly realistic picture of what memory is and how it works.

Unlike Aristotle with his wax tablets and his insistence on the means of memory, Russell is instead interested primarily in the product of recollection itself; the memory-image. Interestingly, he claims that these memory-images do not differ intrinsically from mental images produced entirely through imagination (Russell 1921, p. 186). The only real difference is that the memories are accompanied by a sense of familiarity (Russell, p. 168). This familiarity is similar to an Aristotelian consciousness of 'formerly'. It is a belief-feeling – a sensation, an image or complex of both – in the past existence and experience of the event in question, which may be expressed with the words 'this existed, or happened' (Russell, p. 186). I say that I *remember* Babo coming to speak to my year-11 high school philosophy class only because annexed to my mental image of Babo struggling his way up the three flights of stairs is the belief-feeling in my mind, gut, or soul, that this event truly *happened*. This reference to the past, what makes an image a memory-image, therefore lies not with the content believed but rather with the actual belief-*feeling* (Russell, p. 186). Moreover, this belief-feeling is a connection to a reality, and it is this aspect of memory that sets it apart from pure imagination (Russell, pp. 185–6).

However, does this mean I can then say that I remember Max Charlesworth before I was born, simply because I have various mental-images of this period with the internal belief-feeling telling me that these events – such as Max becoming the Foundation Dean of Humanities at the new Deakin University down in Waurn Ponds – '*did indeed happen*'?

Intuitively most people would seem to want to answer with a flat and direct 'No'. Like Aristotle, most of us would require that a person must have direct experience of an event for Russell's belief-feeling to be annexed to the recollection's mental image. Clearly, I have mistaken the 'this happened' criterion, taking his words too literally (Russell, p. 170). To say 'this happened' does not solely mean that an event has previously occurred, otherwise the whole of history could count as memory. Instead, 'this happened' is the ellipsis of the internal voice asserting, 'this event happened and *I experienced it directly*'. To remember then, to acquire this belief-feeling of remembering, one must have direct experience of the event.

And yet, again, the same question arises; what do we mean by 'experience'? What does it take to fulfil this 'experience criterion'? C.B. Martin and Max Deutscher, in their aptly named article *Remembering*, attempt to answer this very question. Setting aside the question of what 'memory' actually is, they set out to construct a robust definition of what exactly it is to 'remember' (Martin and Deutscher 1966, p. 161).

3.3 What Is It to Remember?

Martin and Deutscher initially separate the large and unruly mess of the many instances of what we call memory into more salient and pragmatic categories. They initially contrast procedural or 'how to' memory – habitual memory of actions, for instance, remembering *how to* ride a bike – with declarative memory, which will be their focus (Martin and Deutscher, p. 161). This declarative memory is further divided along vaguely Aristotelian lines into the sub-categories of propositional and episodic memory; recollection of information and events, respectively.

In terms of propositional memory, Martin and Deutscher argue that a person can be said to remember *that* something happened, even though it occurred before they were born, or within their lifetime though outside their direct experience. This person may have previously worked it out, or heard about it quite independently of their own perception of it (Martin and Deutscher, p. 162).

Of course, this seems obvious. In announcing 'I remember *that* the Carlton Blues won the 1995 AFL Premiership' I am saying nothing controversial. While I was only two years old and did not attend the match at the Melbourne Cricket Ground, I can still have propositional memory of this piece of history. I am simply stating an agreed-upon fact of history, such as that Franz Ferdinand was assassinated in Sarajevo in 1914.

However, the requirements for episodic memory are starkly different. Martin and Deutscher maintain that a person can be said to remember an event only if they have experienced it *directly*, having observed it themselves (Martin and Deutscher, p. 163). It would certainly be false to assert, 'I remember the assassination of the Archduke of Austria', as opposed to the statement, 'I remember *that* the Archduke of Austria was assassinated', for the simple reason that I was not alive in 1914 to be able to experience the event. Whether or not it can be said that I have episodic memory of the 1995 Carlton Premiership is far less straightforward. For while I was young and not present at the actual match, there is a sense in which, especially growing up in Carlton and being a part of the Blues-mad family which Max had raised, I had some aspects of experience of the last of those glory years. Clearly then, the 'experience criterion' of memory needs to be better articulated.

To do this, the authors propose a three-step analysis to determine what exactly it is to remember an event. First, a person must represent that past thing or event, within certain limits of accuracy. Secondly, this person must have *observed* what they now represent, whether this be 'public' (like a sports match) or 'private' (say, an itch). Thirdly, this person's past experience of the thing or event must be *operative* in producing the states within them that eventually lead to their representation, their 'memory' (Martin and Deutscher, p. 166).

In employing the term 'observe' in the second step, Martin and Deutscher thereby seek to restrict the experience criterion to only direct, first-hand experience of an event. However, what does it mean for such experience to be 'operative' in one's remembering?

It is common to describe and reminisce about some past event and yet be uncertain whether the mental image described originated in direct experience or was in fact founded on something one was told after the event (Martin and Deutscher, p. 168). Do I truly remember Babo taking my cousins and me over the road to Optus Oval at three-quarter time? Or is the mental imagery that springs to mind when I think about these events due more in part to my older brother's describing them to me after the fact?

For Martin and Deutscher's strict definition of memory, the prompting of my older brother may disqualify me from having a genuine memory of this event, even if an accurate mental image and Russell's belief-feeling were present. They require the past witnessing – one's direct experience – to be 'causally necessary' to one's present account (Martin and Deutscher, p. 176). Even if I recount this childhood event with perfect accuracy, and I did indeed experience this event (thereby fulfilling Martin and Deutscher's first two criteria), I still may not be strictly-speaking *remembering* the event in question. It must be determined whether I would have given the same story, expressed the same mental-image, had I *not* witnessed this event (Martin and Deutscher, p. 176). If this were the case, according to the authors, my personal experience is not operative in producing the 'memory'. I could only have propositional memory of such events.

Clearly, such an analysis of whether one's experience is casually necessary to one's present recollection is nigh impossible in real life. Moreover, in proposing such a strict analysis, Martin and Deutscher have pushed the determination of what counts as memory away from the subjective self and out of the hands of the internal belief-feeling. What is important, according to these authors, is an external justification and more objective analysis, which is in stark contrast to how we actually use and act upon memory and recollection in our everyday life.

In this sense, Martin and Deutscher would certainly argue that I cannot have memories of a younger Max Charlesworth from before I was born. I may well have a new-found wealth of propositional memories of the life and times of my grandfather – for instance, I am perfectly able to say 'I remember *that* he gave the 1989 Boyer Lectures' (Charlesworth 1989). Nevertheless, it would be impossible for me to claim that I have any episodic memories of such events.

3.4 Familial Memories

Martin and Deutscher's strict definition of memory, and particularly their emphasis on a narrow conception of experience, has, however, missed something essential in the way memory actually functions in everyday life.

It certainly does not feel right, nor is it realistic to say that I *only* have propositional memories of my grandfather before I was born. When I turn my mind's eye to think of Babo, of Max Charlesworth, so much more than a stream of facts rush into my head. All the conversations with family, with his friends and colleagues, the photos, his writings, as well as the videos and recordings match up with my other episodic memories form when he was still alive to offer me rich and intimate mental images that are interconnected and interwoven into a larger picture that constitutes my memory of Babo. When I think of my grandfather, a vast overall complex of image and sensation unfolds within me.

This type of memory then does not obviously fit neatly into the previously defined propositional or episodic categories initially created by Aristotle and reaffirmed by Martin and Deutscher. It sits somewhere between these two traditional groupings, and yet is different again. Memories of this type, which I will tentatively give the name *familial memories*,[2] do not refer to a single event or even single proposition. They are an amalgamation of both episodic and propositional memories; taking their scaffold from this latter type, and the visceral colour, feeling, and sensation from the former. They do not refer to a single and linear event, but are a combination of different memories from different times. They influence and inform each other, coming together to create a holistic memory – one general dynamic image in which one can focus in on particular elements. Most importantly, familial

[2] By offering the term 'familial' I do not mean to restrict such memories solely to family members. Instead this category should be extended to any and all intimate, personal memory-images of close and important relations, which are very often, though not always, connected to a loved one.

memories are infused with a deep personal connection that can profoundly affect the creation and communication of these memories. For when I reminisce about Max presenting his ABC Boyer Lecture on *Life, Death, Genes and Ethics* (Charlesworth 1989), I do not simply remember the *that*. A holistic sensory image springs to mind; the pursed lips I had come to remember so vividly, the sound and texture of his voice that I recall from playing the cassette tapes of this lecture in my car, as well as his stance, emanating a quiet comfort and confidence, which I had seen many times when trawling through photos of Max mid-performance.

Familial memories may not fit precisely into Martin and Deutscher's categories, and they would no doubt argue that I am missing the essential element of direct experience in my formulation. Familial memories, they might argue, still act in very much the same way as episodic memory. While they may not pertain to just one singular event, they still take the form of episodic remembering. That is, the experience criterion must be fulfilled.

However, in my view, Martin and Deutscher's formulation and especially their insistence on direct observation, is far too strict and as such highly unrealistic. While their theory helps distinguish between experience and remembering, it simply sets the bar too high for what can be considered memory. Could not indirect experience via secondary sources be equally operative in producing a memory-image within me? And moreover, is this not in fact a very common source of what many of us would call memory?

3.5 Memory from Indirect Experience

Indirect experience is an experience that does not stem from one's first-hand observation of an event. Instead it is the observation and experience of secondary sources which themselves are connected to the event in question. These secondary sources might include my grandmother's conversations with me about events in Max's life, or more generally, photos, videos or even writings on or about an event. I argue that we rely on many different types of indirect experience to form memories in our everyday lives.

Let me again, unapologetically, use an example of Max and the Carlton Blues to highlight how Martin and Deutscher's formulation is much too rigid to be of any practical use. We would say it is sufficient that Max directly experienced the 1995 Carlton premiership if he attended the match at the MCG. It would also be sufficient, albeit maybe slightly less so, that he directly experienced the match if he was watching it on TV, or maybe on his radio at home in Lang Street. However, say he was out of town, for a conference or holiday, and only had time to watch the replay and read the reports in the newspaper the day after. In such circumstances we may be less inclined to say that he had direct experience of the event. However, to say that Max did not experience the match *at all*, that he did not at all remember the match, would seem equally odd in our everyday parlance. In these cases, Max's observation, gets further and further away from the source of the event, spatially and then temporally, from direct to more indirect experiences.[3] What this shows us is that we have an intuitive idea that the closer one is to the source, the more direct the observation will be, the greater chance for a holistic sensory experience to be impressed. Therefore one should, as is Martin and Deutscher's hope, represent the event in question more faithfully.

What then, about me? Being so young, many would argue that I did not directly experience the match in question. However, let us imagine that some years later I discover the VHS of the Grand Final and obsessively watch and re-watch the game.[4] Moreover, I study the post-match interviews, the celebrations, the compulsive analysis in newspapers, and even have the luck to meet some of the premiership players and hear their various personal insights into the game. I eventually come to have a detailed mental image of the game; the images and sounds of the game itself, the tactical decisions, the added retrospective significance of the occasion, and personal stories that ran through the event. In Martin and Deutscher's analysis, I could still not be said to remember the game. This being so, even if I recall the match *more faithfully* than Max, even if he had attended the MCG that day.

Clearly, this intuition, as represented by Martin and Deutscher, is not *always* correct when it comes to memory. Direct experience and closeness to source does not necessarily translate into faithfulness of representation. Moreover, indirect experience can still be extremely valuable; it can produce faithful mental images, and, I argue, can still be operative in affecting genuine memory.

3.6 Virtues of Secondary Sources

While indirect experience may be further from the episodic source – thus offering a less holistic sensory experience with more room for malleability – this very distance is in some cases its virtue. The fact that secondary sources are detached somewhat from the initial sources enables them to provide a different and unique perspective.

My Nonna often tells me the story of when she, Max and my infant mother were taken in by a convent of Irish nuns for months at a time over summers when Max was studying in Belgium. The large spatiotemporal and personal gap between my grandmother's recounting of the event and the source itself offers to me and my eventual memory the many benefits of hindsight. While I may miss the more visceral feelings, as well as the sights, sounds, and even smells of this experience, what I gain in memory is immense. From this indirect experience I learn what was so special in a longer-term sense to be taken in and cared for by these nuns, and how

[3] Moreover, as it moves further away in spacetime, it seems also to move further from a holistic sensory experience. For instance, watching the game at the ground offers a full gamut of visual, auditory, olfactory, gustatory and somatosensory stimulation. On the other hand, listening to the wireless of course offers a much less holistic sensory impression of the game itself.

[4] For what else is there to do as a Carlton supporter when your team is but a shadow of its former self?

each individual was affected by this event. I am able to grasp and include in my memory how this event was connected to other events before and after, as a catalyst or culmination, which provides a fuller picture of the event's place within a context. Most importantly, and this pertains especially in relation to familial memories, I gain my Nonna's personal subjective take and memory on the event. While some may argue that this sullies the truth-value or faithfulness of the event in question, in this case, I would argue that the subjective twist is itself inherently valuable. To hear my Nonna's feelings of relief and gratitude all these years after the event, communicates something to me that just would not be available to me if I were actually there. Simply put, what my indirect experience lacks in holistic sensory impressions, it gains in retrospective contextualisation and provides a rare opportunity to inject my memories with a subjective interpretation, which in cases with loved-ones is inherently valuable.

This last point touches on a very important aspect of familial memories that previous philosophical discussion of episodic memory has missed. What is most important about a personal, familial memory is the difference in the *aims* of recollection when compared to the types of memory traditionally studied in philosophical arenas. From Aristotle through to Russell and on to Martin and Deutscher, philosophers have typically been concerned with if, and how, a mental-image is indeed a 'genuine' memory. In their epistemological framings, the aim of recollection is to remember something that actually happened, and remember it faithfully. This of course is still an important aspect of any personal memory. However, it is not *always* the immediate nor the most important goal.

Most especially in the context of remembering a now deceased family member or friend, the point of remembering and communicating these familial memories is to commemorate, to celebrate, and for that person's life to live on through those close to them. It is a respect and remembrance of history, a sense of continuation from past through to future. In this way, the aim of these familial memories is contained in the very act of reminiscing and the communicating of such memory itself. When my mother comes together with her four sisters and two brothers to reminisce about the life of their father, questions of the verisimilitude of their personal memories does not initially come into play. Yes, they may light-heartedly argue over their conflicting accounts of certain events (as none of the siblings seem to have inherited the sharp long-term memory of their mother) but all appreciate and understand that what is truly important is the performance of the reminiscing itself. It is this remembering – despite and even because of the various subjective corrections, forgettings and enhancements – and the communication of the memories that is cherished. In fact, imagining a family member wanting to soberly assess the truth-value of a loved-one's recalling of a personal memory (trivial familial bickering aside, of course) would seem extremely odd. One would go as far as to say they are missing the point of the reminiscing entirely.

When my Nonna reminisces to me about stories of her and Max's past, what is important, for both of us, is not the truth-value of the memories in question. It is the very *act* of her communicating these memories to me that is valuable, for both of us. For I trust, as my grandmother, that there is a reason why she wishes to share such intimate moments with me. Because her history, and my Babo's history, is necessarily my history too. Thus, I hope I have shown that indirect experience can indeed lead to genuine memory, and that, moreover, these important secondary sources indeed add certain virtues not available through direct experience rather than simply sullying the memory-image as has traditionally been thought.

3.7 Memory and Imagination

When I am reminiscing about Babo, via indirect experience, I am certainly not trying to argue that the memory-images that come to mind are *exactly* the same as if I had directly experienced the event. I am not reliving direct experience of holistic sensory inputs. Instead, it is the secondary sources – the conversations with Nonna, the scribbled handwriting of Max's ideas, the recordings, the videos – that incite, provoke and stimulate my mind to paint such vivid memory-images. While these may not be identical to the traditional direct-observation memories, all I argue is that these memories from indirect experience are not so fundamentally different from direct-experience memories as to be excluded from being counted as genuine memory.

But from where do these mental tapestries come if they are not from a reliving of sensory experience? Clearly, imagination plays a vital role in not just familial, but in all forms of memory. When I try to remember Max's time in Louvain during his work towards his doctorate, I do not remember his autobiographical scribblings on this period nor Nonna's conversations recalling this time nor the black and white photographs of the snow-lined Belgian boulevards. No, instead I create an interactive, dynamic mental image from these sources with the aid of my imagination. It is this imaginative memory-image that comes to mind when I remember this period of Max's life. And yet it is still memory; there is still a feeling of familiarity, albeit in a slightly different form, that is annexed to the memory-image.

The intuitive objection to this inclusion of imagination into memory presents itself almost immediately. How can a mental image truly be episodic memory if the image is simply a collection of propositional memories propped up by indirect episodic experience and coloured and filled in by imagination? The response here, interestingly, lies in an analysis of what Martin and Deutscher would term 'true' or 'genuine' forms of episodic memory (Martin and Deutscher, pp. 195–6). As we saw earlier, we carry an underlying assumption that direct experience equates to a more faithful recollection of an event. Secondary sources are associated with error, the malleability of indirect experience with unreliability. However, in fact even these 'genuine' memories are themselves constructed in a similar way with the aid of imagination (Sutton 2016). When we reminisce about a past event, we often tell more than we strictly speaking remember. Usually we truly remember only the gist of the event, maybe one or two particularities, and we use our imaginative capacities to fill in the blanks (Ibid.). In this way, our memories are never perfect representations. We use imagination to summarise, construct, interpret, condense, and smooth over to produce a coherent narrative and a 'faithful' picture (Ibid.). Memories, of any type, will *always* be fundamentally reconstructions and it is only with the aid of imagination that we can remember anything in the first place.

Therefore memory-images produced via indirect experience do not differ *fundamentally* from their direct cousins. They are not products of pure imagination, nor of present experience. They are produced, consumed, and acted upon just like any memory. The events that are part of my familial memory of Max's life really did happen and when I think about them, there is a belief-feeling of familiarity that is strongly annexed to them. Such memory-images differ from pure confabulations in that they are rooted in experience, albeit from secondary sources. It is in this sense that I argue that I can indeed have memory of my grandfather's life and times from before I was born.

3.8 A Reformulated Analysis

It is because memories must be grounded in a sense of reality that I would not be justified in pronouncing just any old thing as 'memory', for instance that 'I remember Max supporting the Essendon Football Club'. Even if someone close to Max had told me this, clearly this memory does not cohere with my other available episodic memories, and does not correspond to the propositional memory which I have of my grandfather. Any memory then, even those of a familial variety, is susceptible to questions of justification.

To decide whether a mental image is indeed a memory and not simply a confabulation, a revised form of Martin and Deutscher's analysis is necessary. First, and most obviously, one should represent the past event within certain limits of accuracy (Martin and Deutscher, p. 166). The second requirement, however, should be reformulated slightly with the criterion for experience being extended to include indirect experience as well. Thus, one must have observed what they now represent (Martin and Deutscher, p. 166), *or reference the experience of a secondary source who did observe the original event*. Thirdly, this experience of the event, be it direct or indirect, must be operative in producing the eventual representation (Martin and Deutscher, p. 166).

While building on Martin and Deutscher's analysis, my reformulation sets a lower bar and casts a much wider net as to what can and should be counted as memory. While this may now include some less traditional conceptions of memory, I believe it is a much more accurate reflection of how we define and how we employ memory in our everyday lives. Martin and Deutscher's criteria are far too strict, only permitting the purest forms of memory, whose merits become almost impossible to assess in reality. Moreover, the criteria exclude any experientially indirect forms of memory, including those familial types of memory that are more concerned with commemorating loved-ones and communicating a sense of the continuation of history than with the verisimilitude of a memory.

Furthermore, the ends produced by both forms of memory are almost identical. Even the memories produced from secondary sources, while relying more on imagination than on direct sensory input, still certainly feel and act like any other forms of memory.

The belief-feeling annexed to such memories will be slightly different from the belief-feeling Russell described. In my memories of Max before I was born there still exists a certain consciousness of the 'formerly', albeit a different, less vivacious and forceful version, to borrow some Humean terms, which relies upon the secondary source's connection to the original event. In this sense, trust will play a certain role in the belief-feeling. This is certainly not a problem with more familial memories where one's connection to the secondary source, as well as this secondary source's connection to the original source, is tightly woven with a deep love that easily allows that trust and belief-feeling to develop and be sustained.

I adopt and act upon these indirect memories as I would any other form of more traditional memory. We cannot simply ignore this internal aspect when determining what should count as memory. My familial memory of Max, including the episodic memories I have generated of his younger years, continue to have an influence on my intuition, reasoning, perception and introspection (Frise 2017).

3.9 Concluding Remarks

In this article, I have attempted to explore a question that has been nagging me since I started rummaging around in my grandfather's archives. Is it possible to have memory of Babo's life and times from before I was born? I am in no way suggesting that I could remember the events of his life *as if* I were there at the time. However, to say that I do not *remember* the mental images that so vividly spring to mind would seem to suggest that they fall into the class of pure imagination, and this feels distinctly inappropriate.

I have sought to take the discussion of memory outside a purely epistemological realm and to broaden the scope of what we traditionally count as memory to include those episodic memories that follow from indirect experience via secondary sources. This revised definition is much more in-line with how we discuss and act upon memory in everyday life. This is especially true with more familial forms of memory where the aim of reminiscing and communicating these recollections is to commemorate loved ones and to provide a sense of the continuation of history between family and friends. In such cases, secondary sources are not a poor substitute for direct observation but can offer a unique form of memory that direct experience simply cannot.

Imagination is a necessary component of any memory, not just those stemming from indirect experience. As such, both direct and indirect memories do not differ dramatically in their means. The actual memory-images produced from these different forms of remembering feel very similar and are received and acted upon in almost identical fashions. In this way, I believe one must instead offer an argument as to why memory should be restricted only to cases of direct experience as Martin and Deutscher claim.

Whatever one thinks of my account of memory, I feel terribly lucky that I have been able to take such a rich and intimate look into my grandfather's long, courageous, and productive life. I am very grateful that I have been able to create some memories and imagine what his life was like so as to understand him and his life better and to continue to learn and grow with Max after his death.

In loving memory of Max Charlesworth, my Babo.

References

Bloch, D. (2007). *Aristotle on memory and recollection: Text, translation, interpretation, and reception in Western scholasticism*. Leiden: Brill.

Charlesworth, M. (1989). *Life, death, genes and ethics: Biotechnology and bioethics*. Sydney: Australian Broadcasting Corporation.

Frise, M. (2017, June 30). Epistemology of memory. In *Internet encyclopaedia of philosophy*. http://www.iep.utm.edu/epis-mem/

Martin, C. B., & Deutscher, M. (1966). Remembering. *The Philosophical Review, 75*(2), 161–196.

Russell, B. (1921). *The analysis of mind*. Oxford: Allen & Unwin.

Sutton, J. (2016). Memory. In E. N. Zalta (Ed.), *The Stanford encyclopaedia of philosophy* (Summer 2016 ed.). https://plato.stanford.edu/entries/memory/

Alexander Tomas Charlesworth Linger is one of many grandchildren of Max Charlesworth and has tentatively followed in the large footsteps of his 'Babo' by pursuing philosophical studies. Having recently completed his honours thesis at the University of Melbourne – investigating and defending a Pyrrhonian form of epistemic relativism – Linger is now exploring different ways philosophy can be used and expressed outside the walls of the Academy.

Chapter 4
Max Charlesworth: A Parish Priest Reflects

Michael Elligate

There is a lovely line in Chaucer's "Prologue to the Canterbury Tales" that sums up Max Charlesworth as a man, a scholar, and a Christian searcher. The line refers to "the Clerk of Oxenford":

> And gladly would he learn and gladly teach.

Max and Stephanie were part of life at St Carthage's Parish. They enjoyed coming to pray here, and they enjoyed the diverse congregation that gathers at this place. Often we swapped books and of course many an idea was perused over the meal table at Lang Street and later at The Avenue in Parkville.

Often when people read beyond their own chosen field of expertise, their grasp of the history of ideas is so enriching. Understanding the historical context of a theory or idea was central to Max's appreciation of knowledge.

This gift of openness freed Max from the trap of being an ideologue. Many would have regarded him as the most significant Catholic intellectual in Australia. He understood dogmas and doctrines as our fragile attempts to define mysteries well beyond our full comprehension. It is no surprise that Max found John Henry Newman's writings on The Development of Doctrine quite liberating.

Many years ago I read Max's study on Anselm in the medieval world. Then his clear and practical analysis on matters of reproduction and bioethics were groundbreaking in a vastly different technological world. Max had a profound respect for the ancient civilization of our first people of this land and he wrote with deep sensitivity about their own spirituality.

Recently the family gathered at his grave for a dedication of the memorial stone. We recalled the words from the book of Job:

M. Elligate (✉)
St Carthage's University Parish, Parkville, VIC, Australia

P. Wong et al. (eds.), *Considering Religions, Rights and Bioethics: For Max Charlesworth*, Sophia Studies in Cross-cultural Philosophy of Traditions and Cultures 30, https://doi.org/10.1007/978-3-030-18148-2_4

Ah would these words of mine were written down in stone, inscribed on some monument with iron chisel and engraving tools cut into the rock forever.

After my awakening, he will set me close to him and from my flesh I shall look on God.

Fr Michael Elligate was ordained as priest in 1973 and was appointed to St Carthage's in 1987. He was Chaplain to the University of Melbourne for 18 years. A graduate in Arts and Education, he currently chairs various committees in Human Ethics Research at the University of Melbourne and is Deputy Chair of the Walter and Eliza Hall Institute for Medical Research Ethics Committee. Fr Elligate is Chaplain to St Mary's College, University of Melbourne; Chaplain to Mercy Place Aged Care, Parkville; and Chair of The Council for Chaplaincies in Tertiary Institutions.

Part II
Love of the World

Chapter 5
Community Consultation in a Liberal Society

Loane Skene

5.1 Introduction

This paper considers the process for consultation and deliberation concerning contentious ethical issues in a liberal society. It examines some of Professor Charlesworth's ideas concerning government and society. It illustrates their operation in practice by reference to the process of community consultation in a major Australian review of the law on human cloning and embryo research. It concludes, as Professor Charlesworth did himself, that some agreement may be achieved, even on the most contentious issues, by acknowledging the range of different beliefs, then seeking areas of shared concerns and building upon those areas of agreement can take place.

5.2 Professor Charlesworth's Ideas Regarding Ethics, Government and Society

Professor Charlesworth's book, *Bioethics in a Liberal Society*, was published by Cambridge University Press in 1993. He said that medical ethics should not be considered 'in abstraction from the social and political context in which they arise'.[1] In a liberal society, 'personal autonomy, the right to choose one's own way of life for

[1] These statements are quoted from Charlesworth 1993, pp. 1–2. Later chapters of the book focus on 'Ending life', 'Beginning life', and 'Distributing health care resources', but he mentions 'new procreative technologies' and 'genetic intervention in human life' in his Introduction to the book, and in some passages. He has also written extensively about issues arising in this area in other publications; for example, his Boyer Lectures, *Life, Genes and Ethics* (Charlesworth 1989).

L. Skene (✉)
Melbourne Law School, University of Melbourne, Melbourne, VIC, Australia

P. Wong et al. (eds.), *Considering Religions, Rights and Bioethics: For Max Charlesworth*, Sophia Studies in Cross-cultural Philosophy of Traditions and Cultures 30, https://doi.org/10.1007/978-3-030-18148-2_5

oneself, is the supreme value'. A liberal society is 'characterised by ethical pluralism' since each individual may freely exercise their own autonomy; and indeed must do so if they are acting ethically (Charlesworth 1993, p. 10). There is 'no determinate social consensus about a set of "core values" or a "public morality" which it is the law's business to safeguard and promote'; and members of ethics committees and the broader community ought not 'in the most authoritarian way… tell people what is good for them and… lay down prohibitions on what they may and may not do with their lives'.[2] However, he rejects 'ethical relativism or scepticism, which would mean that no one ethical or moral position is better than any other'; and, quoting Ronald Dworkin, he says that liberalism 'provides that human beings must be treated as equals by their government, not because there is no right or wrong in political morality, but because that is what is right' (Charlesworth 1993, p. 4).

Charlesworth is not alone in holding these views about liberalism, of course. Not surprisingly, he mentions Kant, Mill and 'contemporary liberal thinkers'– John Rawls, Isaiah Berlin, Ronald Dworkin and Joseph Raz, among others (Charlesworth 1993, p. 5). What is of interest in the present context is his proposal for reaching agreement in the development of public policy and law reform. This is an area in which he was prominent for many years, serving with distinction on numerous committees. His contributions were wise, made after careful listening and reflection. He was prepared to compromise where necessary without abandoning his faith and fundamental beliefs; and to show the path for others in order to promote agreement.

5.3 Community Consultation in Australia on Human Embryo Research

Charlesworth's approach may be illustrated by the community consultation undertaken in an Australian review of the law on human cloning and embryo research. This is a matter on which views differ widely. The issues are profound and difficult to resolve. When does human life begin? Should research be allowed on human embryos and, if so, what safeguards should be required? How should a 'human embryo' be defined? Should scientists be permitted to form embryos specifically for research? Is there a difference between forming an embryo by fertilisation of an egg with sperm, or by somatic cell nuclear transfer (SCNT), where a somatic or body cell is transferred into the egg (the 'Dolly the Sheep technique' or 'therapeutic cloning')?

One might expect that it would not be possible to reach agreement on these issues, even in a general way, in a liberal society 'characterised by ethical pluralism' (in Charlesworth's words), giving due weight to all submissions. The people most

[2] In this context, Charlesworth refers to 'some Christians who seem to think they have the right to use the law to enforce Christian morality on divorce, abortion, contraception, assisted procreation, suicide …'—Charlesworth 1993, p. 3.

likely to respond are those with strong views, in this case, based on religious beliefs about the moral status of the early embryo[3]; a desperate desire to accelerate potentially life-saving research to help themselves or family members; fears that the research may exploit vulnerable women who will be asked to donate eggs for the research;[4] and the like. Without careful thought and planning, the consultation process may yield responses that are extreme, widely divergent, unrepresentative of the wider community, and of little assistance to regulators in deciding how to proceed. However, despite the anticipated difficulties, the committee that investigated these issues in 2005 was able to make recommendations that were widely accepted by the community, and by Parliament; and the legislation was amended as the committee recommended.

Before examining the committee's processes, it will be useful to consider more fully the reservations that have been expressed about community consultation in developing policy and law.

5.4 Reservations About Community Consultation

Many people are skeptical about community consultation, especially about respondents being ill informed about the issues; and the weight to be attached to community views. 'Moral majoritarianism' cannot be accepted, they say; that is not 'doing ethics'. A majority of the Australian population reportedly believes in capital punishment for some offences,[5] for example, but their opinions do not dictate that this should be the law. To make good decisions, we must thoroughly analyse the underlying bases of decisions, including risk assessment and cost-benefit analysis. There is a wealth of wisdom in the experience of a wide range of people and that should be taken into account in policy making, to promote widespread acceptance of the ultimate regulation. That approach may be contrasted with the 'principles-based' approach to ethics promulgated by authors such as Beauchamp and Childress (2001) that is widely used in reports of ethics committees and law reform bodies. Where a number of ethical principles are applied in turn in policy-making, they may be listed at the start of a report and then the recommendations may have another basis, perhaps because the ethical principles lead to different outcomes according to which one is applied.

---

[3] Compare Charlesworth, note 2 above.

[4] Charlesworth pointed out that this was only one 'feminist' concern about reproductive for women; he discussed 'the variety of different voices of women' on many occasions; e.g. Charlesworth 1993, note 1 above, pp. 89 ff, citing Carol Gilligan.

[5] A majority of respondents to a Roy Morgan survey in Australia in 2014 approved of capital punishment for deadly terrorist acts (52.5% total – 55% of the men who responded; in Queensland, the overall majority was 57%; in Western Australia, 59% and in Tasmania 63%): 'Small majority of Australians favour the death penalty for deadly terrorist acts in Australia': http://www.roymorgan.com/findings/5814-death-penalty-for-terrorist-acts-september-19-2014-201409190533

Charlesworth supported the broader experience-based approach, drawing on shared values, rather than the application of ethical principles. He acknowledged that some people have strong views, sometimes based on their personal circumstances, or their religion; and that those views must be respected. However, even people with strong beliefs may accept propositions advanced by others that may enable consensual policies to be developed from the shared area of agreement.

5.5 The Lockhart Committee and Its Consultation Process

In 2005, the federal government established the *Legislation Review Committee for the Review of the Prohibition of Human Cloning Act* 2002 *and the Research involving Human Embryos Act* 2002 (the Lockhart Committee)[6] to examine and make recommendations concerning the federal legislation on human embryo research and cloning in 2005.

The Committee undertook very extensive consultation, as required by its Terms of Reference.[7] It published an issues paper to explain the science of stem cell technology in terms that could be understood by a wide audience and established a Review website on which the Issues Paper, submissions and other material could be read by anyone. There were more than 1000 written submissions. The submissions came from private individuals; researchers, service providers and consumers, federal and state government agencies; parliamentarians, lawyers, academics, ethicists, and religious groups. The Committee also held face-to-face meetings with stakeholders, either invited by the Committee or seeking an opportunity to participate. The Committee held public hearings in all capital cities, together with a number of private meetings. It had several site visits, for example to fertility clinics. There was extensive media coverage. Finally, there was an international literature review undertaken so that the Committee could be fully informed about recent scientific developments.

5.6 Seeking Areas of Agreement When There Are Divergent Views

The committee acknowledged from the outset the complexity of assessing community attitudes in a diverse society. It was clear it could not identify the 'Australian community' as a single entity that had one view on issues like embryo donation, stem cell research or SCNT. There are many diverse 'communities' in Australian society, 'with different perspectives, interests and values' (Lockhart Committee

[6] Prohibition of Human Cloning Act 2002 (Cth); Research Involving Human Embryos Act 2002 (Cth). These two Acts are later called 'the 2002 legislation'. See also Lockhart Committee Report 2002.

[7] Committee members later reflected on the process of their deliberations: Skene et al. (2008).

Report, p. xiii). Individuals may be members of a number of different communities at the same time (a church member, a scientist, a person caring for a sick relative, etc.); and different communities may have different moral concerns. Christian communities for example, may give priority to the moral status of the embryo, health communities to care or compassion, and patient communities to health outcomes. Or, as Charlesworth said, 'some people adopt "absolutist" ethical stances while others adopt more pragmatic "consequentialist" stances'.[8] The values and perspectives of those communities and individuals may also change with time, experience and contact with others with different needs, values and perspectives.

Divergent views were therefore inevitable; but, as Charlesworth said, 'it is possible to have a society without consensus upon a substantive set of moral, religious and social values, save for consensus upon the values of personal autonomy, with all that they connote' (Charlesworth 1993, p. 162). Those values may in turn provide the basis for agreement on substantive issues on which views initially differed.

In analysing and reporting on community consultation on embryo research, the committee could have started by listing issues on which there was most likely to be disagreement (such as the moral status of the human embryo and whether it is ever justified to destroy an embryo for 'research'), and then examined ethical arguments that might be made to support that perspective. However, that would have led to conflicts that would be difficult to resolve. That would also happen if abstract ethical principles were set out and discussed in turn – autonomy, beneficence, utilitarianism etc., the 'principles-based' approach to ethics mentioned earlier. Instead, the committee decided to focus on areas of potential agreement, rather than the conflicting arguments based on the ethical beliefs set out in the submissions.

'Hot tubbing'. The Committee members were as much at risk as the wider community of being unduly influenced by their pre-determined beliefs. As Charlesworth warned regarding '"expert" bioethics committees' or 'select groups of quasi-Platonic sages', they are no more likely than the wider community 'to be able to agree upon and formulate a common bioethical code. …they too reflect the ethical pluralism that exists in the community at large' (Charlesworth 1993, p. 162).

The Committee's Chair, Justice Lockhart, suggested early in its deliberations that members should abandon their own philosophical perspective during the Committee's deliberations and take a more open view through 'hot-tubbing'. Instead of arguing with each other about particular issues from predetermined ethical positions removed from the specific complexities of those issues, they should explore together what the solutions might be. Figuratively, they could 'take off their clothes and get into a tub' for frank discussions. This, in turn, might lead to a more robust, honest and transparent conversation and a greater likelihood of consensus. He encouraged some of the people who made submissions to the Committee to do the same, asking those from different sides of the debate how they would resolve the

[8] Charlesworth 1989 (Boyer Lectures). This reflection is accompanied by Charlesworth's comment: 'The Gilbert and Sullivan song has it that everyone is born either a little liberal or a little conservative, but I almost think that people are also born either ethical absolutists or ethical consequentialists'—ibid, p 22.

differences in community views. During this process, he encouraged people to acknowledge for themselves that there were different views and that the committee had the difficult job of trying to reconcile those views.

5.7 Moral Framework and Method used in the Review: Discussion of Ethics, Ethical Theory and Moral Frameworks; Rejection of 'Principlism'

The committee discussed, early in its deliberations and explicitly, the approach it should take in analyzing the ethics, ethical theory and moral frameworks underlying the issues raised in the review. It considered the methods of other reviews involving contentious ethical issues, such as the widely esteemed report of the Australian Law Reform Commission and the Australian Health Ethics Committee, *Essentially Yours: The Protection of Human Genetic Information in Australia* (2003). It noted that some of those reports had a preamble referring to moral theory, or, more often, a reference to broadly accepted ethical principles (the 'principles-based' approach mentioned earlier). However, the moral theory or ethical principles set out in the preamble to such reports were not always evident in the body of the reports or in the recommendations themselves. Indeed, the ethical theory or framework described in the preamble was rarely referred to beyond the introduction. The committee therefore decided not to apply any single normative theory or aspect of 'principlism'.

Instead, the committee chose to adopt an approach based upon fundamental (shared) moral values, an acceptance of pluralism and diversity in community(s), and on processes of deliberative democracy. The ethical approach that the committee adopted was later described by Ian Kerridge,[9] the specialist ethicist on the committee, as an approach of *pragmatic discourse, or communicative morality*, similar to that described by Habermas (1991).

This approach was pragmatic, he said, because it attempted to find a way to reconcile the inevitable conflicts inherent in pluralism and liberal democracy. It was moral because it argued that communities share certain fundamental values, including human flourishing, ontological security and (social) justice; and it assumed that while those fundamental values will remain unchanged, the ethical views or perspectives that communities adopt may change and evolve with time, circumstances, and context and technical feasibility. It was discursive or communicative because it rejected the epistemic and moral authority of any single normative theory (including utilitarianism, deontological approaches or a principles-based approach); it explicitly recognised that different (discourse) communities exist and that they may have different values and perspectives; it recognised that, in areas of complex social or health policy, many moral concerns may be at stake and different communities may give primacy to different moral concerns.

[9] The description of the ethical approach of the committee in this and the next paragraph paraphrases or is based on Kerridge's writing, especially in Skene et al. 2008, p. 135.

5.8 Matters of Potential Disagreement and Agreement

The matters on which there was most likely to be disagreement regarding human embryo research were evident from the start, especially from the submissions to the Committee; in particular, the moral status of the human embryo and whether it is ever justified to destroy an embryo for 'research'. However, instead of discussing those aspects at the outset, the Committee looked for moral values, social principles and matters related to the scientific and medical issues on which the community generally agreed.[10] For example, the submissions showed a good deal of support from both the scientific community and the general public for the regulatory framework put in place to administer the 2002 Acts and that became a significant point of agreement to build on. There was also widespread agreement that some practices that were prohibited by the 2002 legislation should continue to be prohibited, such as reproductive cloning; allowing an embryo to develop for more than 14 days outside the body of a woman; and placing a human embryo in the body of an animal or vice versa. The Committee readily agreed that those practices should continue to be prohibited because of the very strong and widespread feelings in the community about them.

Another matter on which the Committee found broad agreement was a desire to help sick people and infertile couples. As Justice Lockhart said in his Foreword to the Report, 'the Committee found that there is strong community support for medical research to help people who suffer from debilitating or incurable diseases or conditions, through better understanding of the processes of those diseases or conditions, and the development of new treatments' (Lockhart Committee Report 2002, p. v). There was also considerable community support for medical research to help people to have children, including a general acceptance that some 'surplus' embryos no longer needed to achieve a pregnancy will be destroyed.

Having identified points of general agreement, the Committee examined the issues on which views differed, particularly the deeply felt conviction expressed in many submissions concerning the intrinsic moral value of a human embryo. According to this view, a human embryo is an entity deserving full protection from the moment of its creation. It is therefore wrong to create a human embryo except to help a woman to have a baby and an embryo should not be intentionally destroyed, even for research that may benefit many other people. (Allowing an IVF embryo to 'succumb' if it is not needed to achieve a pregnancy is regarded as morally different from deliberately destroying it.)

It might seem that these two views are inevitably inconsistent. However, the Committee was able to make progress in several ways. First, it recognised that we live in a community in which activities are permitted unless they are specifically prohibited by law (in contrast to a community in which activities are permitted only if they are authorised by law). For particular conduct to be prohibited, there needs

[10]The Committee's approach is described in its report (Lockhart Committee Report 2002); and in Skene et al. 2008, from which the following description on the Committee's approach is taken.

to be general agreement in our community that it should be considered a crime. While the Committee respected moral objections to stem cell research and SCNT, members felt that in a liberal, secular democracy where there is a range of moral perspectives, the moral values of one community should not be permitted to override the beliefs and interests of others. Rather, in situations where there is not general agreement but some people have strong moral objections to a particular activity, it may be justifiable to restrict that activity by an appropriate regulatory regime, but without making it a criminal offence. That was the approach of the 2002 legislation which established a federal licensing committee to oversee the research on surplus embryos that was permitted at that time.

Secondly, the Committee agreed that the predominant issue was not whether the potential benefit of the research would override the moral objections of those who opposed it. On the contrary, it rejected a utilitarian approach emphasising that we do not know what the research will ultimately achieve and even the greatest benefits do not always justify the means of achieving them. Indeed, throughout its deliberations, the Committee tried not to be unduly swayed by the potential benefits of the research which are unknown and frequently overstated, at least at this stage. Instead, the Committee focussed on the full range of arguments underlying human embryo research, listening carefully to all of the submissions and trying to evaluate them in forming its recommendations.

Thirdly, the Committee agreed that scientists do not have to prove that their research will produce positive outcomes for health care in order to be permitted to do it. On the contrary, if there is *any* chance that research will help the sick and infertile, then those who oppose that research bear the onus of persuading the regulators that it should be banned. The more likely and promising the treatments that may be developed, the higher the burden becomes of convincing the community that the research should not be allowed. The Committee found it almost inconceivable that a treatment that, for example, would enable people paralysed with spinal injuries to walk, could be denied on the basis of moral objections to the research held by one particular part of the community.

Finally, the Committee tried to 'balance' the competing views concerning the moral status of the early embryo. The Committee found that even those who favour the creation of embryos by SCNT for research acknowledged that SCNT embryos are different from those created by fertilisation of an egg by sperm. SCNT embryos made solely for the purpose of producing stem cells for medical treatment could be regarded as being somewhat akin to culturing a person's own cells for a transfusion, rather than creating a new person. The contrast was especially evident when the Committee heard women in fertility programs talk about the significance of the embryo for them. Their embryo is their future baby, bearing the combined genes of the parents. For this reason, the Committee recommended that the law should continue to prevent the creation of an embryo for research by fertilisation of an egg with sperm, but that SCNT should be permitted to create an embryo for research, provided that it could never be implanted in a woman.

This suggestion will not, of course, persuade all people, some of whom are quick to point out that the SCNT embryo could possibly, if not used in research, develop in the same way as a 'sperm-egg embryo', if it were placed in a woman's uterus. But the crux of the Committee's recommendations was that SCNT embryos created to produce stem cells must *not* be implanted. Indeed one might say that no SCNT embryos have a chance of development because implantation is always prohibited.

Nevertheless, the fact that many people do view early human embryos as having special moral status cannot be discounted. For this reason, the Committee recommended that the use of human embryos in research should continue to be strictly regulated. For example, it should continue to be permitted only with a licence, subject to reporting and careful scrutiny. Scientists should also be required to justify the need to use embryos in research, to use the smallest number of embryos possible and to handle and dispose of the embryos 'with respect'.

5.9 Conclusion

The process of the Lockhart Committee in reviewing the law on human cloning and embryo research in Victoria effectively illustrates how Charlesworth's ideas of decision-making in a liberal society operate in practice. He said that some agreement might be achieved, even on the most contentious issues, by acknowledging the range of different beliefs, and then seeking areas of shared concerns and building upon those areas of agreement. This was the approach of the Lockhart Committee. It was aware of areas of vehement disagreement. Many scientists, and sick people and their families, want embryo research to be permitted in the hope of finding new cures and treatments for serious medical conditions. However, others strongly believe that human embryos have a special moral significance and must be protected by law from the time they are formed; or that vulnerable women may be pressed to donate eggs for research. Those views would be difficult to reconcile.

However, as Charlesworth advocated, the Committee focussed on areas of agreement, rather than dissension. It was broadly accepted that the Australian legislation was effective in banning practices that were widely rejected by the community such as reproductive cloning to produce children identical to their parent; and to strictly regulate other research on reproductive technology. The community also accepted the need for medical research to treat people who are sick. The Committee built on those shared values in formulating its recommendations and, in doing so, explicitly rejected the approach of 'principlism' (setting out a list of ethical principles such as autonomy, beneficence and utilitarianism and then applying those principles seriatim in its reasoning).

The Committee's search for areas of agreement to form the basis of its recommendations was in line with Charlesworth's notion of 'ethical pluralism' both in the general community (in widespread community consultation); and in the committee itself, through the 'hot tubbing' discussion). Each person was able to exercise their autonomy to the maximum extent possible, as Charlesworth said was their right and duty in a liberal society.

References

Australian Law Reform Commission. (2003). Essentially yours: The protection of human genetic information in Australia. *ALRC 96*. http://www.alrc.gov.au/inquiries/title/alrc96/index.htm. Viewed 25 Aug 2016.

Beauchamp, T. L., & Childress, J. F. (2001). *Principles of biomedical ethics* (5th ed.). Oxford: Oxford University Press.

Charlesworth, M. (1989). *Life, death, genes and ethics: Biotechnology and bioethics*. Boyer Lectures. Crows Nest: ABC Enterprises for the Australian Broadcasting Corporation.

Charlesworth, M. (1993). *Bioethics in a liberal society*. Cambridge: Cambridge University Press.

Habermas, J. (1991). Discourse ethics: Notes on a program of philosophical justification. In S. Benhabib & F. Dallmayr (Eds.), *The communicative ethics controversy*. Cambridge, MA: MIT Press.

Lockhart Committee Report. (2002). *The Report of the Legislation Review Committee for the Review of the Prohibition of Human Cloning Act 2002 and the Research involving Human Embryos Act 2002*, 2005. http://www.nhmrc.gov.au/research/embryos/review/index.htm. Viewed 25 Aug 2016. The site of the Lockhart Committee is archived at: http://pandora.nla.gov.au/tep/63190. Viewed 25 Aug 2016.

Prohibition of Human Cloning Act 2002 (Cth). http://www.comlaw.gov.au/Details/C2008C00694. Viewed 25 Aug 2016.

Research Involving Human Embryos Act 2002 (Cth). http://www.comlaw.gov.au/Details/C2008C00689. Viewed 25 Aug 2016.

Skene, L., Kerridge, I., McCombe, P., & Schofield, P. (2008). The Lockhart committee: Developing policy through commitment to moral values, community and democratic processes. *Journal of Law and Medicine, 16*, 132.

Loane Skene is a Professor Emeritus at the Melbourne Law School; and until recently, she was an Adjunct Professor in the Medical Faculty at the University of Melbourne. She was an inaugural member of the Centre for Applied Philosophy and Public Ethics (CAPPE) and a member of the NHMRC Australian Health Ethics Committee. She served on the two federal committees advising the government on legislation regarding research on human cloning and embryo research, the Lockhart Committee, of which she was Deputy Chair, and the Heerey Committee. She was awarded a Centenary Medal by the Commonwealth for 'Service to Australian Society through the Exploration of Legal and Ethical Issues of Health Care'. She is the Inaugural Life Fellow of the Australasian Association of Bioethics and Health Law (AABHL) and a Fellow of Queen's College Melbourne and St Anne's College Oxford.

Chapter 6
Dying in a Liberal Society

Jeff Malpas

> *The essential thing is that people should carefully weigh the price they must pay...*
> – Albert Camus, "Neither Victims nor Executioners"

"Dying", writes Max Charlesworth, "is, in a sense, the most important thing a person does" and he adds that "one should as far as possible be in control of it" (Charlesworth 1993, p. 33). There can be little doubt that the ending of a life is one of the most important events of a life, and what is to be the manner of the ending of our lives is one of the most important questions that faces us all. Most of us would also concur, at least initially, with Charlesworth's claim that the ending of our lives is something over which we should be able to exercise some control. Indeed, issues concerning the end of life, and the control one may have over it, have gained considerable public attention in recent years with the rise of campaigns for the legalisation of assisted suicide in many countries, and, in some cases, the enactment of legislation to achieve just such an outcome – for instance, recent legislation in the state of Victoria, Australia.[1]

[1] 'Voluntary Assisted Dying Bill 2017,' Parliament of Victoria (website), accessed 9 August, 2018, https://www.parliament.vic.gov.au/publications/research-papers/download/36-research-papers/13834-voluntary-assisted-dying-bill-2017. Information is provided here, not only in connection with the enacted Victorian legislation, but also in connection with numerous previous attempts to legislate such laws in Victoria, other states and territories of Australia, and in the Commonwealth of Australia itself. Moreover, this site lists and describes the jurisdictions, worldwide, where voluntary euthanasia and/or assisted dying laws are in effect and, additionally, provides a lengthy list of media releases, news articles, legislation, documents, and websites that relate to the subject.

J. Malpas (✉)
University of Tasmania, Hobart, TAS, Australia

Latrobe University, Melbourne, VIC, Australia
e-mail: jeff.malpas@utas.edu.au

P. Wong et al. (eds.), *Considering Religions, Rights and Bioethics: For Max Charlesworth*, Sophia Studies in Cross-cultural Philosophy of Traditions and Cultures 30, https://doi.org/10.1007/978-3-030-18148-2_6

Death may be the end of life, but it is where the philosophical discussion of life, and especially the ethical discussion, often has its beginning. Charlesworth's comments on the importance of dying appear in his ground-breaking volume, *Bioethics in a Liberal Society.* There the issue of the ending of life is the first of the substantive issues Charlesworth discusses, following immediately after his explication of the liberal ideal and the principle of autonomy that he takes as central to it. Although he acknowledges the ambiguity of the phrase, Charlesworth argues in defence of what he terms "the right to die" and the need for a liberal society to give legal force to that right (Charlesworth 1993, pp. 36–38). Significantly, he also takes this "right to die" to include the right to request assistance from others in exercising that right. Charlesworth argues that whatever one has a right to do is also something with respect to which one can reasonably ask others for assistance in exercising the right to do it (Charlesworth 1993, p. 37). The rights at issue here follow, according to Charlesworth, from the principle of autonomy that he takes to be basic to a liberal society – and his commitment to those rights reflects his claim that our dying is something over which we should exercise as much control as possible. One might even go so far as to say, given the pre-eminence of the ending of life in Charlesworth's account, that the autonomy we exercise in the manner of our dying is the most basic form in which autonomy can be exercised.

Charlesworth points out that the commitment to the principle of autonomy should not be seen as incompatible with the fact that the exercise of autonomy can be a complicated matter or that it may sometimes be unclear the degree to which a decision or action is autonomous – he notes that "autonomy, like all concepts has a 'grey area' of application" (Charlesworth 1993, p. 21). Moreover, he is also at pains to emphasise that the commitment to autonomy does not entail an endorsement of egoism or an asocial conception of the self, nor a rejection of any form of communitarianism or consensus. "There is absolutely no reason" writes Charlesworth, "why an autonomous act must necessarily be self-regarding and cannot be other-regarding… A society of autonomous agents is not necessarily a collection of individualistic, self-contained and self-regarding atoms or 'islands of self-conviction and self-direction'" (Charlesworth 1993, p. 23). The principle of autonomy on which a liberal society is founded is essentially directed at marking out a space of individual action and decision-making free from outside interference – by marking out "a sharp distinction between the sphere of personal moral views and the sphere of state intervention and the law" (Charlesworth 1993, p. 19) – and so "the liberal society is one which promotes and provides space for … self-determining choices to the greatest degree possible" (Charlesworth 1993, p. 22). It is just such a society to which Charlesworth takes his readers to belong, and thus he summarizes the main argument of *Bioethics in a Liberal Society* with the claim "that those engaged in bioethical discussion must become aware of the fact that they are living in a liberal society and take account of its basic values" (Charlesworth 1993, p. 27).

Charlesworth's argument in *Bioethics in a Liberal Society* is admirably clear and accessible, and he is a powerful advocate for the liberal ideal that he espouses. It is notable that although he argues in favour of ensuring that individuals have as much control as possible over the ending of their lives, and even, as I noted above, advocates for the right of an individual to ask others for assistance in enabling such control, he also recognises many of the legal and cultural complexities surrounding these issues. Still, Charlesworth's basic position is that the principle of autonomy is indeed paramount, and responds to those who would warn against making the principle of autonomy 'absolute' in the manner that Charlesworth seems to suggest (McCormick 1991), by asserting that "…to complain of the 'absolutisation of autonomy' is rather like complaining of absolutising personhood. Autonomy is not something one can have too much of" (Charlesworth 1993, p. 34). In spite of the many virtues of Charlesworth's account, this last comment is one that I find somewhat troubling, and it echoes an uncertainty that I have about Charlesworth's opening comment that dying is an event "one should as far as possible be in control of" (Charlesworth 1993, p. 33). Part of my concern here is with the idea of control, as well as with autonomy, but it also connects with a sense that the emphasis on the principle of autonomy, so central to Charlesworth's account, and notwithstanding Charlesworth's own acknowledgement of the complications here, is alone inadequate as a principle to address the issues that face us at the end of life. In this regard, the primary concern of my contribution here can be summarised as follows: if a liberal society is one in which the principle of autonomy is indeed absolute, then what does that mean for dying in a liberal society, and what sort of dying does it entail? Might the absolute insistence on autonomy actually undermine other values that also have relevance to dying as well as to living?

I should begin, however, with a hesitation I have about the society that is being addressed here, or more specifically, about whether the 'liberal society' that is at issue in Charlesworth's discussion is actually identical with our own – about what society it is that is 'our own'. If the test of a liberal society is the degree to which it enshrines the principle of autonomy, then it surely has to be acknowledged that many contemporary societies, including those to which Charlesworth's readers might be thought to belong, are imperfectly 'liberal', just inasmuch as the principle of autonomy is itself only imperfectly enshrined in their legal and institutional structures. Here there is a certain tension within Charlesworth's account, since on the one hand that account seems to be predicated on the assumed 'fact' that we live in a liberal society, where such a society is one committed to the centrality of autonomy, and yet, on the other, the argument for reforming laws and institutions so as to better accord with the principle of autonomy suggests that the society (or societies) at issue is not one in which autonomy is absolutely central (at least not so far as the actual form and structure of its laws and institutions are concerned), and so, by definition, is not entirely 'liberal'. What this surely indicates is that the foundation for the argument for legal and institutional reform in accord with the liberal ideal cannot be based in any simple pre-existing 'fact' concerning the 'liberal' character of the society at issue – which also means that the commitment to the centrality of autonomy cannot itself be assumed without argument. This raises a question that

Charlesworth does not explicitly address concerning the real foundation for the commitment to autonomy in the first place.[2]

Inasmuch as there is an indication of an argument for the centrality of autonomy at work in Charlesworth's thinking it is surely to be found in the idea that the pluralistic nature of modern societies both *precludes* any commitment to more substantive ethical principles (principles, for instance, that concern the nature and content of a 'good' life) and that it also *requires* the commitment to a more procedurally-oriented principle (one that concerns the form of decision rather than its content) of the sort that autonomy seems to exemplify[3] – to a principle, in other words, that marks out an area of decision and action as free from state or institutional interference. Such an argument is a familiar move within liberal theory, and yet it seems to rely on more substantive commitments than might be apparent at first sight – commitments that underlie even the idea of autonomy in its procedural character. Autonomy is itself grounded in a prior assumption, whether or not it is made explicit, that the primary locus of decision and action is the individual person, and even that the person is indeed to be understood as just such a locus of decision and action.

It seems hard to make sense of autonomy, or its significance, independently of the idea of a certain being or kind of being that has autonomy – independently, that is, of the individual person, self, or agent. Charlesworth makes use of the idea of the person as the one who exercises autonomy and who is possessed of certain rights – including the supposed "right to die" – even if he does not ground the notion of autonomy in the idea of the person, nor offer any explicit account of the person, and he rebuts the complaint regarding the absolutisation of autonomy that this is itself "like complaining of absolutising personhood". That the idea of the person is implicated here is significant, since what it shows is that there is indeed a more substantive ethical and even metaphysical commitment at work here. That this is so has an important consequence: if the idea of the person is that in which the notion of autonomy is grounded, then any claim regarding the absolute nature of the principle of autonomy will have to derive from or be dependent on a claim to the effect that what is essentially at issue in the concept of the person is indeed exhausted by the concept

[2] One might say that Charlesworth's point, even though it is not explicitly made in this way, is actually that we have a prior commitment to the liberal ideal, though a commitment that is imperfectly realised, and that it is this commitment that is the starting point for his argument – what Charlesworth argues, on this account, is for making our laws and institutions, as well as our practices, more consistent with that prior commitment. But although this shifts the language of the account, it does not substantially change the issues at stake. What it is that substantiates the claim that we already have a prior commitment to the liberal ideal other than the prior instantiation of that ideal in our laws, institutions, and practices? Moreover, if that commitment is imperfectly instantiated, as it will be if there is need of an argument that our laws, institutions, and practices need to be made more consistent with that ideal, then it cannot be sufficient for the claim that we are indeed a 'liberal' society – at least not without some further argument. Given such an imperfectly instantiated commitment, the question can legitimately be raised as to whether we are, in fact, a liberal society on Charlesworth's own criteria.

[3] So at one point Charlesworth seems almost to characterise a liberal society as a society 'where a plurality of values is not only tolerated, but actively encouraged' (Charlesworth 1993, p. 27).

of autonomy. If it should be the case that the concept of the person involves more than just the notion of autonomy (which is to say that the person is more than just an autonomous decision-maker – a claim that seems at least *prima facie* plausible), then autonomy cannot be the sole or indeed the 'absolute' principle that determines the ethical considerations associated with the person. What becomes evident here is that Charlesworth's claim (and other claims like it) to the effect that the assertion of the principle of autonomy is neutral with respect to the nature of persons or of human lives ("A society of autonomous agents is not necessarily a collection of individualistic, self-contained and self-regarding atoms or 'islands of self-conviction and self-direction'") is not quite so obvious as it may seem. Although it is true that autonomy is not incompatible with a more 'holistic' or 'socialised' conception of the person, this may well not be true of autonomy when taken as absolute. Much depends on how autonomy is taken to stand with respect to other concepts.

It is perhaps significant that although the emphasis on autonomy as a key value tends to be culturally specific (so there are cultures that will emphasise dependence over autonomy or take communal decisions to have priority over the individual, as, for example, in parts of Asia where the Confucian concept of 'filial piety'[4] takes precedence), there is another value that is less specific in this way, and yet can also be seen to be related to the value given to autonomy and, perhaps more fundamentally, to the value accorded to the person. This is the value expressed in the prohibition, admittedly instantiated to varying degrees, against the taking of the life of another. It seems that there could hardly be a more extreme *violation* of personhood than this – and a violation that also exemplifies the most extreme *violence*. In taking away the life of another I take away the very ground of possibility on which the exercise of autonomy depends, and in doing so I also, *prima facie*, assert my own autonomy over that of the other. Interestingly, Charlesworth's discussion of the ending of life does not touch on the question of the taking of the life of another – the question of murder – at all. Perhaps this is because the question might already appear to introduce an element into the discussion that has the potential to prejudice the terms of certain aspects of that discussion – at least in regard to the question of assisted suicide. Yet if we are honestly to address what is at issue in the ending of life, then the question concerning the taking of life surely cannot be avoided.

In fact, Charlesworth's own discussion of the end of life does not ignore the question of the taking of life entirely. That discussion begins, not with any specific cases of untreatable illness or unendurable hardship, but rather with a specific case of the taking of life, namely, the taking of one's own life – self-murder or suicide. Charlesworth's focus is on the traditional prohibition against suicide as present, in particular, in the Judeo-Christian tradition. Beginning with Kant's injunction against

[4] First laid out in the *Classic of Filial Piety* (a Confucian treatise, attributed to a disciple of Confucius, Zengzi, but likely compiled by his disciples), the call of 'filial piety' – including obedience to one's parents, and the responsibility to care for their physical and mental well-being – structurally permeates the culture of China (but also Japan and other parts of Asia), shifting the priority from personal autonomy or independence to obligation to preceding generations – see Zengzi 2015, or, for a more contemporaneous discussion, including a juxtaposition of filial piety with the view of "contemporary liberal individualists," see R. Fan 2006.

suicide on the grounds that it entails a contradiction, Charlesworth argues that suicide can be a thoroughly rational act, and not only that, but an act that also represents a supreme example of the exercise of autonomy – hence Charlesworth's invocation of the idea of the "right to die", which now appears as the right to exercise one's autonomy in the manner and timing of one's dying.

It is worth reflecting, however, on the grounds on which the traditional prohibition against suicide might be based. Although the grounds of the prohibition may vary according to the exact nature of the prohibition and so of the society, the prohibition against suicide is perhaps most strongly based in the idea that a person's life is not entirely their own, not because their lives are indeed 'owned' by another (as in the case of the slave or the prisoner[5]), but because, by their very nature as a person, their life is enmeshed with other lives – perhaps one might try to capture this notion in the idea that if one can speak of a "right to die", one can also speak of a "responsibility to live" (though just what such a slogan might mean is no less in need of clarification, nor any more obviously capable of clarification, than is the idea of the "right to die"). The act of suicide becomes problematic, therefore, just inasmuch as it constitutes an assertion of the individual against those others with whom the individual life is bound up. This way of understanding what has so often been taken as the ethically problematic character of suicide can also be seen to reflect the tremendously destructive effects that suicide (as opposed to death through illness or accident) can have on others.[6] For this reason, even though particular acts of suicide may be strongly grounded in the desire to alleviate suffering, of the one who dies as well as of others, it may nevertheless remain a problematic act – in some cases an act that even retains a sense of violence and violation. One may try to dismiss such language as introducing elements that in virtue of their emotive content distract us from the real issues – that obscure the rationality of what is under consideration – and yet to dismiss the emotional content of what is at issue in dying, or in the ethical more generally, is surely to dismiss something essential and also essentially human.

It is with the issue of the taking of life, and so also of the responsibilities we may have in regard to a life (whether our own or others), that we most directly confront the question as to the values that underpin a life and in which a human life might be founded. The prohibition against the taking of life is perhaps the fundamental limit that founds the structure of human lives as lives that are lived in relation to one another, even as they are also lived in distinction from one another – and this is evident in the problematic character both of murder and of self-murder. High rates of murder, along with other forms of violence, are seen as an obvious indication of

[5] In societies in which some forms of suicide are condoned, the suicide of the slave or prisoner may nevertheless still be disallowed precisely because neither the slave nor the prisoner is taken to have any 'ownership' over their lives. The type of 'ownership' at issue in such cases, however, is to be distinguished from the more fundamental mode of entanglement with others that is a necessary feature of any and every life.

[6] This is undoubtedly one of the reasons why those traditional societies that condone suicide typically do so in a way that situates it within some formalised framework – often as a particular kind of practice that has ritual or other significance.

social breakdown, and high rates of suicide, even in societies in which it is not a criminal act, are also seen as symptomatic of deeper social and psychological ills. In countries like Australia, significant public attention is given (even if the accompanying public resources are considered by many to be inadequate) to the issue of suicide prevention and the treatment of its underlying causes. The very having of suicidal thoughts is seen as *prima facie* evidence of some degree of mental and psychological dysfunction, and this remains so in spite of the fact that in some circumstances such thoughts (to say nothing of the actions to which they might give rise) might also be a rational response to chronic suffering or distress. Charlesworth is himself critical of societies and cultures in which too much emphasis, as he sees it, is given to the value of a life (Charlesworth 1993, pp. 412–45) – a valuation that he takes to issue in a lesser regard for the *quality* of life as against the mere *preservation* of life, and that can itself be seen to lie at the heart of the injunction against the taking of life. But he gives no attention to the consideration that may be adduced in favour of that valuation, the larger context in which that valuation is situated, or indeed to the question as to the nature of the society that might follow from the refusal of that valuation.

It is surely dubious, however, to suppose that Charlesworth intends his criticism of the commitment to the idea of the value of a life to be construed as undermining *all* commitment to that value. Almost certainly what Charlesworth intends to argue against is the absolute commitment to that value such that it over-rides all other considerations. This seems confirmed by the cases he considers and the conclusions that he draws. His focus is the prioritization merely of the preservation of life over anything else. While I do not wish to foreclose on that question, it seems that one could reasonably say that what Charlesworth objects to is the treatment of the commitment to the value of a life as an absolute principle – one that cannot be qualified by any other consideration. What Charlesworth objects to, one might say, is the 'absolutisation' of the commitment to the value of a life. Yet this objection need not impugn the fundamental nature of the commitment – a commitment or principle can thus be fundamental and yet not absolute. There is good reason, then, to retain the commitment, to the value of a life, and so too the prohibition against the taking of life (the latter being closely connected to the former), and yet also to recognise that in some cases that commitment may be over-ridden. The difficulty in cases like this is that, outside of certain well-defined contexts (being a combatant on a battlefield might be one such), it will almost always be difficult to specify in advance just what cases allow the over-riding of the fundamental commitment or breach of the prohibition that is at issue here, and too broad a waiving of that commitment or prohibition may be simply incompatible with its fundamental character (undermining or weakening it to an unacceptable extent). This means that the commitment to the value of a life and the injunction against the talking of a life may remain the legal default, but with discretion being accorded to the courts (and perhaps in some cases to other bodies) to deal with individual cases according to circumstance.

At this point, it is important to note that the commitment to the value of a life, and the injunction against the taking of a life, do not imply that one must seek to preserve life even in the face of the reasoned refusal of one's efforts to do so by the person whose life is at issue. The commitment to the value of a life cannot, for instance, justify the forced treatment of a chronically-ill and suffering patient who has refused that very treatment, nor can it justify the forced feeding of that same patient. There may be cases where forced treatment is acceptable – perhaps where a patient is psychotic or otherwise incapable of making reasoned judgments of their own – and one might also view the rescuing of an attempted suicide as an example of the valuing of a life over the seeming intentions of the one whose life it is (and so of the valuing of the life as more important than the mere affirmation of autonomy), but for the most part, refusal of treatment or assistance is something that ought to be respected. The difficulty, at least in legal and institutional terms, is often in giving context and support to such refusal.

The importance of the ability to refuse assistance is an especially important point when it comes to contemporary medical treatment. In part, the enormous concern that many people have about the end of life relates directly to the fear that medical treatment may itself lead to a loss of control over their dying – that they may no longer have the capacity to refuse treatment and that their lives may be prolonged in ways that are unacceptable to them. Not only may this be a concern for the one whose own life is at issue, but it may also be a concern for those around them, both in terms of the potential distress at the suffering that may be witnessed and the burden of decision that may have to be borne. Yet the irony of this situation – a situation that looms increasingly large in many contemporary societies – is that it often arises out of the increasing control, and desire for control, on the part of contemporary medicine.[7] Moreover, to a large extent, that desire for medical control is not something driven only by those involved in medical practice – we ourselves look to improved medical treatments and procedures, and, indeed, expect them. Our very desire for control through medical intervention is thus part of what gives rise to a loss of control. It is, moreover, doubly ironic, since the solution that is so often looked to (and that Charlesworth himself seems clearly to favour) is itself a further form of medical intervention – assisted suicide through the provision, by a medical practitioner, of lethal medication. Such a solution seems to depend on resolutely ignoring the conditions that give rise to the situation in the first place, and indeed, so long as the situation is described *only* in terms of control, then it seems the situation can only be inadequately described and inadequately responded to. It also seems to be a solution that adds a further set of ethical as well as legal and institutional complications to a situation that is already ethically, and often medically, problematic.

None of this is to say that the desire for control is itself intrinsically problematic – indeed, I would argue that, as seems implicitly to be the case in Charlesworth's argument against the over-emphasis on the value of a life, that the problem is not 'control' as such, but rather the 'absolutisation' of control or the idea that control (or a certain sort of control) is the only thing that matters. There is already a question here as to what 'control' might be: whether, for instance, control involves control

[7] This is not so in every case, of course, but as it relates particularly to illnesses associated with ageing, it is the capacity of modern medicine to maintain life in circumstances in which life would previously have been sharply curtailed that gives rise to many of the difficulties here.

over oneself, and so over one's own attitude and comportment, or whether it involves control over what is, in some sense, 'outside' of oneself, and perhaps happens to oneself – whether control may sometime take the form of a surrender of control, whether it may even involve a giving up of oneself. Yet if control is all that we focus on, then we may well lose sight of other things that also matter – the sorts of things that appear in just those parts of our lives where control is a much less relevant notion, and where it is rather our dependence and our vulnerability that matter most. Moreover, if control cannot be taken to be the only important notion here, then neither can autonomy, since the emphasis on control, as used in this context, and so as Charlesworth also uses it, is essentially derivative of the emphasis on autonomy – to have control is to be able effectively to exercise one's autonomy. Moreover, just as the notion of control can now be seen to be a notion that becomes problematic both as it is absolutised and as the real content of the notion is left ambiguous, so too is this the case with autonomy itself. What is to count as autonomy is a genuine and often inadequately resolved question, and yet it is also central to the sorts of discussions in which autonomy so often figures.[8]

The way we think about dying cannot be severed from the way we think about ourselves, and if we are to do this in a way that is adequate to who and what we are as human beings, then this requires attending to the character of our lives as inevitably bound up with the lives of others – our lives thus have an apartness to them, which is why our decisions are always our own, and yet they also have an essential relatedness, which is why our decisions do not only concern ourselves. It is this apartness and relatedness that appears in the work of a wide range of different thinkers, from Adam Smith, who emphasises the way the ethical relation is founded in sympathy (see Smith 1976) (which can be seen to bring together apartness and relatedness *as felt*), to Hegel and the theory of recognition (in which it is only through the relation to the other that the self emerges as self) (see Hegel 1977, pp. 104–110), and in a very different way, in the work of those such as Buber and Levinas (in which the ethical arises in the direct encounter with the other and the call upon the self that the other makes).[9] While these thinkers can accommodate the

[8] It is often pointed out that the emphasis on autonomy as the key notion in end-of-life situations overlooks the extent to which those situations are most often characterised precisely by our dependence rather than our autonomy. Charlesworth might reply, however, that this is precisely why we need to put measures in place to ensure our ability to exercise our autonomy even in situations where our capacity to act is severely diminished – that is, to ensure autonomy even in situations of dependence – or perhaps to pre-empt such dependence by prior intervention (so one might decide to end one's life rather than risk falling into a situation of dependence). Yet this itself seems to indicate precisely the problems that ensue from an insistence on the absolute value of autonomy, while also seeming to ignore the fact that autonomy is never itself absolute, but always exists alongside dependence (and although Charlesworth might be said partly to acknowledge this, the point does not enter into his accounting in any significant way).

[9] See, for instance Buber 1958, and Levinas 1978. On the sort of general relational account at issue here, see Malpas 2015b (though the argument here is developed in an ontological more than specifically ethical context), and also Benjamin 2015. Levinas is an especially important figure who looms large in the background of my discussion, although he also stands very much outside of the sort of framework assumed by Charlesworth. Significantly, the injunction against the taking of life

notion of autonomy in varying ways, for none of them does autonomy operate as an over-riding principle, nor can it function independently of considerations concerning the actual content and structure of the self or of ethical life as such.

The limits on the principle of autonomy can be seen to follow, in fact, from the very nature of autonomy, especially in Charlesworth's account, as essentially a *procedural* principle. Although it is this that allows Charlesworth to claim that autonomy is compatible with various different substantive accounts of the self and different fundamental values, this means that the manner in which autonomy functions as a procedural principle will itself by conditional on the substantive context in which it is placed. Taken apart from any such context, autonomy is empty and contentless. What this also implies, however, is that precisely because it is a procedural principle, autonomy cannot function as an *absolute* principle (and it cannot even function as an absolute *procedural* principle[10]). Autonomy is thus compatible with an emphasis on the value of a life, and with an account of human lives as encompassing both apartness and relatedness, but the absolutisation of autonomy is not so compatible. As soon as one insists that autonomy is absolute, then one is committed to it as being more than just procedural – and this is just the problem that Charlesworth's account seems to face (as does perhaps any account that tries to insist on a single principle as both absolute and non-substantive).

I noted earlier my discomfort with what appears as Charlesworth's emphasis on the idea of control, and, with that, on the absolute character of autonomy. I have, in the discussion above, tried to sketch out some of the reasons behind this discomfort. To a large extent what troubles me here is what might be termed the *extremity* of Charlesworth's position. This might seem an odd complaint to set against one who otherwise appears as so concerned to avoid extremism, and whose work is so much centred around a plea for tolerance and plurality – an odd complaint to mount against such a 'liberal' position as Charlesworth espouses. The extremity that bothers me, however, is just the extremity that appears in Charlesworth's abolutisation of autonomy – an extremity that disguises itself with the appearance of neutrality with respect to more substantive values. Yet there is an extremity that belongs to liberalism and to modernity, and that is itself directly tied to the focus on the individual as the bearer of autonomy. Perhaps this focus may be said to be characteristic of modernity and of liberalism both. It is an extremity evident in the modern obsessions with 'authenticity' as itself an ethical value that is often set alongside autonomy.[11] It is also an extremity that seems oddly to implicate the idea of suicide, of self-murder, itself. Lionel Trilling points out that the original Greek term from

is a central idea in Levinas' work, and although this reflects its character as rooted in an essentially Hebraic mode of thinking, it is also directly connected with its commitment to relationality. Levinas is well-known for prioritising the ethical over the ontological, but one might also say that what is at issue here is actually the insistence on the fundamental character of ethics and so on the impossibility of an ontology that is not already ethical.

[10] Substantive principles will always have some procedural import, even if not every procedural principle has substantive implications.

[11] See, for instance, Taylor 1991.

which 'authenticity' comes refers to one who has power, perhaps even who has control, and who is "not only a master and a doer, but also a perpetrator, a murderer, even a self-murderer, a suicide" (Trilling 1971, p. 131), and this captures something of Trilling's own argument to the effect that authenticity is indeed a term of extremity, even of violence.[12]

Charlesworth does not himself talk of authenticity, and so the introduction of that notion here may seem utterly gratuitous, and yet the connection between autonomy, control, and authenticity, as well as the old sense that connects authenticity to suicide, seems oddly to reinforce the sense of extremity at work in Charlesworth's emphasis on the absolute character of autonomy, as well as its expression in the act of suicide. Could it be that in a liberal society the act of suicide itself becomes the act that most fully expresses a certain 'liberal' conception of a life – that dying in a 'liberal society' is itself something determined primarily by the degree to which it is under our own control? If that is even a possibility, then it seems we have good reason to ask whether such a 'liberal society' is itself properly consistent with a genuinely *human* form of life – with a form of life in which autonomy has to be understood as itself standing alongside, and even as emerging out of, our *relationality*, our own *humanity*. Perhaps a 'human society' is one in which the ending of a life, no less than the living of it, is always intimately bound up with a sense of our essential interdependence. Moreover, Charlesworth's own thought was not itself confined merely to the scope of 'liberal' thought as narrowly defined – as his work on a range of topics from existentialism to education to aboriginal religion suggests. Consequently, without wanting to be too presumptuous on the matter, and in full acknowledgement of the position he sets out in *Bioethics in a Liberal Society*, one might well argue that there are important elements in Charlesworth's thought more generally (as well, perhaps, in his life and person) that lend support to the idea of a broader conception of the human – one that involves more than autonomy alone – as that which properly ought to be seen to underpin ethical thought and practice in both its public and private instantiations.

References

Benjamin, A. (2015). *Towards a relational ontology*. Albany: SUNY Press.

Buber, M. (1958). *I and thou* (R. G. Smith, Trans., 2nd ed.). New York: Scribners.

Charlesworth, M. (1993). *Bioethics in a liberal society*. Cambridge: Cambridge University Press.

Fan, R. (2006). Confucian filial piety and long term care for aged parents. *HEC Forum, 18*(1), 1–17.

Hegel, G. W. F. (1977). *Phenomenology of spirit* (A. V. Miller, Trans.). Oxford: Oxford University Press.

Levinas, E. (1978). *Otherwise than being or beyond essence* (A. Lingis, Trans.). Dordrecht/Boston, MA: Kluwer Academic Publishers.

[12] For more on the subject of authenticity and extremity see Malpas 2015a.

Malpas, J. (2015a). From extremity to releasement: Place, authenticity, and the self. In H. Pedersen & L. Hatab (Eds.), *The horizons of authenticity: Essays in honor of Charles Guignon's work on phenomenology, existentialism, and moral psychology* (pp. 45–62). Dordrecht: Springer.
Malpas, J. (2015b). Self, other, thing: Triangulation and topography in post-Kantian philosophy. *Philosophy Today, 59*, 103–126.
McCormick, R. A. (1991). Physician assisted suicide: Flight from compassion. *Christian Century, 108*, 1132–1134.
Smith, A. (1976). *The theory of moral sentiments*. Indianapolis: Liberty Classics.
Taylor, C. (1991). *The ethics of authenticity*. New Haven: Harvard.
Trilling, L. (1971). *Sincerity and authenticity*. Cambridge, MA: Harvard University Press.
Zengzi. (2015). *Xiao jing* (Classic of filial piety) (J. Legge, Trans.). Lionshare Chinese Classics.

Jeff Malpas is Emeritus Distinguished Professor at the University of Tasmania, and Distinguished Visiting Professor at Latrobe University. He has published extensively on topics in ethics, phenomenology and hermeneutics, the philosophy of language and mind, the history of philosophy and the philosophy of place and space. He has also written on topics in architecture, art, geography, medicine and sociology. A new, expanded and revised edition of his *Place and Experience* has just appeared with Routledge.

Chapter 7
Moralism and Anti-moralism: Aspects of Bonhoeffer's Christian Ethic

C. A. J. Coady

Max Charlesworth was very likely the first Australian Catholic lay person to be both a committed Christian and a committed academic philosopher.[1] He was the second Catholic to be appointed a Professor of Philosophy in an Australian secular university; the first was Selwyn Grave. I don't say that Max was a Catholic philosopher because this can convey the idea that he was in possession of some uniquely Catholic Philosophy that was to be brought triumphantly into confrontation with the secular world. This idea was very common when I began studying philosophy at Sydney University in the 1950s, and, of course, it has a long history; it was embodied in the teaching of Dr. Woodbury at the Aquinas Academy in Sydney, as it was amongst many seminary teachers, priests in religious orders and common clergy. Church authorities in the nineteenth century had basically canonised what they took to be the philosophy of Thomas Aquinas, widely known as Thomism, as an official bulwark against the hostile 'modern world'. Some struggled valiantly to give their personal twist to the inheritance and some brave souls amongst the Franciscans chose to give more weight to their order's medieval hero, John Duns Scotus. Max was respectful of the achievements of the medieval Schoolmen but not bound to

[1] Selwyn Grave, Professor of Philosophy at the University of Western Australia from 1961 to 1981, is a contender for the honour, but he was originally, at least, a New Zealander. Julius Kovesi was another Catholic who practiced philosophy with distinction, first at the University of New South Wales and then at the University of Western Australia, but that was slightly after Max. Dr. Vernon Rice at Melbourne University was another with claims and roughly contemporary with Max, but he published very little and was in the Thomist camp with his own personal twist to it. He was an eccentric but influential figure with some of the brighter students but not as well known in the wider world as Max.

C. A. J. Coady (✉)
University of Melbourne, Parkville, VIC, Australia
e-mail: t.coady@unimelb.edu.au

P. Wong et al. (eds.), *Considering Religions, Rights and Bioethics: For Max Charlesworth*, Sophia Studies in Cross-cultural Philosophy of Traditions and Cultures 30, https://doi.org/10.1007/978-3-030-18148-2_7

them in that way. His was thus a relatively lonely and much scorned position for a time until a later generation of Australian lay Catholics also became philosophers in the secular universities. A common understanding amongst most of these (including Max) was that philosophy had its own intellectual norms and integrity that could not be dictated by external political or religious imperatives.

Max was an inspirational figure during his time at Melbourne University and Deakin University and in his writings. His inspiration covered a number of fields: religious studies, continental philosophy, church and state, bioethics and contemporary politics, to name a few. When I first knew him he struck me, perhaps in the brashness of my relative youth, as fairly conservative in some of his theological and moral views, on contraception and abortion, for instance, but he was (and remained so to the end) a genuine Millian liberal who respected personal autonomy, favoured open discussion and was suspicious of all authoritarian tendencies. He was also open to intellectual change and development so that his intellectual career gave the lie to old sayings about youthful radicalism inevitably giving way to the conservatism of maturity.

So far as I know, Max never wrote on the thought of Dietrich Bonhoeffer, but Bonhoeffer's role as a public intellectual confronting power with truth in the darkest of times and showing exceptional courage as he grappled with the moral perplexities of those times must have appealed to him. So, I thought it a reasonable subject to explore in a tribute to Max, especially as my discussion overlaps with one of his abiding concerns, namely, the relations between religion, morality and politics.

I should say at the outset that I venture on this discussion with no pretension to significant expertise in the thought of Dietrich Bonhoeffer or to theological expertise more generally. I approach my task today as a moral philosopher and as a Christian impressed by the depth and force of what I know of Bonhoeffer's work but sometimes puzzled by its meaning. As I read it, Bonhoeffer's account of ethics, at least in his book *Ethics* and in the earlier essay 'Basic Questions of a Christian Ethic', is a brilliant, complex, sometimes paradoxical treatment that raises questions about the nature and importance of ethics and even the very existence of Christian ethics. In what follows, I shall explore some important aspects of this outlook, but I shall begin with some background reflections on distinctive challenges posed by the idea of a Christian ethic.

7.1 Some Background to the Discussion of Christian Ethics

To begin with, we should be clear that there is something problematic about the term 'Christian Ethics'. It may suggest that there is some Christian propriety over ethics itself, so that what genuine ethics there is must be itself somehow special to Christians, or, on the other hand, it may suggest that there is a plethora of ethics each special to its own group, and the Christian ethic is one amongst so many others, such as the Marxist ethic, the bourgeois ethic, the working class ethic and so on. In Bonhoeffer's ethics we will see shadows of both these suggestions. In the second suggestion, we face the looming danger of cultural or group relativism about morality: there are all these different moralities local to their groups and insulated by their cultural or confessional location. Whatever utility this outlook might have for anthropologists (and I think it even somewhat limited there), it understands behaviour in terms of mores rather than morality. It makes it impossible to criticise the prevailing values of some foreign group or culture, but, even more importantly, it makes it impossible to criticise one's own. It is descriptive of what various groups have held morality to be rather than normative about the right way, or ways, to live morally. These and other problems associated with cultural relativism have been well criticised by many philosophers so I will not elaborate such criticisms further here. But the first case is also problematic since it is deeply implausible to think that only Christians have access to a genuine realm of the moral or ethical.[2]

What I mean by this implausibility is that non-Christians and non-believers more generally cannot be supposed to be ignorant of ethics. Everyday experience counts against any such a claim and indeed St. Paul explicitly teaches that unbelievers can have access to moral truths. As he puts it (in Romans 2, 14–15), 'For when the Gentiles, who have not the law, do by nature those things that are of the law; these having not the law are a law to themselves: Who shew the work of the law written in their hearts, their conscience bearing witness to them, and their thoughts between themselves accusing, or also defending one another'.[3] The Catholic tradition of natural law, drawing upon Stoic philosophy, enshrines the idea that natural reason can determine at least a great deal of moral truth, and although in modern times (and even to an extent in Aquinas himself) the insights of this approach have been gravely distorted by a mechanistic application of the concepts of the natural function of bodily organs to sexual ethics, the tradition has both philosophical and theological merit. Its philosophical merit consists in the way it allows the idea of human flourishing a central place in moral thinking and hence provides a hinge on which public debate on moral issues can move. Its theological merit resides in the fact that Christianity, committed as it is to a doctrine of Incarnation and a Creator who looked on the world and found it good, cannot afford to view the created order as wholly hostile or indifferent to revealed truth, but should more plausibly see the workings of 'natural' reason, sensitivity and imagination as themselves capable of revealing truths in morals, as in much else.

But if non-Christians can discover moral truths (or engage in adequate moral understanding) and live good lives in consequence of that, then we need to think more profoundly about what a Christian ethic could be. One answer to the question of course is to say that a Christian ethic has things to say about moral requirements with respect to God, e.g., requirements of worship, that are no part of an ethic for those who don't believe in God. This is, of course, true as far as it goes, but one might expect more. Another answer concerns the additional motivation for good

[2] In what follows, I shall use the terms 'moral' and 'ethical' as synonyms. There is some point in distinguishing them in some contexts but those issues are not directly relevant to my discussion here.

[3] The quotation is from the Douay-Rheims Catholic Bible.

behaviour that a religious outlook can provide. There is, I think, something in this but it needs a good bit of unpacking, and it needs also to meet certain difficulties to do with the moral adequacy of motives such as fear of punishment. Another deeper answer would address the question of how to see the moral life in toto, as it were. Here a Christian answer might resort to explanations that place love at the centre of responses to the needs of others, takes a distinctive view of suffering, and perhaps much else. It might help to think of these matters, in a fashion I have briefly explored elsewhere, as belonging to ethos rather than ethics (Coady 1993). But I do not hope to answer fully these difficult questions here. Rather, I want to try to progress some way towards answers by exploring the vice of moralism in the light of some of the things that Bonhoeffer has to teach us.

7.2 Bonhoeffer's Dismissal of 'The Ethical' and The Critique of Moralism

In his *Ethics*, Bonhoeffer at various points is contemptuous of what he calls 'the ethical'. In his chapter on 'The "ethical" and the "Christian"' he targets several distortions or misunderstandings of life and its moral dimensions that a certain sort of emphasis upon ethics can produce. These represent common ways in which the Christian, and indeed anyone, can be led astray by high-minded attention to moral principles, prohibitions, or permissions. Bonhoeffer, at his best, does not want to deny any place for ethics; as he says:

> Certainly there is a necessary time and place in human existence for the so-called 'ethical phenomenon' that is to say, the experience of obligation, the conscious and deliberate decision between something which is, on principle, good and something which is, on principle, evil, the ordering of life in accordance with a supreme standard, moral conflict and moral resolve (Bonhoeffer 1964: 'The "Ethical" and the "Christian" as a Theme: The Warrant for Ethical Discourse', p. 265).[4]

His point rather is to warn against 'the pathological overburdening of life by the ethical, if one is to prevent that abnormal fanaticization and total moralization of life which has as its consequence that those processes of concrete life which are not properly subject to general principles are exposed to constant criticism, fault-finding, admonition, correction and general interference' (Bonhoeffer 1964, p. 265). To my mind, Bonhoeffer's comments here and his further elaborations on the theme in this chapter of his book are strictures against what I have called elsewhere 'moralism'. (See especially Chaps. 1 and 2 of Coady 2008.) This is a certain sort of vice that needs to be contrasted with genuine morality even though it mimics several features of morality in a distorted way.

---

[4] There is a hardback version of this Bethge edition (Macmillan, New York, 1964) in which unfortunately the pagination and the arrangement of chapters differ (Bonhoeffer gave no real guide to the best arrangement). My references will be to the Fontana paperback, but I will give chapter and section headings to guide those who use the hardback.

Moralism is not one simple thing for it takes several forms: it is a family of tendencies that can masquerade as morality and draws its power from the respect due to moral thinking, but is basically destructive of what is important in such thinking. One form that it takes is that of over-moralising life. This is what I have called in my book *Messy Morality*, 'moralism of scope'. Another form I have identified is 'moralism of abstraction', which occurs when an agent is dominated by abstract principles, prohibitions and injunctions in such a way as to be wholly or partially blind to the particular circumstances in which they must take effect and be embodied (p. 453). Bonhoeffer is concerned to criticise both of these (though not in those words). So, in the passage already quoted, he seems to be insisting that much of the value in ordinary pursuits can be undermined by intruding ethical categories where they do not belong. This is a prime failing of moralism of scope. In the same vein he says:

> …the 'ethical phenomenon', in the sense which we have just described, is fundamentally misunderstood if the unconditional character of the experience of obligation is taken to imply an exclusive and all-embracing claim. To understand it in this way is to injure and to destroy the creaturely wholeness of life (Bonhoeffer 1964, p. 265).

He follows up these comments by the homely remark: 'Big guns are not the right weapons for shooting sparrows'. This strand in his comments connects with recent work in analytical philosophy (not only my own) that is apprehensive of the blighting effects that a certain picture of morality can have on the full enjoyment of otherwise innocent and wholesome activities in life. Susan Wolf has criticised the way that utilitarian and also Kantian pictures of the moral life can intrude the heavy hand of obligations into a person's life in inappropriate ways (Wolf 1982). Kant certainly seems to be in the background of Bonhoeffer's remark about 'the unconditional character of the experience of obligation' and his fear that its 'all-embracing' scope can 'injure and destroy the creaturely wholeness of life' (Bonhoeffer 1964, p. 265). People who are obsessed with such 'unconditionality' will actually fail to experience the richness of life and hence miss out on much that is the material for moral life, though moral life needs to be understood in a more relaxed and nuanced fashion than is common in those whose mind is overwhelmed by concepts of stern duty and strict obligation. Bonhoeffer is very anxious to reject a role for the ethical as a sort of constant nagging presence, hence the reference to the negative aspects of morality as 'constant criticism, fault- finding, admonition, correction and general interference' (Bonhoeffer 1964, p. 265). He thinks that 'the moralists' promote 'the fiction' that 'at every moment of his life man has to make a final and infinite choice…a conscious decision between good and evil. They seem to imagine that every human action has had a clearly-lettered notice attached to it by some divine police authority, a notice which reads either "permitted" or "forbidden" ' (Bonhoeffer 1964: 'The "Ethical" and the "Christian" as a Theme: The Warrant for Ethical Discourse', p. 264). Bonhoeffer thinks that this outlook 'represents a failure to understand that in historical human existence everything has its time (Eccl. 3), eating, drinking and sleeping as well as deliberate resolve and action, rest as well as work, purposelessness as well as the fulfilment of purpose, inclination as well as duty, play as well as earnest endeavour, joy as well as renunciation' (Bonhoeffer

1964, p. 265). Here the endorsement of inclination over duty has a clear reminder of Kant's demotion of inclination and elevation of duty.

Bonhoeffer is also emphatic about the moral significance of the concrete circumstance of life and is acutely aware of the ways in which abstract principles can take such a hold of the mind that they obscure relevant details of the reality to which they are meant to apply. As I read him, he is concerned that concentration on general, abstract principles or moral categories can draw the mind away from the complex human situations and circumstances that are a proper concern of conscientious action. The same can happen when someone is captured by abstract moral categories other than principles – concepts, phrases, condemnatory or laudatory expressions – and uses them peremptorily without regard for close attention to the circumstances of their application. The former Australian Prime Minister, Kevin Rudd, regarded Bonhoeffer as a hero and publicly cited his influence upon him, but some of Mr. Rudd's pronouncements on various actions, people or cultural objects appeared to have the lofty, off-the-cuff remoteness from actual circumstances that verges on such moralism, or at least this is the gist of some common criticisms of him.

Bonhoeffer's discussion of the commandment of God is instructive about his view of moralism. He regards it as different from 'the ethical'. It is 'the only possible object of a "Christian ethic", an object which lies beyond the "ethical", namely the "commandment of God" ' (Bonhoeffer 1964: 'The "Ethical" and the "Christian" as a Theme: The Commandment of God', p. 277). The commandment of God is essentially concrete. As Bonhoeffer says:

> Unlike the ethical, the commandment of God is not a summary of all the ethical propositions in the most general terms. It is not the universally valid and timeless in contrast to the historical and temporal. It is not principle, as distinct from the application of principle. It is not the abstract as opposed to the concrete, or the indefinite as opposed to the definite (Bonhoeffer 1964, p. 277).

So Bonhoeffer rejects what I have called the moralism of abstraction and emphasises instead a living understanding of our circumstances in which God guides us towards right conduct. Given this rejection of abstract moralism and his embrace of the significance of the concrete, it is not surprising that Bonhoeffer shows some otherwise surprising, though muted, sympathy for the Catholic tradition of confession. His sympathy is related to the way that confessors were supposed to be trained in 'casuistry', namely with close attention to the way that moral principles, rules and prohibitions needed to be understood in relation to the special difficulties of application thrown up by the complexity of actual experience. Although he calls upon the Protestant church to rediscover 'the divine office of confession' with its emphasis upon the importance of concrete 'cases', he also warns against the dangers in the confessional tradition of 'reducing the divine commandment to a mere code of laws and pedagogic method' (Bonhoeffer 1964: 'The "Ethical" and the "Christian" as a Theme: The Commandment of God in the Church', p. 293). Again, the danger is one of moralism, and it is ironic that a technique for avoiding moralism should itself create the very dangers it seeks to subvert.

In this emphasis on the concrete, Bonhoeffer's thought is also close to that of contemporary philosophers who call themselves 'particularists'. These philosophers make no reference to God or his commandments, but they emphasise that ethical insight operates primarily at the level of the concrete and particular in experience. Simplifying considerably, their position is that particular judgments about what is right or wrong are prior logically and morally to judgments about general principles and values. Such generalisations have their uses but the priority lies with insight into the morality of particular acts. So the mischief of this or that particular act of deception is prior to the wrong proclaimed in the principle or prohibition against lying. There is clearly an affinity between this outlook and Bonhoeffer's, but there are also differences. One is that Bonhoeffer's stress is more upon the positive value of living freely in the domain of God's inspiration than on the more negative or imperative flavour of 'do' and 'don't' or, as he puts it, 'shall and should'. He thinks that 'ethicists' would do well to:

> ...help people to share in life not out of the motive of 'shall' and 'should', but from the full abundance of vital motives, from the natural and organic, and from free acceptance and will, not in humourless hostility towards every vital force and towards every weakness and disorder (Bonhoeffer 1964: 'The "Ethical" and the "Christian" as a Theme: The Warrant for Ethical Discourse', p. 269).

There is thus more emphasis on the spirit in which one lives life, encounters opportunities and engages with basic institutions in society. So, Bonhoeffer draws upon his theory of the four 'divine mandates', which are: the Church, marriage and the family, culture, and government. These areas of life, or institutions, are not, he says, 'in any sense products of history'; instead they are 'not earthly powers, but divine commissions' (Bonhoeffer, 1964: 'The "Ethical" and the "Christian" as a Theme: The Concept of the Mandate', p. 288). Through a relationship to these (and through friendship, which he finds difficult to accommodate to the schema of the mandates) a Christian discerns the commandment of God in specific circumstances and lives out what might be called a Christian ethic.

7.3 The Difficulties in Bonhoeffer's Account

This is a rich account of an ethic, and indeed a Christian ethic, and it is specifically aimed at avoiding the vices of moralism to which I have drawn attention. But it is not without difficulties of its own. One of these concerns the doctrine of the mandates. In the first place, it is not at all clear what Bonhoeffer means by denying that marriage/ family, culture and government are in no sense 'products of history'. It is one thing to insist that all good things are from God, that family life, cultural values and political rule are God-given and have a certain Divine endorsement. Equally legitimate from a Christian point of view is the insistence that Christ is the source of all authority and that the validity of the four mandates stems from Him. In this broad sense, no good things are merely 'products of history'. But it is another thing altogether to make that fact so powerful as to claim that the 'bearers of the mandate do not receive their commission from below' but 'hold their commission from God, they are deputies and representatives of God' (Bonhoeffer 1964: 'The "Ethical" and the "Christian" as a Theme: The Concept of the Mandate', p. 289). In the case of politics, this is to echo the rightly discredited seventeenth-century political doctrine of 'the divine right of kings'. I doubt that Bonhoeffer would be comfortable with this, but when he says that the task of bearers of the mandate 'is not to expound and execute desires of the human will' (Bonhoeffer 1964, p. 289), he comes close to denying that role for 'the will of the people', which has a central position in the theory of democracy. He goes on to say that the relations of superiority and inferiority that the divine warrant establishes shouldn't be confused with mere earthly relations of superior and inferior power. But if they are to play a part in our ethical responses to one another in the order of government, then we need an account of how the divine relations and earthly relations are connected. So, there remain puzzles and ambiguities in his account. Bonhoeffer is prepared to insist that the mandates are 'conjoined' (as he puts it, Bonhoeffer 1964: 'The "Ethical" and the "Christian" as a Theme: The Concept of the Mandate', p. 291) so that no single one 'is sufficient in itself or can claim to replace all the others' (Bonhoeffer 1964, p. 291) since they are for one another. Thus he tries to reject any dominance of the church over the government, culture or family or vice versa, but the nature of this interconnection remains somewhat opaque. He is insistent that there is no 'kind of autonomy of the secular sphere' (Bonhoeffer 1964: 'The "Ethical" and the "Christian" as a Theme: The Commandment of God in the Church', p. 297) and this could be seen as rightly posing a challenge to what I have elsewhere called an exclusionist picture of politics that treats religion as having no place at all in the public arena. It may also be an attempt to rid himself of the influence of some dubious elements in Luther's strict separation of Church and State and the accompanying difficulties that arose for German Lutherans about criticising the Nazi state. Many German theologians, including Martin Niemoller, seemed to have been influenced by this doctrine in their support for Hitler in the early years of his rise to power (though nationalist motivations were also important) but Bonhoeffer's instincts about the evil of Hitler's regime were far sounder far earlier than most of his confreres. Nonetheless, the question remains what Bonhoeffer thinks about apparently autonomous secular goals and values, such as the freedom, equality and prosperity of all citizens regardless of religion.

This raises a wider problem about Bonhoeffer's position and for my account of it as a rejection of moralism. I have framed his position as a rejection of moralism in favour of a more realistic and contextualised version of morality, but the difficulty with this is that Bonhoeffer vacillates between a rejection of what I have called moralism and a rejection of morality itself. His often-repeated rejection of mere ethics in favour of fidelity to the perceived commands of God in concrete circumstances is clearly influenced, as Matthew Kirkpatrick has pointed out, by his admiration for Kierkegaard and to some extent by his reading of Nietzsche (Kirkpatrick 2013). Like Kierkegaard, he was fascinated by the *Akedah,* the Biblical story of Abraham's readiness to sacrifice his beloved son at God's command, and he saw this as showing, for the Christian, the way in which obedience to God's command overturned ordinary ethical considerations. The conclusions to which this often drove him can be seen most starkly by reference to his early work, 'Basic Questions of a Christian Ethic' (Bonhoeffer 2008, pp. 359–378). After characterising ethics in a strongly relativistic way as 'a matter of blood and a matter of history' so that 'there is a German ethic as well as a French ethic and an American ethic. None is more or less ethical than the other, for all remain bound to history…' (Bonhoeffer 2008, p. 366), he echoes common nationalist or fascist invocations of the soul of the people (Volk) and the degeneration of culture. His relativist understanding of ethics (or as he once calls it, 'secular ethics') makes him fear that a Christian ethic will be just one more such relativised ethic so he agonises: 'Does the so-called Christian ethic not thereby become merely one along- side others, one of many, perhaps a bit better or even a bit worse, but in any case now drawn wholly into historical relativity?' (Bonhoeffer 2008, p. 362). This leads to the resounding conclusion:

> If our line of argument is correct to this point, then the conclusion seems quite clear. Christianity and ethics have absolutely nothing to do with each other. There is no Christian ethic. From the idea of Christianity, there is absolutely no transition to the idea of ethics (Bonhoeffer 2008, p. 363).

Bonhoeffer immediately retreats somewhat from this, however, by saying that he has been drawn off track, since he needs to account for the abundance of ethical regulations in the Christian scriptures. Indeed, he does. After more discussion he produces the idea already mentioned above about concrete fidelity to the commands of God replacing ethical principles, and indeed ethics itself. Here, he draws upon St. Paul in insisting that the Christian is free from the Law and draws a parallel between the Christian and Nietzsche's 'Overman' since 'only Christians themselves provide the justification for their acts, just as they alone bear responsibility for them' (Bonhoeffer 2008, p. 366).

The antinomian flavour of much of Bonhoeffer's writing on ethics can be criticised on several grounds. First, to the degree that it rests upon a shallow relativist picture of what ethics might be, it is rejecting a morality that is something of a straw man, since very few philosophers, and few reflective thinkers of any sort, would identify a plausible morality with the kind Bonhoeffer imagines in 'The Basic Questions'. Second, the emphasis that Bonhoeffer puts upon concrete, contextual judgements of a 'particularist' kind is not merely available to those who wait upon God's command – this point will be developed more fully below. Third, any wholesale rejection or even disparagement of 'the ethical' and a serious role for moral principles or rules makes it difficult to see how moral education or the development of stable character can be achieved, and yet these are not only necessary for personal fulfilment but for social stability. The moral education of children can hardly be achieved simply by telling them to listen attentively for the commands of God. Certainly, it won't do to approach such an educational task with Bonhoeffer's confident assertion ringing in one's ears: 'There are no acts that are bad in and of themselves; even murder can be sanctified' (Bonhoeffer 2008, p. 367). It may be that the doctrine of the mandates is part of an attempt by Bonhoeffer to meet these difficulties but we have already seen that there are serious problems with that.

7.4 The Christo-Centric Problem

This worry is connected with a certain nervousness I have about the precise way to understand the Christo-centric nature of his discussion of these matters. Bonhoeffer says in the *Ethics* that 'it is vain to seek to know God's will for created things without reference to Christ' (Bonhoeffer 1964: 'The "Ethical" and the "Christian" as a Theme: The Commandment of God in the Church', p. 296) and again, 'All the powers of the world are made subject to Him *(i.e., Christ)* and must serve Him, each in its own way' (Bonhoeffer 1964: 'The "Ethical" and the "Christian" as a Theme: The Commandment of God in the Church', p. 298). Now, in the light of other things Bonhoeffer says, I think there are ways of understanding such utterances that free them from the worries I have, but first let me articulate the worries. On the face of it, remarks like those quoted, taken in conjunction with his theory of mandates, would seem to give too little credit to the capacities of non-Christians to live morally good lives in the context of family, government, culture and possibly religion – if not Church in Bonhoeffer's sense. The conquistadors who pillaged in the newly discovered Americas in the sixteenth century claimed a right to violent conquest because the natives they sought to dispossess and plunder were pagans and hence had no political legitimacy over their land and its treasures. We may well wonder how much of this theological appeal was seriously part of their motivation, given that their racism, greed and venality would probably have sufficed to explain and motivate their activities, but in the European climate of the time, they needed a theological argument. That argument invoked the idea that only those who acknowledged the dominion of Christ could legitimately claim sovereignty over their lands and peoples. Any account of the centrality of Christ to ethics and particularly to the mandate of government must avoid such hegemonic claims. To their great credit, some of the leading Catholic theologians of the day publicly rejected the religious argument of the conquistadors and their supporters. Two of the most outspoken of the New World prophets, as these critics were to be known, were Bishop Bartolomeo de Las Casas and the Dominican Thomist theologian, Antonio Montesinos. Montesinos preached publicly against the genocidal activities of the Spanish colonists and, as reported by Las Casas, denounced 'the cruelty and tyranny that you practice on these innocent people. Tell me: by what right or justice do you hold these Indians in such cruel and horrible slavery? By what right do you wage such detestable wars on these people who live mildly and peacefully in their own lands, where you have consumed infinite numbers of them with unheard of murders and desolations?' (Goodpasture 1989, p. 12). These New World prophets relied in part upon a Christian revulsion from cruelty, murder and enslavement, but also upon the tradition of natural law that, by the time they wrote, had developed a sophisticated account of political authority grounded less in Divine authorisation and more in the consent of the governed. While recognising that the existence of a political order and its accompanying authority was part of God's providential order, they argued, following Aquinas, that the pursuit of the common good was what unified a people and legitimated their governance. The details of this common project were open to the determination of natural reason exercised even by citizens who had never heard of Christ.

The lessons of this critique of the conquistadors are relevant to the multicultural societies in which so many of us live today. Any suggestion that only those who explicitly proclaim a commitment to Christ should have some dominant position in our political life must be rejected, as also the idea that only an explicitly Christian understanding of our common political life can be authentically ethical. Beyond politics, the same must be said surely of the central institutions of such a society, namely those 'mandated' areas of the family, church and culture. There are many arguments that can be given for freedom of religion (or irreligion), freedom of expression, and even freedom to form unorthodox marriages and families. Indeed some of these arguments seem to me capable of being Christian in inspiration, even if not proclaimed or even denied as doctrine by some Christian authorities.

Before considering what those arguments might be, let us ask: does Bonhoeffer want to deny any of this? I have said that some of his Christo-centric rhetoric and argument might incline a reader to think so. Indeed, he seems at one point thoroughly opposed to the natural law tradition that partly underpinned the Spanish theologians' critique of the conquistador theology. So, he says:

> There can be no legitimate proclamation by the Church which is not a proclamation of Christ. The Church does not proclaim two different messages, a message of universal reason and natural law for unbelievers, and a Christian message for believers (Bonhoeffer 1964: 'The "Ethical" and the "Christian" as a Theme: The Commandment of God in the Church', pp. 295–6).

Yet, the Spanish theologians did not really do this. They proclaimed a message of universal reason and natural law for all people, believer and unbeliever alike, and they took it that such reason was in no respect hostile to the Christian message. Indeed, one might take it as helpful to the interpretation and understanding of the Christian message and the command of God. If natural reason combined with the experience and imagination that should enter into any of the concrete encounters that Bonhoeffer regards as crucial can contribute to the living of a genuine ethic why should we not see it as making a contribution to the Christian's living of an ethical life? Why should we not regard such exercises of reason and discernment as part of that Christian engagement in the world that Bonhoeffer was so anxious to promote? In spite of Bonhoeffer's hostile comment about natural law and his emphasis on the Church as the vehicle or instrument for the proclamation of Christ, there are elements in his thought that suggest a positive answer to such questions. One significant element is contained in earlier chapters of the *Ethics*, especially the chapter on 'Last and Penultimate Things', where he discusses specific moral problems such as suicide, contraception, abortion and sterilisation in ways that make perfectly standard recourse to forms of thinking that are, for the most part, accessible to the reasoning of non-religious people. (Incidentally, he there challenges some part of those standard Catholic arguments against contraception that I intended to signal rejection of earlier as distortions of natural law thinking.) Another pertinent consideration is what he says of church-state relations: 'the mandate of the government is certainly not to confess Christ; the government is concerned rather with quite concrete abuses which its divine mandate requires it to remedy' (Bonhoeffer 1964: 'The "Ethical" and the "Christian" as a Theme: The Commandment of God in the Church', p. 296). This suggests that the government has access to ways of dealing with its specific task that are peculiar to it and these constitute a kind of autonomy under the rule of reason. This interpretation is perhaps reinforced by the following passage:

> The Christian congregation stands at the point at which the whole world should be standing; to this extent it serves as deputy for the world and exists for the sake of the world. On the other hand, the world achieves its own fulfilment at the point at which the congregation stands. The earth is the 'new creation', the 'new creature', the goal of the ways of God on earth (Bonhoeffer 1964: 'The "Ethical" and the "Christian" as a Theme: The Commandment of God in the Church', p. 301).

There is at least a hint here of the idea that Christian insight and ordinary human reason and understanding are not only potentially compatible but also potentially reinforcing. The passage indeed may be viewed as expressing what the modernist Catholic thinker Baron von Hugel once said in explication of the relation of Church and world. Von Hugel explained it in terms of 'Christ in the Church calling to and answered by God in the world'.

7.5 The Mandates, the Natural Order and Political Authority

But if this is conceded, then it raises a further, difficult question about how it is that non-Christians can live an ethical life in the absence of any explicit input from Christianity. If moving beyond moralism and the merely ethical essentially requires our obedience to the command of God as revealed by Christ, how could non-Christians and their involvement in the mandates ever achieve such authenticity? Indeed, how could their families, culture, governments and religion ever be genuine mandates rather than mere historical phenomena? One possible response for Bonhoeffer is to treat the message of Christ and its salvorific import as already indirectly available to the non-Christian world (both before and after Christ's life on earth) without its explicit teaching by the Church. In Bonhoeffer's terms, 'the command of God' can be present in the lives of sincere, thoughtful people of other religious persuasions or of none even if they have never heard of the Christian message or have been unmoved by its explicit presentation by Christians. If von Hugel's insight is taken seriously then the unfolding of Christianity is a matter of dynamic confrontation and collaboration between the Church's self-understanding and the divinely inspired workings of the world it exists in. Of course, not all the intellectual, moral and religious developments in that world are good or divinely inspired, but neither are all the workings of the Christian community. A picture such as this seems to me to make much more sense of how the hesitant growth of moral and religious insight both within and beyond Christianity has actually occurred. It also helps to provide a Christian understanding and rationale for the sort of firm tolerance that must underpin the working of pluralistic, liberal democracies. Under the pressure of the dynamic mentioned above, Christians have slowly come to see that the freedom given by the Gospel has connections with the political liberty that lies at the heart of liberal democracy. Bonhoeffer's emphasis upon freedom in the ethical sphere and his stress on its Christian endorsement, as well as his positive attitude to some forms of 'worldliness' should make him sympathetic to the response I am suggesting on his behalf. His comments on what he regards as the positive features of the Enlightenment and the French Revolution also provide some support for this. So he says:

> Intellectual honesty in all things, including questions of belief, was the great achievement of emancipated reason and it has ever since been one of the indispensable moral requirements of western man. Contempt for the age of rationalism is a suspicious sign of failure to feel the need for truthfulness (Bonhoeffer 1964: 'Ethics as Formation: Inheritance and Decay', p. 97).

There is however an aspect of Bonhoeffer's use of 'the mandates' that I find puzzling and that might block the path to the response I have been suggesting. This is the way that the mandates are said to establish what he calls 'an unalterable relation of superiority and inferiority' (Bonhoeffer 1964: 'The "Ethical" and the "Christian" as a Theme: The Concept of the Mandate', p. 289). The relation is said to apply in each of the mandates and it clearly has some connection with the idea of authority in government, family, culture and church. Although Bonhoeffer is at pains to make it clear that he does not identify this relation with what he calls the earthly one of superior and inferior power, his account of the relation nonetheless seems exposed to the danger, to put it provocatively, of making authority too authoritarian. It is true that he places three 'limitations' upon the relation he favours (Bonhoeffer 1964: 'The "Ethical" and the "Christian" as a Theme: The Concept of the Mandate', p. 291). The relation is to be limited by God, by the other mandates, and by the relation of inferiority (Bonhoeffer 1964, p. 291). As far as I can see, Bonhoeffer does little to explain how these limitations are supposed to work to negate what seem obviously dangers of the superiority/ inferiority relation, and no plausible interpretation of them seems nearly sufficient to dispel fears about the excessively inegalitarian implications of his position across the four realms covered by the mandates. What Bonhoeffer might mean can be illustrated by the case of government. The inferiority relation is supposed to work to moderate abuses of authority by reminding the superior that he or she is inferior in other ways, for example, if he has governmental authority he will usually be inferior to those above in government. And even if he is supreme in government then he must be conscious of God's power, governance and command over him. Perhaps also the incumbent authority's relation to cultural, family and church authority will moderate the temptations of power. And so on for problems with the other mandates. It should be conceded that these limitations can sometimes have the desired effect, but given the history of political, domestic, cultural, and clerical corruption and abuse, it is surely fanciful simply to rely upon this.

Indeed, it is precisely a realisation of the corruptions and abuses of 'earthly' power that has produced the radical reformation of politics that goes by the name of liberal democracy. For liberal democrats, Acton's dictum that 'all power tends to corrupt and absolute power corrupts absolutely' not only warns against kingly or governmental power (especially in their absolutist versions) but also against institutional and personal power more generally. We are very conscious (or should be) in today's world of the great abuse and corruption of the powers that reign in the world of corporations, banking and the media, but the church and even the family are not exempt from such dangers. Indeed, the key concepts of theological and religious discourse are apt to dazzle those who use them to the extent that they can be blinded to the mundane realities in which the concepts and their referents must abide. Those mundane realities are just the occasions for distortion and abuse that we need protection against. Invoking mandates is insufficient for such protection; what is needed are the specific safeguards and constraints that the liberal political tradition, in particular, has striven to develop. These are no doubt imperfectly embodied in present democratic societies, but they are far better than the non-liberal or anti-liberal alternatives.

The tensions and difficulties in Bonhoeffer's account of ethics and Christian ethics point to underlying contrasts between theological outlooks that have been in contention since the earliest years of Christianity. At heart, they concern answers to Tertullian's famous question: 'What indeed has Athens to do with Jerusalem? What has the Academy to do with the Church?' (Tertullian: Chap. 7). Those Christians who answer 'nothing' or 'very little' look with scorn upon the feeble efforts of 'the world' to address great questions of life, especially those that ethics at its best attempts to answer such as: 'What is it to live well?' The contempt for the non-Christian intellectual world implicit in Tertullian's question and the preference for a total reliance on what is understood as the undiluted word of God as either revealed in Scripture, or given individually in Christian attentiveness to God's concrete command or (in some versions) in deference to Christian tradition or authority have always appealed to Christian thinkers and movements. Very roughly, we can see Tertullian, Augustine (in some moods) and of course Luther as subject to this appeal. Luther's debate on free will with Erasmus (a fellow Christian, but a humanist philosopher) shows this temperament at work in the starkest fashion. In more modern times, Karl Barth seems to stand in this tradition, especially in his suspicion of any role for philosophy in theology. But another strand in Christianity has been more open to the non-Christian intellectual world and to some of its practices and attitudes. We might cite Origen, Augustine (in other moods), Aquinas and many of the Scholastics, Hooker and Erasmus. Of course, the two strands sometimes interweave: even Tertullian has recourse to Athens when he attempts a theological account of the Trinity by employing Greek philosophical concepts of 'hypostasis' and 'homoousios' (in English: 'person' and 'substance'), but it is useful nonetheless to distinguish them. We might call the first the rejectionist position and the second the integrationist. In Bonhoeffer's discussion of ethics the rejectionist strand is often present, as it was in Kierkegaard who was a significant influence upon him. It stems in part from a very bleak view of the Fall and the effects of Original Sin in which there is little or no persisting value seen in human nature and its fruits in reason, instinct and culture. By contrast, the integrationist stance sees human nature as damaged by the Fall but not totally corrupted; in need of restoration and redemption but not abandonment; in the phrase of Aquinas 'Grace builds upon Nature and does not destroy it' (Aquinas 1920: I Qu. 1 Art 8 reply to objection 2).[5]

The above is a simplified picture offering an ideal typology rather than an intricate mapping, but I think that tensions between the poles so broadly described are at work in Bonhoeffer's account of ethics and help in understanding much that is puzzling in it. These tensions also seem at work in Bonhoeffer's concern with and use of with the *Akedah*, but I will not develop this point further here.[6]

7.6 A Parallel with 'Emergency Ethics'

Earlier I discussed briefly the similarities and differences between Bonhoeffer's approach and that of the particularist school of moral philosophy in analytic philosophy. Similarities can also be found in some of the writings of the existentialist school, especially in Sartre's reflections on ethical choice. But I want to conclude by sketching a point of connection with some contemporary philosophical writings on what has come to be called 'emergency ethics'. One of the principal stimuli for this development is the work of the American political theorist Michael Walzer who has coined the terms 'supreme emergency' and 'dirty hands' for situations in which 'necessity' requires that profound moral prohibitions be overridden even though the required actions remain immoral. Walzer gives several examples in his influential paper, 'Political Action: The Problem of Dirty Hands' (Walzer 1973), including a resort to torture in extreme situations, but the most developed example occurs in his book *Just and Unjust Wars* where he argues that the Allied carpet bombing of German cities in the early stages of World War II was clearly immoral in terms of the version of just war theory that he accepts, but was nonetheless justified by the necessity of defeating the great evil of Nazi Germany. Walzer argues however that it was not similarly justified in the later stages of the war where the bombing was simply immoral. In the early stages, however, it was just as immoral but justified by the imminent danger of a catastrophic Nazi victory (Walzer 1977).

This 'dirty hands' story feeds, to some extent, off another category much discussed in modern analytic philosophy, that of a tragic moral dilemma. The idea is that of a choice facing the agent in which whatever course of action she decides upon is profoundly morally wrong. A common example is that presented in the novel (and subsequent film) *Sophie's Choice* where a mother is confronted by a

[5] The full sentence indicates even more the relevance of natural philosophy to faith: 'Since therefore grace does not destroy nature but perfects it, natural reason should minister to faith as the natural bent of the will ministers to charity.'

[6] I have discussed the complexities of the Akedah for religion and moral knowledge, and general problems of religion and morality, in Coady 2019.

Nazi officer at the gates of the concentration camp where she is to be confined with her two young children and asked to choose which of the children will be taken away to die and told that both will be killed if she refuses to choose. It is a feature of moral dilemmas (in this strict philosophical sense, which is not equivalent to the common use of the phrase to mean difficult moral problem) that there is a moral equivalence between the choices so that both are morally wrong and neither is morally preferable. The dirty hands story goes further in insisting that, though both choices may be morally wrong, one (the 'necessary' one) is clearly preferable. There are many puzzles in the category of 'dirty hands' or 'supreme emergency' (the latter spells out the circumstances in which the hands must get dirty) and I have discussed the category at length in several places, suggesting that we need to be very cautious about characterising and even admitting it. (See Coady 2008: Chap. 4, 'Engagement in Evil: Politics, Dirty Hands, and Corruption'; and Coady 2018.) Walzer himself in later writing on the topic has expressed some nervousness about how the category could be abused and has attempted to make the conditions of supreme emergency more stringent so that only genocidal threats or threats to a community's way of life can legitimate dirty hands (Walzer 2004).

The relevance of the philosophical discussions of dirty hands (and moral dilemmas) to Bonhoeffer is that some of his critique of ethics may be connected to his sense of the tragic choices that emergency situations can provide to an agent. This has particular salience in the context of resistance to the horrors of the Nazi regime in Germany, and it could also be used to throw light upon the emergency situation facing Abraham in the choice he confronted between disobeying what he took to be the command of God and murdering his son. There is much more that could be said about this analogy, but I want to conclude by pointing out a disanalogy between the dirty hands/supreme emergency category and Bonhoeffer's general attitude to ordinary ethics. Emergency ethics cannot rescue Bonhoeffer from my earlier criticisms precisely because it is concerned only with emergency situations whereas Bonhoeffer's scorn is also and principally directed at everyday ethics. To invoke the dirty hands debate on his behalf would be to confuse the exceptional with the normal; to overdramatise the role and nature of morality in one of the distorting ways that I have referred to as moralism and that I have argued may be seen as a principal target of Bonhoeffer's own criticisms of what he calls 'the ethical'.[7]

---

[7]This essay was originally published in 2012, the Special 50th Anniversary Issue Tribute to Max Charlesworth in *Sophia 51*(4), 449–464. It has been revised by the author for publication here.

References

Aquinas, T. (1920). *The summa theologica of St. Thomas Aquinas* (Literally translated by Fathers of the English Dominican Province, 2nd and Rev. ed.).

Bonhoeffer, D. (1964). *Ethics* (Ed.: Bethge, E. & Trans: Smith, N. H.). London: Fontana.

Bonhoeffer, D. (2008) Basic questions of a Christian ethic. In *Barcelona, Berlin, New York – 1928–1931*: *Dietrich Bonhoeffer works* (Vol. 10, pp. 359–378). Edited by R. Staats and H. C. von Hase (English edition edited by C. J. Green). Minneapolis: Fortress Press.

Coady, C. A. J. (1993). Ethos and ethics in business. In C. A. J. Coady & C. J. G. Sampford (Eds.), *Business, ethics and the law* (pp. 149–171). Leichhardt: Federation Press.

Coady, C. A. J. (2008). *Messy morality: The challenge of politics*. New York: Oxford University Press.

Coady, C. A. J. (2018 (2009)). The problem of dirty hands. In E. N. Zalta (Ed.), *The Stanford encyclopedia of philosophy* (Fall 2018 Edition). https://plato.stanford.edu/archives/fall2018/entries/dirty-hands/ (First published Wed Apr 29, 2009, substantive revision Mon Jul 2, 2018, accessed 4/8/2019).

Coady, C. A. J. (2019). Religion and moral knowledge. In A. Zimmerman, K. Jones, & M. Timmons (Eds.), *The Routledge handbook on moral epistemology* (pp. 537–551). New York/Oxford: Oxford University Press.

Goodpasture, H. M. (1989). *Cross and sword: An eyewitness history of Christianity in Latin America*. Maryknoll: Orbis Books.

Kirkpatrick, M. (2013). Bonhoeffer, Kierkegaard, and the teleological suspension of the ethical – The beginning or end of ethics? In A. Clark & M. Mawson (Eds.), *Ontology and ethics: Bonhoeffer and contemporary scholarship* (pp. 86–101). Eugene: Pickwick Publications.

Tertullian, Q. S. F.. *The prescription against heretics*. Available online: http://www.tertullian.org/anf/ index.htm. Accessed 8 Aug 2012.

Walzer, M. (1973). Political action: The problem of dirty hands. *Philosophy and Public Affairs, 2*(2), 160–180.

Walzer, M. (1977). *Just and unjust wars: A moral argument with historical illustrations*. New York: Basic Books.

Walzer, M. (2004). Emergency ethics. In *Arguing about war* (pp. 33–50). New Haven: Yale University Press.

Wolf, S. (1982). Moral saints. *The Journal of Philosophy, 79*(8), 419–439.

C. A. J. (Tony) Coady is Emeritus Professor of Philosophy at the University of Melbourne. He there served as Founding Director of the Centre for Philosophy and Public Issues (1990–2000) and then, until 2003, as Deputy Director and Head of the University of Melbourne division of its multi-university replacement the ARC Special Research Centre for Applied Philosophy and Public Ethics (CAPPE). His book *Testimony: A Philosophical Study* (OUP, 1992) was widely praised and pioneered a new area of research in epistemology. He has also written extensively in political philosophy on issues concerning war and terrorism. In 2005, he gave the Uehiro Lectures on Practical Ethics at Oxford University, and in 2012 he was Leverhulme Visiting Professor at Oxford lecturing on Religion and Politics. He regularly contributes to public debate on ethical and philosophical dimensions of current affairs. Coady's other books include *Morality and Political Violence* (CUP, 2008) and *Messy Morality: The Challenge of Politics* (OUP, 2008).

Chapter 8
Love and Affirmation of the World: Inaugural Max Charlesworth Memorial Lecture, Deakin University, Melbourne, 2015

Morny Joy

8.1 Introduction

In paying tribute to the life and work of Max Charlesworth, I have chosen to introduce specific aspects of the work of two scholars: the French philosopher Paul Ricoeur (1913–2005), and German-born Hannah Arendt (1906–1975), who preferred to call herself a 'political thinker,' rather than a philosopher. I have chosen them because they both are closely associated with Continental Philosophy. Ricoeur has even a closer philosophical affiliation with Max Charlesworth in that he was an early advocate of Edmund Husserl's work and wrote a book on his phenomenology (1967). Ricoeur even taught courses in the early 1970s at the Université de Louvain (now Leuven University), where Dr. Charlesworth obtained his doctorate.

Arendt and Ricoeur first met at the University of Chicago in the late 1960s. In an interview with Charles Reagan, Ricoeur observes: 'I met Hannah Arendt at the home of Paul Tillich. My friendship in those days with Paul Tillich and Hannah Arendt played a major role in the decision of the University of Chicago to invite me to regularly give courses there' (Ricoeur in Reagan 1996: 132). They had each journeyed to the United States to escape difficult situations. Both Arendt and Ricoeur were victims of World War II. Arendt barely escaped from Nazi Germany, first to Paris, where she spent a number of years as an activist for Jewish causes prior to the German Occupation. She was then forced to flee again to the United States, arriving there in 1941. Ricoeur, who was a French officer, spent 5years as a German prisoner

Sections of this paper have been published in a Journal. They are printed with permission of the publisher: Symposium, Canadian Society for Continental Society, Spring, 2016.

M. Joy (✉)
University of Calgary, Calgary, Canada
e-mail: mjoy@ucalgary.ca

P. Wong et al. (eds.), *Considering Religions, Rights and Bioethics: For Max Charlesworth*, Sophia Studies in Cross-cultural Philosophy of Traditions and Cultures 30, https://doi.org/10.1007/978-3-030-18148-2_8

of war.[1] It was, however, his numerous invitations to give lectures after the 1968 Paris student riots that were responsible for Ricoeur's increasing presence in the United States. Both Arendt and Ricoeur strove to counter the horrors of war and violence, which they both viewed as a manifestation of evil. They each used their prodigious intellectual strengths and physical energies to investigate and provide profound insights into its occurrences. They strove to provide a means that would help to prevent further such irruptions. They did not always concur, in fact Ricoeur, in his book of essays, *The Just* (2000: 94–108), took Arendt to task for her work on imagination and judgment. Nevertheless, a comparison and contrast of their ideas and published work provides a valuable account of their respective commitments to the betterment of human existence.

What is most relevant in my choice of these two scholars is that Arendt and Ricoeur both based their lives on a strong affirmation of hope in the human capacity for renewal and regeneration. Such affirmation did have a basic religious influence – albeit qualified from Arendt's perspective as a non-observant Jew[2] – and both thinkers were also given to continuous speculations on both the provenance and the persistence of evil. One could say that they were not overly optimistic in their respective outlooks, as both comment often on the fragility of personal and collective human efforts. Such a fragility was not regarded as simply the result of human finitude *per se* but also resulted from their acute awareness that evil, though not considered by either of them as innate or original, could never be discounted from disruption and interference in human affairs.

8.2 Ricoeur on Birth and Living

Ricoeur's strong affirmation of life in this world became evident from his earliest writings. It featured initially in his important book, *The Voluntary and the Involuntary*, a phenomenological study of the human will. This was published in France in 1950 but was not translated into English until 1966. Ricoeur was only too well aware of human faults and failings, but, instead of emphasizing this, he proposed that: 'The phenomenon of the voluntary and the involuntary appeared to me to be capable of accounting only for the weaknesses of being exposed to evil and capable of doing wrong, but not of actually doing evil' (Ricoeur 1995a:15). For Ricoeur, a human being, however fallible, was never considered as predetermined in his or her actions, especially in the direction of wrong-doing and dereliction.

Perhaps the principal reason for his commitment to such a position can be found toward the conclusion of *The Voluntary and the Involuntary* in a chapter entitled

[1] Ricoeur has described how he spent part of his years in a German prisoner-of-war camp in Pomerania translating Husserl's *Ideen 1* into French.

[2] In her time at Marburg University, Arendt, as a non-practising assimilated Jew, was nonetheless a strong defender of Jewish identity. While at the university, she studied with a number of professors, including Romano Guardini, a Catholic priest, and Martin Heidegger.

'The Way of Consent.' Here Ricoeur examines the manner in which body and mind have been separated into what he describes as 'the virulent form of dualism of freedom and necessity' (1966: 444). Ricoeur refuses to assent to such a rigid dualism. Consequently, while he concedes that birth could be considered as associated with determinism and an involuntary perspective, given that it 'is not available to consciousness,' it can also indicate another dimension. Ricoeur acknowledges birth as something that is both wondrous and compelling. He declares: 'My birth is the beginning of my life: in it I was placed, once and for all, into the world, and placed in being before I was able to posit anything voluntarily' (433). He also allows that something powerful can result. This is because, for Ricoeur, birth denotes the emergence of consciousness – it initiates an orientation toward freedom. He declares: 'I have always begun to live when I say "I am" ' (441). He is quite adamant that human beings can consent to life, and the commitment of this first choice of life makes all choice possible. Conceding that he would not go so far as to claim that 'this is the best of all possible worlds,' Ricoeur concludes with a strong affirmation: 'This unique world, uniquely for me, this incomparable world is good with a goodness which itself knows no degrees, with a goodness which is the *yes* of being'(475).

In an interview with Azouvi and de Launay in the last decade of his life, Ricoeur revisits this early work, reminiscing: 'I had not wanted to be crushed by the problem of death: I wanted in this way to give its rightful place to the theme of birth' (1998: 93–94). Later in this same book of interviews, Ricoeur expands on these ideas, placing them in a more contemporary context: 'I therefore project not an afterdeath but a death that would be an ultimate affirmation of life ... what is important is to be living until the moment of death' (156). Such a sentiment is further developed in a posthumously published book of his thoughts during the last years of his life: *Living up to Death* (2009).

It was a similar profoundly felt dedication to human existence and life in this world that would captivate Ricoeur when he discovered Hannah Arendt's writings on 'natality' in *The Human Condition*. He describes this discovery as inducing 'a certain sense of amazement' when he read her words, quoting the Gospels, to support her understanding of natality: 'A child has been born to us' (Ricoeur 1998: 157).[3] This discovery alerted him to the existence of a kindred spirit, as he relates: 'For her, too, birth signifies more than death. This is what wishing to remain living until death means' (157). Ricoeur was also intrigued by the fact that for Arendt 'natality' had an ontological resonance that manifested itself in a commitment to strive for the well-being of humankind.

8.3 Arendt on Natality

In *The Human Condition* (1959), Arendt introduces her understanding of the neologism 'natality.' She first celebrates the fact of its various intimations of birth and beginnings. The creation of human beings – 'male and female he created them'

[3] See the actual statement of Arendt in *The Human Condition* (1959: 223).

(1959:10) – as Arendt insists – is a gift (1959: 222). At the same time, 'natality' is an extremely evocative term, summoning other attributes that are expressive of various forms of generativity, of renewal, and not only the affirmation of life itself. In her biography of Arendt, *Hannah Arendt: For Love of the World*, Elisabeth Young-Breuhl quotes Arendt's statement from a letter to Karl Jaspers on 6 August 1955: 'I've begun so late, really only in recent years, to truly love the world.... Out of gratitude, I want to call my book on political theories *Amor Mundi*' (Young-Breuhl 2004: xxiv). Instead, the book was assigned the more prosaic title, *The Human Condition*. Nonetheless, this volume still resonates with Arendt's celebration of human existence and her efforts to safeguard its flourishing.

Arendt's own appreciation of life itself elicits the statement: 'that men, though they must die, are not born in order to die but in order to begin' (1959: 222). From this perspective, Arendt appreciates natality not simply in relation to physical birth but also as an intrinsic element of all creative human activity. A figurative form of natality introduces this second, more conscious mode of birth, of human renewal. It designates the possibility of initiatives in thought and action that can result in continual forms of creative productivity. As Arendt describes it: 'With word and deed we insert ourselves into the human world, and this insertion is like a second birth, in which we confirm and take upon ourselves the naked fact of our physical appearance' (157).

Arendt modified the term 'natality' from the work of St. Augustine, on whom she wrote the equivalent of a master's thesis (*Der Liebesbegriff bei Augustin* (1996 [1929]).[4] She amplified his understanding of life, however, from its specific religious setting, to align it with her own vision of human beings acting together for the common good of this world. For Arendt, 'To act, in its most general sense, means to take the initiative, to begin…to set something in motion' (1959: 157). Such an observation may seem straightforward, but it has extensive repercussions. Natality, in conjunction with action, has the potential to interfere with what Arendt, similarly to Ricoeur, describes as the order of necessity or the involuntary – 'the inexorable automatic daily course of life' that follows the law of mortality (222). Action, particularly when exercised as communal enterprise, after due reflection, is central to Arendt's vision of politics. Human beings, in relationship with others, can exercise their political participation and act in ways that allow them to realize the fullness of human freedom. For Arendt, these collective political endeavours are intimately implicated in a fundamental sense of responsibility.[5] Such a radical revision of established norms presumes an entirely different way of establishing human political priorities. Arendt anticipates this in her declaration: 'Moreover, since action is the

[4]Arendt adapts Augustine's word from *The City of God: "Initium ergo esset, creatus est homo, ante quem, nullus fuit"* (*De civitate Dei*: 11: 20). She revised this thesis, written in 1929, in the late fifties and early sixties in America. This revised version was published in English in 1996.

[5]Arendt regarded responsibility as basically a political rather than a legal or moral activity, though she also deemed that each person needed to take personal responsibility for their actions. See Arendt (2003).

political activity par excellence, natality and not mortality may be the central category of the political, as distinguished from metaphysical thought' (Arendt 1959:11).

Yet, because natality is associated with freedom, for Arendt, it can also be unpredictable. 'It is in the nature of beginning that something new is started which cannot be expected from whatever may have happened before' (1959: 157). As Arendt describes this predicament, it has both advantages and liabilities. There is an 'inherent boundlessness' in human activity that is creative and can dismantle existing obstacles and limitations. It is in this connection that Arendt introduces the term 'frailty' to describe the inherent instability of human affairs in the body politic and institutions, as distinct from the actual state of human nature as necessity and human finitude itself.

Arendt, however, is equally eloquent in her appraisal of possible interventions: 'It is the very nature of every new beginning that it breaks into the world as an 'infinite improbability'' (1968: 169).[6] Such effects signal that, for Arendt, natality, as *initium*, together with freedom, can achieve momentous, and perhaps precarious, outcomes(1959: 171; 209).Yet, such consequences need not necessarily forecast disaster. This is because, concurrently, for Arendt, natality can also indicate the possibility that unexpected consequences, or what she names as 'miracles,' can result, i.e., results that are not governed by necessity. 'Every act, seen from the perspective not of the agent but of the process in whose framework it occurs and whose automatism it interrupts, is a 'miracle' – that is, something which could not be expected' (Arendt 1968: 169). From Arendt's perspective, miracles and unpredictability are the close associates of human freedom.

Ultimately, for Arendt, it is natality, in its original and generative guise, that can also provide a safeguard against the incursions of evil. This is because, in Arendt's view, natality has a close relation with narration, and, together, these elements support the meaning and coherence of human existence. Narrative, in this guise, is thus, for Arendt, intimately aligned with history and its inspirational exemplars. These observations of hers would in time have a powerful influence on Ricoeur's work.

8.4 Ricoeur and Arendt on Narrative

Ricoeur was stimulated by a number of other ideas introduced by Arendt in *The Human Condition*, but he was especially taken by her appreciation of narrative as bearing witness to human existence and activities as dimensions of natality. Arendt

[6] Arendt expanded on this topic elsewhere: "The fact that man is capable of action means that the unexpected can be expected from him, that he is able to perform what is infinitely improbable. And this again is possible only because each man is unique, so that with each birth something uniquely new comes into the world. With respect to this somebody who is unique it can be truly said that nobody was there before. If action as beginning corresponds to the fact of birth, if it is the actualization of the human condition of natality, then speech corresponds to the fact of distinctness and is the actualization of the human condition of plurality, that is, of living as a distinct and unique being among equals" (1959: 158).

proposes that aspects of human life can be related by a story – a narrative that traces the episodes of one's life. The emphasis here is on the 'who' of identity and the vibrancy of human existence, rather than on the 'what' afforded by empirical data (1959:159). In Arendt's view, individuals reveal who they are by their actions, and these actions can also have a profound influence on the web of human relationships, or plurality, as she termed it. Narratives witness to many diverse activities. They can also provide paradigms of past happenings, both as instructive ideals and as cautionary tales. A narrative account of a person's life can illuminate their own contribution to the betterment of the human world and supply models for future constructive action. In Arendt's view, such narratives constitute a key component of an historical record but can also contribute standards for political guidance (184–85).

In his own subsequent three volumes on *Time and Narrative* (1984–88), Ricoeur, focussing also on the 'who' as an aspect of human identity, launched his investigations in a somewhat different direction. He was primarily preoccupied with the question of the 'narrative self,' especially as it concerned the nature of identity. At that time, he was also disturbed by the anti-humanist direction of the 1970s development of postmodern thought, where notions of the 'self' and the 'subject,' as well as 'grand narratives,' were being contested by deconstruction. As a remedy to this challenge, Ricoeur explains his own recourse to the postulate of a 'narrative self' as a response to what he termed the 'wounded cogito' (2007:243). This latter mode of the *cogito* was, according to Ricoeur, the result of the criticism levelled at the cogito's presumption in articulating the certainty or transparence of knowledge. Ricoeur attempted to take a mediatory role in order to provide an alternative version of the self. He observed:

> Without recourse to narration, the problem of personal identity would in fact be condemned to an antinomy with no solution. Either we must posit a subject identical with itself through the diversity of its different states, or following Hume and Nietzsche, we must hold that this identical subject is nothing more than a substantialist illusion whose elimination merely brings to light a pure manifold of cognitions, emotions and volitions. (1988: 246)

Ricoeur, employing this construct of a 'narrative self,' introduced a sense of self that was not static and imperious but rather flexible and dynamic: an identity that allowed for both revision and expansion.[7] For Ricoeur, a narrative identity will always be a qualified and provisional one. This non-didactic version of the self could also be considered as a type of emendation of Ricoeur's own earlier definition of the type of self that was to engage in a hermeneutic exercise. It was a 'non-egotistic, non-narcissistic, non-imperialistic mode of subjectivity which responds and corresponds to the power of a work' (1975: 30). It was this particular insight that had lead to Ricoeur's own rejection of the 'Cartesian and Fichtean – and to an extent Husserlian – ideal of the subject's transparence to itself' (1991a: 17), as well as any apodictic claims to certainty. What becomes obvious as a result of the above definitions and

[7] In his work on narrative Ricoeur introduced two forms of identity: *idem* which coincided with the "what" element, and ipse with the "who" element. These variations which interact as elements of narrative will not be discussed in this article as they are not absolutely necessary to the issues at hand.

qualifications is that Ricoeur's work was not in the service of absolutes, either in the sense of authorial domination or definitive interpretations. In this regard, he was clearly in agreement with Arendt's position on the modified role of the author, though his approach differs.

It is on this topic of authorship that Arendt proclaims: 'everybody started his life by inserting himself into the human world through action and speech' (1959: 164). These activities then become the basis of narratives. But Arendt then modifies this position by making a rather striking observation to the effect that: 'nobody is the author or producer of his or her own life story' (164). With such an amendment, Arendt seeks to establish that no one author can unequivocally pronounce the final version of a narrative account of his or her life. This stance is in keeping with Arendt's taking a panoramic historical perspective. While she admits that a protagonist may initiate this process, the ultimate outcome of any narrative is unpredictable. The reason she provides for this situation is that human beings are in constant interaction in diverse relationships, the extent of which avoids final encapsulation by any one person. It will be up to others to review and ultimately describe our accomplishments. Arendt also states that: 'Because the actor always moves among and in relation to other acting beings, he is never merely a 'doer' but always and at the same time a sufferer. To do and to suffer are like opposite sides of the same coin, and the story that an action initiates is composed of its consequent deeds and sufferings' (190). Such a perspective implies that Arendt views the consequences of actions as having long-term results, if not interminable ones. This also implies that, for Arendt, any action, although it may arise autonomously, can instigate a continuous series of reactions. Yet, even in these endless reverberations, 'one deed, and sometimes one word, suffices to change every constellation' (1959: 190). Arendt implies that even these subsequent effects may still produce miracles. In this way, natality is always dynamically present.

Initially it is apparent that Ricoeur is in accord with Arendt's position on narrative when he states: 'Action, connected with speech, reveals man as an agent, i.e., the one who initiates change in the world.'[8] He follows this statement with a qualification, similar to that of Arendt, affirming that, despite such agency, a person does not necessarily become the author who is in control of one's life-story. Indeed, Ricoeur virtually mirrors Arendt's words:

> We learn to become the *narrator of our own story* without completely becoming the author of our life. It could be said that we appropriate in the application to ourselves the concert of narrative voices that make up the symphony of the great works, of the epics, the tragedies, dramas, and novels. The difference is that in these works the author has disguised himself as narrator and bears the mask of his many *personae* in whose midst he is the dominant narrative voice telling the story we read. We can become our own narrator, following these narrative voices, without becoming authors. (1986a, 131–32)

[8] Quoted from "Action, Story and History: On Re-Reading *The Human Condition*," *Salmagundi* 60 (1983a: 65). This article is an English translation of Ricoeur's "Préface" to the French edition of Arendt's *The Human Condition* [*Condition de l'homme moderne* (1983).

Ricoeur will extend the range of narrative possibilities with his emphasis on imaginative explorations of 'a proposed world, a world I might inhabit' (1977: 25). He will also expand on Arendt's depiction of 'acting and suffering human beings' in his move to ethics (to be discussed later). It become evident that the insistence by both Arendt and Ricoeur on lack of a single controlling authorship and the immersion in a plurality of voices and views will have further important, though distinct, repercussions for their work. Yet this is where their paths will diverge. Arendt will insist that it is only from a collective perspective, where the 'who' is embedded in a web of human relationships, that a particular process can be discerned and enacted. For Arendt, this inevitably involves a move into the political realm. It is in this manner that the "who," which action discloses, belongs as a citizen in the polis; one whose life in intricately interconnected with others (1959: 163). Arendt is more concerned with story-telling as establishing an historical precedent, rather than salvaging a construct of personal identity. This distinguishes her work from Ricoeur, who, in contrast to Arendt, will prefer to focus on ethics as a way of introducing his commitment to recognition.

It is obvious that, for Arendt, narrative or story-telling is not a naive exercise. For her, story-telling comes to the rescue when traditional thought/philosophy has lost contact with reality. Narratives can be appreciated as evidence of her rejection of traditional philosophy and her describing herself as a 'political thinker.' She specifically did this as a protest against German philosophers who did not publicly oppose the Nazi regime. In such circumstances, narratives, from Arendt's perspective, can come to the rescue. They address the contingent and the particular, especially in the context of revealing instructive guidance for action. In addition, as observed above, they can provide models from our heritage for consideration, not only about everyday matters, but also in unprecedented times such as that of the Shoah. Lisa Disch provides a helpful insight into Arendt's understanding of stories: 'By stories, Arendt meant everything from the casual anecdotes told by friends over dinner or by parents to children, to novels and short stories, to the narratives and essays that she herself wrote for *The New Yorker* and *Commentary*' (Disch 1993: 2). Many regard such story-telling as at the heart of Arendt's later teaching and writing. Seyla Benhabib explains the crucial relation between action and narrative for Arendt: 'Action, unlike things and natural objects, only live in the narratives of those who perform them and the narratives of those who understand, interpret and recall them' (1990:187). Melvyn Hill further clarifies its importance: 'I believe that Hannah Arendt's concept of storytelling – the fundamental form of thinking about experience – is central to the relationship between thinking and acting in her work, though the point is not always clear in her writing and its significance has not been realized' (Hill 1979).

Nevertheless, narrative itself is not sufficient to direct political decisions and actions. As Hill mentions, it is thinking and narrating that form a type of symbiotic relationship for Arendt, specifically insofar as they can have an influence on action. But 'thinking,' as Arendt defines the term, has quite different resonances from those that inform everyday usage.

8.5 Arendt on Thinking

Arendt defines the activity of thinking as being self-reflexive in a manner that questions received habits, definitions, or orders.[9] Her version of 'thinking' also moves beyond Heidegger's formulation so as to incorporate a distinctly self-reflexive dimension. Thinking is part of the troika of action, thinking, and judging that Arendt intended to comprise her unfinished book, *The Life of the Mind* (1981 [1978]). Here Arendt describes thinking as a capacity, or 'an independent human faculty, unsupported by law and public opinion, that judges in full spontaneity every deed and intent anew whenever the occasion arises' (2005:41).[10] Such a mode of reflection was vital to Arendt's requirement for a human being's establishing a strong sense of integrity. In addition, such thinking enabled human beings to grow deep and strong roots. Such thinking, however, was not only designated for an elite. Arendt states that 'The dividing line between those who think and therefore have to judge for themselves, and those who do not, strikes across all social, and cultural or educational difference' (2003: 45). In her later work, Arendt regarded thinking, when placed in collaboration with judging, as an absolutely necessary task to be performed before any action could be undertaken.

This understanding of thinking is not the same as knowledge or the search for certainty. Richard Bernstein clarifies Arendt's stance: '[A]lthough we must not identify or confuse thinking with knowing, genuine knowing would be *impossible* without thinking' (Bernstein 2000: 283). He elaborates: 'Thinking is the faculty by which we ask unanswerable questions, but questions that we cannot help asking. It is the faculty by which we seem to understand the *meaning* of whatever we encounter. And in the quest for meaning there is no finality' (283).[11] From Arendt's perspective, this form of thinking is exactly what is required when the times are out of joint, as during the Shoah.

For Arendt, the activity of thinking has both personal and collective elements. As she observes: 'It needs the presence of others 'in whose place' it must think, whose perspectives it must take into consideration, and without whom it never has the opportunity to operate at all' (1977: 220–21). Arendt will recommend that we need to take seriously the views and thoughts of others, an activity which she describes

[9] In *The Life of the Mind*, Arendt observes that: "Clichés, stock phrases, adherences to conventional, standardized codes of expression and conduct have the socially recognized function of protecting us against reality, that is, against the claim on our thinking attention which all events and facts arouse by virtue of their existence" (1981 [1978]: 4).

[10] Arendt delivered her Gifford Lectures in Aberdeen between 1972 and 1974 where she presented two of her three planned lectures, on "Thinking," and "Acting." Her third lecture on "Judging" was not presented or ever published as she suffered a heart attack in Aberdeen in 1974 and then a second fatal coronary on 4 December 1975. The first two lectures were edited by her literary executor, Mary McCarthy, and posthumously published as *The Life of the Mind* in 1978. Arendt's work on judgment is represented in a number of earlier minor works but she had not even begun to write her later views.

[11] Again, Bernstein captures Arendt's intention: "The search for knowledge and truth, and the quest for meaning are by no means totally unrelated" (2000: 283).

as 'going visiting' (1982: 43), even if we do not agree with them. Such an 'enlarged mentality' (43) a term that she borrows from Kant, fosters a cosmopolitan awareness and tolerance. This demanding communal activity characterizes for Arendt the life of a genuine *polis* – a public space for all concerned people – re-envisioned as distinct from the limited version of ancient Greece, where it applied solely to elite males. It also marks the fulfillment of natality as both an ontological and a political category for human beings who participate in such an exercise.

Thinking also exemplifies for Arendt an essential criterion by which she evaluated the integrity of a human being:

> Thinking and remembering … is the human way of striking roots, of taking one's place in the world into which we all arrive as strangers. What we usually call a person or a personality, as distinguished from a mere human being or a nobody, actually grows out of this root-striking process of thinking (2003: 100)

It was in accordance with this criterion of thinking, as will be presented later, that Arendt would judge Eichmann.

8.6 Ricoeur and Critique

Ricoeur neither adopted nor commented on Arendt's views on thinking. Before meeting Arendt, however, he had spent at least 15 years exploring the intricacies of hermeneutics, which led him toward a different model of self-reflexivity. One of the predominant themes in Ricoeur's hermeneutic studies was an attitude toward reading that questioned texts in a critical manner – assessing the accuracy of both texts and their author's pronouncements. He referred to this approach as a 'hermeneutics of suspicion.' His first reference to this term appeared in his work *Freud and Philosophy* (Ricoeur 1970). There, he named the 'three masters, seemingly mutually exclusive, [who] dominate the school of suspicion: Marx, Nietzsche, and Freud' (1970: 32). With this term, Ricoeur wanted to alert readers to the possibility that they might not be fully in control of what they understand, let alone say and do. This lapse can be attributed to various subtle influences, be they either external impositions or unconscious needs and desires. Ricoeur developed this form of criticism in diverse directions.

Perhaps most relevant for this essay is his introduction of the movement of 'distanciation,' which he has described as 'a condition of understanding' (1991a: 88). This movement of distancing oneself from identification with a text encouraged a mode of evaluation that Ricoeur regarded as crucial for both self-reflexivity and deeper understanding. It was a continuation and qualification of Ricoeur's earlier-mentioned 'non-narcissistic self,' recommended as the appropriate model of a self who undertook a hermeneutic approach. In this manner, a person, as a reader, was prevented from uncritically incorporating either his or her own prejudices, or those of an author. This movement allowed the text, unmoored from an author, to speak for itself. Such a discipline fosters a sense of open-mindedness and a lack of dogmatism in interpreting the meaning of texts (1991a: 88).

As Ricoeur observes: 'It is the task of hermeneutics … to reconstruct the set of operations by which a work lifts itself above the opaque depths of living, acting, and suffering, to be given by an author to readers who receive it and thereby change their acting' (1984:53). Ricoeur does not finalize his work of evaluation with this remark, but will further qualify the future-oriented results that may develop from this expansive interactive method. For Ricoeur, the dynamics of self-understanding, however, must always involve such a moment of critique before any move to incorporate new ways of acting. This latter moment in the repertoire of one's hermeneutic activities was designated by Ricoeur as 'appropriation.' In Ricoeur's lexicon, appropriation involves a modality both of insight, derived from a self-reflexive attitude, together with a deeper self-understanding that is constantly cultivated by such a process. Ricoeur describes this evolution: 'By 'appropriation,' I understand this: that the interpretation of a text culminates in the self-interpretation of a subject who thenceforth understands himself better, understands himself differently, and simply begins to understand himself….hermeneutics and reflective philosophy are correlative and reciprocal' (1991b:118).

It may seem that Ricoeur waxes somewhat too lyrically in this context by not acknowledging certain obstacles that can prevent people from fully participating in such activities. In time, however, he will address these issues. But before focussing on this topic, there is one more subject that needs to be carefully examined –this is the role of imagination – where Ricoeur and Arendt share a remarkably similar interest. The role of imagination, particularly as described by Kant, is of profound significance in enriching the work both thinkers in their respective agenda.

8.7 Imagination in Arendt and Ricoeur

It is fascinating to note that, during the early 1970s – the years that marked their short friendship – both Ricoeur and Arendt were lecturing and writing on imagination. At the heart of both Arendt's and Ricoeur's innovative excursions into text, narrative and/or story, the imagination played a considerable role, specifically as depicted in Kant's interpretations of imagination in the First and Third *Critiques*. Imagination was not regarded as fantasy or wishful thinking by either Arendt or Ricoeur, but as a means of entertaining alternative ways of thinking – a method of thought experiment that could change a person's views and, ultimately, even their actions. Sadly, neither of them published a detailed study of imagination, despite many tantalizing passages in their writings. Arendt was scheduled to give a course on Kant's *Critique of Judgment* at the New School in New York in 1976, but she died before she could present it. For Arendt, it is imagination that enables a person to 'go visiting,' to take into consideration the viewpoints of others. Ricoeur's own lecture notes from his courses on Kant and imagination in the early 1970s at the

University of Chicago are due to be published in the near future. It is nonetheless tempting to consider the conversations that they may have had on this topic.

While imagination does not appear in Arendt's work, *The Human Condition* (1959), it is addressed in *The Life of the Mind* (1981 [1978]) with an Appendix on judging, as well as her writings on *Lectures on Kant's Political Philosophy* (1982). With Ricoeur, imagination made a number of important appearances in *The Rule of Metaphor* (1977), with metaphor regarded as an innovative element. It became more pronounced in the three volumes on narrative (1984–88), especially in connection with the creative role of a novel's plot (*muthos*) as proposing an alternative reality that could be entertained. Finally, in certain of his essays featured in *From Text to Action* (1991a), Ricoeur offers insights into his appreciation of Kant's work on the productive imagination.

It is in their creative focus on the vital work of imagination – with its affirmative and constructive influences – that both Arendt and Ricoeur share much in common, though there are also definite disparities in their applications. There remain many more complex details that could be explored than I can present in this essay, but I will attempt to provide at least some initial insights.

8.8 The Work of Imagination

It is worth noting that when Arendt does appeal to imagination in her work, especially in *Lectures on Kant's Political Philosophy* (1982), she employs only the reproductive imagination from Kant's *First Critique*. Quoting Kant, she states: 'Imagination is the faculty of representing in *intuition* an object that is not itself present' (1982: 79). Nonetheless, Arendt is quite creative in her experiments with imagination. In contrast, Ricoeur himself criticized this reproductive definition of an image with its primary designation as an indicator of something absent– citing similar deficient definitions in the works of Hume, Sartre, and, to an extent, Gilbert Ryle. Ricoeur develops his own theory of the imagination mainly in relation to the productive imagination of Kant's *Third Critique*. In his Chicago courses, however, he makes certain amendments to the First *Critique*, which are accomplished only with some fancy footwork. In fact, both Arendt and Ricoeur could be said to indiscriminately combine elements of Kant's two *Critiques* to help make imagination work to their own advantage.

Arendt introduces the work of imagination as part of her advocacy of the notion of entertaining as many viewpoints of other people as possible. This is an adaptation of Kant's idea of 'enlarged thinking' as a capacity of a cosmopolitan imagination. Such a capacity, as presented in Kant's Third *Critique*, is regarded by Arendt as crucial for training one's imagination 'to go visiting' (1982: 43).In this manner, one can take into consideration multiple perspectives that allow for the consideration of diverse ideas held by fellow humans in the public arena. Yet Arendt stresses that one need not necessarily agree with them. Arendt describes this procedure: 'The more people's standpoints I have present in my mind, while I am pondering a given issue, and the better I can imagine how I would feel and think if I were in their place, the stronger will be my capacity for representative thinking and the more valid my conclusions' (1961: 241). In this situation, Arendt is not prescribing empathy, or urging agreement with others' views. Nor does she advocate an assembly of only like-minded people. Her imaginative consideration of others' viewpoints informs and enriches Arendt's own position by encouraging plurality and tolerance – regarded as essential elements of any *polis*.

Arendt has been criticized for this position, where it is alleged that she is merely conjuring up what she imagines to be the positions of others, rather than actually visiting people and having real discussions with them.[12] But Arendt does not view this venture as being a mere invention. She argues that she does not blindly adopt the views of those whose standpoints are distinctly different. Instead, she explains her endeavour of representing diverse standpoints as an exercise in trying to appreciate why people might hold such views. For Arendt, it is a sign of a healthy democracy that such issues can be considered and openly debated. In fact, this process informs one of the charges that she levels at Eichmann and his ilk. Not only did she charge that Eichmann did not think deeply in the way that Arendt has proposed, but he also failed to imagine himself in the place of all the unfortunate victims whom he dispatched to their deaths. This lack of fellow-awareness was one of the most serious of charges Arendt raised against him: 'A more specific, and also a more decisive flaw in Eichmann's character was his almost total inability ever to look at anything from the other person's point of view' (1963: 49). Arendt's own verdict of Eichmann on charges of both not thinking and of not imagining himself in another's place has been contested, but it is a damning charge that Arendt levels at Eichmann – one that results from her own far-reaching investigation of human motivations. Even if her decision results from an imaginative project of an 'enlarged mentality' that is a result of 'going-visiting,' Arendt indicts Eichmann for his failure to abide by measures that promote the well-being of his fellow humankind. He was, in her view, a man who lacked roots. Drawing on her metaphor of human thinking as integrity that has developed a deep 'rootedness', Arendt emphasizes: 'Limitless, extreme evil is possible only where these self-grown roots, which automatically limit the possibilities, are entirely absent' (101).

Ricoeur, in contrast to Arendt, is quite expressive in his own appeal to a productive imagination. This is obvious in his tribute to the impetus of creativity that animates the productive imagination. For Ricoeur, imagination is the crucial agent in reading texts, whereby one is inspired to entertain alternative ways of living and acting. He explains: 'Imaginative variations, play, metamorphosis – all these expressions point to a fundamental phenomenon, namely, that it is in the *imagination* that this new being is first formed in me' (1991a: 101).

In his essays on imagination in *From Text to Action* II (1991a: 25–52),[13] Ricoeur examines in greater detail the influence of Kant and his ideas on imagination in both

[12] In one sense, Arendt could be described as using the productive rather than reproductive imagination in this exercise.

[13] See also *From Text to Action* II, 53–74, 75–88, 89–101, 168–87.

the First and the Third *Critiques*. In his own adaptation, Ricoeur first appeals specifically to Kant's use of *schematism* as an agent of the productive imagination. This, in turn, supports his choice of metaphor as a *schema* that stimulates creative thought. Ricoeur's theory is that a metaphor with its 'cognitive dissonance' can disrupt assumed meanings/ideas.[14] He further explains:

> Through this approach, we rediscover the basic aspects of the Kantian theory of schematism. Schematism, Kant said, is a method for giving an image to a concept. And again, schematism is a rule for producing images.... In what sense is imagination a method rather than a content? In the sense that it is the very operation of grasping the similar, by performing the predicative assimilation answering the initial the original semantic shock. Suddenly, we are seeing as....To be sure we have not yet accounted for the quasi-sensorial aspect of language. But at least we have introduced Kantian productive imagination into the field of language. In brief, the work of imagination is to schematize metaphorical attribution. Like the Kantian schema, it gives an image to an emerging meaning. (1991a:173)

Kant's work on imagination also informs Ricoeur's later developments in expanding the creative role of narrative. Ricoeur enlarges on Kant's depiction of imagination so that the creative impulse is now ordered not only to the effects of words but to the plots of narratives, which, in their depiction of human action, function also as a mode of schema. Ricoeur then delineates the process: 'For the power of allowing oneself to be struck by new possibilities precedes the power of making up one's mind and choosing. Imagination is the dimension of subjectivity that responds to the text as a *poem*' (1991a: 101). It is here that Ricoeur turns to the productive imagination of the *Third Critique* to envisage the way that imagination can potentially change our lives. It involves the 'free-play of imagination,' which Kant introduces in the *Critique of Judgment*. Ricoeur employs this creative process to envisage other possible worldviews and behaviours that could be adopted (1991a). He elaborates on this development:

> Imagination is involved in the very process of motivation. It is imagination that provides the milieu, the luminous clearing, in which we can compare and evaluate motives, as diverse as desires and ethical obligations, themselves as disparate as professional rules, social customs, or intensely personal values....Finally, it is in the realm of the imaginary that I try out my power to act, that I measure the scope of 'I can'. (1991a: 177–78)

It is a major shift to move from talking of living metaphor and lively expression to describing texts as reverberating with a creative dynamic. It is a further giant step to appreciate that this liveliness/aliveness continuum can constitute a new poetics/praxis merger. Yet another level altogether is required if one is to act on the incentive so provided. Ricoeur explores these innovative developments in his works on narrative. In *Time and Narrative*, vol. 1, he had heralded this venture: 'For some years now, I have maintained that what is interpreted in a text is the proposing of a world that I might inhabit' (1984: 81). Yet, after completing his three volumes on

[14] Ricoeur was troubled by Kant's move from his use of the term "productive imagination" in the Introduction of first edition of the *Critique of Reason*, to his use of "reproductive imagination" in the second edition. Ricoeur basically decided to explore the "productive imagination." I draw these ideas from a set of class notes from a course that Ricoeur taught at the University of Chicago. n.d.

narrative, a distinct change was to occur in Ricoeur's work. A further development would also appear in Arendt's work. These proposed activities, however, would emphasize quite divergent strategies.

8.9 The Move to Action in Ricoeur and Arendt

Imagination, thinking, and critique, while supplying important aspects of awareness about the injustices evident in human society, are not sufficient in themselves to effect any substantial political change. Both Hannah Arendt and Paul Ricoeur, primed by their respective explorations in imagination, introduced specific activities they believed would help ameliorate the less-than-satisfactory conditions of human existence. In Ricoeur's case, it was a deliberate turn from celebrating imagination to a more cautious approach in the direction of ethics. Arendt's work would orient itself to investigate aspects of judgment from a political perspective.

In the final volume of *Time and Narrative*, Ricoeur indicates a major change in his interpretation of narrative texts, which reflects his increasing concern with the undiminishing scale of human suffering in the world. Having become somewhat dissatisfied with his construct of the narrative 'self,' Ricoeur refines this definition by proposing an acting and ethical self, specifically in relation to non-narrative features. 'It belongs to the reader, now an agent, an initiator of action, to choose among the multiple proposals of ethical justice brought forth by reading. It is at this point that the notion of narrative identity encounters its limit and has to link up with the non-narrative components in the formation of an acting subject' (1988: 249). In addition, Ricoeur acknowledges what he now regards as omissions in his earlier work: 'I left unclear the face of impotence owing not only to those infirmities of every sort that may affect the human body as the organ of action, but also the interference of outside powers capable of diminishing, hindering or preventing our use of our abilities' (1997: xi). As a result, ethical issues now become an essential element in his approach. Ricoeur's own anguish at the unceasing and unmerited suffering in the world is graphically evident in his cry of distress. 'The question becomes: What shall we do with this fragile being, what shall we do for him or her? We are directed towards a future of being in need of help to survive and grow' (1996: 16). This statement indicates a change in Ricoeur's attitude to imagination – though he had already issued warnings of its possible pathologies in *Lectures on Ideology and Utopia* (1986b).

In Ricoeur's movement toward ethics, beginning with *Oneself as Another* (1992), a person now encounters an entirely different entity, that of another human being, who replaces the text as constituting the other with whom one interacts. In addition, in such an encounter, Ricoeur depicts a human person as now participating in the 'dialogical constitution of the self' (2000: xii). He will insist that: '*Oneself as Another* suggests that, from the outset, one's selfhood of oneself implies otherness to such an intimate degree that one cannot be thought of without the other, that instead one passes into the other, as we might say in Hegelian terms' (1992: 3).

This extraordinary proposition of human symmetry, involving a relation of mutuality, establishes an extremely radical claim. It marks a new understanding of recognition that surpasses the Hegelian model. This is because Ricoeur revises the nature of recognition as it pertains to human beings. He states that one is ultimately oneself only insofar as one is, at the same time, other. Such a relationship implies that a person attains self-worth only insofar as the incomparable worth of others is equally respected. A claim of this nature surpasses that of Hegel because what Ricoeur proposes is not simply that recognition of others as necessary for growth in knowledge and self-awareness but that recognition requires a sense of identification with others in their uniqueness, i.e., their 'irreplaceability' (1992: 193). This allows that the difference or otherness of another human being exists not to be ignored, or even subsumed, let alone eradicated. It is these observations that will undergird Ricoeur's ethical aspirations with its modification of Aristotle: 'To live well with and for others in just institutions' (1992: 352).

After establishing the foundations of this integral model of intersubjectivity with personal and ethical implications, Ricoeur undertakes ethical evaluations of the work of Heidegger, Husserl, and Levinas so as to explicate his difference from their respective positions. Given the constraints of length for this essay, I cannot undertake a detailed examination of Ricoeur's analyses, which occur in diverse places in his texts. I can, however, outline the basic arguments that Ricoeur develops in comparing his position with those thinkers mentioned above.

Ricoeur has always looked upon Heidegger's work with some diffidence. In *The Rule of Metaphor*, he admits that 'Heidegger's philosophy steps forth as intermingled and [an] inescapable attempt and temptation' (1977: 309). This ambivalence was first evident in two essays published in *The Conflict of Interpretations*, 'Existence and Hermeneutics' (1974a), and 'Heidegger and the Question of Hermeneutics' (1974b), where he initially worried about Heidegger's taking a short-cut to ontology. At the heart of Ricoeur's difficulty was Heidegger's move in his proposed 'new ontology' of identifying philosophy with poetry, and rejecting all other ontologies as reflecting an outmoded metaphysical approach (1977: 311). Ricoeur observes that ontology is in no way separate from interpretation. The necessity of interpretative mediation by hermeneutics will be Ricoeur's own preferred longer route. Most especially, however, Ricoeur is also concerned about the status of *Dasein* as presented in Heidegger's new ontology. Ricoeur questions the notion of the self that is implied by Dasein, especially in relation to self-knowledge or self-reflexivity, as well as to evidence of any intersubjective dynamics (1974b: 227). All of these elements that indicate his unease will combine in a stark statement that is found in *Oneself as Another* (1992), where Ricoeur, directing his attention to ethics, is discussing Heidegger's position as it is 'related to our concernful Being with Others' (349). Ricoeur remarks: 'Unfortunately, Heidegger does not show how one could travel… from ontology toward ethics' (249). In a later interview with Richard Kearney, Ricoeur succinctly reflects on what he was attempting to clarify in this final chapter:

> It is no accident that the title of the last chapter of *Oneself as Another* is in the form of an interrogation rather than an assertion – 'Towards which Ontology?'. Here I try to explore the possibilities of an ethical ontology beyond the Heideggerian model of *ontology without ethics* and the Levinasian model of *ethics without an ontology*. By trying to think ethics in terms of action (*praxis/pragma*) and action in terms of being as potency and act I am seeking ways beyond the either/or of Heidegger/Levinas. (Ricoeur in Kearney 2004: 167)

Unfortunately, there is not sufficient space left to investigate in any depth these ideas of Ricoeur about action in relation to ethics, together with his concomitant task to outline the requirements of a just society. One productive source that helps to understand what Ricoeur is aiming to achieve can be found in another of his engagements with the thought of Husserl and Levinas in *Oneself as Another*. In this context, Ricoeur claims that there is a lack of reciprocity in human encounters as depicted by both these thinkers. In Husserl's model, Ricoeur discerns a merely theoretical model of 'appresentation' (333) on the part of the subject who encounters another. This mode of interaction, where the subject imposes his or her own ideas on another, does not allow for the absolute integrity of the other person as a fully capable human being who both acts and suffers. All initiative is on the part of the subject, who simply attributes what Ricoeur terms an 'alter-ego' to the other person, based on a projection from his or her own ego. Thus, there is no recognition accorded to the other. Neither is the capability of the other as an ethical agent in his or her own right acknowledged. In Ricoeur's view, mutual recognition does not take place.

In the case of Levinas, Ricoeur regards any ethical injunction that impels one person to be utterly responsible the other as imbalanced. For Levinas, in contrast to Husserl's model, all initiative originates from the other person. Ricoeur assesses this demand, issued by the other, as denying the integrity of the subject. Because he or she is required to respond pre-reflexively, the subject is denied any moment of reflection. On Ricoeur's account, such a subject acts under duress. Ricoeur regards such a demand as imposing a limited relationship, as one of the participants is unable to act from the fullness of their being.[15] This orientation would also preclude mutual recognition, where each person is regarded as irreplaceable.

Ricoeur will classify both of the above forms of intersubjectivity (i.e., those of Husserl and Levinas) as manifestations of what he terms a 'unilateral dialectics,' instead of the dialogical model he wishes to promote. To advance beyond the 'modified solipsism' of Husserl, and the 'absolute imperative' of Levinas, as well as to lessen the obvious dissymmetry, Ricoeur observes: 'A two-pronged conception of otherness remains to be constructed here, one that does justice in turn to the primacy of self-esteem and also to the primacy of the convocation coming from the other' (1992: 331).[16] In Ricoeur's view, what is lacking in both of above cases is the recognition that results from the self-esteem of a person that holds him- or herself

[15] Ricoeur observes: "If the injunction coming from the other is not part and parcel of self-attestation, it loses its character of injunction, for lack of the existence of a being enjoined standing before it as its respondent. If one eliminates this dimension of auto-affection, one ultimately renders the meta-category of conscience superfluous; the category of the other suffices" (1992: 355).

[16] Ricoeur will add a final qualification to his analysis of Husserl and Levinas in *The Course of Recognition* (2005: 260–62).

ethically accountable to the other person for their own actions.[17] Such recognition witnesses to the fragility, to the mutual suffering, which all human beings share. In a particularly poignant passage, Ricoeur portrays his own exemplar of such fellow-feeling.

> In true sympathy, the self, whose power of acting is at the start greater than that of its other, finds itself affected by all that the suffering other offers to it in return. For from the suffering other there comes a giving that is no longer drawn from the power of acting and existing but precisely from weakness itself. This is perhaps the supreme test of solicitude, where unequal power finds compensation in an authentic reciprocity in exchange, which, in the hour of agony, finds refuge in the shared whisper of voices or the feeble embrace of clasped hands. (1992: 191)

Ricoeur will undertake further fine-tuning of his own journey from theory to action and then to ethics in his final philosophical work, *The Course of Recognition* (2005 [2004]). In this exploration, he carefully differentiates between the various gradations appropriate for solicitude as the expression of love and concern for those who are familiar, and for recognition and justice on the institutional level. Institutions are allotted for dealings with all those with whom we do not have a close affinity. In concluding, Ricoeur admits, however, that the struggle from misrecognition to recognition will continue to provide a major challenge to all who seek to establish a just world.

8.10 Arendt and Political Action

There is unfortunately little room here to describe the intricacies of Arendt's move to include the faculty of judging within her model of democracy. Nor can there be a comprehensive comparison of Ricoeur's ideas with Arendt's advocacy of this act of judging within a democratic politics. These two developments mark the culmination of Arendt's endeavours to establish ways of avoiding the degradation that both Arendt and Ricoeur had experienced in their lifetime. In this connection, Arendt places judging at the heart of the democratic process. In seeking to replace deliberative judgments, with their appeals to cognitive universals and absolutist rules (and which reflect the philosophical tradition she had rejected), Arendt adopts Kant's productive imagination from his *Critique of Judgment*. By locating notions of taste

[17] The important factor sustaining solicitude is an attribute that Ricoeur calls self-esteem. The term could be easily misunderstood as meaning "pride," but Ricoeur clarifies its meaning: "We call *self-esteem* the interpretation of ourselves mediated by the ethical evaluation of our actions. Self-esteem is itself an evaluation process indirectly applied to ourselves as selves" (Ricoeur, *The Narrative Path*: 1989: 99). But it is not only self-referential: "I cannot myself have self-esteem unless I esteem others *as* myself. 'As myself' means that you too are capable of starting something in the world, of acting for a reason, of hierarchizing your priorities, of evaluating the ends of your actions, and having done this, of holding yourself in esteem as I hold myself in esteem" (1992: 193).

and aesthetic ideals with politics, however, Arendt's borrowing is quite at odds with Kant's own approach, as he never produced a political philosophy.

In order to make a political judgment, Arendt proposes that one adopts a reflective position, with moves similar to those of aesthetic judging. Many thinkers disagree with this change, asserting that judgments henceforth would depend solely on personal sentiments. In introducing reflective judging entry into the public space of the contemporary *polis*, however, Arendt will also incorporate plurality and impartiality as core elements. These qualifications allow for a more expansive range of decision-making. Arendt's position can then be appreciated as an extension of the activity of an imagined 'enlarged mentality' where the views of multiple others are taken into consideration. As noted previously, such inclusiveness, which Arendt views as encouraging plurality and tolerance – hallmarks of a society where natality can flourish. As Seyla Benhabib observes: 'What Arendt saw in Kant's doctrine of aesthetic judgment was ... a procedure for ascertaining intersubjective agreement in the public realm' (Seyla Benhabib 1996:188–89).

But this is not the only outcome that political judgment can produce. Such judgments assist one in more deeply understanding human experience. As Linda Zerilli, who has attentively followed and illuminated Arendt's work on imagination and her adaptations of Kant, remarks: "We feel our freedom,' as Kant put it, when we judge aesthetically or, as Arendt shows, politically. If the pleasure that obtains in a judgment arises not out of the immediate apprehension of an object but out of reflection (that is, it arises in relation to nothing other than the judgment itself), then we are thrown back on ourselves and our own practice: we take pleasure in what we hold (e.g., that these truths are self-evident)' (Zerilli 2005: 163). Ideally, in such judgments, human persons learn how to participate in democracy and its benefits. In addition, they\come to an appreciation of the wonders of an existence shared in common with fellow creatures.

8.11 Arendt, Ricoeur, and Judgment

Ricoeur did not write a large treatise on justice, but there are a number of occasional essays in both *The Just* (2000) and *Reflections on the Just* (2007) where he discusses specific issues. One of these essays, 'Aesthetic Judgment and Political Judgment according to Hannah Arendt,' appears in *The Just* (2000: 94–108). In this essay, Ricoeur expresses several reservations about Arendt's work on judgment. It becomes obvious that, on the question of the distinctive merits of reflective judgment and deliberative judgment, Ricoeur and Arendt part company.

In the essay in *The Just*, Ricoeur initially focuses on certain problems he has with Kant's arguments in the *Third Critique,* rather than Arendt's own work. In addition, in criticizing Kant's work, Ricoeur also spends time in supplying Kant with a suitable political philosophy – something Kant never wrote. Ricoeur develops ideas from Kant's *Toward Perpetual Peace*, as providing him with an acceptable teleological aim. This amendment will then influence Ricoeur's appraisal of Arendt, inferring that her work on taste and aesthetic judgment as a model for political judgment exhibits similar weaknesses as those of Kant. Although he does acknowledge Arendt's unfinished project, it is unfortunate that Ricoeur does not mention that Arendt did not even commence writing her section on judging for inclusion in *The Life of the Mind* (1981 [1978]). Ricoeur's views were based on his reading of Arendt's posthumously published and edited lectures from a course she gave on Kant at the New School in New York in 1970, *Lectures on Kant's Political Philosophy* (1982: 50–85). Certain of Arendt's close readers have argued that in writing *The Life of the Mind* (which she did not live to complete) she had nonetheless developed positions that were not totally in agreement with Kant. They even argue that Arendt has made a constructive contribution to contemporary political thinking. (See Bernstein 1986; Disch 1993; Zerilli 2005.)

Ricoeur, however, would prefer that Arendt include a teleological direction in her adaptation of Kant's *Critique of Judgment*. This is because he assesses that her emphasis on plurality and toleration do not supply sufficient strength to sustain a just society – his own teleological ideal. Nor does he recommend that a reflective judgment, based on what he regards as the views of a single onlooker/spectator, even one who has 'gone visiting' and has a cosmopolitan outlook, be regarded as decisive. It appears that Ricoeur is fearful of an individual losing his or her way without sufficient (teleological) guidelines by which to contain the power of what he regards as an 'undisciplined imagination.' In contrast, Arendt, who is suspicious of any agenda imposed by a political decree, takes an alternative position, foregoing any requisite ideals of progress or pre-determined future goals. This debate definitely requires a more extensive and finely observed analysis because it seems that, on a number of issues concerning polity and pluralism, Arendt and Ricoeur do concur. Individually, each of their contributions still stand as beacons of wisdom flashing in the fading light.

8.12 Concluding Remarks

It has been a compelling exercise, tracing the respective interactive paths of Hannah Arendt and Paul Ricoeur through some of the most significant issues that have engaged humanity during the past century. It has been even more engrossing to witness these two great thinkers, who were both totally committed to the affirmation of life in this world and its continual betterment, engaged in both dialogue and debate about their respective visions. Their specific goals are dedicated to lessening human suffering and promoting the ideals they attributed to natality. Their respective agendas were dedicated to envisaging the world as one where justice and freedom could thrive, and human beings flourish, although they well understood the hazards and the unanticipated pitfalls that ever lay in wait to threaten human existence. In concluding, I would propose that Professor Max Charlesworth was a philosopher whose motivations and activism aspired to achieve the same inestimable ideals.

References

Arendt, H. (1959). *The human condition*. Garden City: Anchor Books.

Arendt, H. (1961). *Between past and future*. New York: Viking Press.

Arendt, H. (1963). *Eichmann in Jerusalem: A report on the banality of evil*. New York: Penguin.

Arendt, H. (1968). *Men in dark times*. New York: Harcourt, Brace, Jovanovich.

Arendt, H. (1977). *Between past and future*. New York: Viking.

Arendt, H. (1981 [1978]). *The life of the mind. 1. Thinking; 2. Willing*. New York: Harcourt, Brace Jovanovich.

Arendt, H. (1982). *Lectures on Kant's political philosophy* (ed.: Beiner, R.). Chicago: University of Chicago Press.

Arendt, H. (1983). *Condition de l'homme moderne*. Paris: Calmann-Lévy.

Arendt, H. (2003). *Responsibility and judgment* (ed: Kohn, J.). New York: Schocken.

Arendt, H. (2005). *The promise of politics* (ed: Kohn, J.). New York: Schocken.

Benhabib, S. (1990). Hannah Arendt and the redemptive power of narrative. *Social Research, 57*(1), 167–196.

Benhabib, S. (1996). *The reluctant modernism of Hannah Arendt*. Thousand Oaks, CA: Sage.

Bernstein, R. J. (1986). Rethinking the social and the political. *Graduate Faculty Philosophy Journal, 11*(1), 111–130.

Bernstein, R. J. (2000). *Arendt* on thinking. In D. Villa (Ed.), *The Cambridge companion to Hannah Arendt* (pp. 277–292). Cambridge: Cambridge University Press.

Disch, L. J. (1993). More truth than fact: Storytelling as critical understanding in the writings of Hannah Arendt. *Political Theory, 21*(4), 665–694.

Hill, M. A. (1979). The fictions of mankind and the stories of man. In M. Hill (Ed.), *Hannah Arendt: The recovery of the public world* (pp. 275–300). New York: St. Martin's Press.

Kearney, R. (2004). Dialogues: On life stories (2003). In *On Paul Ricoeur: The owl of Minerva* (pp. 157–169). Aldershot: Ashgate.

Reagan, C. (1996). *Paul Ricoeur: His life and work*. Chicago: University of Chicago Press.

Ricoeur, P. (1966 [1950]). *Freedom and nature: The voluntary and the involuntary* (trans: Kohák, E. V.). Evanston: Northwestern University Press.

Ricoeur, P. (1967). *Husserl: An analysis of his phenomenology*. (Edward G. Ballard and Lester E. Embree, translators, editors and introduction). Evanston: Northwestern University Press. This book is a selection of articles previously published in French. There was no French edition.

Ricoeur, P.. (1967 [1960]). *The symbolism of evil* (trans: Buchanan, E.). Boston: Beacon Press.

Ricoeur, P. (1970 [1965]). *Freud and philosophy: An essay on interpretation* (trans: Savage, D.). New Haven: Yale University Press.

Ricoeur, P. (1974a [1968]). Existence and hermeneutics. In *The conflict of interpretations: Essays in hermeneutics* (ed: Ihde, D. & trans: McLaughlin, K., pp. 3–24). Evanston: Northwestern University Press.

Ricoeur, P. (1974b). Heidegger and the question of the subject. In *The conflict of interpretations: Essays in hermeneutics* (ed: Ihde D. & trans: McLaughlin, K., pp. 223–31). Evanston: Northwestern University Press.

Ricoeur, P. (1975). Philosophical hermeneutics and theological hermeneutics. *Studies in religion/Sciences religieuses, 5*(1), 14–33.

Ricoeur, P. (1977). *The rule of metaphor: Multidisciplinary studies of the creation of meaning in language* (trans: Czerny, R., McLaughlin, K., & Costello, J.). Toronto: University of Toronto Press.

Ricoeur, P. (1984). *Time and narrative* (Vol. 1, trans: McLaughlin, K. & Pellauer, D.). Chicago: University of Chicago Press.

Ricoeur, P. (1983a). Action, story and history: On re-reading *The human condition*. *Salmagundi 60*, 60–72.

Ricoeur, P. (1983b). Préface. *Condition de l'homme moderne* (French translation by G. Fradier, pp. i–xxviii). Paris: Calmann-Lévy.

Ricoeur, P. (1986a). Life: A story in search of a narrator. In M. C. Doeser & J. N. Kraaj (Eds.), *Facts and values: Philosophical reflections from western and non-western perspectives* (pp. 121–32). Dordrecht: Nijhoff.
Ricoeur, P. (1986b). *Lectures on ideology and utopia* (ed: Taylor, G.). New York: Columbia University Press.
Ricoeur, P. (1988). *Time and narrative* (Vol. 3, trans: Blamey, K & Pellauer, D.). Chicago: University of Chicago Press.
Ricoeur, P. (1989). *The narrative path: The later works of Paul Ricoeur* (ed: Peter Kemp, T. & Rasmussen, D.). Boston: MIT Press.
Ricoeur, P. (1991a). *From text to action: Essays in hermeneutics II*. Evanston: Northwestern University Press.
Ricoeur, P. (1991b). Appropriation. In M. Valdés (Ed.), *A Ricoeur reader: Reflection and imagination*. Toronto: University of Toronto Press.
Ricoeur, P. (1992 [1990]). *Oneself as another* (trans: Blamey, K.). Chicago: University of Chicago Press.
Ricoeur, P. (1995a). *The philosophy of Paul Ricoeur* (ed: Hahn, L. E.). Peru: Open Court.
Ricoeur, P. (1995b). *Figuring the sacred: Religion, narrative, and imagination* (ed: Wallace, M. & trans: Pellauer, D.). Minneapolis: Fortress Press.
Ricoeur, P. (1996). Fragility and responsibility. In R. Kearney (Ed.), *Paul Ricoeur: The hermeneutics of action* (pp. 15–22). London: Sage.
Ricoeur, P. (1997). A response. In M. Joy (Ed.), *Paul Ricoeur and narrative: Contexts and contestations* (pp. xliii–xxliv). Calgary: University of Calgary Press.
Ricoeur, P. (1998). *Critique and conviction* (Ed: Azouvi, F. & de Launay, M., trans: Blamey, K.). New York: Columbia University Press.
Ricoeur, P. (1999). Memory and forgetting. In R. Kearney & M. Dooley (Eds.), *Questioning ethics: Contemporary debates in philosophy* (pp. 5–11). London: Routledge.
Ricoeur, P. (2000). *The just* (trans: Pellauer, D.). Chicago: University of Chicago Press.
Ricoeur, P. (2004 [2000]). *History, memory, forgetting* (trans: Blamey, K. & Pellauer, D.). Chicago: University of Chicago Press.
Ricoeur, P. (2005 [2004]). *The course of recognition* (trans: Pellauer, D.). Cambridge, MA: Harvard University Press.
Ricoeur, P. (2007). *Reflections on the just* (trans: Pellauer, D.). Chicago: University of Chicago Press.
Ricoeur, P. (2009). *Living up to death* (trans: Pellauer, D.). Chicago: University of Chicago Press.
Young-Bruehl, E. (2004). *For love of the world*. New Haven: Yale University Press.
Zerilli, L. (2005). We feel our freedom: Imagination and judgment in the thought of Hannah Arendt. *Political Theory, 33*(2), 158–188.

Morny Joy is Faculty Professor in the Department of Classics and Religion at the University of Calgary, Canada. Morny's BA is from Sydney University, MA from University of Ottawa and PhD from McGill University, Montreal. She also spent a 2-year postdoctoral fellowship at the University of Chicago studying with Paul Ricoeur. She researches and teaches in the areas of philosophy and religion, postcolonialism and intercultural studies in South and Southeast Asia, as well as in diverse aspects of women and religion. In recent years, she has published three edited volumes, *Continental Philosophy and Philosophy of Religion* (Springer 2011); *After Appropriation: Explorations in Intercultural Philosophy and Religion* (University of Calgary Press 2011); *An Abundance of Riches: Women, Religion, and the Gift* (Springer 2016). Her latest volume, *Explorations in Women, Rights, and Religions* (Equinox) will be published in January 2020. In 2011 she received an Honorary Doctorate from the University of Helsinki, and she is also a Life Fellow at Clare Hall, University of Cambridge.

Part III
Life of the Mind

Chapter 9
St. Anselm's Argument

M. J. Charlesworth

I suppose that no one now is likely to be taken in by St. Anselm's argument for the existence of God in the *Proslogion*. However, if the argument is inadequate and inconclusive, it does not deserve to be dismissed in the quick and facile way which some of its critics (Aquinas and Kant among them) have used. If the *Proslogion* argument is wrong, it is important to have the right view of why it is wrong, for, despite its flaws, it brings up in a very vivid way certain quite fundamental points about the logic of the concept 'God' and about the structure of arguments for the existence of God.

As every schoolboy knows, in chapter II of the *Proslogion* St. Anselm defines God as 'something than which nothing greater can be thought', and he goes on to say that this notion is meaningful or understandable and, in this sense, 'exists in the mind'. Now what exists in actual reality ('in re') is distinct from what merely exists in the mind. It is one thing for a picture to be thought of or in the mind of the painter, and another thing for it actually to exist after the painter has painted it. And, more importantly, what exists in actual reality is 'greater' than what exists in the mind alone. God, defined as 'that than which nothing greater can be thought', must therefore exist in actual reality, for if he did not so exist but merely existed in the mind he would not be, precisely 'that than which nothing greater can be thought' since it would be possible to think of a greater, namely, something-than-which-nothing-greater-can-be-thought existing in actual reality as well as in the mind.

It is important to notice that this is an argument or train of reasoning involving several premises. In other words, St. Anselm is not pretending that the proposition 'That than which nothing greater can be thought actually exists' is an analytic proposition such that its denial would be immediately self-contradictory. The denial of

Originally published in 1962, *Sophia 1*(2), 25–36

M. J. Charlesworth (✉)
Philosophy Department, University of Melbourne, Melbourne, VIC, Australia

P. Wong et al. (eds.), *Considering Religions, Rights and Bioethics: For Max Charlesworth*, Sophia Studies in Cross-cultural Philosophy of Traditions and Cultures 30, https://doi.org/10.1007/978-3-030-18148-2_9

this proposition only becomes self-contradictory *on the supposition* that what actually exists is greater than what merely exists in the mind. Unless we suppose this latter premises then there is no self-contradiction involved in the proposition 'That-than-which-nothing-greater-can-be-thought does not actually exist'.

Aquinas is plainly wrong, then, when he interprets St. Anselm as claiming that the proposition 'God exists' is self-evident ('per senotum') (*Sum. Cont. Gent.* Bk. I. ch. x.). (It has been claimed that Aquinas was not considering Anselm's proof as such but rather later formulations of it. However, Aquinas must have known of Anselm's *Proslogion* argument, and he nowhere bothers to distinguish the formulation of it which he rejects from St. Anselm's own formulation. We may suppose, then, that he thought that his criticisms of it were fatal to St. Anselm's proof as such.)

If, however, the *Proslogion* argument is a real argument, there is no doubt that, for Anselm, the premises of it were so evident that it would be impossible not to be convinced by it. If one admits that God is definable as that than which nothing greater can be thought, and if one admits the obvious premises that what exists in actual reality is greater than what exists in the mind alone, then, under pain of self-contradiction, one cannot but conclude that God must actually exist. Or, put in another way, the proposition 'God does not exist' is seen to be self-contradictory on the assumption that God is defined as 'that than which nothing greater can be thought', and on the further assumption that it is greater to exist in reality than in the mind alone.

This, then, is the elegant and ingenious argument which Anselm proposes, and we must now examine more closely the elements from which it is composed. What, first of all, is to be said of the definition of God as 'that than which nothing greater can be thought'? As we have seen, St. Anselm supposes that we are able to conceive of a being so great that nothing greater than it could be conceived. Of course, Anselm admits that we cannot have determinate or positive conception of such a being, but he claims that we can, nevertheless, still form some conception of the greatest conceivable being. Now, what is the sense of 'greater' as it is used in the Anselmian formula? It is obvious that it is not being used in any quantitative sense, but rather as meaning 'more perfect' in the neo-Platonic sense, that is to say, having a higher level or 'degree' of existence, (In his *Reply to Gaunilo*, for instance, Anselm uses 'greater' interchangeably with 'better', e.g. supratemporal things are metaphysically 'greater' and 'better' than temporal things). It is in this sense that, in the *Monologion*, St. Anselm claims that a horse is 'more perfect' than a tree, and that a man is 'more perfect' than a horse. For St. Anselm, this whole neo-platonic notion of metaphysical 'perfections' was so familiar and so seemingly self-evident that it needed no justification. However, for the modern thinker the notion of a 'perfection' is a puzzling one. We can, obviously, compare things *in particular respects*; for example, we can say that, in respect of strength, a horse is greater or more perfect than a man, but that in respect of doing sums, a man is greater or better or more perfect than a horse. But can we say that, *absolutely* speaking, a man is greater or better or more perfect than a horse, in that he has a 'higher degree' of being or existence? Of course, if there were a relation of *causal dependence* between the things compared, then, perhaps, it would be possible to give a meaning to the notion of 'greater' or 'more perfect' used in this metaphysical sense. For example, if we established that things of finite temporal duration (as in Aristotle's *Physics* sub-lunar things are dependent upon the movers of the spheres); or that temporal things (whether finite or infinite) were dependent upon supra-temporal things (as in Aristotle's universe the temporal universe is causally dependent upon the supra-temporal Prime mover); or, again, that contingent existents were causally dependent upon a necessary existent then we could, perhaps, compare these things in an absolute sense and speak of one thing being 'greater' or 'more perfect' than another.

The notion of 'greater' or 'more perfect' may, then, be given some sense in the context of causal dependency. However, the notion of causal dependence plays no part at all in the *Proslogion* argument. From this point of view, the validity of the *Proslogion* proof depends upon the possibility of comparing things as 'greater' or 'better' or 'more perfect' in an absolute sense, and, as we have seen, outside the context of causal dependence it is difficult to see exactly how such absolute comparisons can be made. Within our experience we can only make comparisons in particular respects, and it would have to be *proved* or demonstrated in some way that it is possible and licit to make absolute comparisons.

Put in another way, we can say that, within our experience, no being can ever be so great that no greater can be thought. Of course, a being can be *de facto* the greatest in some respect; for example, the velocity of light is, as a matter of fact, the greatest velocity. But the velocity of light is also a finite velocity, and we can quite well conceive of a greater velocity; it is not, and cannot be, that velocity than which a greater cannot be thought. And, this, of course, is true of everything else within our experience; nothing can ever be so great that a greater cannot be thought. It would, then, have first to be shown that the things within our immediate experience are not the only kind of things, if we are to give, a meaning to the notion of a being so great that no greater can be thought. In other words, we would have first to prove the existence of God before we could give a sense to the notion of a being so great that no greater can be thought. In other words again, we have, in a sense, to *prove* that the notion is meaningful, for it is not immediately evident that it is meaningful. Of course, this means that equally it cannot be immediately evident that it is *meaningless*; for if, as we have seen, the notion of a being so great that no greater can be thought is only meaningful if it is first shown that the things within our experience are not the only kind of things, then equally the notion could only be meaningless if it were first shown that the things within our experience were necessarily the only kind of things. In short, if we cannot *a priori* affirm the logical possibility of the existence of God, equally we cannot *a priori* deny the logical possibility of the existence of God.

We must now examine the second premises of St. Anselm's argument, namely that what exists in actual reality is greater than what exists in the mind alone. It is this premise which allows us to infer from the notion of 'that than which nothing greater can be thought' to its instantiation in actual existence, and it is absolutely essential to the argument.

First of all, it is obvious enough that when St. Anselm speaks of 'that than which nothing greater can be thought' existing in the mind, he does not mean this to be taken in any psychological sense, as though there were existents of two distinct kinds, real existents and mental existents. For something to exist 'in the mind' simply means, for St. Anselm, that it is thinkable or conceivable or intelligible or logically possible; in other words, we know what it would be like for that thing to exist, but we do not know whether it actually exists or not. Now, in what sense can we *compare* something in the mind – something conceivable or logically possible – with something existing in reality? And, again, assuming that we can compare them, in what sense can we say that for something to actually exist is *greater than* that same thing merely existing in the mind, or existing conceivably or possibly?

First, can we really *compare* something in the mind with that something existing in reality; can we, for example, compare £1000 as conceived in the mind and £1000 actually existing in my pocket? There certainly is a difference between thinking of having £1000 and actually having that £1000, but simply because there is a *difference* does not mean that they are *comparable* as 'greater' and 'lesser'. First of all, it could be objected that if we were to take this principle at its face value we would be led to say that actually having cancer was 'greater' or 'better' or 'more perfect' (qua having cancer) than merely possibly having cancer or thinking about having cancer. Perhaps St. Anselm might admit this and say that an actual evil was in fact a *greater* evil than a merely possible evil. However, it would surely be paradoxical to speak of it as a 'more perfect' evil.

But, apart from this, in what sense can we say that actual existence are greater *absolutely* than possible or conceptual existence? Of course, it may be that something actual is greater or better or more perfect *in some particular respect*; for me, poor and in need of the money, an actual £1000 is greater than £1000 merely thought of, but how can we say that *in itself* the actual £1000 is greater or more perfect?

A possible £1000 is the possibility of there being an actual £1000; it is not some queer, ghost-like kind of (actual, real) money. A possible £1000 is not a sum of money, albeit of a peculiar kind; it is the possibility of there being a sum of money. And the fact that I am aware of the possible £1000, or my having it 'existing in my mind', does not make me any richer than one who is not aware of the possibility of this £1000, or who does not have it in his mind.

Put in another way, the difference between a possible £1000 and an actual £1000 is not the latter has all the properties that the former has *plus* the additional property of actual existence. As every schoolboy knows once again, Kant showed conclusively that the *concept* of possible £1000 and an actual £1000 is exactly the same. 'By whatever and by however many predicates we may think a thing even if we completely determine it – we do not make the least addition to the thing when we further declare that this thing *is*. Otherwise, it would not be exactly the same thing that exists, but something more than we had thought in the concept; and we could not, therefore, say that the exact object of my concept exists'. (*Critique of Pure Reason*, p. 505). Expressed more generally, existence is not a property or attribute on a par with other properties and attributes of things.

The principle 'existence is not a predicate' is commonly thought to be fatal to St. Anselm's argument. However, in the form in which it is usually proposed, 'existence is not a predicate' means no more than that 'exists' is not a predicate *of the same kind* as other predicates, 'round', 'six feet tall', 'red', 'to the left of' etc., and that it cannot be 'contained' analytically in the notion of any subject *in the same way* as, say, the notion of 'plane figure containing two right angles' is contained in the notion of 'triangle'. Taken in this way, it is clear that St. Anselm's argument (and that of Descartes, for that matter,) is not touched by the principle, for St. Anselm admits (as does Descartes) that it is only *in one unique and extraordinary case* that 'exists' can be analytically contained in the notion of a subject. (*Reply to Gaunilo*, Sec.III; Descartes, *Meditation* V).

However, the principle 'existence is not a predicate' may be couched in a more rigorous form. Thus, it may be said that 'exists' does not function as a true predicate in sentences in which it is used, but is rather used to set up or posit or propose a logical subject – of predication which it sets up. In other words, 'X exists' may be translated as 'X can function as a logical subject to which predicates may be applied', so that 'exists' itself cannot be one of the predicates which may be applied to 'X'. From this point of view, it is all one whether we say either that 'exists' is not a predicate, or that it is a meta-predicate (that is to say, it predicates something of 'X', namely, that something may be predicated of 'X'). Now, of course, interpreted in this way, existential statements do not say anything about anything, but merely tell us that it is possible to say something about something. And, again, it is obvious that, in this sense, 'exists' may be used of conceptual or imaginary or fictional subjects as well as of really existing subjects. Anything useable as a subject-of-predication in any 'realm of discourse', whether conceptual or fictional or real, will, in this sense, be said to exist, Mr. Micawber exists in that , in a piece of fiction, certain predicates are applied to him; and the dragon I dreamed of last night also exists in that I may apply certain predicates to it.

This sense of 'exists' is, then, a purely formal or 'logical' one and may be thought to be quite trivial. However, it is useful to make it explicit because it helps us to discern another function of 'exists', namely, that of distinguishing conceptual and fictional and imaginary subjects-of predication on the one hand, from real subjectsof-predication on the other. Thus, 'Dragons do not exist' may be translated as, 'The term "Dragons" does not function as a subject-ofpredication in a real "realm of discourse" '; or, more colloquially, 'You can't talk of dragons as you do of real things; you can only talk of them in stories or as you do of imaginary things'. Again, 'Poltergeists exist' may be translated as, 'The term "poltergeist" can function as a subject-of-predication in a real "realm of discourse", as contrasted with fictional or imaginary "realms of discourse" '; or, 'You can talk of poltergeists as you do of real things'. This way of putting things is, it is obvious, simply a circumlocution, for, though we have translated talk about real and conceptual *things* into talk about subjects-of-predication in real and conceptual 'realms of discourse', the latter distinction is defined in terms of the former. Thus, to be a subject-of-predication in a real realm of discourse means that we can apply predicates to it or talk of what it refers to as we do of *real things*. However even if, in one sense, the circumlocution gets us no further forward, it does, all the same, bring out in what sense 'exists' functions as a predicate and in what sense it does not; or, put in another way, in what sense we can distinguish between real and conceptual existence without supposing that existence is a predicate in the ordinary sense.

Now, it is clear that St. Anselm and Descartes, in their respective ways, might reformulate their arguments in terms of this account of existential statements, so as to escape the objection that they both supposed that 'exists' was a real predicate. Thus , Anselm might say that his premises 'what exists in reality is greater than what exists in the mind alone' can be translated as 'to function as a subject of predication in a real "realm of discourse" is greater than to function as a subject of predication in a fictional or imaginary or conceptual "realm of discourse" '. This translation makes it clear that 'exists' is not being used as a predicate, but that nevertheless some distinction is being made between real and conceptual existence.

We may conclude from this, therefore, that the 'existence is not a predicate' dogma is not of itself fatal to St. Anselm's argument. However, we are still left with the problem of giving a sense to the *comparison* between real and conceptual existence. It is clear from our analysis that 'exists' can function, in certain contexts, to *distinguish* real subjects-of-predication from fictional and conceptual subjects-of-predication, but it is also clear that it is difficult to give any sense to a *comparison* between real and conceptual existence. Indeed, it might be asked once again whether the very possibility of comparison between the two does not presuppose that a real existent has some 'property' (namely, the 'property' of existence) which the conceptual existent lacks. In other words, if we admit with Kant that existence is not a real predicate, have we not thereby admitted that no comparison at all is possible, for the very notion of comparison involves, by definition, that two similar subjects have different predicates?

However, Anselm might reply that it is, of course, obvious that any comparison between real and conceptual existents cannot be of the same kind as other comparisons. What are being compared here are, to put it crudely, two different kinds of existents, and a comparison *between* different kinds of existents cannot be made in the same way as a comparison *within* the respective kinds of existents. We can compare a *conceptual* £50 with a *conceptual* £100, and we can compare a real £50 with a *real* £100, but we cannot compare *in the same way a conceptual* £50 with a *real* £100. A conceptual £100 is greater than a conceptual £50, and a real £100 is greater than a real £50; but, it, Anselm's sense, a real £50 is 'greater' than a conceptual £100. Indeed, a real 5p is greater than a conceptual £50.

Put in another way, what we are comparing here are real and conceptual 'subjects-of-predication', and therefore, by definition, the comparison cannot be made in terms of predicates as all other comparisons are made.

By definition, then, the comparison which Anselm is making between real and conceptual existents is not like any other kind of comparison. But does that mean, therefore, that no kind of comparison at all can be made; does it necessarily exclude the possibility of any such comparison? Surely, St. Anselm might object, there is a perfectly clear sense in which the real and actual is greater than the conceptual and possible. Thus, if X really exists, X is both conceivable and real, and is thus greater than X as merely conceivable; or, if X is actual, then X is both actual and possible, and is thus greater than what is merely possible. What is real and actual, then, seems to have a certain 'priority' over what is conceptual and possible. But, what sort of priority is this? Is it not a purely *logical* priority? Does it not simply mean that, if I know that something actually exists, then I may infer that it is possible ('ab esse ad posse valet illatio'); but that, if I know that something is possible, I may not infer that it actually exists ('ab posse ad esse non valet illatio')? From this point of view we may certainly say that to exist in reality is (logically) greater than to exist conceptually or possibly or 'in the mind' alone. But then it is difficult to see that this logical sense of 'greater' is the same as the metaphysical or ontological sense of 'greater' (things being greater in respect of their 'degree of being') implied in the definition of God as 'that than which nothing greater can be thought'. However, it might be replied in turn to this that the logical priority of real and actual existence over conceptual and possible existence reflects on ontological priority. In other words, we may infer from real existence to conceptual existence (but not vice-versa) *because* real existence is in some way prior to (greater than) conceptual existence. One way of showing this, perhaps, would be to show that it is not possible for only possible beings to exist, but that it is necessary for at least one real and actual being to exist. In other words, it would have to be shown that 'All existents are conceptual or possible existents', (or 'No existents are real or actual existents', or 'Nothing (real or actual) exists'), was self-contradictory, so that 'Some existents are real and actual existents' ('something (real and actual) exists') was a necessary proposition. If this could be shown then we could say that real and actual existence was ontologically prior to conceptual and possible existence.

But this, of course, is what can only be proved by proving or disproving the existence of God. Part of the point of the theist's proof of the existence of God is to prove *eo ipso* that 'Nothing (real and actual) exists' is necessarily false: and, likewise, the point of the atheist's disproof is to prove that 'Something (real and actual) exists' is not and cannot be a necessary proposition.

If, then, we had first proved the existence of God, we could say that real and actual existence had an ontological priority over conceptual and possible existence. But, of course, Anselm wants first to establish the priority in order to prove the existence of God.

Despite all these considerations, however, St. Anselm's premises that real and actual existents are 'greater' than conceptual and possible existents seems to be so intuitively evident and commonsensible that one hesitates to reject it with complete confidence. At any rate, we may at least say that the comparison between real and conceptual existence is such a different kind of comparison from those we ordinarily make, that we may reasonably place the onus on St. Anselm to show what sense can be given to it.

I should like to return now to St. Anselm's definition of God as 'that than which nothing greater can be thought'. I said before that the notion of an absolute 'greatest' is not self-evidently meaningful, as St. Anselm supposed, and that he would have to *prove* in some way that it was meaningful. Put in another way, St. Anselm's proof allowing for the moment that it is valid – will only work for the sort of atheist who understands by the proposition 'God does not exist', something like the following, 'We know what it would be like for God to exist but actually he does not exist', or 'God could possibly exist but actually does not exist', or 'the concept "God" is meaningful but it is not instantiated', or 'The proposition "God exists" is meaningful but false'. But it will not work against the logical atheist who denies that the concept 'God' has a meaning; in other words, who maintains that 'God does not exist' is not logically similar to 'Unicorns do not exist', but rather to 'Square circles do not exist'. As against the logical atheist Anselm must first show that the notion of 'That than which nothing greater can be thought' is a meaningful one. This implies that the onus is upon St. Anselm rather than upon the atheist. But there is a difficulty here which it is worth exploring because it helps to point up the logical peculiarity of the propositions 'God exists' and 'God does not exist'.

The difficulty is this: if St. Anselm has to show that the concept 'that than which nothing greater can be thought' is meaningful, does not the logical atheist have equally to show from his point of view that it is meaningless? In other words, does not the logical atheist have to say not merely that *within our experience* we do not compare things as absolutely greater or more perfect, (while tacitly allowing that it might be possible to give a sense to the notion of absolute perfections *outside* our experience), but that *necessarily* it is the case that things are not greater or more perfect in an absolute sense, or that it is *self-contradictory* to suppose that things can be compared as absolutely greater or more perfect? In other words, to put it crudely, is not the logical atheist compelled to say that the things within our experience (spatio-temporal and contingent beings which allow only relative comparisons, so that no being is ever such that a greater cannot be conceived than it) are *necessarily* the only things. Then, of course, the concept of God, defined as 'that than which nothing greater can be thought' would be meaningless by definition; in other words the logical atheist would be committed to an 'ontological disproof' of the existence of God.

If the atheist, St. Anselm might continue, does not wish to claim 'that than which nothing greater can be thought' is logically meaningless, then he must allow that it is meaningful (though not instantiated). And then he is in the position of the 'factual atheist', and then of course the *Proslogion* argument will work!

The categories 'Meaningful/meaningless' and 'true/false' function in an eccentric way, then, when applied to the proposition 'God exists', for one of the morals to be drawn from St. Anselm's discussion is that we cannot both admit that the proposition is *meaningful* and yet at the same time false. From another point of view, St. Anselm's discussion also shows that the possibility which the theist claims is realized when he affirms that God exists, and the possibility which the atheist denies or excludes when he denies that God exists , is a very queer kind of possibility. Put in another way, the onus of proof of the existence or non-existence of God seems to lie equally on both sides.

The same point arises with regard to St. Anselm's complementary argument in chapter III of the *Proslogion*. There, in place of the premise 'what exists in actual reality is greater than what exists in the mind alone', we have the premise 'what cannot be thought not to exist is greater than what can be thought not to exist', or, as we may legitimately translate it, 'what exists necessarily is greater than what exists contingently'. From this, St. Anselm proves that God, defined as 'that than which nothing greater can be thought', must exist necessarily. The immediate objection to this, of course, is that it assumes that the notion of 'necessary existence' is meaningful. But, if Kant is right, the notion cannot be meaningful, for, to assert that God is a necessary existent is equivalent to asserting that the proposition 'God exists' is a logically necessary proposition, so that it would be self-contradictory to assert the proposition 'God does not exist'. But it is not self-contradictory to assert this proposition, just as it is never self-contradictory to deny any existential propositions which, in Kant's terms, are always synthetic. (*Critique of Pure Reason*, pp. 502, 504). As is well known, Kant's criticism has been developed by certain contemporary philosophers and combined with the doctrine that all necessity is reducible to logical necessity, which in turn, it is claimed , simply reflects the conventions of language. From this it follows, so it is argued, that the notion of a necessary existent is a self-contradictory one. As Professor J. N. Findlay has put it 'If God is to satisfy religious claims and needs, He must be a being in every way inescapable, One whose existence and whose possession of certain excellences we cannot possibly conceive away'; but, he goes on, 'modern views make it selfevidently absurd (if they don't make it ungrammatical) to speak of such a Being and attribute existence to Him. It was indeed an ill day for Anselm when he hit upon his famous proof. For on that day he not only laid bare something that is of the essence of an adequate religious object, but also something that entails its necessary non-existence' (Findlay 1955, p. 55).

Now Anselm might reply both to Kant and to his contemporary followers that their objections prove too much, for they do not simply assert that the existence of all the things within our experience is contingent, so that all existential propositions about things within our immediate experience are synthetic, (a point which St. Anselm admits, 'Everything other than you (God) alone can be thought of as not existing'), but they go further and claim that it is logically necessary that all existential propositions are synthetic. In other words, they maintain paradoxically that it is logically impossible for the proposition 'God exists' to be a *logically necessary* one, and end by espousing an 'ontological disproof' of the existence of God.

We may conclude, then, that if we have no right to assume that the notion of 'necessary existence' is meaningful, without further argument, equally we have no right to assume that it is meaningless, without further argument. Merely logical analysis of the notion one way or another cannot decide whether the notion is meaningful or not; or, in other words, if there cannot be an *a priori* 'ontological' proof of the existence of God, equally there cannot be an *a priori* 'ontological' disproof. Once again, it is difficult to see where the onus of proof lies here: and once again it is difficult to see what kind of possibility the theist wishes left open for the notion of 'necessary existence', and the atheist wishes to exclude. In any case, no purely logical considerations will serve to break the deadlock between theist and atheist over the meaningfulness of 'necessary existence' – the theist demanding that the atheist demonstrate that the notion is self-contradictory, and the atheist demanding that the theist demonstrate that the notion is not self- contradictory.

It would be possible to break the deadlock if other extra-logical considerations were brought in. Thus, for example, the theist might argue that, by reflection upon the contingent existents in the world, we are led to ask for an ultimate causal explanation of them, and thus we are constrained to postulate the existence of a 'necessary existent' as cause of the contingent existents. In other words, we do not presuppose that the notion of 'necessary existence' has meaning, but rather the argument forces us to postulate *that* the terms 'necessary' and 'existent' may be conjoined and *that* the notion of necessary existent is meaningful, that we do not know *how* the terms 'necessary' and 'existent' are conjoinable (as we do with 'triangle' and 'figure containing two right angles') nor how the notion of 'necessary existent' is meaningful. (As Aquinas says, *Sum. Cont. Gent.* I, XI, the proposition 'God does not exist' is not, for us, a self-contradictory one. However, this does not imply that God is a contingent being, but rather that God's existence must be proved or demonstrated from his effects. The necessity of God's existence is seen only as the conclusion of a demonstration. As Aquinas puts it, 'God can be thought not to be', is not a statement about the mode of God's existence, but rather about the deficient mode of our knowledge of God.)

In conclusion, then, it is difficult to see how St. Anselm's proofs, both in chapter II and chapter III of the *Proslogion* can be made to work unless some kind of causal or 'cosmological' argument is presupposed, both to give meaning to the definition of God as 'that than which nothing greater can be thought', and to the two premises 'what exists in actual reality is greater than what exists in the mind alone' and 'what exists necessarily is greater than what exists contingently'. But then, of course, if St. Anselm's argument presupposes a causal argument, this makes it redundant and defeats his whole purpose in the *Proslogion.*

References

Findlay, J. N. (1955). Can God's existence be disproved? In A. Flew & A. Macintyre (Eds.), *New essays in philosophical theology*. London: SCM Press.

Kant. (1929). *Critique of pure reason* (trans.: Kemp Smith, N.). London: Macmillan.

Chapter 10
That Anselm's God Exists and Gaunilo's Island Does Not

Richard Campbell

Max Charlesworth began his 1962 paper on 'St. Anselm's Argument' with:

> I suppose that no one now is likely to be taken in by St. Anselm's argument for the existence of God in the *Proslogion*.

That is an odd remark, coming from a man who was working on a new translation of Anselm's *Proslogion* (and his *Reply*) together with a commentary on it. He added:

> However, if the argument is inadequate and inconclusive, it does not deserve to be dismissed in the quick and facile way which some of its critics (Aquinas and Kant among them) have used.

Maybe in 1962, the argument might have had few, if any, who believed it to be cogent, but since Charlesworth wrote that negative assessment, interest in this allegedly 'inadequate and inconclusive' argument has gathered pace, with at least nine books having been published in the past 12 years.

Charlesworth is to be commended for undertaking that translation and commentary. At the time, the only English translation widely available was Sidney Deane's from 1903. Anyone who has been following the scholarly debates in English about this famous argument cannot fail to notice how indebted scholars were to Charlesworth's slim volume. At the time, it provided in easily accessible form the essential textual material, in both Latin and English, for anyone who seriously wanted to understand this most intriguing and subtle argumentation. We were all in Max's debt. More recent work has, however, shown that, unfortunately, *crucial parts of his translation can no longer be endorsed*, as we will soon see.

R. Campbell (✉)
Australian National University, Canberra, ACT, Australia
e-mail: richard.campbell@anu.edu.au

P. Wong et al. (eds.), *Considering Religions, Rights and Bioethics: For Max Charlesworth*, Sophia Studies in Cross-cultural Philosophy of Traditions and Cultures 30, https://doi.org/10.1007/978-3-030-18148-2_10

10.1 Stage One

In 1976, I published my first book on Anselm's argument, *From Belief to Understanding*, because I had discovered that the argument so often attributed to him is simply not in the text. Most commentators, ancient and modern, wrongly locate his argument in a passage which is not about God at all. They focus their attention almost exclusively on *Proslogion* 2 (hereafter P2), the conclusion of which is:

> There proves to be [*Existit*] beyond doubt something-than-which-a-greater-cannot-be-thought both in the understanding and in reality.[1]

That conclusion does not mention God. Anselm does not identify this something-than-which-a-greater-cannot-be-thought with God until halfway through the next chapter. And he *never* writes that God exists in reality. Consequently, for over 940 years, almost all commentators, including Thomas Aquinas, and almost all contemporary critics, base their assessment on a fundamental misreading and misunderstanding of what he has written. In fact, he does not produce any argumentation which mentions God until midway through P3. And when he does, what he concludes is not that God exists in reality. Rather he announces two conclusions:

> You are something-than-which-a-greater-cannot-be-thought.
>
> You so truly exists that You could not be thought not to exist.

Of course, those conclusions imply that God exists. But Anselm never ascribes to God such a crass predicate as "is in reality". Having established that first conclusion, he drops the qualification "in reality" from the second.

That needs some explanation. That predicate expresses a binary conception of existence; it treats "exists" as subject to the Law of Excluded Middle. Something either exists, or it does not, and there no third option available. Therefore, to say that God exists in reality is to treat God as a thing, that is, as a *res*: the Latin word for the 'thick' substantial sense of "thing". And to do that is to regard God just as a thing alongside other things, all of which exist within the universe of things. For Anselm, God's mode of existence is so much more exalted than that of His creatures that he concludes that God has existence the most truly and maximally of all.

To reach those genuine conclusions, he first imagines that the Fool who is quoted in the Psalms as saying in his heart, "God does not exist", has wandered into the chapel of the monastery at Bec, in Normandy, and has been listening to Anselm's pouring out his heart in prayer, imploring God to give him some understanding of

---

[1] Readers who are familiar with this text will be surprised by my translating the beginning of this sentence as "There is proven to be …" instead of "There exists…". Of course, by concluding that something-than-which-a-greater-cannot-be-thought 'is in reality', Anselm is concluding that it exists. But the verb with which he begins this sentence, "Existit", only looks like it means "exists". The Latin verb, "existit" is a form of "exsistere", the root meaning of which is "to come forth", "to appear". Only later, as that Latin verb migrated into English, did it lose the nuance of 'coming forth'. Since Anselm was writing in the eleventh century, he is more likely to have used "existit" in its original sense. His argumentation has brought forth, i.e., proven there to be, a conclusion that is beyond doubt: that this something is both in the understanding and in reality.

what he believes. Anselm immediately specifies the first belief he wants to understand. He writes:

> We certainly believe You to be something-than-which-nothing-greater-can-be-thought.

Despite the fact that Anselm makes it perfectly clear that here, at the outset, he does not understand that belief, it is commonly misreported that Anselm is here presenting a definition as the first premise of his argument. Charlesworth's remark is typical (1962: 25):

> As every schoolboy knows, in chapter II of the *Proslogion* St. Anselm defines God as 'something than which nothing greater can be thought".

I would like to read that remark as ironic, but, unfortunately, it is more likely to be meant seriously, since in the commentary accompanying his 1965 translation, Charlesworth again misreports Anselm's argument as beginning with a definition of God.

Some commentators recognize that such a sentence would never pass muster as a definition and describe it as "something like a definition" (Brian Davies 2004: 168), or as an assumption (Jasper Hopkins 1981: 136). In a quite different way, Karl Barth treats this sentence as expressed 'the revealed Name of God' so as to ground Anselm's argument in a rather radical notion of faith that gives rise to thought (1931/1960: 102). But that, too, is to treat this sentence as declaring a premise. All of that speculation is illogical and misconceived. Anselm has learnt from Boethius enough of Aristotle's teachings on logic to know that definitions are of *kinds* of things and the proper way to frame a definition is to locate the kind to be defined in some genus, distinguished from other species also belonging to that genus by some differentiating characteristic. If Anselm were offering a definition, he would have had to frame it in that way, and he knows full well that God could not be a species of some larger genus. Even if that Aristotelian criterion is relaxed, the content of this belief could never pass muster as a well-formed definition, since it contains an *indefinite* description.

Nor is Anselm treating the content of that belief as a premise, as is so often alleged. His text elsewhere shows him to have too finely-tuned a sense of logical propriety for it to be credible that he has propounded an argument of the following form:

x is something *F*;
Something *F* is *G*;
Therefore, *x* is *G*.

That form of argument is fallacious. Consider the following:

King Arthur is a legendary character;
Some legendary characters actually existed;
Therefore, King Arthur actually existed.

Difficult historical questions are not settled so easily! To attribute such an invalid form of reasoning to Anselm can only be described as a serious misrepresentation. He clearly had a firm grasp of logic.

The text of the *Proslogion* is a much more subtle and sophisticated argument than that caricature. His argument is not located in P2; rather, that passage is the first stage of a single extended argument which he develops over *three* distinct but logically connected stages. The proposition which he says that 'we believe' cannot be the first *premise* of his argument, since it is a *conclusion* he validly draws in P3. What his argument begins with is a sentence which reports what 'we believe'. That premise has the form of a historical fact, namely:

> Anselm says, 'We certainly believe You to be something-than-which-nothing-greater-can-be-thought".

Thereafter, apart from mentioning that the Fool has said in his heart: "God does not exist", neither the word "God [*deus*]", nor "You" appears in the text until the middle of P3.

Rather, in the little scenario Anselm presents, he imagines that the Fool has overheard himself uttering aloud that belief. He then argues that the Fool understands what he hears, and that what is understood exists in the understanding. He concludes from this that even the Fool is bound to concede that this something is in the understanding.

This last inference is the only one where Anselm's reasoning appears somewhat shaky. Let us grant that the Fool has heard the words Anselm has uttered, and that he understands the meaning of those words. It does not necessarily follow that the Fool is convinced that such a thing is in the understanding. All that Anselm can reasonably claim is that the Fool *can* have it in his understanding, that is, that he *can* be thinking of such a thing.

And there appears to be a second problem. Anselm's claim that the Fool is thinking of such a thing is ambiguous. It is possible that the Fool is vaguely thinking of something-or-other than which nothing greater can be thought, without that thought being specifically about any particular thing. As Peter Geach pointed out, it does not follow from "John is thinking of a dragon" that John is thinking of a particular dragon, say, Fafner. John could, as we ordinarily say, 'just' think of a dragon, but not of any particular dragon. Some occurrences of "some *F*" are specific, as in the case of Brutus killing some man, but in intentional cases, like Geach's example of thinking of a dragon, the thought might well only be generic.

As a general point, Geach's objection is sound. But, as in the case of Anselm's argument, the context can make a difference. It is Anselm who has written this scenario, and it is he who has uttered that belief. So, when Anselm utters that belief, *he* is attributing the indefinite description, "something-than-which-nothing-greater-can-be-thought" to a particular subject. What he says is that "we believe You to be something-than-which-nothing-greater-can-be-thought." So, the text makes it clear that Anselm is thinking of some specific something, not some generic, indeterminate something-or-other. So, he is licensed to proceed on the basis that this something is understood to be something specific. And that legitimates his claiming that it has at least the status of being in the understanding. And, as he makes clear in the *Reply*, his argument only needs something weaker than that: that such a thing can be thought.

The rest of P2 is taken up with arguing that this something cannot be in the understanding alone, since it can be thought to exist also in reality, which is greater. Countless objections have been made to this seemingly innocuous claim. It is said that Anselm is treating existing in reality improperly as a 'great-making' predicate. It is said that he must be appealing to some hidden premise to justify the phrase "which is greater", and there have been numerous proposals as to what that hidden premise might be. It is said that he is illegitimately assuming that "is in reality" is a 'real predicate', whereas Kant has shown that "exists" is not a real predicate. And it is said that he is regarding existence in reality as a 'perfection', when it is not in all other cases. And so on.

None of these objections succeed, because they are all beside the point. In a recent paper Günther Eder and Esther Ramharter (2015) have taken seriously the fact that Anselm is comparing that-than-which-nothing-greater-can-be-thought *with itself* under two different conditions: (a) that it is only in the understanding, and that (b) that it has all the positive properties as in (a), plus the additional property of being in reality. That comparison involves a counter-factual conditional proposition, which is notoriously difficult to express in our current standard systems of logic. To express how Anselm is reasoning when he makes that claim, they formulate two definitions in second-order logic.

The first definition facilitates the comparison of the same thing with itself when there is a non-essential difference between how it is in one condition and in another. This definition is a modified form of Leibniz's Laws of Identity. They call it 'Quasi-Identity', which I think is a somewhat unfortunate label, so I am calling it 'Essential Identity'. With a quite minor tweaking, it states the conditions under which something is essentially-identical with something:

> *x* is essentially-identical to *y*, *modulo* the properties in the sub-set of non-essential properties in *D*, if and only if, for all consistent, primitive, and positive properties *F*, then *x* and *y* have the same properties *F* if and only if *F* is not in the sub-set of non-essential properties *D*.

Secondly, Eder and Ramharter propose that *x* is greater than *y* if, and only if, *x* has all the consistent, primitive and positive properties *y* has, but it has one more which *y* does not. This definition suddenly made Anselm's reasoning transparently clear and simple. On reflection, I recognized that while it also needs a little tweaking, it enables a rendering of Anselm's reasoning which is both faithful and plausible. Anselm explains in *Reply* 8 how any rational mind can come to think of such a thing as something-than-which-nothing-greater-can-be-thought. To exist in reality is not the only property he considers to be good to have, and thus relevant to something's being greater. He suggests that there are both lesser goods and greater goods in the world. Then, if there is something good which has a beginning and an end, something which has a beginning but does not cease is better, and what does not have a beginning, nor an end is better still, and so on. In this way, he argues anyone with rational mind can ascend in thought from thinking of lesser goods to thinking of greater goods, culminating in thinking of something-than-which-a-greater-cannot-be-thought. Clearly, he is not according existing in reality a peculiar (in both senses of that word) relation to greatness. He manifestly has a quite *general* concept of what makes something greater than another, namely, having some additional property which is good. So, I have amended Eder and Ramharter's definition by including as a requirement for being greater that the extra property has to be one which it is good to have. With that amendment, this definition supplies what Anselm's argument needs:

> If P is the class of consistent, primitive and positive properties, anything x is greater than anything y if, and only if, x has all the properties in the class P which y has, plus some additional property in P which is good, but which y has *not*.

That Anselm holds that being greater implies being good is manifest in the explanations he gives in the *Reply*. And it is obviously true. It clarifies what Anselm means when he asserts that the thing can be thought to have an additional property, and if it does, it is greater.

This becomes clear once the definition of Essential Identity is applied to this case. Anselm says that-than-which-nothing-greater-can-be-thought can be thought to exist in reality, and if it does, it would be greater than if it exists only in the understanding. So, if this thing exists only in the understanding, then something essentially identical to it, can be thought to exist in reality. Two significant implications follow from this.

Firstly, since Anselm, like Kant, requires that it is *the same thing* which exists in the understanding which can be thought to exist in reality, it follows from the definition of Essential Identity that existing in reality is a non-essential property.

Secondly, if this thing were to exist in reality, it would have an extra good property which it is good to have, and which would not have if it exists only in the understanding. Therefore, it follows from the definition that, in that circumstance, it would be greater. So, even if it does not exist in reality, it can nevertheless be thought to be greater. But that shows that if that-than-which-a-greater-cannot-be-thought does not exist in reality, that-than-which-nothing-greater-can-be-thought is not that-than-which-nothing-greater-can-be-thought.

No peculiar claims are being made here about existing in reality, other than it is good. That it is good to exist, and better to exist than not to exist, is widely accepted. That assessment underlies the joy people express at the birth of a baby, the grief they express when someone dies, the universal condemnation of murder as a crime, the desire to preserve wilderness, the reaction of horror at wanton destruction, and many, many other everyday judgements.

And with those few premises Anselm validly deduces that beyond doubt something-than-which-a-greater-cannot-be-thought is both in the understanding and in reality. Indeed, implicit in this reasoning is a stronger conclusion. Since Anselm infers that conclusion from deducing a conditional proposition with a contradictory consequent, it follows the antecedent is not just false, but impossible. The assumption which implied that contradiction is that that-than-which-a-greater-cannot-be-thought does not exist in reality. So, Anselm is entitled to conclude that:

> It is necessary that that-than-which-a-greater-cannot-be-thought exists in reality.

There is considerable evidence that he was aware of this stronger conclusion, although he only claims the weaker version in P2. That is Stage One of the argument. It says nothing about God.

10.2 Stage Two

Stage Two occupies the first half of P3. It begins with a premise, the translation of which is controversial. The Latin sentence is:

> *Nam potest cogitari esse aliquid quod non possit cogitari non esse, quod maius est quam quod non esse cogitari potest.*

Charlesworth (1965: 119) translates the first clause of that sentence as:

> For something can be thought to exist which cannot be thought not to exist.

Other translators, e.g. Jasper Hopkins (1986: 227) and Ian Logan (2009: 34), translate it as:

> For there can be thought to exist something which cannot be thought not to exist.

Both translations are possible renderings of Anselm's Latin clause. But since this clause serves as a premise, both translations are unacceptable. Neither mentions something-than-which-nothing-greater-can-be-thought, whereas something so described is the subject of the conclusion which Anselm claims. So, readers and commentators have to introduce that subject in another assumption. They can justify doing so because Anselm writes, immediately after the sentence quoted above:

> Therefore, if that than which a greater cannot be thought can be thought not to exist, that very thing than which a greater cannot be thought is not that than which a greater cannot be thought, which cannot be consistent.

So, he must have also supposed that than which a greater cannot be thought can be thought not to exist, if only to negate that supposition. Now, it is easy enough to assume that this singular term refers to the same thing as in Stage One, but there is nothing in the text to justify that assumption. Nevertheless, the sentence translated as above, together with a second premise which is alleged to be a background premise, suffice to prove validly that:

> Something-than-which-nothing-greater-can-be-thought could not be thought not to exist.

But that is not the conclusion which Anselm announces. For, according to him, what follows is:

> Something-than-which-nothing-greater-can-be-thought *so truly exists that it* could not be thought not to exist.

If we accept either of those ways of translating the major premise, there is nothing in the text which would justify that conclusion although it is arguable that Anselm could have argued that what cannot be thought not to exist is unable not to exist, and therefore exists. But the text gives no indication of that. There is nothing in the text which justifies concluding that the something mentioned in that premise *exists*. All the premise says, according to these translations, is that it *can be thought* to exist.

The trouble is that whether Anselm's clause is translated as Charlesworth has, or as Hopkins and Logan have, this P3 argument has no logical connection with the argument in Chap. 2. A few commentators, such as Gregory Schufreider and David Smith, have noticed that this is a serious problem. These translations rendered Anselm's Stage Two argument invalid. The conclusion he claims does not follow from the premise as it is translated. And if that conclusion does not follow, it appears that he has no valid argument for the existence of God.

For that reason, I argued in *From Belief to Understanding* that the translations above must be rejected, and the Latin clause be translated as having an implicit subject. The clause should be translated as:

> Something-than-which-a-greater-cannot-be-thought is both in the understanding and in reality, it can be thought to be something which could not be thought not to exist.

The consequent in that conditional sentence is exactly what Anselm has written. Interpreted that way, this premise does make it possible validly to deduce the conclusion Anselm claims.

Now, in the opening sentence of his commentary on P3, Charlesworth says (1965: 73):

> It is not clear whether St. Anselm means his argument in this chapter to be a complement to the argument advanced in Chapter II, or whether it represents an independent proof in its own right.

His own answer is that Anselm "probably regarded the argument in Chapter III as a complement to the basic argument in Chapter II".

That comment was reasonable in 1965. But it has now become clear that Anselm's arguments in P3 are *not* independent of the argument advanced in P2. There is now a precise sense in which they 'complement the basic argument in P2'. I have recently made another discovery about Anselm's argument. In section 9 of his *Reply* to Gaunilo, he presents a rather obscure argument which can be readily adapted so that the major premise of Stage Two, as I have stated it above, is validly deduced from the conclusion of Stage One.

The first premise in this R9 argument is:

> What cannot not exist can be thought of and understood.

In R1, he had already proved that something-than-which-a-greater-cannot-be-thought can be thought, it cannot not exist, which is one way of expressing the stronger version of one of his conclusion in P2. The premise in R9 is a generalization of that.

His second premise in R9 is:

> He who is thinking of what cannot not exist is thinking of something greater than what he who is thinking of what is able not to exist is thinking of.

That follows from the argumentation in P2, where he argues that if that-than-which-a-greater-cannot be-thought is in reality, it is greater than what is essentially the same, but is only in the understanding. i.e., not in reality. Since that proposition does not depend on any assumptions which mention that-than-which-a-greater-cannot be-thought, it can legitimately be universalized, and from that the second premise in R9 follows, given the three following logical truths:

(i) What is in reality exists;
(ii) Whatever necessarily exists exists; and
(iii) What does not exist is able not to exist.

From those two premises, he then deduces in R9:

> He who is thinking of [what is something]-than-which-a-greater-cannot-be-thought cannot be thinking of what is able not to exist, but must be thinking of what is not able not to exist.

This argument can easily be adapted to deduce the major premise of Stage Two, as follows. Anselm also holds it to be logically true that:

(iv) What is able not to exist can be thought not to exist.

Of these four logical truths, (i) is implicit in his assuming that the Fool's denial, that God does not exist, is to be understood as asserting that God does not exist in reality. (ii) is true in any system of modal logic. And Anselm explicitly asserts (iii) and (iv) in *Reply* 5. Since these four extra premises serve only to facilitate his inferences, and are obviously sound, they are acceptable. So, from the two premises he deduced in R9, plus (iv) it follows that:

> He who is thinking of [what is something]-than-which-a-greater-cannot-be-thought cannot be thinking of what can be thought not to exist, but must be thinking of what cannot be thought not to exist.

And that implies:

> It is not possible that something-than-which-a-greater-cannot-be-thought is something which can be thought not to exist; rather, it is something which cannot possibly be thought not to exist.

And that is equivalent to:

> Something-than-which-a-greater-cannot-be-thought can only be thought to be something which cannot possibly be thought not to exist (i.e., something which *could* not be thought not to exist).

Now this deduction follows from the fact that the same premises which entail Anselm's conclusion in P2 entail that that conclusion is necessary. Therefore, by conditional proof, the following is true:

> Something-than-which-a-greater-cannot-be-thought is both in the understanding and in reality, it can be thought to be something which could not be thought not to exist.

The consequent in that conditional sentence is word-for-word what Anselm has written. Accordingly, I now insist, in order to make what is implicit explicit, that that conditional proposition is the premise of Stage Two, and must be translated as

I have maintained.[2] Interpreted that way, this premise does make it possible validly to deduce the conclusion Anselm claims for Stage Two:

> Something-than-which-nothing-greater-can-be-thought *so truly exists that it* could not be thought not to exist.

10.3 Stage Three

That conclusion proves to be very powerful. For Anselm clearly uses it as a premise in the arguments he announces in the second half of P3, where the line of argumentation begun in P2 comes to its first major conclusions. Regrettably, Charlesworth's commentary says nothing about the second half of P3, where the line of argumentation begun in P2 comes to its first major conclusions. That was a very serious omission. Perhaps he passed over this passage without comment because he assumed that Anselm must have finished his argument, because he has resumed praying! Yet this is the very passage where Anselm proves the existence of God, for this is where he announces the two conclusions already mentioned. He writes:

> And this is you, Lord our God. You, therefore, Lord my God, so truly exist that You could not be thought not to exist.

Unfortunately, Charlesworth is not alone in ignoring the very passage where Anselm proves the existence of God; it is also ignored by almost all the commentators, friends and foes alike. Of the few who take note of this passage one, Richard La Croix (1972: 13), dismisses it, suggesting "that it is simply intended to be a digressive address to God concerning certain of Anselm's beliefs about the nature of God". Two others, Jasper Hopkins (1978: 151–152, 1986: 11) and David Smith (2014: 14) believe it is question-begging and circular. And Ian Logan believes (2009: 96), as do La Croix and Hopkins, that it takes Anselm the whole of the *Proslogion* to justify his claim that God is something-than-which-a-greater-cannot-be-thought. I disagree with all of them. When we look at the text, we see that he offers two independent reasons for these conclusions.

The first is a theological argument:

> For if some mind could think of something better [*melius*] than You, the creature would rise above the Creator, and judge the Creator, which is completely absurd.

[2] There are two other passages where Anselm explicitly asserts that his Stage Two depends on the conclusion of Stage One. In *Reply 1* he writes: "[Something] than which a greater cannot be thought, if it exists, cannot be thought not to exist. Otherwise, if it exists, it is not [something] than which a greater cannot be thought, which is not consistent." And in *Reply 3* he writes: "Moreover, it has already been seen plainly that [something] than which a greater cannot be thought, which exists by such certain reasoning of truth, cannot be thought not to exist. Otherwise it would in no way exist".

This argument is valid, but would not impress anyone who did not already believe that God created the heavens and the earth. That does not mean that it is unimportant. Anselm has gone out on a limb, being much more daring than Augustine, in setting out to prove deductively that God exists. He needs, therefore, to demonstrate his orthodoxy, and this argument does just that.

The second reason he offers is metaphysical in character. It is true that he does not spell out the arguments which are entailed, but the reason he articulates, once properly understood, validly entails not only his two conclusions, but also that they are true of God alone. Unfortunately, once again, how the sentence should be translated is controversial. In Latin, it reads:

> *Et quidem quicquid est aliud praeter te solum; potest cogitari non esse.*

Charlesworth translates this sentence as:

> In fact, everything else there is, except You alone, can be thought of as not existing.

Most other translators render this premise in similar terms.

Interpreted that way, Hopkins and Smith can both reasonably argue that that this premise does indeed beg the question. For while the main point of the sentence is that almost everything can be thought of as not existing, the parenthetical clause, "except You alone", seems to be making an additional claim, that God alone cannot be thought of as not existing. So, yet again, if that translation faithfully renders the sense of what Anselm has written, he does not have a valid argument for the existence of God.

Ian Logan, however, translates Anselm's Latin sentence differently. His alternative translation is (2009: 34):

> And indeed, whatever is other than You alone can be thought not to exist.

There is much to be said in favour of this translation. The most obvious and straightforward way of reading the first clause in this sentence is that its subject is "*quicquid* [whatever]" and its predicate is the phrase "*est aliud praeter te solum*". The simplest translation of that predicate is "is other than you alone". That also has the merit of preserving Anselm's word order. It takes the subject to be "whatever is other than You alone". It reads the verb "*est*" simply as a copula introducing the predicate qualifying whatever [*quidquid*], not as asserting existence. And it presents the sentence as a simple subject-predicate structure, without any parenthetical clause.

But most decisive reason for accepting Logan's translation, and rejecting the others, is that, when this sentence is read minimally, there can be no doubt that it does not beg the question of God's existence. The premise Anselm requires is simply: "Whatever is other than God can be thought not to exist". The word "alone" plays no role in this argument; it anticipates one of the consequences he is about to prove. Since whatever is other than God can be thought not to exist, and something-than-which-a-greater-cannot-be-thought so truly exists that it could not be thought not to exist, it follows validly that:

(a) that God, and only God, is something-than-which-a-greater-cannot-be-thought.

(b) God, and only God, so truly exists that he could not be thought not to exist.

Lest there be any lingering doubts about whether this Stage Three premise is somehow begging the question, I report that I have been able to demonstrate that if, for the sake of the argument, we adopt the Fool's disbelief, and assume that God does not exist, we can infer a thoroughly sceptical hypothesis: If God does not exist, then everything can be thought not to exist. From that sceptical hypothesis, together with the conclusion of Stage Two, it follows that God exists. Given that, Anselm's stated premise reverts to its original formulation, and all the other conclusions about God then also follow validly.[3]

Anselm ends P3 by asserting another validly inferred conclusion:

God exists most truly of all, and maximally of all.

That conclusion reveals that Anselm has been working with two different conceptions of existence. In P2, his argument involves what I have called the binary conception of existence; anything either exists or it does not. In the two stages in P3, his arguments involve a conception of existence derived from Plato, via Augustine. It understands that there are varying degrees of existing; some things exist more intensely than others. To modern ears that does sound rather strange, but I submit that that is only because we are accustomed to think of existence as binary only. Our natural languages, however, contain many adjectives which have three forms: simple; comparative; and superlative. Think of light, lighter, lightest; good, better, best; great, greater, greatest, etc. Furthermore, in the world there are many properties which are had more or less intensely. One of the clearest examples of this is found in colours; two things can be the same colour, in the sense that their colour is the same hue, but differ in how saturated that hue is. I submit that to think of existence in that way is not bizarre either. Some things are more vulnerable than others; their 'hold' on existence is not so strong. This especially true of all living things, whose way of being is far-from-equilibrium. They maintain themselves in existence, more or less successfully, through their interactions with their environment. But unless living things maintain those interactions in optimal balance over time, they fall prey to disease and aging, and die. Other things are energy wells; so stable and cohesive that it takes a great deal of energy to disrupt and destroy them. Their continuing to exist is not so precarious; it takes a lot of energy to destroy them.

Accordingly, I have no difficulty in finding these concepts to be intelligible in our contemporary world. It is not the case that Anselm's argument is plausible only within a medieval context. Indeed, his most crucial premise – that whatever is other than God can be thought not to exist – is easier to endorse today than in his day, when thinkers like Boethius and Thomas Aquinas believed that the sun, moon and stars were necessary beings, because they had no matter. For us, however, everything in the universe stems from the Big Bang, which happened about 13.8 billion years ago, according to the best estimates. So, everything in the universe that has

[3]This is demonstrated in my *Rethinking Anselm's Arguments: A Vindication of his Proof of the Existence of God* (Leiden: Brill, 2018).

ever existed, does now exist, or will exist, has come into existence at some time, and so, adopting what Anselm argued in the *Reply*, there was a time when everything in the universe did not exist – and at some time later it will cease to exist. That implies that it can be thought not to exist.

Since that seems indisputable, the issue of the soundness of Anselm's argument for the existence of God turns on the premises of Stage One. His premises about the Fool can be stripped down to a minimum, as he himself does in various places in the *Reply*. He says in *Reply* 9, for example, that:

> Even if someone is so foolish as to say that something-than-which-a-greater-cannot-be-thought does not exist, still he would not be so shameless as to say that he could not understand or think what he said.

Concede that, and one needs only to add the following premises:

- If anything than-which-a-greater-cannot-be-thought is only in the understanding [that is, if it is in the understanding but not in reality], it can be thought that something essential to it exists in reality;
- To exist in reality is good;
- To be unable not to exist is good;

Plus the four logical truths stated above, and the two definitions: of 'Greater Than' and of Essential Identity.

Given those premises, it follows validly that something-than-which-a-greater-cannot-be-thought so truly exists that it cannot be thought not to exist. What objection could any rational mind make to that set of premises? That conclusion, together with just one more premise, namely:

- Whatever is other than You can be thought not to exist.

is all Anselm needs to prove not only that God exists, but also that:

- You, and You alone, is something-than-which-a-greater-cannot-be-thought;
- You, and You alone, so truly exists that He could not be thought not to exist;
- You exists most truly and maximally of all.

10.4 Gaunilo's Lost Island

But does that set of premises not prove too much? Soon after publication of the *Proslogion*, it elicited a commentary from someone usually thought to be also a monk, named Gaunilo, although the evidence for his name is rather thin. He proposed a counter-example which was intended to prove that from Anselm's premises an obvious falsity can also be deduced. Most modern commentators concede that Gaunilo's argument needs 'tidying up', but when it is, it is a decisive refutation of Anselm's argument.[4]

[4] For example, Graham Oppy (1995, 2011), Sandra Visser and Thomas Williams (2009), and Brian Garrett (2013).

> Certain people say that there is somewhere in the ocean an island, which because of the difficulty or, rather, the impossibility of discovering what does not exist, some call 'lost'.

His contention is that Anselm's premises entail that, nevertheless, this island exists in reality. His first premise is:

> It is not difficult to understand, "An island more excellent than all other lands".

From that, mimicking the assumption with which Anselm begins the second phrase of his argument in P2, he infers that:

> An island more excellent than all other lands exists in the understanding.

And from that, he claims to prove that the Lost Island exists in reality.

His contention is that Anselm's premises entail that, nevertheless, this island exists in reality. Because Gaunilo described this island as "greater than all other lands", Anselm protested that an argument with that formula could not succeed in mimicking his own. Anselm was right about that. Because Gaunilo's formula does not contain the phrase "can be thought" he is unable to deduce the contradiction from which Anselm infers his conclusions in P2 and P3. But that error is easily fixed. Once his formula is 'tidied up', a counter-example can be constructed which is said to be exactly parallel to Anselm's argument.

Now, when Gaunilo infers that his island exists in the understanding. he is making an assumption, which his supporters never mention. And when they amend his argument, they too are in fact relying on a background assumption. They generally amend Gaunilo's formula to make it closer to Anselm's; they propose that he should have described his lost island as "An island than which no greater island can be thought". When an argument is being assessed for its validity, all background assumptions have to be articulated explicitly, since they function as premises. So, with that amendment, they too are assuming that:

> It is legitimate to substitute "An island than which no greater island can be thought" for "Something than which a greater cannot be thought" in Anselm's argument.

From that assumption, and the amended form of Gaunilo's first premise, it follows that:

> An island than which no greater island can be thought is in the understanding.

Since that premise has an indefinite description as its subject, to infer anything from it, one must introduce as an assumption a singular proposition which echoes it. Gaunilo can still call the subject 'the Lost Island', so, the requisite assumption is:

> The Lost Island is an island than which no greater island can be thought, and it is in the understanding.

With that change, and the fact that this Lost Island does not exist, Anselm's premises in P2 entail:

> If the Lost Island does not exist in reality, then it can be thought that some island is greater than that island than which a greater island cannot be thought.

And from that, it does follow that the Lost Island exists in reality.[5] Since the Lost Island does not exist, but this argument has entailed that it does, this contradictory outcome is taken to show that Anselm's argument is fallacious.

Now, to constitute an effective refutation of Anselm's Stage One argument, the Lost Island argument must be exactly parallel to Anselm's. Is that so? There remain, in fact, some significant differences between the two.

The first difference concerns the identity of something-than-which-a-greater-cannot-be-thought. There is nothing in Anselm's argument to say what it is, or even what kind of thing it is, until Stage Three. He *believes* that it does exist, and that it is God, but he is troubled by the fact that, given his own initial belief, the Fool's denial implies that it does not exist. But in Gaunilo's parody, right at the beginning, it is identified as an island. That will prove significant.

The second difference concerns the status of the Lost Island. Gaunilo *knows* that it does not exist; he says so explicitly. That fact must remain true once this island has been re-described as an island than which no greater island can be thought. But although it is true, Gaunilo's amended argument shows that truth to be false. That, of course, is Gaunilo's very point: Anselm's reasoning has been shown to produce falsehoods from truths. On the other hand, Anselm does *not* know, at the beginning of his argument, whether something-than-which-a- greater-cannot-be-thought exists, or not. That is why he *supposes*, for the sake of the argument, that that-than-which-a- greater-cannot-be-thought does not exist. That assumption is then negated, because it has turned out to imply an impossibility. The dialectical role of these parallel propositions is therefore quite different.

A third point follows from the second. Because those parallel propositions serve different dialectical roles, negating the proposition that the Lost Island does not exist is arguably an improper use of *reductio ad absurdum*. That style of argument works by deducing a contradiction from a series of propositions assumed as premises, and negating the one identified as responsible for generating the contradiction. When an argument is valid, the falsehood of an implication must have been introduced by at least one of the premises. But logic alone does not determine which premise is the culprit. That is a choice made by the author. In this case, it is improper to choose to negate the assumption that this 'lost island' does not exist, since it is true. Therefore, some other premise must be the one which is false.

But which premise is false? The deduction of the contradiction is dependent upon six premises; there are five others besides the proposition that this island does not exist. Since that proposition is known to be true, and has to remain true, the contradiction must be due to at least one of those other five premises. The two definitions – of Essential Identity and of the relation of 'Greater Than' are reasonable, and were not available before 2014, so neither of them could be the culprit. That leaves the three others. It would be hard to object to the one which licenses the inference from 'is in the understanding alone' to 'it can be thought that something essentially identical to it is in reality'. So that leaves two which do not appear in Anselm's argument.

One possibility is to choose the assumption that:

[5] I also set out this deduction in my *Rethinking Anselm's Arguments* (2018).

> The Lost Island is an island than which no greater island can be thought, and it exists in the understanding.

That is, instead of using Conditional Proof with a view to negating a premise known to be true, it would have been more appropriate to infer:

> If the Lost Island is an island than which no greater island can be thought, then it can be thought that some island is greater than that very island than which no greater island can be thought.

To infer that conditional proposition is as *equally valid* as the deduction of the conditional proposition with "The Lost Island does not exist in reality" as its antecedent. Each of those conditional propositions can be inferred by applying the Rule of Conditional Proof, but the rules of Natural Deduction do not determine which is these two is the appropriate assumption to negate. Since the consequent in each of those conditional propositions is contradictory, it not only follows by conditional proof and *modus tollens*, that:

> It is not true that the Lost Island does not exist in reality,

but it also follows, with equal validity, that:

> It is not true that some island is such that no greater island can be thought.

So, when tidied up, Gaunilo's version of Anselm's argument can, with equal validity, be interpreted as showing that his counter-example is incoherent. For what his amended argument can be taken to prove is that, for any island, it is possible to think of an island which is greater. Gaunilo's argument can with equal legitimacy, and more plausibly, be construed as *demonstrating* that his 'Lost Island' is what he himself would call a *falsum*.

That is, in effect, the response of Alvin Plantinga and Kenneth Himma. They have claimed that Gaunilo's parody fails because it is not analogous to Anselm's argument in this respect. Alvin Plantinga (1974: 90–1) argues that God's great-making qualities (e.g. omnipotence, omniscience and perfect goodness) are maximal. But most of the qualities that make for greatness in islands – number of palm trees, amount and quality of coconuts, for example – have no intrinsic maximum. Brian Garrett (2013), on the other hand, argues that, properly understood, the great-making qualities of an island are maximal. He proposes that we can make this explicit by defining the perfect island as the island of ideal size, possessing the ideal number of coconuts, ideally white sand, ideal sea and air temperature, etc. Since these qualities are intrinsically maximal, he claims, Plantinga's riposte to Gaunilo's parody collapses.

It is not as clear as Garrett assumes that the qualities listed in his definition of the greatest conceivable island suffice to define one and only island. What sized island would be ideal for everyone? There are probably many answers, depending on the lifestyle preferred by different people! Could it be guaranteed that an island ideal for growing coconuts would not also be liable to be hit by typhoons, which is not ideal? Would an island ideal for growing coconuts also be ideal for growing apples? If, to be ideal, an island have to be suitable for growing a wide variety of fruit, it might not be an ideal size. The more we think about it, the fuzzier becomes the concept of an island than which a greater island cannot be thought.

But whether that is a coherent concept is not the most critical issue. Rather, we need to examine more carefully how that concept is introduced in Gaunilo's counter-argument. This is where the first point of difference noted above concerned Gaunilo's identifying Anselm's something-than-which-a-greater-cannot-be-thought as an island becomes crucial. Anselm's argumentative strategy is to leave the question of what his formula describes until the end of his argument. Gaunilo identifies it right at the beginning. Recalling that difference reminds us that there is another assumption involved in 'tidying up' this Gaunilo's counter-argument. This is the background assumption that:

> It is legitimate to substitute "An island than which no greater island can be thought" for "Something than which a greater cannot be thought".

This implicit assumption highlights an issue concerning Gaunilo's counter-example more severe than those already identified. It is, in fact, the decisive issue. The problem with the Lost Island is a consequence of the most significant difference between this counter-argument and Anselm's original. This difference, of course, is that the two formulae are *not* the same.

Now, the discussion above took the appropriate premise to be negated as the assumption:

> The Lost Island is an island than which no greater island can be thought, and it is in the understanding.

But that assumption was introduced in order to infer a conclusion from a prior proposition which has an indefinite description as its subject, namely:

> An island than which no greater island can be thought is in the understanding.

And that proposition is an implication inferred from that background assumption and Anselm's premise. Since this background assumption is the actual starting point of the parody, when conditional proof is properly applied to the parody, what ensues is:

> If it is legitimate to substitute "An island than which no greater island can be thought" for "Something than which a greater cannot be thought", then it can be thought that some island is greater than that very island than which no greater island can be thought.

Since that consequence is not possible, it follows that:

> It is not legitimate to substitute "An island than which no greater island can be thought" for "Something than which a greater cannot be thought".

Consequently, whether the idea of the greatest conceivable island is coherent becomes a secondary issue.

In stark contrast, the conclusion of P2 neither asserts nor implies what something-than-which-a-greater-cannot-be-thought is. Not only does has Anselm said nothing about what in particular it is; he has nothing in his argument which could even inform anyone as to *what sort* of thing it is. Visser & Williams, who are generally sympathetic to Anselm, allege that it could be any sort of thing: not only an island, but a live oak tree, or a cockroach (2009: 77). Anselm, of course, *believes* it is God, but at the end of P2 he does not yet have any justification for that belief, and therefore he neither claims nor assumes that it is God. Gaunilo, however, does say what sort of thing it is: it is an island. And Visser & Williams propose that what Gaunilo should have said is that it is 'an island than which no greater can be thought', in order to make his argument exactly parallel to Anselm's.

But that identification of Anselm's wholly indefinite 'something' as an island is what ensures that that substitution is illegitimate. That substitution in Anselm's Argument suffices to ensure that Gaunilo's parody, even when 'tidied up', is self-refuting.

Brian Garrett seems to be aware that there is a deeper issue at stake than whether islands can have maximal qualities, for he concludes by asserting:

> Nor, incidentally, is there any force to the quite different rejoinder that Gaunilo's parody fails since God is a necessary being whereas islands are contingent. An Anselmian argument for the necessity of God's existence ('Suppose that God existed contingently. Then we could conceive of a being greater than God – one with all God's traditional qualities who existed necessarily. But...') can be parodied by Gaunilo to show that the perfect island exists of necessity.

But this 'incidental' comment does not suffice to rescue the Lost Island. Anselm is not just one, but three steps ahead. The first step is that Anselm is well aware that not only is his P2 conclusion true, but it is necessarily true, since it is derived from the impossibility of a contradiction. That is evident from his argument in *Reply* 9, which I invoked earlier. So, if it is legitimate to specify that Anselm's 'something' is some island, it also follows that:

> It is necessary that some island-than-which-a-greater-island-cannot-be-thought exists in reality.

But Anselm has not yet finished his argument. All those commentators and critics who think his argument for the existence of God in located in P2, are in error. After all, at the end of P2 he has not yet drawn any conclusion about what sort of thing something-than-which-a-greater-cannot-be-thought is, let alone that it is God.

Since it is indeterminate what sort of thing Anselm's something might be, let us say it is an *F*. Then, if it is not possible that something-*F*-than-which-a-greater-*F*-cannot-be-thought does not exists in reality, it also follows that it can be thought to be something which could not be thought not to exist. That is because, as noted above, Anselm's conclusion in P2 entails the premise with which he resumes his argument in P3. Therefore, those who, like Gaunilo, adopt Anselm's premises in order to construct a disproof, thereby commit themselves to accepting the conclusion of Anselm's Stage Two as well. There are no rational grounds on which to resist extending this argument to a further stage. That is, they are committed to accepting as a conclusion:

> Because it is necessarily true that something-*F*-than-which-a-greater-*F*-cannot-be-thought exists, it could not be thought not to exist.

This form of argument can be deployed once *any* descriptive term is substituted for "*F*" to produce Gaunilo-style formulae. Since those who try to construct a parody along such lines accept thereby Anselm's P2 premises, they cannot avoid the conclusion that their preferred counter-example so truly exits that it cannot be thought not to exist, whether that be an island, or a live oak tree, or a cockroach. And that is absurd.

The obvious retort from defenders of Gaunilo is to say: So much the worse for Anselm's Argument! There just has to be something wrong with it. But its logic is impeccable. So, they say, the fault must lie with the premises.

Ironically, that is precisely how Anselm would reply to such a critic. He would contend that altering his formula is responsible for the argument going awry. Given Anselm's premises in P2, amending his formula to specify what sort of thing is being introduced, entails these absurdities. Therefore, the assumption that altering his formula is legitimate must be rejected.

However, I said that Anselm was three steps ahead. The first was that his argument in P2 also establishes that something-than-which-a-greater-cannot-be-thought necessarily exists in reality. The second is that it follows from that that it could not be thought not to exist. His third, and clinching point is his Stage Three premise:

> Whatever is other than You can be thought not to exist

Since that is true, it follows that if any such thing is other than God, it both can and could not be thought not to exist. That conclusion is not just absurd; it is an explicit contradiction. This is Anselm's decisive response to Gaunilo. If it is legitimate to substitute any description other than "divine" into his formula, running through his entire argument, and not just the first stage of it, necessarily entails contradictions. Therefore, by *reductio ad absurdum*, it follows that:

> It is *not* legitimate to substitute "An island than which no greater island can be thought" for "Something than which a greater cannot be thought" in Anselm's argument.

Anselm has thus forestalled every such alleged Gaunilo-style disproof. Adding to his formula some descriptive term – indeed, any term describing something which possibly does not exist – necessarily turns a plausible argument into a *reductio ad absurdum.*

Gaunilo, and his latter-day supporters, might try to avoid this negative outcome by insisting that all that is required for their disproof is that his premises in P2 entail the existence of something we know does not exist. Up until now, that might well have been thought to be a plausible rejoinder, since it was often believed that the premises Anselm introduces in P3 are independent of P2. If that belief were true, it would be possible to adopt, purely for the sake of constructing a disproof, his P2 premises, but reject his P3 premises. But it is now clear that that is not possible; it is demonstrable that the major premise of Stage Two is not independent of those in Stage One, but is entailed by them. Because of that, any Gaunilo-type parody cannot block Anselm's argument running through to at least the end of Stage Two. And the absurdities generated by this assumption are enough to license the invocation of the Rule of *reductio ad absurdum*.

But Anselm's Stage Three premise – Whatever is other than You can be thought not to exist – converts those absurdities into direct contradictions. A critic might deny that premise. However, as I have already said, it is even more certain nowadays, than it was in Anselm's day, that that premise is true. That premise is sufficient to blow Gaunilo's counter-example out of the water, and any other counter-example which replaces Anselm's "Something" with "Something *F*", where "*F*" is any descriptive term applicable to something other than God. And together with the conclusion of Stage Two, it suffices to prove all the conclusions about God which Anselm asserts in P2 to P4.

Some might find my assessment of the truth of this premise too generous. Some commentators have objected that, since the subject of this premise mentions God, it begs the question of God's existence. Such an objection can be brought only by someone who has not fully analysed the argument. This premise makes no assertion about God; its subject is "whatever is other than God". The Latin phrase "*aliud praeter*", translated here as "other than", occurs elsewhere in Anselm's texts, where it has the force of "Setting aside". What he is doing by including that phrase in this premise is bracketing the question of God's existence. The premise means, "Leaving the contested issue of God's existence aside, and referring only to whatever remains, everything can be thought not to exist". Nevertheless, even if we modify Anselm's premise, by replacing this subject, his conclusions still follow.

That crucial premise is what enables Anselm to deduce that God exists – indeed that God exists so truly that he could not be thought not to exist. And that premise also implies the God exists most truly of all, and that nothing other than God can be thought to be something-than-which-a-greater-cannot-be-thought. And only God can be shown by this argument to exist: not Gaunilo's Lost Island; not cockroaches; nothing other than God. This premise, along with the conclusion of Stage Two, entails that God is the only being of which Anselm's formula is true.

10.5 What Kind of Proof?

There is another significant consequence of our analysis. The appellation 'the ontological argument' is supposed to label any argument which purports to deduce an existential conclusion from premises known purely *a priori*. On that basis, Anselm's proof is not a version of the 'ontological argument', since it begins with his saying something and someone's hearing what is said. We have to learn those facts *a posteriori*. But that is not all.

So, if Anselm's proof is not a version of the Ontological Argument, what kind of proof is it? Let me begin to answer that question by establishing some agreement with those modern commentators who find fault with it, just as Anselm begins his argument by establishing common ground with the Fool. For I am not so sanguine as to believe that all his critics will be convinced by my exposition. For many will insist that it is not possible to deduce that *anything* actually exists just from its being thought of.

Nevertheless, it is reasonable to ask such sceptics how they understand the fact that Anselm has a valid argument which deduces that something-than-which-a-greater-cannot-be-thought exists in reality. A reasonable answer is that he has shown that this something has to be thought of *as existing*, but that does not imply that it actually exists. Likewise, in Greek mythology Pegasus has to be thought of as a flying horse, but it does not follow that some horses have wings. So, let agree on that. Both Anselm and the sceptics can accept that this something proposition cannot be thought not to exist, where that does not imply that it actually exists.

Next, to ensure that our reconstruction of Anselm's argument cannot be accused of begging the question of God's existence, let us suppose that the Fool is correct: God does not exist. So, what follows now?

Since we are supposing that God does not exist, it is relevant that Anselm has asserted in *Reply* 5 that what does not exist can be thought not to exist. Consequently, God can be thought not to exist. That consequence alters Anselm's Stage Three premise, which said that, "Whatever is other than God can be thought not to exist". Since our supposition implies that God also can be thought not to exist, it has the effect of transforming that premise into a thoroughly sceptical hypothesis. For, if God does not exist, it follows that *everything* can be thought not to exist. Given this transformed version of Anselm's premise, there can now be no question of its being question-begging, or circular.

What is surprising is that, even with these concessions to the sceptics, Anselm's conclusions still follow. For while they deny that Anselm has proved that God exists, they in turn have to concede that he has shown that something-than-which-a-greater-cannot-be-thought cannot be thought not to exist. But given that, it is false that everything can be thought not to exist, since this something cannot be thought not to exist. Now, our sceptical hypothesis says that if God does not exist, then everything can be thought not to exist. Since even the sceptics have to concede that Anselm has shown that the consequent of that hypothesis is false, it follows, by *modus tollens*, that God does exist. So, even when we suppose that God does not exist, it still is demonstrable that God exists. And this demonstration does not rely on the disputed argument in Chap. 2, because we set that aside. All Anselm's argument requires is the interim conclusion of Stage Two, which we are conceding to the sceptics for the purposes of this argument, does not depend on the conclusion of Stage One, and which he also deduced in *Reply* 9 without assuming that anything exists. From that proposition, and his Stage Three premise, it follows validly that God exists, and consequently, all his other conclusions in P3.

With that outcome, Anselm becomes entitled to proceed with the original version of his premise. Since everything which is other than God can be thought not to exist, it follows that God and only God is this something-than-which-a-greater-cannot-be-thought, and God, and only God so truly exists that it cannot be thought not to exist. It was because Anselm knew that he had proven those two conclusions that he was so dismissive of Gaunilo's counter-example. Nothing other than God can be something than which a greater can be thought.

That brings us back to the question of what kind of proof has he devised. I have been calling Anselm's argument a proof, because he uses the verb "*probare* [prove]" 11 times in his *Reply* to describe it. Significantly, in every one of those occurrences that verb is preceded by the phrase "*quod dicit* (what is said)". His proof is not like the proofs of theorems in Euclidean geometry; rather it takes the form: "Concerning what it said, it is proved that …". He is not interested in impersonal propositions; because his quest is to understand what he believes, he is only interested in what someone sincerely asserts.

Our analysis has shown that his Stage Three premise is crucial. That is the one which proves that God exists. So, I will finish by asking: Is it true? That is, setting aside the question of God's existence, is it true that everything else can be thought not to exist? When Anselm was alive that was a somewhat difficult question, since even he agreed that the heavenly bodies move by necessity. Because he also believed that God created the heavens and the earth, he believed that everything other than God had come into existence, and therefore could be thought not to exist. But he did not try to justify this premise by invoking the doctrine of creation. But nowadays, we have our own reasons to believe, beyond reasonable doubt, that the universe, and everything in it, has had a beginning, and, most likely, an end. In the 1950s, cosmologists debated whether the universe began with the Big Bang, or was in a state of constant creation. The former view has now prevailed and is being confirmed by more and more observations. So, we have more than enough factual evidence to accept that Anselm's Stage Three premise is true. His proof relies on that factual evidence. So, it is not a case of deducing that something actually exists just from its being thought of. His proof does not depend on premises all of which are known *a priori*. Its most crucial premise is derived from a proposition which is as empirically verifiable or falsifiable as any current scientific postulate, in the light of factual evidence. I finish by drawing the following unexpected conclusion:

> Anselm's argument for the existence of God is not a version of the Ontological Argument; it is a valid and plausible version of the Cosmological argument.

References

Barth, K. (1931/1960) *Anselm: Fides quaerens intellectum.* (I. W. Robinson, Trans.). London: SCM Press. (Zurich: Evangelischer Verlag, A.G.).

Campbell, R. (1976). *From belief to understanding: A study of Aselm's arguments for the existence of God.* Canberra: ANU.

Campbell, R. (2018). *Rethinking Anselm's arguments: A vindication of his proof of the existence of God.* Leiden: Brill.

Charlesworth, M. (1962). St. Anselm's argument. *Sophia, 1*(2), 25–36.

Charlesworth, M. (1965). *St. Anselm's Proslogion.* Oxford: Clarendon Press.

Davies, B. (2004). Anselm and the ontological argument. In *The Cambridge companion to Anselm.* Cambridge/New York: Cambridge University Press.

Deane, S. N. (1962). *St Anselm – Basic writings* (2nd ed.). La Salle: Open Court.

Eder, G., & Rambarter, E. (2015). Formal reconstructions of St. Anselm's ontological argument. *Synthese, 192*, 2795–2825.
Garrett, B. (2013). On behalf of Gaunilo. *Analysis, 73*(3), 481–482.
Geach, P. T. (1977). Review of Campbell (1976). *Philosophy, 52*(2), 234–236.
Hopkins, J. (1978). On understanding and preunderstanding St. Anselm. *The New Scholasticism, LII*(2), 243–260.
Hopkins, J. (1981). On an alleged definitive interpretation of Proslogion 2-4: A discussion of G. Schufreider's *An introduction to Anselm's argument. The Southern Journal of Philosophy, 19*(1), 129–139.
Hopkins, J. (1986). *A new interpretative translation of Anselm's Monologion and Proslogion*. Minneapolis: A.J. Banning Press.
La Croix, R. (1972). *Proslogion II and III: A third interpretation of Anselm's argument*. Leiden: E.J. Brill.
Logan, I. (2009). *Reading Anselm's Proslogion: The history and Anselm's argument and its significance today*. Farnham: Ashgate.
Oppy, G. (1995). *Ontological arguments and belief in God*. Cambridge: Cambridge University Press.
Oppy, G. (2011). On behalf of the fool. *Analysis, 71*(2), 304–306.
Plantinga, A. (1974). *God, freedom, and evil*. Grand Rapids: Eerdmans Publishing Company.
Schufreider, G. (1978). *An introduction to Anselm's argument*. Philadelphia: Temple University Press.
Smith, A. D. (2014). *Anselm's Other Argument*. Cambridge, MA: Harvard University Press.
Visser, S., & Williams, T. (2009). *Anselm* (Great medieval thinkers). Oxford: Oxford University Press.

Richard Campbell AM, is an Emeritus Professor of Philosophy at the Australian National University, Canberra. Educated at the Universities of Sydney and Oxford, he was appointed to the Department of Philosophy at the ANU in 1967 and was engaged in teaching, research and administration until he retired in 2003. During that time, he served 5 years as Dean of the Faculty of Arts, followed by 4 years as Pro-Vice-Chancellor at the ANU. Also, for 15 years he was involved in restructuring the system of public education in the Australian Capital Territory, including 6 years as Chairman of the ACT Schools Authority. In recognition of those services, he was installed in 1986 by Queen Elizabeth as a Member of the Order of Australia. He is the author of *Secondary Education for Canberra* (1973), *From Belief to Understanding* (1976), *Truth and Historicity* (1992), *The Concept of Truth* (2011), *The Metaphysics of Emergence* (2015) and *Rethinking Anselm's Arguments* (forthcoming 2018) and numerous articles.

Chapter 11
Intentionality – Evolution of a Concept

Maurita Harney

"The idea of intentionality is a liberation" (Levinas 1998 p. 135). These words of Levinas resonate with my own response to the concept when I was introduced to it in Max Charlesworth's undergraduate philosophy course in 1962 at the University of Melbourne. The concept was an eye-opener: It illuminated the exciting new ideas of the existentialists like Sartre, Beauvoir, and Merleau-Ponty, as expressed in their literature and activism. The intentionality of human behaviour implied actions that are open to possibilities, to the idea of freedom of choice – in Sartre's case, a freedom that was held to be absolute; in Beauvoir's that "anatomy is not destiny."[1] Without the premise of intentionality, it makes no sense to speak of the moral dimension of human experience.

To insist on the intentionality of human action is to commit to a deeply humanist orientation, and for this reason, we might say that this concept has been an implicit theme through all of Max's work. It is not a concept he wrote about explicitly. Nor did it enter his discourse to any great extent. However, if there is a common thread through the diversity of his interests and intellectual pursuits, it has surely been the quest to understand human actions as meaningful, significant and deeply ethical. Intentionality is central to understanding the ideas and preoccupations of those philosophers belonging to phenomenological, existentialist and hermeneutic schools of philosophy – the 'contemporary European Tradition' – and it is a theme which links his interests in other areas such as mediaeval philosophy, and informs his engagement with the religious and the spiritual as well as with ethics.

[1] This is the popular slogan used to summarise Simone de Beauvoir's thesis in *Le Deuxième Sexe* (1949).

M. Harney (✉)
School of Historical and Philosophical Studies, University of Melbourne,
Melbourne, Australia
e-mail: mharney@unimelb.edu.au

P. Wong et al. (eds.), *Considering Religions, Rights and Bioethics: For Max Charlesworth*, Sophia Studies in Cross-cultural Philosophy of Traditions and Cultures 30, https://doi.org/10.1007/978-3-030-18148-2_11

I have found that intentionality is one of those irrepressible concepts that keeps intruding on just about every intellectual project I have ever undertaken. Since those early days as an undergraduate, my own philosophical journey has focussed more explicitly on the notion of intentionality. It is a journey that has taken some very unexpected turns, however. It has in my case, involved diverging from Max's teachings of intentionality as a specific feature of being human to a naturalised version which allows us to extend the concept to living things generally – a development now associated with what is known as "*post*humanism." (Braidotti 2013).[2] I have every confidence, however, that this is a position that Max would have embraced, because of its commitment to a more inclusive conception of what it means to be human.[3] As homage to Max, I now offer some of the insights about intentionality that I have been able to glean along the way.

***

If I engage in conscious acts like thinking, perceiving, believing, hoping, there is always some*thing* that I am thinking about, perceiving, etc. My thoughts, perceptions and hopes are directed to some object. This directedness or "aboutness" of my conscious acts is called intentionality. Intentionality is usually characterised as a distinguishing feature of mind or consciousness: Inanimate objects like stones, chairs, and thermostats don't have this property. The *locus classicus* for the modern theory of intentionality is Brentano, who in turn credits the Scholastics of the Middle Ages as his source. Brentano's thesis of intentionality was, in turn, a main inspiration behind Husserl's phenomenology. However, this notion was very much alive in the early Middle Ages, in the Aristotelian writings of the Arabic philosophers like Ibn Sīnā (Avicenna) and Ibn Rushd (Averroës). Whilst these philosophers are well-known as translators of the writings of the ancients, they were also responsible for developing their own autonomous teachings on a variety of philosophical topics. Amongst these is a proto-typical version of the intentionality thesis. It is important to acknowledge this, as it is not irrelevant to some of the contemporary directions to which the concept of intentionality has led. I shall return to this later.

Brentano famously stated his intentionality thesis as follows:

> Every mental phenomenon is characterized by what the Scholastics of the Middle Ages called the intentional (or mental) inexistence of an object, and what we might call, though not wholly unambiguously, reference to a content, direction toward an object (which is not

[2] The "posthuman" refers to those currents of thought which, following Foucault's "death of Man" and thinkers like Deleuze, Derrida, and Irigaray, have initiated a critique of the concept of "Man" or "the human" inherited from post-Enlightenment thinking. Posthumanist thinkers and fields of study show how these concepts mask important assumptions and biases relating to gender, race, colonialism, and our relationship to nature including the role of science and technology. They seek new ways of thinking about what it means to be human, enlisting perspectives of those minorities traditionally excluded from our Eurocentric, gendered, and anthropomorphic approaches (Braidotti and Hlavajova 2018).

[3] Especially in the form espoused by prominent thinker on this topic, Rosi Braidotti, who argues for a new (posthuman) way of preserving subjectivity without the implicit biases (Braidotti 2013, p.12).

> to be understood here as meaning a thing), or immanent objectivity. Every mental phenomenon includes something as object within itself, although they do not do so in the same way. In presentation, something is presented, in judgment something is affirmed or denied, in love loved, in hate hated, in desire desired and so on.
>
> This intentional inexistence is characteristic exclusively of mental phenomena. No physical phenomenon exhibits anything like it. We can, therefore, define mental phenomena by saying that they are those phenomena which contain an object intentionally within themselves. (Brentano 1973, pp. 88–89)

The most important features singled out by Brentano were first, the object-directedness of mental acts, the fact that my thinking, hoping for, believing, etc. always involves a relation to some object. Second is the fact that these objects need not exist in reality. This gives the intentional object a special status which Brentano called *intentional inexistence* and which the Scholastics had called *esse intentionale*. Since Brentano, the status of the intentional object has been a source of protracted debate raising issues of both an ontological and a logical kind for many mainstream philosophers. The intentional object cannot be the same thing as an object in the real world, for I can think about objects, like "Pegasus" or "the present king of France" that do not exist in reality. However, to assign to it some kind of existence-in-the-mind does not solve the problem, for when I think about the rock, Uluru, it is the real rock that I am thinking about – not just a mental replica of it. As we shall see below, these ontological problems have their counterpart in puzzles of a logical kind relating to entailment relations in the case of the logical and linguistic representations of psychological phenomena.

Brentano was not unduly concerned with ontological issues however as his aim was psychological. This brings us to a third important claim in Brentano's formulation of the intentionality thesis: He states that intentionality characterises *all and only* mental (i.e., conscious) phenomena. In other words, Brentano saw intentionality as the distinguishing feature that marked the mental off from the physical. Brentano aimed to develop a descriptive psychology, one that examined psychological processes not from the point of view of physiological and causal 'external' factors, but from a first-person perspective. This meant a study of *conscious* processes or consciousness as we experience it. Intentionality is identified with consciousness.

Brentano was a major inspiration for his student, Edmund Husserl. For Husserl, however, coming from a background in mathematics and logic, the intentionality of consciousness was to be put to a philosophical end, and a very radical reformist one at that. He sought to develop a philosophy which would provide a secure basis for science, one free of any presuppositions of the "natural attitude" which he took to be characteristic of the existing sciences (Husserl 1965 p. 75ff, 1969, p. 101; p.105). One such presupposition was that of a separation of subject and object, or the duality of subjective versus the objective, with the concomitant presumption of an independently existing reality. It is represented in modern science by the dichotomies of man versus nature, and the knower versus the known. Husserl sought to return to "the things themselves" (Husserl 1965, p. 108 n46), and his phenomenology required a description of phenomena as they were given to consciousness, with the aim of seeking out the necessary structures of acts of consciousness. This meant suspending any considerations about the existential status of the intentional object. In the light of Frege's criticisms of his early work, this also meant avoiding psychologism or conflating the intentional with the purely mental, thereby committing the fallacy of reducing the logical to the psychological. In his *Ideen I* (Husserl 1969), devoted to a study of the acts and objects of consciousness, Husserl finds that the intentionality of this relation needs to be analysed triadically as a relation between the act (*noesis*), its meaning content (*noema*) and the object (if there is one) (Husserl 1969, 255ff.). Our relationship to the world is always mediated by the *noema* or meaning. To reduce intentionality to a dyadic relation of act and object, means either reducing the intentional object to the particular psychological process in the mind of the perceiving subject, in which case it is immanent to that act, or else severing it from the act altogether, thereby introducing an unwarranted duality of subject and object.

In the 1970s, it became popular to conceptualise Husserl's notion of intentionality using the tools of linguistic philosophy.[4] Husserl himself saw parallels between aspects of his own account of intentionality of perception and the linguistic notion of sense (*Sinn*) (Husserl 1969, 346–48; 367–69). This invites a comparison with Frege's theory of linguistic meaning in his essay, "On Sense and Reference" (Frege 1970). Frege's tripartite distinction of linguistic sign, sense *(Sinn*), and reference (*Bedeutung*), seems to be a counterpart of Husserl's tripartite analysis of act (*noesis*), meaning (*noema)*, and object (Føllesdal 1969): Linguistic sense or meaning, like Husserl's *noema*, is not the same thing as the object referred to. So, as with the *noema*, an expression like "The present king of France is bald' can have a meaning – be meaningful – even if there exists nothing that it refers to. For Frege, sense is the means by which we refer to some object, analogously to the way the *noema* mediates the relation between an act of consciousness and its object.

Frege saw the notion of *Sinn* as important for distinguishing the different cognitive values of linguistic expressions containing co-referring expressions with different senses (Frege 1970, p.56). For example, the expressions, "creature with a heart" and "creature with kidneys" refer to the same set of things (same *extension*), but differ in respect of their meaning or sense (different *intensions*). We would normally expect these expressions to be interchangeable within sentences without disturbing the truth value of the overall sentence. For example, if I shoot a creature with a heart then I have shot a creature with kidneys. This entailment pattern does not hold, however, for the language we use to talk about intentional objects, for example, if Amy believes that lions are creatures with hearts, we can't infer therefore that Amy believes that lions are creatures with kidneys. In this respect, the language we use to describe psychological states shares certain logical peculiarities with other contexts – e.g., modal contexts[5]. These are said to be *intensional* or *non-extensional*

[4] Smith and McIntyre (1982), Mohanty (1982), and Harney (1984).

[5] For example, "it is necessary that…" These are said to be intensional contexts – characterised by failure of substitutivity *salva veritate*. See Caston 2001, for entailment patterns that are violated by intensionality.

contexts. In these sentences, the non-equivalence of meaning and object of reference must be preserved. Linguistic meaning *qua* Fregean *Sinn* cannot be reduced to the object (reference), and it can exist even in the absence of there being any object referred to.

This parallel in turn meant that links could be forged between the intentionality of acts and the intensionality of language, and to some extent, this parallel meant working against mainstream analytical thinking of philosophers like Russell, Quine, and Frege (in his works on logic) who, like Husserl, argued for a clear separation of psychology from logic. For these philosophers of the analytic tradition however, the solution was to insist on the primacy of *extensional* languages – thereby excluding notions of meaning or sense from this domain (Harney 1984). This was because 'sense' or 'meaning' was regarded as 'psychological' in the sense of being a content of the subjective individual mind. It was therefore inaccessible to scientific inquiry with its requirement that beliefs be expressed in a language that was univocal and context-independent, and able to be represented in a system governed by binary logic.

Although the parallel between Fregean linguistic meaning (or *Sinn*) and Husserl's *noema* suggests a way of bridging a gap in understanding between the continental and analytical traditions, it can in retrospect be seen as a very limited exercise, one that locks intentionality into a very circumscribed sphere of human language and cognition, closing it off to some creative developments within the continental tradition associated with the '4EA' approaches to cognition – that is, the non-Cartesian idea of cognition as embodied, embedded, enactive, extended, and affective. Before turning to these developments, it is necessary to say more about the fortunes of intentionality within the analytic tradition.

Intentionality and associated concepts of mind, consciousness and cognition have been a source of protracted and intractable problems in analytical circles. One of the main reasons for this is the domination of a representationalist view of mind traceable to a Cartesian-derived dualism that persists in some quarters of the analytic community.

Broadly speaking representationalism is the view that the mind and its contents are in some sense *representations* of reality – a view premised on a dyadic ontology which pits subject against object in our understanding of the world. It is often implicit rather than explicit, and finds expression in such oppositions as mind *vs* nature, language *vs* reality, knower *vs* known, culture *vs* nature.

Representationalism is exemplified in information-processing models of mind and cognition which flourished especially during the 1970s and 1980s with the rise of cognitive science and its star attraction of artificial intelligence. The mind as information processor builds on the idea that the mind consists in representations of the world or of reality, and that thinking and other cognitive activities consists simply in the manipulation or 'processing' of these representations. It is a view premised on a Cartesian-derived distinction between subject (mind) and object (world) such that mental representations can be true or false of reality and hence submitted to evaluation in terms of binary logic. In some recent analytical writings, the intentionality thesis becomes a thesis of *representation* (for example, Seager and Bourget 2007). In some versions, a distinction is drawn between access and phenomenal consciousness[6] or between conceptual and nonconceptual mental contents. 'Access consciousness' includes those mental states which are characterised by propositional content (and therefore computable), for example, my thought that the earth is round, my belief that there is life on Mars, etc. which can unproblematically be represented linguistically and subjected to truth-conditional evaluation. Phenomenal or nonconceptual consciousness is more difficult. It includes perceptual experiences or *qualia* such as the experience of redness or pain – the 'what-it-is-like' consciousness which machines and zombies lack. The essentially private and subjective nature of phenomenal consciousness gives rise to what is famously known as the 'hard problem of consciousness.' The hard problem is the problem of finding a scientific explanation for such phenomena. It is better described as the 'wrong' problem. The weakness here, is seeing consciousness as something that entities *lack* – something that can be *added on*. Constructing the problem of consciousness in this way means that a science of consciousness is forever beyond the grasp of science because Descartes' "ghost in the machine" has not been exorcised.

The real problem is not that of consciousness *per se* but of an underlying Cartesianism: It is not just that consciousness is mysterious. It is also that the body *sans* consciousness remains as a meaningless machine something devoid of any form of animation, meaning, or agency in its own right. It is a view of the body well-suited to reductionist forms of explanation like extreme behaviourism which attempt to construct a science of human behaviour in reductionist stimulus-response models.

A critique of these Cartesian-derived approaches to mind and body are the basis of Merleau-Ponty's theory of intentionality as it is developed in his *Phenomenologie de Perception* (Merleau-Ponty 1962). Here he rejects both the representationalist view (what he calls *intellectualism*) as well as stimulus response behaviourism (what he calls *empiricism*). He does this to pave the way for his very important notion of *bodily intentionality*, a notion deriving from Husserl's *Ideen II* and later works.

Merleau-Ponty's bodily intentionality de-couples meaning from the 'mind' and begins the process of 'naturalising' intentionality. Intentionality becomes a property of biological that is, *natural,* processes when these are understood in a non-reductionist and non-mechanistic sense. Intentionality as a property of sensory experience is exhibited by human and non-human animals alike, in the form of touching, looking, smelling, hearing, feeling within their environment. Bodily intentionality is best understood as a *pre*-conceptual or *pre*-reflective intentionality that structures our relationship to the world. Merleau-Ponty calls it a "motor intentionality" (Merleau-Ponty 1962, p. 110). It is expressed in our actions and movements and our potentialities for these movements as we make our way around the world and encounter other people. This is not to deny that humans have the capacity for reflective consciousness or intellectual cognition, but this is not something privileged in respect of its intentionality. Merleau-Ponty sees motility as "a basic

[6] See, for example, Siewert 2011.

intentionality," meaning that "consciousness is in the first place not a matter of 'I think that' but of 'I can.'" (Merleau-Ponty 1962, p. 137).

Throughout his works, Merleau-Ponty makes constant reference to the Estonian ethologist, Jakob von Uexküll (Uexküll 1957), whose account of the animal's relation to its environment provides a starting point for a non-reductionist biology. Uexküll coined the term *Umwelt* to describe an organism's environment or *milieu*. Under this description, an animal's environment is not some static, meaningless backdrop, but something which *means something* to the animal in terms of food, threat, reproduction, etc. "The *Umwelt* is the world implied by the movement of the animal, and that regulates the animal's movements by its own structure" (Merleau-Ponty 2003, p.175). The sheep's perception of the wolf's hostility is not reducible to an interaction of mere physical mechanisms such as a response to a stimulus. Rather, the wolf *means* threat and hostility to the sheep, and it is because it perceives the hostility in the wolf that it runs away. *Contra* Descartes, animals are not to be understood as automata, responding mechanically to stimuli around them. Rather, they sense things in their environment, they seek out and move towards some things and recoil from others. Even instinctual behaviour can be seen as intentional in this respect. It is *because* the environment is meaningful to them that they move. This is not, of course, to say that these organisms are exercising consciousness in the form that humans are capable of doing, however they are engaging in sensory activities which in an important biological sense are meaningful.

In the relational ontology of the *Umwelt* there is a complementarity between organism and environment and this is evident also in Merleau-Ponty's description of bodily intentionality. Merleau-Ponty speaks of the *attunement* of the organism to its environment, meaning an anticipatory behavioural orientation towards the world (Merleau-Ponty 1962, pp. 75 ff.), and a reciprocal receptivity on the part of the environment. The environment complements the organism's movements and potentialities for movement in the form of what has come to be called *affordances*: just as a cricket ball as a ball-to-be caught *affords* catching, so, too, water affords swimming for the fish, air affords flying for the bird, earth affords walking for humans and mammals. Organism and environment form a system of reciprocities, "a system of meanings whose reciprocities, relationships and involvements do not need to be made explicit" (Merleau-Ponty 1962, p.129). A relational ontology of this kind signals not just an inter-connectedness between all living things, but an inter-*dependence*.

Merleau-Ponty's later works are marked by a 'turn to the object' or 'turn to ontology' – a shift of focus from the embodied subject to the object of those acts (Merleau-Ponty 1968, 2003). For Merleau-Ponty, this means a turn to nature: "nature is the expression of an ontology" (Merleau-Ponty 2003, p.204). Merleau-Ponty ceases to use the word "intentionality" in these later works because of its ties to the notion of subjective consciousness so important in Husserl's *Ideen I*. However, there is a good case for claiming that his ontology is an extension of embodied intentionality and a generalisation of the relational ontology of the *Umwelt* to all of nature: in short, that the intentional 'object', in this case is nothing less than nature itself. Nature, here, is the dynamic, evolving world of living things: "There is nature wherever there is a life that has meaning, but where, however, there is not thought; hence the kinship with the vegetative…" (Merleau-Ponty 2003, p.3). It is the sensed and sensing world that is disclosed not in the exercise of reason but in our "animality" – the pre-reflective, sensory mode of being that we share with the animal world. Human being is "not animality plus reason" (Merleau-Ponty 2003, p. 208). He states: "the relation of the human to the animal will not be the single hierarchy founded in addition… but by an *Ineinander*" (Merleau-Ponty 2003, p.214). *Ineinander* means "intertwining," and it is used to designate the unique relation of the sensing and the sensible. This notion is introduced as part of Merleau-Ponty's ontology of the flesh which is articulated in *The visible and the invisible* (Merleau-Ponty 1968, pp. 133ff). Here Merleau-Ponty seeks to explain relations of intersubjectivity in the human domain. These are "intercorporeal" relations (Merleau-Ponty 1968, p.143) that cannot be reduced either to the external relation of discrete things or to some kind of immaterial spirit. It is, rather, an intertwining (*Ineinander*) of the sensing and the sensible. This intertwining is exemplified in the different patterns of intentionality involved in touching. (Merleau-Ponty 1968, Pp. 133; 141; 147–148). When I touch one of my hands with the other, the boundary between subject (the touching hand) and object (the touched) dissolves in the unity of the body; however this is not complete coincidence – the touching does not completely coincide with the touched – there is still a phenomenological difference between "subject" and "object" when these terms are understood as "sentient" and "sensible." There is no privileging of the sentient over the sensible; there is reversibility in this relation as when the toucher becomes the touched: "Things touch me as much as I touch them." (Merleau-Ponty 2003, p. 224). Merleau-Ponty introduces his ontology of the flesh to help us make sense of this relation: Flesh is an elemental category of being that "is not matter, is not mind, is not substance" (Merleau-Ponty 1968, p.139). In his *Nature* lectures (2003), Merleau-Ponty draws on this unique relation of intertwining to describe our relations first with non-human animals and then with nature, generally. The flesh of the body makes us understand the flesh of the world, for nature is the "sensible" correlate of the body's "sensing." (Merleau-Ponty 2003, p. 218). In this way, Merleau-Ponty's ontology of the flesh, freed of any theory which privileges human consciousness can nonetheless be said to retain and extend intentionality, albeit in a *naturalized* form (Harney 2015, p143).

A second justification for retaining the notion of intentionality in Merleau-Ponty's turn to ontology can be offered by returning to the precursors of Brentano's celebrated thesis and locating the seeds of this notion in the works of the ancient and mediaeval philosophers. For many of these thinkers, great attention was given to the processes of sensation and perception – processes which are the basis for any theory of embodied intentionality. For many of these earlier thinkers, however, the framework was one associated with the understanding of living things generally, rather than Brentano's distinction of the mental from the physical which implicitly owes a great deal to the influence of Descartes and which has shaped so many of the subsequent debates about intentionality, particularly among analytical philosophers.

Continental philosophers like Merleau-Ponty are heirs to a very different tradition, one closer to Aristotle who links perception with sensation and motion rather than to intellection or cognition (Aristotle 1961). Within an Aristotelian framework the operative distinction is that between the living and non-living, and when intentionality is considered in the light of this distinction rather than that of the mental *versus* the physical, representationalism of the Cartesian kind has no place. Amongst living things, Aristotle distinguishes three categories of beings. In ascending order these are, first, those with the power of nutrition and reproduction (plants); second are those who, in addition, have the power of sense-perception and self-motion (animals); finally those who exhibit also the powers of intellection and rationality (humans). The capacities in question form a nested hierarchy, such that those at the lower level are still included in the higher orders of living things (albeit in a re-organised form).

If there is anything resembling bodily intentionality in Aristotle's philosophy, it would have to be his account of perception. Aristotle's controversial view of perception as the reception of a form without matter has received considerable attention and was even suggested by Brentano to be a source of the modern notion of intentionality. For our purposes, however, it is his account of the key role of sensation and movement – capacities shared by beasts and humans – that is important.

For Aristotle, all perception has an object, and is always true of its object. In this respect it differs from 'thinking' (*dianoeisthai*) of the kind associated with human reasoning which can be true or false (Aristotle 1961, III-3, 427b 8–14). We perceive things through the senses (sensation). Acts of sensing such as touching, seeing, hearing, smelling, etc. are, in turn, defined by their objects. For example, if the object is colour then it is seeing, if it is sound, hearing. Aristotle gives a very rich and complex account of the objects of sensation and perception. These include not just the "direct" objects specific to each sense, but also those that are 'common' in the sense that they can be perceived by more than one sense, for example, shape, size, motion. Finally, there are the "incidental objects" which are the things perceived "indirectly" as part of my directly perceiving "a white thing." "The son of Diares" is perceived "incidentally since the thing you perceive is incidental to the white thing" (Aristotle 1961, II.5418a20–23). However this is still a sensed object and not something inferred.

The senses are not passive receptacles. They involve activity at a number of levels. They can involve a kind of judgment or discerning (*krinein, κρινεῖν*) (Aristotle 1961, I.4), such as discriminating dark from light. Furthermore, the activity of sensing includes not just the sensed object but what we would now call an awareness of sensing: "… in the act of sensing something else, we do also sense *that* we sense" (Aristotle 1961, III.2). Unlike thermostats or smoke alarms, we "know" that we sense. "Knowing", here, is inherent in the sensing, not something additional to it. As Gendlin remarks: "In the modern West we might say that we "know" that we sense, but for Aristotle we sense that we sense." (Gendlin 2012, III-4, p.10). With Descartes this "Sensing that we sense" is equated with 'consciousness,' and is separated out from sensing as the agency of cognition. As a property of the cognizing "I", it becomes the agency responsible for interpreting and organising the "input" of the sense-organs in the form of concepts. A consequence of this was the radical separation of humans and animals (man and beast) and, for Descartes, the relegation of animals to the category of mere machines.

Whilst Aristotle's very rich and fertile accounts of sensation and perception provide a grounding for the idea of a biologically-based approach to intentionality, a more developed approach to this notion can be found in the works of the Arabic philosophers of the early Middle Ages, Ibn Sīnā (Avicenna) and Ibn Rushd (Averroës)[7]. These philosophers were not mere translators of Aristotle, but extended and elaborated his ideas and built onto them in original ways. One such novel development was a theory of cognition that arose from Avicenna's study of Aristotle's theory of perception. Avicenna's concern was to explore the inter-relationships between sensory-based and intellectual cognition (Black 2004, p.311). As part of this, he developed what might arguably be called a prototypical theory of intentionality. As with Aristotle, perception, which is common to humans and animals, is explained in terms of the capacities of the senses, these senses being in turn distinguished by their objects. To Aristotle's external senses, whose objects are essentially material or "sensible" objects such as shape, colour, sound, smell, Avicenna added a set of internal senses whose objects were not perceivable by the external sense organs of vision, hearing, touch, smell, and taste, but which were nonetheless in some sense related to them. (McGinnis 2010, p.98–99). Avicenna's celebrated example of this is the hostility of the wolf that is perceived by the sheep (Avicenna 1952, Ch III p.30, 10–20). An object like the wolf's hostility is not perceptible in the same way as the wolf. It is not essentially material but nonetheless such objects are perceived *through* the sensible forms. In this respect, they are very similar to and include Aristotle's incidental sensing (perceiving the white thing as "the son of Diares"): "what is first perceived by the [external] sense and then by the internal faculties is the form, while what only the internal faculties perceive without the external sense is the *intention*" (Avicenna 1952, Ch III p.30)[8].

Because objects like "hostility" cannot be perceived by the external senses, Avicenna postulated the inner sense known as the '*estimative*' faculty or *wahm* whose objects include 'the *intentions* of the sensible' (*ma'nā*) (Avicenna 1952, ch III p. 30; Black 1993, p.220).[9] The hostility of the wolf is such an object. "Intention," here, comes from the Latin *intentio* which is, in turn, the commonly accepted translation of the Arabic word *ma'nā.* It was this notion of *intentio* that was subsequently taken up (with subtle modifications) by mediaeval Latin scholars such as Aquinas in the form of the doctrine of *esse intentionale.* As we have remarked, this was later

---

[7] For present purposes, I am confining the discussion to Avicenna's theory of perception with particular reference to his account of the estimative faculty (*wahm*) and intention (*ma'nā*) as these are developed mainly in his *Al-Najat* (Avicenna 1952) and his *Al-Shifā* (Avicenna 1959). Averroës, along with others contested many of Avicenna's ideas including the status and scope of the estimative faculty. A full discussion of these debates is beyond the scope of this paper.

[8] Other inner senses include the common sense (*sensis communis*) responsible for integrating the individual sensations such as touching and seeing into a unity; imaginative power (*imaginativa),* imagination (*phantasia),* and memory (*memoria).*

[9] *Wahm* is a highly contentious notion which stimulated lively debates amongst Avicenna's contemporaries, and continues to do so in contemporary scholarship.

equated by Brentano with "intentional inexistence," and became the core of later mainstream theories of intentionality in the west (Black 2004, 2010; Hasse 2000).

For Avicenna, intentions of the sensible include properties relating to appetition and affection such as pleasantness, painfulness, hostility, friendliness, etc. The estimative faculty or *wahm* is, as the name suggests, a kind of judgement or estimation: "The estimative faculty … perceives the non-sensible intentions which exist in the particular sense-perceptible objects, like the faculty existing in sheep judging that the wolf is something to flee from and that this child is something to have affection for" (Avicenna 1959. I.5, p.43). Because we are focusing on animal perception, the judgment here is not yet a rational or intellectual judgement, the latter being unique to humans, and whose proper object is a *concept* (of hostility, agreeableness, etc.,). However, it is because of the exercise of the estimative faculty in particular encounters (such as the wolf), that concepts can be formed by the intellect. Rahman (1952, p. 84) states: "the most important function of *wahm* according to Avicenna is to judge pleasure and pain, agreeableness and disagreeableness of objects and thus to produce appetence and movement."

The role of the estimative faculty in relation to other forms of cognition is further explicated by Avicenna, first in relation to degrees of abstraction, and then by reference to universals and particulars: The estimative sense involves a greater degree of abstraction from the material object than does imagination, but a lesser degree than that of intellection, for example conceptualization of good and evil, agreeableness and disagreeableness (Avicenna 1952, ch VII p. 39; Avicenna 1959, p.60, 10ff). "The faculty of estimation… receives the intentions which in themselves are non-material, although they accidentally happen to be in matter." (Avicenna 1952, p.39). He adds that because such attributes *can* be conceived of apart from matter, they cannot be essentially material. When conceived apart from matter, they are concepts. Concepts are universals and, as such, can only be grasped by the intellect, never by the senses whose objects always inhere in particulars. (Avicenna 1952, Ch VIII, p. 41).

Hasse (2000), in a very detailed and comprehensive analysis of *wahm* and intentions, argues that Avicenna's *intentio* has "hardly anything to do with intentionality" (Hasse 2000, p.124). His preferred translation is "connotational attributes"[10] rather than "intentions" on the grounds that "the intention is not in the perceiver but in the object" (Hasse 2000, p.130), and hence cannot qualify as an *intentional* object. There is an implicit reliance here on Brentano's notion of intentionality as the 'mark of the mental' – a definition that we have rejected in favour of the non-Cartesian notion of embodied intentionality. Moreover, the wolf's hostility is not something intrinsic to the wolf but must be seen as a property of the sheep's relation to the wolf. (It may not, for example, be an attribute of the wolf as perceived by a she-wolf, or its cub).

The important point for our purposes is that in this context, intentionality comes from "a focus on activities that are common to animals and men and which, as a consequence, are concerned with the practical activities of motion and appetition"

[10] McGinnis (2010, pp.97–99) also adopts this terminology.

(Black 1993, p.221). If there is a proto-typical form of intentionality here in the object-directedness of acts of perceiving, and in the special 'mode of being' of the objects, understood as "intentions of the sensible" in the case of the estimative faculty, then it is one closer to the embodied intentionality of Merleau-Ponty than the narrowly mentalistic characterisation of Brentano. Perception, in the form of the estimative faculty, involves a form of knowing. However it is not intellectual knowledge (which is unique to humans); rather, it is sensory-based or perceptual knowledge common to humans and animals alike. This is a view which can be comfortably juxtaposed with the description of the *Umwelt* and its relational ontology and through this, the naturalized intentionality we can attribute to Merleau-Ponty.

Descartes radically transformed this notion of sensing as something shared by human and non-human animals by appropriating it to the category of human thought or 'cogitation'- this by virtue of its being an act of the representing conscious and thinking "I" (Heller-Roazen 2007, p.165). As a result, sensation was seen to be untrustworthy and passive and for this reason separated from cognition proper. The repercussions of this on the subsequent western intellectual tradition have been immense. Gendlin observes: "In modern science 'the idealized observer' unifies space and time and provides the grid for scientific constructions. Motion, size, figure, and unity are considered conceptions, and must be brought to sensations to give them structure and connections. For Aristotle the basic concepts of physics such as sensibles, motion, size, figure, and unity are derived within sensation. Modern philosophy since Descartes has considered them to be external relations imposed on sensations" (Gendlin 2012, III-I, p 10).

However at the same time as Descartes, another lesser-known current of thought developed most notably by Calabrian, Tommaso Campanella (1568–1639). A strident critic of Aristotle, he rejected the classical doctrine of sensation in terms of "in-forming" or passing of the sensible form from the perceived to the perceiver, and developed instead a 'materialist' theory of perception inspired by the empiricist approach of his forbear, Bernardino Telesio (1509–1588) in which perceiving is seen as the transfer of tactile impressions through the nerves to the brain. Self awareness or knowledge of self was implicit in this process: "To feel an external object is to feel within oneself the very force of that which one feels outside" (Heller-Roazen 2007, p. 170). For Campanella, however, this "awareness" is not something separable from sensitive being which unites us with other forms of life, and is simply a matter of degree of complexity rather than something qualitatively different as it becomes for Descartes.

Sensing that we sense is necessarily tied to self-preservation: "Every being displays a tendency toward the conservation of its own life and for this purpose is endowed, in varying proportions, with sense. This consists of the capacity to distinguish that which is positive and conducive to its life, and is consequently to be pursued and sought after, from that which is perceived as negative and destructive, and consequently to be shunned and avoided" (Ernst 2014).

From Telesio, Campanella adopted a form of *pansensism* meaning that this tendency was present in all existing things. Hence, the power of perceiving is extended to all of nature and is summed up in the statement "the world is an extremely sensitive animal" (Heller-Roazen 2007, p. 172). Pansensism is demonstrated in the reciprocal action by which all things move towards what they desire and hence lack and flee their opposites. Plants move towards the sun; water, air, and magnetism also move towards what's lacking: "an unbroken chain of perception…stretched from matter which senses in desiring the forms it lacks, to the sensations of the astral bodies that circulate in the sensing heavens" (Heller-Roazen 2007, 171–172).

A growing body of contemporary popular literature, much of it stemming from environmentalist concerns, express very similar ideas attributing agency to nature itself – for example, the idea of the planet as a super-organism or as Gaia, that a plant "knows", that trees can communicate, and so forth.[11] These are not to be conflated however with the pan*psychism* of those physicists and philosophers who speak of "consciousness" as permeating the universe. For these thinkers, it is very much the Cartesian consciousness split off from the senses that is postulated. And for this reason, such ideas are still plagued with the mysterious 'ghost in the machine.'

It is sensing and movement, rather than disembodied Cartesian consciousness, which is central to Merleau-Ponty's idea of embodied intentionality, and this is already present in Husserl. Although he does not use terms like "embodied,"[12] he is nonetheless talking about animate being, a point made forcefully by Sheets-Johnstone. Referring to Husserl, she states: "Animation is the ground floor, the ontological as well as epistemological bedrock of human self-understandings and indeed of human pan-animate understandings, *understandings that include but do not separate out cognition as the point of entry to those understandings*" (Sheets-Johnstone 2010, p.219) (my emphasis).

By linking sensation with movement, we can begin to see the historical roots of phenomenological naturalism. Ironically, it is Husserl, teacher of Merleau-Ponty, who establishes this connection – ironic because of Husserl's anti-naturalism. However, as Merleau-Ponty argues, phenomenology (including Husserl) "denounces the natural attitude and at the same time does more than any other philosophy to rehabilitate it" (Merleau-Ponty 2003, p.72). What Merleau-Ponty is suggesting here is that Husserl and phenomenology commit us to a reconceived view of nature, one which is free of the dualistic presuppositions of the natural attitude. It is a view that sees us as part of nature, not separate from it. But, as the concept of *Umwelt* reminds us, we are not thereby reduced to mere mechanisms.

Intentionality plays a key role in shaping a perspective on nature that is at once very new and also very old. It restores the ancient idea of nature as living, animate, creative, and evolving rather than static or dead; it creates a space for Aristotle's final causation or teleology – not as something imposed from without but as something inherent in natural processes, exemplified by Darwin's observation that all living things are in some sense striving towards that which will promote their

[11] There are, of course, developments of this in scholarly research as well. See in particular, Hoffmeyer 2012.

[12] Sheets-Johnstone (2010, p. 219) points out: "Husserl wrote of action, but he did not write of active or enactive organisms; he wrote of bodies, but he did not write of embodied organisms…"

survival and their flourishing. It also affirms a view of nature consistent with the findings of ecology marked by interdependencies of all living things, be they vegetative, animal, or human.

This is not a way of anthropomorphising nature, but an affirmation of nature as primarily living, animate, evolving, and of seeing us as part of that. It is more a case of 'naturalising' that species, *anthropos*. The idea of a naturalised intentionality by way of phenomenology is as liberating as its presence in the writings of twentieth century existentialist philosophers. While it is still the source of that view of the human associated with choice, moral significance, and responsible action, it is not a mark of our species as disconnected from other living things and for this reason – arguably – it augments and deepens the significance of those choices and responsibilities.

References

Aristotle. (1961). *De anima*. Edited, with introduction and commentary by W. D. Ross. Oxford: Clarendon Press.

Avicenna. (1952). *Psychology* (Kitāb Al-Najat Book Two, Chapter VI) (F. Rahman, Trans.). London: Oxford University Press.

Avicenna. (1959). *De anima. Being the psychological part of Kitāb Al-Shifā'* (F. Rahman, Ed.). London: Oxford University Press.

Black, D. (1993). Estimation (*Wahm*) in Avicenna: The logical and psychological dimensions. *Dialogue, XXXII*, 219–258.

Black, D. (2004). Psychology: soul and intellect. In Peter Adamson & Richard C. Taylor (Eds.), *The Cambridge companion to Arabic philosophy* (pp. 308–326). Cambridge companions to philosophy. Cambridge: Cambridge University Press.

Black, D. (2010). Intentionality in mediæval Arabic philosophy. *Quaestio, 10*, 65–81.

Braidotti, R. (2013). *The Posthuman*. London: Bloomsbury.

Braidotti, R., & Hlavajova, M. (Eds.). (2018). *Posthuman glossary*. London: Bloomsbury.

Brentano, F. (1973) [1874]. *Psychology from an empirical standpoint* (C. Rancurello, D. B. Terrell, and Linda McAlister, Trans.) (from the second edition, of 1924) (first edition, 1874.). London: Routledge.

Caston, V. (2001). Connecting traditions: Augustine and the Greeks on intentionality. In D. Perler (Ed.), *Ancient and medieval theories of intentionality* (pp. 23–48). Leiden: Brill.

de Beauvoir, S. (1949). *Le Deuxième Sexe* (The second sex). Paris: Gallimard.

Ernst, G. (2014). Tommaso Campanella. *The Stanford encyclopedia of philosophy* (Fall 2014 Edition). (Edward N. Zalta, Ed.). https://plato.stanford.edu/archives/fall2014/entries/campanella/. Accessed 27 Aug 2016.

Føllesdal, D. (1969). Husserl's notion of the noema. *Journal of Philosophy, 66*, 680–687.

Frege, G. (1970) [1892]. On sense and reference (*Uber Sinn und Bedeutung*). Translated by M. Black. In P. T. Geach & M. Black (Eds.), *Translations from the philosophical writings of Gottlob Frege* (pp. 56–78). Oxford: Basil Blackwell.

Gendlin, E. T. (2012). *Line by line commentary on Aristotle's* De Anima (Books I, II and III). Spring Valley: The Focusing Institute.

Harney, M. J. (1984). *Intentionality sense and the mind*. The Hague: Dordrecht Martinus-Nijhoff.

Harney, M. (2015). Naturalizing phenomenology – A philosophical imperative. *Journal of Progress in Biophysics and Molecular Biology 19*(2). Special theme issue on Integral Biomathics. Guest edited by P. Simeonov, S. Rosen and A. Gare.

Hasse, D. (2000). *Avicenna's De anima in the Latin West*. London: Warburg Institute.
Heller-Roazen, D. (2007). *The inner touch: Archaeology of a sensation*. New York: Zone Books.
Hoffmeyer, J. (2012). The natural history of intentionality: A biosemiotic approach. In T. Schilhab, F. Stjernfelt, & T. Deacon (Eds.), *The symbolic species evolved* (Biosemiotics 6) (pp. 97–116). Dordrecht: Springer.
Husserl, E. (1965 [1910–1911]). Philosophy as rigorous science. In *Phenomenology and the crisis of philosophy* (Quentin Lauer, Trans.). New York: Harper and Row.
Husserl, E. (1969 [1913]. *Ideen I* (Ideas). (W. R. Boyce Gibson, Trans.). London: Allen and Unwin.
Levinas, E. (1998). Intentionality and sensation. In *Discovering existence with Husserl* (pp. 135–150). Edited, and chapter translated by, Richard A. Cohen and Michael B. Smith. Evanston: Northwestern University Press.
McGinnis, J. (2010). *Avicenna*. Oxford: Oxford University Press.
Merleau-Ponty, M. (1962). *Phenomenology of perception* (Phénoménologie de la perception) (Colin Smith, Trans.). London: Routledge & Kegan Paul.
Merleau-Ponty, M. (1968). *The visible and the invisible* (Le visible et l'invisible). Edited by Claude Leforte, translated by Alphonso Lingis. Evanston: Northwestern University Press.
Merleau-Ponty, M. (2003). *Nature: course notes from the Collège de France.* (*La nature: notes, cours du Collège de France,* Paris: Gallimard, 1995.) Compiled with notes by Dominique Séglard (Robert Vallier, Trans.). Evanston: Northwestern Unversity Press.
Mohanty, J. N. (1982). *Husserl and Frege*. Bloomington: Indiana University Press.
Rahman, F. (1952). *Avicenna's psychology*. London: Oxford University Press.
Seager, W., & Bourget, D. (2007). Representationalism about consciousness. In M. Velmans & S. Schneider (Eds.), *Blackwell companion to consciousness* (pp. 261–276). Oxford: Blackwell.
Sheets-Johnstone, M. (2010). Body and movement: Basic dynamic principles. In S. Gallagher & D. Schmicking (Eds.), *Handbook of phenomenology and cognitive science* (pp. 217–234). Dordrecht: Springer.
Siewert, C. (2011). Consciousness and intentionality. *The Stanford encyclopedia of philosophy* (Fall 2011 Edition) (Edward N. Zalta, Ed.). http://plato.stanford.edu/archives/fall2011/entries/consciousness-intentionality/
Smith, D. W., & McIntyre, R. (1982). *Husserl and intentionality: A study of mind, meaning, and language*. Dordrecht/Boston: Reidel.
von Uexküll, J. (1957) [1934]. A stroll through the worlds of animals and men. In *Instinctive behavior: The development of a modern concept* (pp. 5–80). Edited and translated by Claire H. Schiller. New York: International Universities Press.

Maurita Harney is Honorary Senior Fellow in Philosophy at the University of Melbourne, having previously taught philosophy at the Australian National University and Swinburne University of Technology. She was an undergraduate student of Max Charlesworth's in the early 1960s. Although her earlier specialisation was in analytic philosophy, in the 1970s she was drawn to the continental tradition, largely as a result of Max's influence. She joined the small group of philosophers developing teaching and research in this area, and in 1976 she convened Australia's first phenomenology conference. Her PhD thesis (1980) on Husserl and Frege sought to bridge a gap in understanding between the analytic and continental traditions. Maurita's recent interests include the intersection of phenomenology with neuroscience and with biosemiotics – an approach to nature, biology and 'embodied' cognition, which draws its philosophical inspiration from the philosophy of Charles Sanders Peirce.

Chapter 12
'Is and Ought': Yet Again

Patrick Hutchings

> I cannot forbear adding to these reasons an observation, which may, perhaps, be found of some importance. In every system of morality which I have hitherto met with, I have always remarked, that the author proceeds for some time in the ordinary way of reasoning, and establishes the being of a God, or makes observations concerning human affairs; when of a sudden I am surprised to find, that instead of the usual copulations of propositions, *is*, and *is not*, I meet with no proposition that is not connected with an *ought*, or an *ought not*. This change is *imperceptible* [Italic added]; but is, however, of the last consequence. For as this *ought*, or *ought not*, expresses some new relation or affirmation, it is necessary that it should be observed and explained; and at the same time that a reason should be given, for what seems altogether *inconceivable* [Italic added], how this new relation can be a *deduction* [Italic added] from others, which are entirely different from it. But as authors do not commonly use this *precaution* [Italic added], I shall presume to recommend it to the readers; and am persuaded, that this small attention would subvert all the vulgar systems of morality, and let us see that the distinction of vice and virtue is not founded merely on the relations of objects, *nor is perceived by reason*. (*A Treatise of Human Nature*. David Hume, 1739–1740)[1]

Hume's real discovery in the famous passage at the end of Section 1 of Book III of *The Treatise of Human Nature*, was the ***precaution***, the small attention, that he recommended that we take, or pay, whenever we encounter an 'imperceptible' change from the assertion of fact to the asseveration of value.

Because he was concerned to show that morals were not a matter of reason but of something else such as sentiment,[2] Hume – at least half – mistook his own

[1] Epigraph: David Hume, *A Treatise of Human Nature*, ed. L.A. Selby-Bigge, Oxford at the Clarendon Press, 1888, and many subsequent editions. There is a revised edition by P.H. Nidditch, Oxford, 1978, in which the original pagination is, virtually, preserved. Or, see Ernest C. Mossner's edition, Pelican 1968, Penguin 1985. Epigraph (Hume, 1958, Bk III, Part I, p.469); (Hume, 1985, p.521).

[2] One used in a literature and philosophy course Henry Mackenzie's *The Man of Feeling* 1771. (It happened that Mackenzie also wrote a *Life of John Home*, the Scottish dramatist, – whose *Douglas* is still eminently readable – a relative of Hume's. The Scots pronounce the family name 'Home' as 'Hume'.) Reprints of *The Man of Feeling* are still available, notable is the Oxford 'World's

P. Hutchings (✉)
SHAPS, The University of Melbourne, Melbourne, VIC, Australia
e-mail: sophia@philosophy.unimelb.edu.au

P. Wong et al. (eds.), *Considering Religions, Rights and Bioethics: For Max Charlesworth*, Sophia Studies in Cross-cultural Philosophy of Traditions and Cultures 30, https://doi.org/10.1007/978-3-030-18148-2_12

discovery. The cramp that he found himself in because he denied the place of reason in morals, a cramp of which he does not himself at all seem to have been conscious, we shall discuss *ambulando*. For a start let us stick to the crux of '*precaution*'. Of course from a certain point of view it seems altogether inconceivable how this new relation of value can be a '*deduction*' from matters of fact which are entirely different from it in ontological and axiological kind. But so concerned is Hume to have morals no kind of deduction at all – because for him morals are not a function of reason at all – that he overlooks that we can indeed conceive this 'inconceivable' new relation out of an old one, since in the first place we do it all the time as he himself suggests; and in the second place it is notoriously the stuff of 'vulgar systems of morality'. Systems of morality had better be vulgar too, if the populaces are to be moral. So much for vulgarity, what of the deduction?

Any deduction of value from fact may occur when there is, *an intervening axiological premise*. And if we took Hume's 'precaution', we would not halt 'imperceptible' changes from fact to value we would simply: (a) perceive them and, (b) understand how they are in fact effected.

Much of the reading of Hume's crux has turned on the phrase 'a deduction'. And theories of the kinds put forward at various times notably by Professor R.L. Stephenson, have turned on finding a deduction; finding a 'deduction' and finding one and only one that will do for all cases. Or they have turned on finding some substitute for the missing deduction. Emotive and command theories of ethics can get generated from this kind of interest in an absolute, one size fits all 'deduction' which is not even in any sense a *deduction*. The ground is simply shifted. The analysis of 'this is good' into 'I approve of this' and 'snap to it and approve too!', gets the *good* pasted onto whatever '*this* is' in the context in a drillmasterish kind of way. But as has been argued many times before, and as I myself argued rather a long time ago, a command is quite a different thing from an evaluation. Evaluations appeal 'to a candid world'. Commands are given to inferiors, thralls and so on.[3]

It is not just that the tone of these emotivist command theories is tiresome, it is the case that the desire to find a single solution is in fact mistaken. What is notable is the number of enabling principles that vulgar systems of morality severally exhibit. Which they exhibit to theory, and in the last resort which they exhibit in the lived world. The lived world trumps theory by being prior to it. Theory reflects on what it is given to reflect on.

There is in a sense not a 'deduction' from fact to value; but there are many 'deductions'. There is not *a* 'deduction' though of course there are always *some*. Or, to put it another way: There is a 'deduction' in so far as there is, and always must be an authorizing premise, making legitimate – and often perspicuous – any change from fact to value. A slogan might be '*At least one premise: and on any occasion perhaps just one premise, but overall many premises*'. Every vulgar or non-vulgar system of morality contains many principles or premises which will authorise

Classics' ed. The book is as fine an example as one may get of eighteenth century sentimentalism: although it may feel on occasion a parody of it.

[3] See my 'What does "good" tell me?' (Hutchings, 1965).

changes from fact to value. Hume's 'Observations concerning human affairs' are crucial, and not to be sidelined as he sidelines them. (For the phrase 'human affairs', see the epigraph. See also 'When in the Course of Human Events…')

12.1 Take a Case

Hume's 'precaution' must be taken not just because as Hume has been almost universally understood to imply there is no principle enabling and authorizing a change from fact to value, but simply because there are many such principles. And the seriousness of values makes it necessary that we always know what is afoot when any particular transition from fact to value is being made to occur.

Here is a case: the following is a simple factual sentence 'Identical twins have been born in the village'. This sentence in a number of natural languages might be said to represent a simple fact. It is the case that birth has been given to identical siblings in the village of 'N'.

But of course notoriously the value implications of this fact – this mere fact? – will vary: and they will be strong or weak, nice or nasty according to the geographical/cultural location of the village N.

If 'N' is the village of the culture A, then both twins will be put down and the gods who are obviously very cross at the villagers, so cross as to send a monstrous birth, will be placated according to the appropriate rites. If the village 'N' is a culture B village, then one twin will be put down and the gods will be placated with slightly different rites. If 'N' village is of the culture C people, there will be great rejoicing and much feasting and merrymaking. And the gods who are obviously on the side of the village at this moment will be asked for further favours. They will be asked for further increases in fertility especially in the coconut and breadfruit plantations. If 'N' is a village in Shropshire in the twentieth century, then Lady X may say to Sir John X 'We must offer the woman the perambulator that we used for Simon and Jane.' If 'N' is a village in Australia 'a' will say to 'b' "What village do you mean?" "Yes, twins do you say?"

Anthropology, sociology, and other intellectual and pragmatic disciplines are much, and usefully, given to discovering and exfoliating the vulgar principles which obtain in our five villages. And they will even explain why nothing much happens in our Australian village. We haven't got villages, we haven't got squires, and we haven't got perambulators. We have small towns, big cities and bigger suburbs, and we use 'strollers' to move infants about in. And we lend or give 'strollers'.

The disciplines which explain the particular transitions from fact to value which occur in the particular villages, will also explain the difference between the villagers.

Of course anthropology and sociology, as we all learnt to say at Oxford in the 50s, are not philosophy. Nevertheless, Hume's doing philosophy may have pointed us inevitably by means of his crux of 'precaution' towards these non-philosophical disciplines.

But Hume's crux has been read as a challenge to philosophers to find the denied deduction. This may simply be a function of the tendency proper, or anyhow endemic, to persons doing philosophy to find single and generalisable solutions of a philosophical kind to whatever possibly real-life problem is presented to them. But it may be that there is no philosophical solution to this philosophical crux, because it is not a crux in real life. There is simply a move which is always useful to keep a sharp eye on, this one from fact to value.

12.2 Cases and Shapes

The notion that we need to go straight for Hume's precaution into sociology, or into models of the lived world, is not a particularly original one. At least one of the Oxford positivists in the 50s had it: as I recall it was Patrick Noel Smith who said in a lecture that '*...the justification of a single ethical maxim could involve one in the total description of the way of life of which it forms a part*'. Now this remark was made with a mixture of insight and despair. Insight because it is a true and sensible one, and despair because giving descriptions of whole ways of life does not seem to be the proper activity of a philosopher. Nor does it seem that a philosopher is particularly well qualified to do it: rather the contrary.

Again, positivists *en bloc* admitted that if at the end of some real life moral suasion or formal ethics seminar your interlocutor remains unconvinced then all that you *can* do (and importantly something that you *may* do) is to tell him or her – 'Alright, go away and re-read *Anna Karenina*'. We would do well, writing of Hume to begin with where the novel itself more or less begins, that is with things like *Pamela*: and indeed, with *Pamela*. It could be argued, and the argument will be sketched very roughly in the rest of this paper, that Pamela as the eponymous heroine takes Hume's 'precaution' of seeing where the 'is' becomes an 'ought'. Pamela, in her own case, knew: as Masie in quite a different case knew.

The dates mesh quite prettily, *Pamela* is 1740, Hume's *Treatise* is 1739–1740, and both works are of course prosaic, empiricist and in an eighteenth century way rational and enlightened. They are superficially, and perhaps a little more deeply, comparable. *Pamela* is indeed an odd piece of pure fiction. As everybody knows, Richardson began by writing a how to-do-it letter-book; he began by telling us how to cope with small situations in the real world, and he ended up by producing a work of art which became a model of larger sections of the world as it was in his day. A form of life was exhibited in a fable which trenched on fact. Poor young women in service were often enough sexually harassed by their employers or their employers' sons. This is a commonplace, and the proper subject of any number of novels.

Pamela might have been written, though it was certainly not written, *to order* for Hume. But if it had been written to order for Hume it would have been in a sense too good a work for him in one way. It really renders his 'precaution' unnecessary. We do not need to take Hume's precaution in order to see how Pamela gets from fact to value for she tells us as she writes in letter XV '[I am] a poor creature [to be pitied] who knows nothing of her duty but how to cherish her virtue and her good name'. And this cherishing of virtue and good name she refers to on the same page as 'The first duty which shall ever be the **principle** [bold added] of my life'.[4] We shall return to principles at the end of this paper: Section 12.5, Hearts & Principles.

As Kinkead-Weekes reminds us in the introduction to the 1962 Everyman edition of *Pamela*, just cited, Europe in the eighteenth century was divided into Pamelists and anti-Pamelists. The Pamelists thought her an innocent girl who had indeed, with simplicity, kept her virtue. The anti-Pamelists, taking their cue from the sub-title of '*Pamela: or Virtue Rewarded,*' and taking many cues from the text, thought that Pamela was a sly minx who was determined to sell her virtue at a high going rate: marriage. And the highest going rate was marriage to 'Mr B', and so elevation from a humble station in life to a proper place among the gentry. Henry Fielding, who really should have known better,[5] published a parody called *An Apology for the life of Miss Shamela Andrews* (1741) which mines the calculating minx vein. The answer of common sense to the issue between the Pamelists and the anti-Pamelists, and the answer of the text itself is of course: Pamela herself was a bit of both, a 'nice girl' and prudent. No young woman however innocent or silly, unless a perfect idiot, could in the eighteenth century have failed to realise that virtue – in its contextual sense – is a commodity at once absolutely withholdable and, under certain circumstances, advantageously saleable. To withhold for whatever reason including the ones recommended by parents and the clergy might under some circumstances be to raise the odds. And again Pamela is a simple young woman of 15 years of age who believes the doctrines of sentiment: she believes in romantic love and she believes in one of its riders which for her would cash out as something like this –'If "Mr B" wants my body why doesn't he want the rest of me? And why doesn't he want me as his wife?'. Now by living up, innocently or calculatingly, or innocently and calculatingly, to that notion Pamela makes it come to be, the romantic thing. In the end she does marry 'Mr B' – and why not? The daughter of a poor but lettered man is good enough in eighteenth century England to 'marry up', if the chance is offered her. 'Mr B' says to Pamela – not meaning it at the time 'I will make a gentlewoman of you' (Letter XI) but later does just that (Richardson 1974, p.12). Pamela in *Pamela* avows a principle of value-enablement and of value disenablement in terms of her 'virtue' and her good name which must at all times be cherished: and she is quite clear what 'cherish' cashes out at. If 'Mr B' wants her, he must take her as she is – and marry her. Of course Hume – of an aristocratic family – and Samuel Richardson of a lesser line – inhabited the same – or similar – *lived worlds*. It is all a neat fit. The Novelists and the Philosopher shared *a form of*

[4] Richardson, *Pamela*: the most readily available reprint is the 'Everyman' edition in two volumes. Dent, London & Dutton, New York ed. M. Kinkead-Weekes [1914] and 1974 (*etc*). The quotations in text are from p.19 of Vol. I of this printing; *q.v.* for a Select Bibliography. Kinkead-Weekes' introduction is dated 1962 so will not be found in earlier editions.

[5] Fielding should have known better. Perhaps he did; whether he wrote *Shamala* has been a matter of controversy. I do not know the present state of the case. However how could one of the foundation writers of the English novel have been a parodist of another man's work before becoming himself a – better – novelist?

life then current. One in which Pamela's elevation into the gentry was possible, if not altogether likely.

Modern feminists will undoubtedly see 'Mr B' as a most unpleasant fellow. He was. He was monstrous as someone given to sexual harassment in a quite obsessive way. Feminists may relish, as half of Europe relished, 'Mr B's' come-uppance. 'Mr B' is made to pay the highest going rate for what he wants: he has to marry Pamela. But he not only marries Pamela, he becomes under her influence a tolerable enough country gentleman. Except that in the second half of *Pamela* 'Mr B' remains a womanizer. A Romantic and Enlightenment happy ending, still to be found, with variations, in many Mills and Boon novelettes, but usually without the serial adultery. 'Vulgar systems of morality' indeed!

In *Pamela* virtue is not only rewarded, in Pamela its rewarding is exhibited as a social as well as a private good.

Richardson may have been a prosaic printer, but as *Pamela* shows he was no fool. We are meant to read the text in which Pamela's avowal of principle occurs as not just the locus of that avowal. We are expected to measure her innocent expression of principle against the context in which it occurs. And we are expected to see this expression of principle in the light of the events which the novel exhibits, and see these events themselves in the light of Pamela's self-observation. The Pamelists and anti-Pamelists did not know perhaps that this was the way, or that it was to be the way, in which to read novels. After all, *Pamela* was probably the first novel that they had encountered. And it is interesting to notice that Fielding after writing a parody of *Pamela*, goes on to write the admirable *Joseph Andrews* (1742), *Tom Jones* (1749) and sometime later, the really quite splendid *Amelia* (1751). He discovers what novels are about by writing them. And he must have discovered how really to read novels by writing them: and they give us some useful account of eighteenth century mores, as well as the entertainment that literature offers.

We know nowadays almost to the point of being bored by it that this is the way in which to read novels: as exhibitions of forms of life, as models of the real, as models or fantasies of an alternative life, as models of a futurable state of affairs, or whatever. But though the doctrine that we read novels as models of the real is not itself an interesting one but has become boring – 'Oh! Leavisite still?' – the activity of reading novels remains interesting.[6] In the late twentieth century and early twenty-first century, novels are 'about adultery in the suburbs'. Consider John Updike, and John Cheever. Hume, would if he took his own account of reason and the passions seriously, not be too shocked by sex in the suburbs.

[6] David Foster Wallace's *The Pale King* transcends the 'interesting' of the novel by being unfinished, plotless, and being about the boring life of a tax office persons: and by directly raising the question of boredom, never to settle it. Except by forcing us, so to speak, to read with pleasure passages on the face of them boring, boring. See Wallace 2012, pp.383, 176, 488, 461, 504 & *546*: etc. The David Foster Wallace sentence-form is considered by Wallace and others to be the only one suited to the USA as it presently is. It seems, 2013, to be as mannered and laborious as are the 'letters' in *Pamela*. One now reads both as a duty as much as a pleasure. The point is obvious: both content and style change between *Pamela*, *What Masie Knew* and *The Pale King*. How content and style interact is a matter of interest for serious literary criticism.

If all this sounds a dull, empiricist view of literature, it is. Or, it may be empiricist, but it's not dull. Taken straight or deconstructed, novels inform us.

And Hume's famous crux gives precise and permanent point to the reading of literature in this way, of plumbing it for a form of life. Literature becomes a way of exhibiting whatever it is that we must take as pains when we take Hume's 'precaution'. How we read *Pamela* is how we read an Updike novel: the world has changed since Richardson and we, now, live in that new world. As society changes, so do its representations, in content and in style.

12.3 Hume's Cramp and Moral Reflection

At the end of his crux passage Hume comes back again to his central thesis: that morals have nothing to do with reason. This thesis is notoriously less clear than it sounds and we cannot go into all the issues here, but two points must be made. Point 1. Given Hume's definition of 'reason', it is not at all hard to see why morals have nothing to do with it. Reason is 'the discovery of truth or falsehood. Truth or falsehood consists in an agreement or disagreement either to the real relation of ideas or to the real existence and matters of fact'.[7] And that's it.

Why Hume adopts this restrictive definition of reason is a large question. That the definition will not do has, of course, often been suggested in the past.

We are left however with a smaller issue, and it is just this. Point 2: What were I to call – if not 'reason' – the kind of intellectual activity which does concern morals? What are we to call the kind of intellectual activity that goes on when persons find themselves in moral situations? Well, Hume himself calls it variously 'consideration' as in the sentence 'when a character is considered in general….then it causes such a feeling or sentiment as denominates it morally good or evil' – having a little of it both ways. And he uses such words as 'invention, 'thought', and 'reflection'. He uses these words in a kind of back-handed way and the context in which this back-handed use occurs we shall examine a little later in this paper.

Hume needs some word if he rules out 'reason' to refer to whatever activity it is that we exhibit in moral situations, because if he doesn't have an equivalent word for 'reason', he is caught in an obvious cramp. We *do* move from fact to value, and this needs an account. If reason has nothing, but absolutely nothing, to do with morals, how can Hume reasonably write a book on morals, since writing a book about the relationship or non-relationship of reason to morals is itself a, reasonable, meta-activity, an activity meta to actual moral reasoning. Hume's *Treatise* almost says that there is no such thing as moral reasoning. This I think is not very helpful. To be *meta* on this matter of moral reasoning will not do. And there is a sense in which Hume himself seems to realise this. One may read him with ironical reserve. He almost invites us to.

[7] 'Reason is the discovery of truth or falsehood' (Hume, 1958, p.458); (Hume, 1985, p.510).

All that Hume could sensibly object to about reason in morals was perhaps rationalism in morals. Reasoning about moral issues exists at the baseline level and at the meta level: both. And there is nothing that Hume can do, or the, opposing, doctrine of moral sentiments can do, to alter the baseline existence of moral reasoning. That is, there is nothing that a meta analysis of moral reasoning can do to make its own baseline go away.

But what, although very obscurely, Hume was really concerned about comes out perhaps when he uses the backhand terms 'reflection' and 'thought'. Two things must be noted about them. The first point is that if reason is not allowed, after Hume, to run in morals, then we had better find a word for what it was that we used to call 'reason', and 'thought' and 'reflection' will do. And the second point is that these terms 'thought' and 'reflection' do in fact point up something cognate with the issue of the 'precaution' crux itself. Let us look at another text. Hume is writing about an issue which seems in a way separate from the ones about reason and reasoning in morals. But when one reads the passage carefully with the crux of 'precaution' at the forefront of one's memory, things apparently separate come together. Hume's particular topic is the non-naturalness of justice as a virtue, and this is what he says:

> To avoid giving offence, I must here observe, that when I deny justice to be a natural virtue, I make use of the word *natural*, only as opposed to *artificial*. In another sense of the word, as no **principle** [bold added] of the human mind is more natural than a sense of virtue, so no virtue is more natural that justice. Mankind is an inventive species; and where an invention is obvious and absolutely necessary it may as properly be said to be natural as anything that proceeds immediately from original **principles**, *without the intervention of thought or reflection* [Italic added]. Though the rules of justice be *artificial*, they are not *arbitrary*. Nor is the expression improper to call them *Laws of Nature*; if by "natural" we understand what is common to any species, or even if we confine it to mean what is inseparable from the species. (Part II of Hume's *Treatise*)[8]

The crucial phrase here is: 'Without the intervention of thought or reflection'. We might reply that: Thought and reflection may be taken for granted when what is second nature to us issues in a judgement which we may – notably – regard as natural. However we must not let Hume get away with his offhand 'invention'. If invention does not imply the use of reason, what does? Even what is blindingly obvious – certain devices of justice – what are they blindingly obvious to if not to reason? That society must banish murder is obvious to the reason – as well as to the sentiments – of anyone who understands the basic conditions of society itself. We are dealing in the passage cited, as Hume notes, with another sense of 'principle' than the one that the fictional Pamela used, but Hume's vaguely Natural Law use of the word "natural" lies well within the range of things to be recognized and judged by reason. 'Original Principles' are open to reason, and their applications to its critique. Hume's own use of 'principle' in the passage quoted almost echoes the

[8] 'To avoid giving offence…' Part II of Hume's *Treatise* (Hume, 1958, p.484); (Hume, 1985, pp. 535–36).

Stoic-Scholastic 'principles' of Natural-Law, Human Nature, about which Hume may be very doubtful, with his 'separation' of 'is' and 'ought'. But to explore Stoic hauntings of Hume would require another paper.

Man is the only thinking being, as far as we can tell, and she is the only being who has rules of justice, as far as we can tell. And the conjunction implies a connection which is at least prima facie and which will be needed to be talked away more skillfully than Hume talks it away. But what Hume says about reflection and invention on the other hand makes more sense than what he says about thought. Rules of justice which are practically thought up, that is thought up by practical people and devised, and so on, are products of 'reflection', but may or may not be always subsequently reflected on. Reflection after reflective-invention is the task of philosophy or the task of some other intellectual operation which will apply the Humean precaution. The Law Reform Commission and Parliamentary Commissions are more inventive and reflective than is the daily business of civil justice. The Humean precaution is a reflective activity which elucidates practical thought, which elucidates structures which are not themselves yet explicit or explicitly analysed, but which are going to become so in the light of persons' taking Hume's proper precaution.

Now fictional models of the moral universe may do this exhibition of structures, do this analysis of structures, as well as other kinds of reflection do it.

Anna Karenina may exhibit, in its large and altogether rich texture, morally relevant structures. More profound and less obvious than those of *Pamela*. Tolstoy is after all a deeper man than Richardson. And, or 'and' and 'but', he writes in a form of life different from Hume's or ours. Nevertheless we find him Universal and Timeless. Or, so the story – old lit. crit. story – went.

And this is why we used to say in the 1950s at the end of an unsuccessful moral suasion or at the conclusion of a fruitless ethics seminar, "Oh good gracious, go away and reread *Anna Karenina*". We have not space in this paper to 'reread' *Anna Karenina*: we have not even time to gut it as mercilessly and perfunctorily as we gutted *Pamela*. But it is apt perhaps to close these reflections with one of Tolstoy's own *pensées*, a thought which catches splendidly the relationship between reason and morals. Tolstoy writes "Reason prescribes nothing, it simply enlightens" (Tolstoy, 1910).

When Hume wrote that:

> Reason is, and ought only to be the slave of the passions, and can never pretend to any other office but to serve and obey them.[9]

he rather excelled himself. Much of the Humean subtext however has the flavour of Tolstoy's *pensée*. The passions move us, sometimes too far. They are at once the impulsions to action, and a problem. As we all know, the passions can gang aft aglay

[9] 'Reason is, and ought only to be the slave of the Passions.' *Treatise*, Part III, Section III (Hume, 1958, p.415); (Hume, 1985, p.462).

without the moderation of reason. *Precautions* are always to be considered. Ordinary as well as Humean ones.

12.4 Multiculturalism

It is easy to link Hume's *Treatise* with Richardson's *Pamela*: they were written in a culture of more or less common assumptions. Sentiment could 'replace' reason because sentiment and reason were – the supposition goes – very close. But in the twentieth and twenty-first centuries societies' *consensus,* (feeling-together), of an eighteenth century sort is not easily to be found. Sentiments/reasons sometimes no longer chime together or cohere. Refugees in Sweden have recently – 2013 – rioted. And Sweden is the prime example of a good society. The Australian government has already had to make female circumcision a crime, it not being native to the place. And Parliament is presently considering increasing the jail-time of convicted offenders to make sure that the practice is discouraged in the Antipodes. Multiculturalism[10] is just an attempt to reconcile different forms of life: or at least get them to knock along together. For the – brief – moments of Post Modernism the assumption was: 'All cultures are equal: and, more to the point, incommensurable'. There was a nice comic segment in a BBC TV show a few years ago: an immigrant Indian housewife in London was complaining to a visiting social worker that her husband had chased her around the kitchen with a knife. The PoMo social worker had asked, in an earnest voice, 'Are you sure it was not some kind of *ritual* knife?' The answer was 'It was a bloody great cleaver from the kitchen knife-box!' Ritual knives given, they would be of no account to the unfortunate policemen sent to try to settle this 'domestic'.

Even Kant's great Enlightenment Categorical Imperative won't cover all forms of life, *equally*. Some years ago in the 1970s in Cambridge I attended a talk by Professor Hare, whose Oxford lectures I had gone to in the mid-1950s. Hare struggled with the thought that a committed Nazi *could* will that his Nazi oppressor *could will*, 'as a universal law', some piece of Nazi beastliness, and so-by will that he the convinced Nazi himself would be the victim-subject of it. Some might consent to nastiness being visited on them in a very nasty culture.[11] The same thought experiment could be run without the consolation that the Nazis are gone: contemporary examples of the like kind abound: Even Sweden in the 2018s now has hard right ratbags elected to its Parliament. Hare had by 1970 painted himself into a Kantian corner; and not a cosy one. The Categorical Imperative works beautifully within a

[10] Kwame Anthony Appiah mistrusts the word 'multiculturalism': see his excellent *Cosmopolitanism: Ethics in a World of Strangers* (Appiah, 2006). See also Appiah's *The Honor Code: How Moral Revolutions Happen* (Appiah, 2010).

[11] See 'The Horror, the Horror', Gary Saul Morson on Isaac Babel in *The New York Review of Books* (Morson, 2018). On p.30, col.a, Morson quotes Babel: "Must penetrate the soul of the fighting man. I'm penetrating, it's all horrible *wild beasts with principles*". [Italic added.]

given form of life: it does not however universally dictate any particular one. So: multiculturalism to a degree is a negotiation between forms. The Enlightenment hope of the absolute universality, of the principle of universalizing maxims totally informing, and so reforming a cosmopolitan morality was premature. Mozart's opera *The Abduction from the Seraglio* illustrates the hope. Deprived of a concubine the Pasha freely allows her to go back to where she came from, in a speech of such a high-minded sort that this Turkish gentleman becomes a very figure of the Enlightenment Ideal. The Pasha exhibits '[a] rational idea of a cosmopolitan sentiment' which Kant ascribes to Frederick the Great, in *The Critique of Judgment* where he analyses a fragment of 'the great king's' French poetry: See side number 316 of the Third Critique. Jefferson expresses the same notion when he appeals, in *The Declaration of Independence,* to the judgment of 'a candid World'. The World is still with us, less candid, and with the 'cosmopolitan sentiment' still to be realized. One needs to be careful about the precise import of this sentiment. There is a danger of a false entailment when one looks at Kant's rule 'universalize maxims'. The false entailment would be: 'universalizing maxims cashes out as Universalizing *one* form of life'. Mozart's Pasha remains a Turk: his rational magnanimity does not mean that he has accepted all the cultural assumptions and mores of Vienna. This then does not mean that the Enlightenment rested upon a logical mistake. But it does mean that one needs to be careful not to fall into a false entailment, and treat Cosmopolitanism as a project of universal uniformity.

One cannot overlook the exact wording of Jefferson's *Declaration*: it is counter-Hume:

> The History of the present King of Great-Britain is a History of repeated Injuries and Usurpations, all having in direct Objects the Establishment of an absolute Tyranny over these States. To prove this, let *Facts* be submitted to a candid World.

The boring bits of the *Declaration*, the *Facts*, (Italic added) which nobody can remember easily, all the 'Injuries and Usurpations', are the *facts* on which The American Revolution 'dissolve[d] the Political Bands' with Great Britain. A very clear move from fact to value, from *is* to *ought.*

Many years ago I published a book on Kant's moral philosophy and its axiology,[12] in which I argued that the Categorical Imperative was simply Utility retro-engineered. If one cannot universally will that maxim M become a law, this is because one could not live with – or under – its being so willed. Everything would be so dreadful. Utilitarianism itself presumes the – possibility of – agreement on what might constitute 'the greatest happiness of the greatest number'. Different forms of life may very well come up with different notions of 'greatest happiness'.

---

[12] P. Æ. Hutchings *Kant on Absolute Value* (Hutchings, 1972). See particularly pp.234*ff* and: 'The categorical imperative *says* nothing about utility, but it – *draws our attention to it* most effectively by requiring us to test maxims against their own possible harmfulness. Showing something to be harmful makes, perhaps, a stronger case for its being wrong, than showing it to be useful does for its being right. This kind of *negative Utilitarianism* is effective, while making smaller claims, and needing infinitely less elaboration and defence, than does Mill's rather more ambitious scheme of positive utilitarian morality: p.241.

Different forms of life inhabiting the one nation state could make Utilitarianism problematic. This aside from the other well-known philosophical difficulties it may face, and may or may not, withstand. The pragmatics of Jurisprudence have to face, if they cannot iron out, the conflicts of forms of life in a multicultural society.

For a post-Enlightenment-Enlightenment-Liberal: Act A as an act of female circumcision gets the 'ought-not' out of the 'A *is* or *would be*', in a trice. What practically to do would be a problem for lawmakers and judges. It is not obvious that philosophy could come up with a solution, either readymade or painfully thought through.

We move from 'is' to 'ought' in terms of our form of life. That does not mean that ratiocination is ruled out: rather we must rule it in. But we rule it in for what it is worth. It is a process for dealing with ordinary and with hard cases, but there is no guarantee that it can easily solve the latter.

Hume's 'imperceptible' change from an 'is' to an 'ought' is not noticed in form of life F, because it happens as it were by second nature. In from of life F∗ where second nature is different, the move may happen differently. We ought to be able to resort to 'the Opinion of a Candid World' to moral reasoning or to Human Nature to settle the 'imperceptible' moves from 'is' to 'ought' in confrontations between F and F∗. We may try: but success is not guaranteed. Sentiments abound, but are not always convivial. Hence civil law: 'artificial' but not 'arbitrary'. A trickier negotiation than that between 'is' and 'ought', is the one between 'artificial' and 'non-arbitrary'.

12.5 Hearts & Principles

Towards the end of Henry Mackenzie's *The Man of Feeling* (1987 [1771]) there is a curious passage: an unidentified character tells a tale to Mr. Harley who is *the man of feeling*. The story begins with what seems to be the Humean 'passions' 1739–40. Here is the prologue. It goes:

> THE PUPIL. A Fragment
>
> ∗ ∗ ∗ ∗ But as to the higher part of education, Mr. Harley, the culture of the Mind;–let the feelings be awakened, let the heart be brought forth to its object, placed in the light in which nature would have it stand, and its decisions will ever be just. The world
>
> Will smile, and smile, and be a villain;
>
> and the youth, who does not suspect its deceit, will be content to smile with it.–Men will put on the most forbidding aspect in nature, and tell him of the beauty of virtue.
>
> (*The Man of Feeling*. Mackenzie 1987 [1771], p.118)

The latter part of this is unclear – stylistically – but the overall point is obvious: Hume rides again, some 30 years on from the *Treatise*.

Of Miss Walton, whom Harley loves but does not – through ill fortune – marry, Mackenzie writes:

> Her beneficence was unbounded; indeed the natural tenderness of her heart might have been argued, by the frigidity of a casuist, as detracting from her virtue in this respect, for her humanity *was a feeling not a principle*: but minds like Harley's are not very apt to make this

> distinction, and generally give our virtue credit for all benevolence which is instinctive to our nature.[13]

The section which I have put in Italic is stunning: 'a feeling not a principle'. Here Mackenzie's writing seems to be a reverberation of Hume on the passions; an echo rather than a restatement. The trouble with Hume's 'passions' is that they might put under one umbrella great benevolence and unbridled lust.

One wishes that one could be as optimistic about benevolence and instinctiveness as is Mackenzie. And moral reasoning may from time to time involve us in 'casuistry': forms of life entail the production of **principles of action**, and casuistry seeks to resolve possible and actual conflicts between principles. The 'benevolence which is instinctive to our nature' cannot always be relied on.

We are all persons of feeling: we are also reasonable. So: moral reasoning obtains. It is not superseded by the passions, rather it moderates them. Even benevolence might go too far, and the over-generous person impoverish hirself.

The present writer is a 'casuist' in the sense of being one who expects 'humanity' and 'sentiments' to generate – under reason's moderations – *principles*. And principles go two ways: to command *e.g.* p 'Be charitable', and to censor p 'Do not commit fornication', p 'Do not yield to a seducer'. Pamela's **principle** in these respects was 'Be-very-prudent': and in her circumstances it was an excellent principle. 'Mr B's' sentiments were excessive: and – on occasion – Pamela's became so. Nevertheless she repulsed her suitor until he became a *proper* suitor: then – and only then – did she give rein to her sentiments. Anyone could understand this from reading *Pamela*. Hume included.

12.6 Hume's 'Precaution': Kant's 'Maxim'

Hume's 'virtue [is not] perceived by reason' is torpedoed by Kant's 'Act only on that maxim that you could at the same time will to become an universal law'. It is reason which must decide what maxim could become an universal law. That Hume's *principle* is the same thing as *maxim* seems self-evident.

Kant's whole system requires, in the first place that principles/maxims, (a) become clear to the putative agent of their employment, and (b) that the agent subject them to the critique of *universalizability.*[14]

---

[13] See Mackenzie, 1987 [1771], p.16. For an informative account of Mackenzie see *Capital of the Mind: How Edinburgh changed the World*, by James Buchan, Chapter 11, 'The Man of Feeling' (Buchan, 2003). The book contains a portrait of Mackenzie by Raeburn with a sharp remark by Buchan. Buchan also observes 'In [*The Man of Feeling*] '… incessant floods of tears … there are forty-three separate instances of weeping' (Buchan, 2003, p.306). Adam Smith's book on Moral Sentiments is much more sober. His *The Theory of Moral Sentiments* was published in 1759 (Our Hume here, 1739–1740) Smith's *The Wealth of Nations* was published in 1776: the year of a notable event in the whole future history of Capitalism!

[14] See Immanuel Kant, *The Groundwork of the Metaphysic of Morals* and *The Critique of Practical Reason,* any edition.

That – in a room full of Conference-going persons who have presumably all read Kant – one had to suffer through laborious papers on 'Getting an *ought* from an *is* – was one of the tedious things about being a teacher of philosophy. Kant sinks the question of '*ought* from *is*'. That he then raises other questions of his own is not unexpected. Consider the footnote to the previous paragraph of this essay. And recall Professor Hare's problem of the Nazi who might 'universally will' Nazi nastiness being inflicted on himself.

It is of course very 'Enlightenment' of Kant to hope that actual living agents can – in all sincerity – formulate the maxims of – pressingly urgent – actions. Self-deception has been around as long as humans have. Further: after Freud – name your favourite other theorists – the possibility of the Ulterior, the Unconscious, may in many cases obscure an agent's formulation of hir maxim. This is well known: but it is not to the point of the present essay.

Pamela's enunciation of her *principle* has – although it may seem naïve – the great virtue of being clear. In fiction – and possibly in real life – it could, as well, be effective.

12.7 Passion in Jane Austen: Marriage Among Gentlefolk

> It is a truth universally acknowledged… (Jane Austen: the first sentence of *Pride and Prejudice*)

…That Jane Austen offers more enjoyment to the judicious reader than do *Pamela* or *The Man of Feeling*. Had Austen read David Hume's, 'Reason is and ought only to be the slave of the passions…'[15] she would have found in it neither sense nor sensibility. 'What use would Hume's idea be to a serious novelist? None whatsoever!' Even a pornographer might find it excessive if the ambiguity of 'the passions' included the nastier ones.

In his *Becoming Jane Austen: a Life*[16] Jon Spence observes '[T]he old and abiding theme so central to Austen family thinking: [is] the conflict between reason and passion': The whole family were anti Humean whether they had read him or not. In the very first chapter, paragraph 10, of *Sense and Sensibility* we find, in the description of Elinor Dashwood:

> Elinor, the daughter whose advice was so effectual, possessed a strength of understanding, and coolness of judgment, which qualified her, though only nineteen to be the counsellor of her mother, and enabled her to counteract, to the advantage of them all, that eagerness of mind in Mrs. Dashwood which must generally have led her to imprudence. She had an excellent heart, her disposition was affectionate, and her feelings were strong: but she knew how to govern them: it was a knowledge which her mother had yet to learn, and which one of her sisters had resolved never to be taught. (*Sense and Sensibility* (Austen, 1811, Chapter I, paragraph 10))

[15] Cited above, Ref. *Treatise*, Part III, Section III (Hume, 1958, p.415); (Hume, 1985, p.462). In his 'Reason *is* and *ought* only to be…' one might feel that Hume is getting his *ought* out of his *is* at a considerable discount. Special rates for sceptics perhaps.

[16] *Becoming Jane Austen: a Life*, by Jon Spence, 2007, p.91.

It is to be hoped that the unnamed sister, who had resolved never to be taught, was never brought into the company of a James Boswell WS to whom 'Reason is and ought only to be the slave of the passions,' would be *carte blanche* for immoderate flirtation and plain venery. Austen does not use the word 'passion' in the passage quoted, but 'eagerness of mind' is coupled with 'imprudence': this is suggestive of Mrs. Dashwood's lacking the essential sensibility which her own daughter had. Elinor knows 'how to govern' feelings, and doubtless, passions.

In the first chapter of *Sense and Sensibility* the springs of the novel's action are named 'cold heartedness', 'selfishness' and – obliquely – avarice and niggardliness. All passions apt to lead to actions best avoided.

Jon Spence observes, justly:

> However much Austen's reticence and control of style may suggest otherwise, passion is the centre of Jane Austen's novels. The primacy of passion links *Pride and Prejudice* to the three novels of her later career. Fanny Price and Anne Elliot stake everything on passion and reject marriage to men to whom they feel no passion…

On the other hand:

> The heroines may validate their passion in a rational way by their respect for their lovers' moral character, and these qualities may be – like their social and financial positions – desirable in prudent, practical ways, but passion is always the animating factor in the heroines' decision to marry. (Spence, 2007, pp.103–104)

Austen by no means discounts passion – how could any novelist – but it does not run as wild as Hume would, perhaps, have us believe. Good sense governs the passions: this is 'sensibility' in Austen's idiom. Sensibility is passion in leading strings. If passion is strong wine, reason's soda water makes it a *spritzer*. Reason is not the slave of the passions, since sensibility includes reason. It is a great pity that Hume did not read *Pamela* or live to read Austen. Austen – as, later George Eliot – is a fair model of real life.

Sensibility is defined in the – Australian – *Macquarie Essential Dictionary* (ie the shorter one) in a positively Janeite way under sense 2, 'Sharpness of emotion and fine feeling'. Sense 1 was the – primitive – 'Quality of being able to appreciate and respond to complex emotional or aesthetic influences' – this itself is a refinement of the *root* notion of sensibility as the power to receive impressions from the world and persons about one. *The Oxford English Dictionary* says of the – fundamental – sense of 'sensibility' 'Capability of being perceived by the senses' that it is 'rare after the seventeenth century'. The OED gives the etymology of *sensibility* 'State of being capable of sensation' as Middle French from Old French, 1314. In the Online Etymology Dictionary of 2010 Douglas Harper gives the date of 1751 for the sense of, 'Sensibility: Emotional consciousness, capacity for higher feelings or refined emotion'. One gratefully acknowledges Harper. This although both the OED and *Robert* – the big one – give instances of the sense of 'sensibility' and *sensibilité* as slip-sliding as one might expect usages to.[17]

[17] As might be expected Diderot and J-J. Rousseau provide interesting uses of 'sensibilité'.

Where Jon Spence puts 'passion', meaning erotic passion we might put 'sensibility': 'Sense [good sensibleness] and Sensibility' present us with passion no longer wild but already house-trained. Hume's 'the passions' are moderated in the drawing-room to 'sensibilities'. Spence takes up Jane Austen's civilization of passion even as he writes 'passion(s)'.

When gentlemen carried swords, excessive politeness would guard against any passion-driven use of them. In most cases anyhow.

Like Pamela, Austen's heroines were faced with the task of finding suitable husbands. But they did not endure sexual harassment, and worse, as Pamela did.[18] Instead Austen models the lives of young women of sensibility and sense getting – or not – suitable men to marry. Mr. Darcy at best: at worst an Officer of the Navy or Army – and if that failed, a Clergyman of the Established Church.

There is a book on Jane Austen (Walker, 2017) of which I have read only reviews, which maintains that Jane had a teenage crush on D'Arcy Wentworth, a surgeon and occasional highway man who eventually emigrated to Australia. For a moment the real Jane looks like a character from a novel by Fielding. The surgeon-highwayman was – I think – one of the Wentworths who prospered considerably in New South Wales. Would Austen have ended up as the first – and best – Australian novelist? As it is, D'Arcy Wentworth is probably the man who gave Mr. Darcy his surname.

Had the young barrister Tom Lefroy, with whom Jane Austen seems to have been in love, married Jane before he went back to Ireland[19] – of which he later became Chief Justice – we might have had Anglo-Irish novels by Austen. These would have been haunted by the animosity which both native and many Norman-Irish had against *Albion perfide*. The novels which Austen wrote in England could not have had their present tone if penned in Éire.

12.8 Hume and the Passions on the Cusp of the Era of Sensibility

In many years I have, in the course of grading Ethics 202 essays, developed an animus against *le bon David* and his 'Reason *is* and *ought* only be the slave of the passions,' because dull undergraduates have taken this as an axiom sufficient to solve all ethical problems. The less dull have disappointed me by – if they reject the axiom on other grounds – not noting the tendentious '*is* and *ought*' in Hume's famous proposition. The logic of this *is* > *ought* might be defended as rhetorically proper to the case: but to let it slip by un-noticed has seemed to me lax.

[18] That in the lived world young gentlewomen might have been sexually harassed one don't doubt. But it is not Austen's style to have dwelt on this possibility. In *Pamela* it is the engine of the whole plot.

[19] See Jon Spence, 2007, pp.104–105; 110–*111*.

What one is entitled to say of 'Reason *is* and *ought* to be the slave of the passion' is that "passions" is too open: it covers a range of things, from benevolence to unbridled lust. And this Hume – a sensible skeptic – should have noticed. "Passions" should have been in some way qualified.

Hume was one supposes a man of sensibility himself: and should – then – have spoken up for sensibility, as firmly as he did for taste. Taste being after all sensibilities' first cousin. The challenge 'get an *ought* from an *is*' sets a useful task for undergraduate philosophers. However Kant sank it: and Literature from Austen to now shows both how the thing is done, and the bad consequences of not doing it. As for Hume's 'precaution': *ça va sans dire*. It's a done deal, done daily, as a matter of sense and sensibility.

12.8.1 Coda

Kant might not have insisted that we constantly and on each occasion of action avert to our maxims then attempt to universalize them. He could have settled for Aristotle's advice to develop good moral habits – 'tho Aristotle's virtue being the mean between two vices is simply too artificial: it don't work.

Since Kant there have been many books on moral reasoning, and this is not the place to name or summarize them. My intent has been merely to scotch Hume. Nobody really believes that reason ought only be the slave of the passions. Nobody? Well at the time of writing 2018, the Australian Royal Commission into the Banks reveals that some at least of our Bankers make reason the instrument of their devising devious ways of better serving the passion of avarice. They are absolute deplorables, robbing people of the savings of a lifetime, often. They foreclose on farmers whose fields are made barren by drought, calling-in loans that in normal times could be serviced. Then they undervalue the estates which they have now taken over and sell them for quick peanuts. This covers what the farmer has borrowed – the remainder of the loan – but may leave the erstwhile agriculturalists, zilch! This is on the public record: one sees snippets of the Commission on the TV news. How bad it is all over we shall discover when the Report is published. These bankers are not moral-reasoners of any kind. Jail would be a good place for them – they just might reflect on the reasons why they ended up there. The Report has now, 2019, been published, and things have been tidied up a bit. But no thieving Banker has ended up behind bars. Alas!

The world has always had decent moral agents and scoundrels. And most of us can tell the difference: one does not need to be a Royal Commissioner, but sometimes one wishes that one were. I would not recommend that *le bon David* be the Honourable Mr. Commissioner Hume, for all that he had been a minor diplomat, as a philosopher he pushes his contrarian notions too far. The present Commissioner is a man of icy cool, and quick mind. As is the young woman, a SC who asks the unaskable questions. The bankers seem driven by avarice and management principles – selling off a farm foreclosed on as soon as may be is called 'file churning'. Orwellian! And – as I say – reported on TV.

One cannot resist closing with a real example from life today: *The Sydney Morning Herald* 11 May 2018 ran the following headline, slightly redacted: 'Banker stole millions but Banco Poltrona let him go free'. Hume himself would have had no difficulty about getting *ought* from these two *facts*: a brace of *is*. No more difficulty than the Procurator Fiscal would have had. The Procurator Fiscal would have 'artificial but not arbitrary' rules of justice under which Mr. Ladro – the banker in question who stole the millions, and confessed to it – could have been arraigned. These 'artificial but not arbitrary' rules of Commercial Law seem, even *natural* to a person of a moral disposition. (I have cited Hume on 'artificial' v 'natural' and 'artificial but not arbitrary' above: from Hume's *Treatise* Part II, p. 484, Oxford edition; Penguin pp. 535–36.) The Procurator would have charged the complicit bankers who looked the other way at the theft of X million, for Criminal Conspiracy, or under some such Scots Law statute.

Should the appropriate Director of Public Prosecutions not act in this case, here in Australia, against Mr. Ladro and the Poltrona Bank's, employees and directors, s/he should be made to read again for a pass-mark in jurisprudence, the branch of legal studies which deals with *oughting* from *is-ing*. Jurisprudence is 'artificial but not arbitrary'. Moral principles may be various and variously named, from culture to culture – but are not arbitrary. Nor does any adult person taking Hume's *precaution* have much difficulty in getting hold of an appropriate *principle*.

Moral principles are to be looked for in a natural space between the weepy *The Man of Feeling* and the louche *Boswell's Journal*. Indeed in the – on the whole rather tedious – *Pamela*.

The Australian Royal Commission[20] looking into the dubious dealings of the banks discovered things which made my gorge rise – 'These fellows make me sick'. From 'made my gorge rise' and 'they make me sick', good examples of demotic English (or Scots) we may – without too much philosophical argument – learn that, in real life, reason and passion may come ready-made as an amalgam. Reason here tells us what to be cross about, and cross we become. When not in contentious mood, Hume might have noticed this for himself.

12.8.2 Envoi

In a *Non Sequitur* the splendid cartoonist Wiley has an elderly couple looking down a street of modest houses with real estate placards in their front yards: 'FORECLOSURE: For Sale'; 'FOR SALE BY BANK'; "FORECLOSED, FOR SALE' et cetera. One of the elderly couple is saying to the other, 'I miss the time when "Bank Robbery" meant people robbing banks' (Miller 2018).

[20] See 'Other People's Money' 2018.

References

Appiah, K. A. (2006). *Cosmopolitanism: Ethics in a world of strangers*. New York/London: W.W. Norton & Company.

Appiah, K. A. (2010). *The honor code: How moral revolutions happen*. New York/London: W.W. Norton & Company.

Austen, J. (1811). *Sense and sensibility*. London: T. Egerton, Whitehall.

Buchan, J. (2003). *Capital of the mind: How Edinburgh changed the world*. London: John Murray.

Hume, D. (1958 [1888]). *A treatise of human nature* (L. A. Selby-Bigge, Ed.). Oxford: Oxford University Press (Clarendon Press).

Hume, D. (1985 [1888]). *A treatise of human nature* (Ernest C. Mossner, Ed.). Penguin Classics.

Hutchings, P. (1965). What does 'good' tell me? *Ethics, 76*(1), 47–52.

Hutchings, P. Æ. (1972). *Kant on absolute value*. London/Detroit: George Allen & Unwin/Wayne State University Press.

Mackenzie, H. (1987 [1771]). *The man of feeling* (Brian Vickers, Ed.). Oxford/New York: Oxford University Press.

Miller, W. (2018, August 7). Non sequitur: 'I miss the time when "Bank Robbery" meant people robbing banks' [Cartoon]. *The Age*, p. 29.

Morson, G. S. (2018, February 8). The horror, the horror. *The New York Review of Books 65*(2).

Other people's money. (2018, July 21). *The Age: Good Weekend,* pp. 15–19.

Richardson, S. (1974) [1914]). *Pamela* (M. Kinkead-Weekes, Ed.). London/New York: Dent/ Dutton.

Spence, J. (2007 [2003]). Becoming Jane Austen: A life. London/New York: Hambledon Continuum.

Tolstoy. (1910). *Les pensées de Tolstoi*. Vol. I. *Pensée* No.370 (Ossip-Lourié, Ed.). Paris: Alcan.

Walker, W. (2017). *Jane and D'Arcy: Vol. I: Folly is not always folly*. McMahon's Point, Sydney: Arcana Gallery.

Wallace, D. F. (2012). *The pale king*. Penguin Books Australia.

Patrick Ælfred Fitz Gerald Hutchings was educated in Literature and Philosophy at the University of New Zealand and in Philosophy at University College, Oxford. He has lectured at the Universities of London, Edinburgh and California. He was Reader in Philosophy at the University of Western Australia and later at Deakin University. He taught the course 'The Philosophy of Art' at the University of Melbourne. He is Member of the International Association of Art Critics. His research interests are in literary criticism, philosophy of religion and aesthetics. He is an Editor of *Sophia*.

Chapter 13
Why Is There Nothing Rather Than Something? An Essay in the Comparative Metaphysic of Nonbeing

Purushottama Bilimoria

13.1 Part I

In the beginning, there was Neither Non-Being (asat) nor Being (sat)
– ṚgVeda X.129

The Big Q, and the Neglected '?'

Leibniz's oft-quoted Question reads '… [W]hy is there something rather than nothing, since nothing is easier than something?' Whatever the merits of the first

*This essay was originally published in the Special 50th Anniversary Issue Tribute to Max Charlesworth, *Sophia* vol 51, no 4, December 2012, 509–30. I thought it appropriate to include the essay as a chapter in this volume so as to celebrate the life and work of Max Charlesworth. This is a fitting tribute to the founding editor of *Sophia* and my mentor Prof. Max Charlesworth, as he taught me Aquinas and much of the Western disquisition on being and non-being I discuss herein. In the course of preparing study material and teaching courses in Philosophy of Religion in the years that I worked with him, I was faced with questions about being and nothingness. Charlesworth gave me my first university job! So my *karmic-ruṇas* are immense to this amazingly dedicated and unique master amongst us. See also note 10 below. I also like to thank Anand Vaidya of San Jose State University Comparative Philosophy Group for valuable critical comments to this version. I am also indebted to J. N. Mohanty, J. L. Mehta, Keiji Nishitani, J. L. Shaw, Wilhelm Halbfass, Morny Joy, and the late Bimal K. Matilal and Ninian Smart, for certain inspirations toward developing my thoughts on this metaphysic; I also have fond memories of conversations with Jack (JJC) Smart, especially his reading of Śankara's 'Māyā-Brahmanism' that he aligned to Bradley's Idealism (well, not quite so, as we'll see). A longer version of this paper was presented at 'Beyond the Possible: in Memoriam of Richard Sylvan' (ARC/Logic Group), July 2011, University of Melbourne; I am grateful to those present for helpful comments.

P. Bilimoria (✉)
School of Historical and Philosophical Studies, University of Melbourne, Melbourne, Australia

Graduate Theological Union and University of California, Berkeley, CA, USA
e-mail: p.bilimoria@unimelb.edu.au; pbilimoria@berkeley.edu

P. Wong et al. (eds.), *Considering Religions, Rights and Bioethics: For Max Charlesworth*, Sophia Studies in Cross-cultural Philosophy of Traditions and Cultures 30, https://doi.org/10.1007/978-3-030-18148-2_13

horn of the question – his principal concern and the only part represented in philosophical literature (cf. Kołakowski 2008, 144) – the flippant inclusion of the second horn has largely gone unnoticed. It is in part this rhetorical dismissal of 'nothing' – and all that comes under '*n*,' negation, nothing, non-entity, no-thing, non-existence, nullity, nihility, nihilism – that has led to the neglect of the importance of nothing-ness in philosophy proper, i.e., in the enterprise of philosophy extending from the historically retraced Greco-Hellenistic to Judeo-Christian roots and contemporaneously in analytical fields. This is the scenario, notwithstanding the increasing inclusion and recognition of 'nothingness' in Continental and Comparative philosophies, and in certain quarters of theoretical sciences, such as quantum mechanics, and naturalistic or Big Bang cosmologies contra Kalām cosmology. But the reverse question, albeit imitatively in bad faith, that I scandalously pose: 'Why is there likely Nothing rather than Something?' – echoing Heidegger's finalé, 'Why are there beings at all, why not rather nothing?' (Freiburg lecture, 1929) – like the radical thesis of Metaphysical Nihilism – is probably false, because trivially there is always something, or at least as a pervasive human perception that remains *prima facie* unfalsified, even if we feel justified in believing the obverse, as we are oft-times unjustified in believing what is, in fact, true. Hence, for one given to realism (in the Dummett-McDowell re-articulation), it would be difficult to provide truth conditions for an indefeasible deliverance of the cognitive contents of the proposition in question, short of warranted assertability, which is the way of anti-realism. But then the Davidsonian difficulty is also there for understanding (any) reality in terms of truth conditions. The epistemological embarrassment of realism leading to skepticism is however grist to the mill for a Nāgārjunian (whether Buddhist or broadly Indianist). A logical positivist might also retort that the very utterance of nothing/ness is a self-contradiction or too fuzzy (as Carnap charged Heidegger with on the telling passage we return to in Part IV). Although, one may as well note, Nāgārjuna (the second-century Indian-Buddhist dialectician) would not buy into this retort in his analogous claim that everything, including the claim he is about to pronounce – *that there is only ever emptiness* – (only just, though not quite, in parity with the Liar's Paradox about all Cretans) is not self-defeating: this utterance too therefore is empty, as is the retort. Hence, the self-erasing expression: emptiness is of emptiness too! We are for the most part held ransom to our concepts grounded in practices that constitute reality – reality of things – for us. Realism is no better for it. Thus, neither realism nor antirealism would be adequately suited to clinch the knowledge of Nothing were such to be the case, for that state would be prior to language and mind (being or not-being independent of the mind is not the issue). How things are, as Leibniz would concur, is distinct from how we investigate them: the principle of 'verification or falsification transcendence' – votes vis-à-vis pebbles. So why did Leibniz presume the unassailability of 'something' in his stock-taking question? Could the source of knowledge of nothingness be some kind of Heideggerian disclosedness (*Erscholossenheit*)? But that might be an even more embarrassing route for the non-metaphysicians or neo-metaphysicans among us. Nonetheless, this does not make our question any less philosophically *uninteresting*. Quite the contrary, particularly when we confront *this* 'Big Negative Q' in the cross-cultural currents as well.

Instructively, even though the Buddhists believed that the idea of self as *ātman* (mistranslated often as 'soul') of [pre-Hindu] Brāhmaṇism, as a permanently abiding entity, enduring presence, hence being, is a false belief to which there is no corresponding reality – being a conceptual-social construct, or as Hume would have put it, *constituted by our habits and practices* – and this imaginary in fact produces harmful effects – such as, ego, selfish desires, cravings, suffering, etc. It did not stop Buddhist and Indian philosophers from engaging in speculations as to what the Brāhmanical idea of self and various permutations of their own counter-doctrine of non-self might look like. '*In virtue of what counterfactual is the former doctrine false*?' might just pass the test, and you have the answer. I submit, there is no such clear non-trivial answer to the question I have paused contra Leibniz – 'Why is there likely Nothing?' – in the traditions I will draw from at least, for the quandary is perhaps on a par with Kant's imponderables, namely, 'God,' 'Freedom,' and 'Immortality'; being neither an *a priori* truth nor so warranted by empirical or epistemological investigations. One might look toward a metaphysical or conceptual argument nevertheless.

However, as will be clearer, I don't intend nothing/ness to be an entirely free-standing category in all respects and cases – that would be risking Metaphysical Nihilism (*Vernichtung*); rather I see its connection with thinking on 'zero' – the mother of all natural numbers, cardinal numerals and decimal (positive and negative) integers that Indian mathematicians (and possibly Chinese also around the same time[1]) are said to have first discovered and for which they used the same term '*śūnya*' as the Buddhists later called their insight into void/emptiness: *śūnya/ śūnyatā*. The Sanskrit symbol also registers the function of pure negation – as cognate to the negative copula (*nañ*, '*na*', '*niḥ*', or '*a*', as in *nāsti*, *niḥkāma*, *akārya*) – in Jaina, Buddhist, and later Nyāya logic, as well as in certain ontologies of non-existence and extinction, and frays into suggestive or at best speculative tropes that tend to arrest rather than affirm the inexorable *being-there* (*da-sein*), indefeasibly, of something/being.

Here, for heuristic purposes, I could well draw on the Converse Barcan conclusion (BFC): *if something x is such that it is possible that x does not exist, then it is possible that something x does not exist* $\Box\forall xFx \rightarrow \forall x\Box Fx$. At least the antecedent is plausibly true, and for the consequent one could appeal to possible worlds, or the Routley-Meinongian metaphysics of hyper-real non-existents via the *Noneism* thesis (Priest 2005). Tim Williamson (1998) derives the following (modified) conclusion by first pointing out the falsity of a crucial premise in BFC, which goes as follows, but does not fully refute the overall argument:

- If there exists an X that is possibly an F, then it is possible that there exists something that is an F.

[1] D.P. Chattopadhyaya (2006, 190) cites Jacob Needham as saying that the symbol of zero (0) was well established in India and Indo-China (via Buddhism) during the seventh to ninth century CE; while many principles of numerations were known in ancient Mesopotamia, the sexagesimal place-value order was mixed up with other principles for values below 60. The place value in China was decimal, not sexagesimal. The decimal place value was extensively used in the mathematics developed by *Āryabhaṭṭa* (b. 476CE), the author of *Āryabhaṭīya*; p. 190.

- If there is something that could have been such-and-such, then there could have been something that was such-and-such.
- (1) It is not possible that there exists an X that does not exist.
- (2) There does not exist an X that possibly does not exist. (modus tollens)
- (3) Everything that exists necessarily exists. (restating 2)
- (4) Everything that exists exists in every possible world. (restating 3)
- is false; it is only true if it seems: 1′) It is not possible that there exists an X that does not *possibly* exist. Wittgenstein, though he died issueless, has a possible non-existent child in some possible world; conversely, the river Inn is such that if no part of the earth's surface had ever been covered by water, nothing would have been it, so something is such that possibly nothing is it; the Inn could have been nothing in the sense that it might not have existed, as a non-existent possibilia.
- Also, in 3, 'contingency' is mistaken for 'necessarily'; everything that exist today, here & now, necessarily exists; but may not have 2 years ago, or in the future. How does it follow if I say, *I exist*, that *it is not possible that I do not exist.* (2,3)?
- And I would add: Richard Routley stamped his existence when he changed his name to 'Sylvan'; but neither Routley nor Sylvan exists necessarily now, nor in the future; except as a non-existent avatar of Routley-Sylvan in all possible worlds, noneistly (Sylvan via Routley 1966, 1976, 1980, 1997).

I might also want to bolster some insights from similar debates in compositional nihilism (the view that denies 'table' exists apart from the simples that are arranged table-wise[2]) fraying into indeterministic counterfactuals (e.g., in quantum mechanics, chancy probabilistic decision theories) wherein the universe we observe is thought possibly to come out of a pre-physical, lawless singularity (at $t = 1 \times 10^{-43}$ sec.) and reflects an indifferent, un-designed, grandly purposeless (except for local ends, mostly of survival) existence. Even though the improbability is higher than the probability (1 to zero) that the universe with random matter around and some meta-laws actually came about, i.e., creation actually happened, the universe appears to have emerged by way of 'natural selection, the blind, inconspicuous automatonic process which Darwin discovered,' with 'no purpose in mind' and without sufficient reason to impute a causal Agency outside of the process.[3] This is of course from the over-stewed Dawkins-Dennett rhetoric, but it has some heuristic value for my argument here, because it echoes some possibilities within ancient Vedic cosmologies and quantum mechanics informed by the uncertainty principle, etc., as illustrated in the Smith-Craig-Oppy debate (Bilimoria 2011a[4]).

[2] For a critical discussion, see David Grimes (2010): http://forums.philosophyforums.com/threads/compostional-nihilism-41359.html

[3] See, R. Dawkins (1988) p. 5; Dawkins elaborates: 'The basic idea of *The Blind Watchmaker* is that we don't need to postulate a designer in order to understand *life, or anything else in the universe*' (147; italics added); really his 'basic idea' is nothing more than just shameless assertion.

[4] This debate will be treated of in more detail in a subsequent paper; the 2011 paper merely gives an outline.

Thinking about Nothing has its own charms and challenges, as do the traditions that have bothered to engage with this im/probability in the many permutations and nuances that have inflected this terrain: cashed in terms, such as of non-existence, non-existent, non-being, negation, nihility, *ex nihilo*, and even certain ways of talking about contingency, fictionalism, etc. Here, from the West, I would include Aquinas because he, albeit momentarily (in his third 'proof' toward the cosmogenic necessity), pondered on the radical contingency of the created universe and therefore its likely non-existence at some time in the remote past or in the future (Charlesworth 1970a; Kenny 1969, 66), as did Nietzsche, Heidegger, and their Continental cohorts from very different angles. So did the eighth-century doyen of Indian philosophy, Śaṅkara, while seriously considering the Nāgārjunian question of why the process of 'superimposition' (*adhyāsa*) of the imaginary (the illusions, *mithyā*, our world is made of) could not occur on an 'empty' (*śūnya*, non-abiding, universally self-negating) substrate (Bilimoria 1997, 2017). They all moved on because of the stark threat of nihilism: nonetheless, none have found it that easy, or 'easier,' to think nothingness, unless of course one takes 'something' as a given and for granted – then tautologically all that one needs to ask is 'what can we say of x?' 'What is it for something to be?' But suppose – as Descartes in the West and Śaṅkara, again, and Nāgārjuna to Vasubandhu in India entertained – we encounter through a thought experiment that 'something x' might only be there by virtue of some grand deception, which itself is a figment of another grander deception, interdependently (*pratītyatva*), as in a fictitious rumour, and so on and so forth. Would it not behoove us to chase that 'something x' all the way, beyond the very last turtle, into the abyss of an inexplicable nothingness even as it – shadows of 'something x' – recedes into oblivion and its existence, much less self-existence, can no longer be assured; indeed, also all inferences to its necessity begin to sound hollow [as Aquinas stared into, but only for a frightful moment, before turning his gaze back upon the altar (Charlesworth 1970b); as did also Śaṅkara, whose gaze turned on the elusive Concept – of which no greater or smaller could be thought – he named, again, 'Brahman,' before taking voluntary enlightenment, *samādhi-maraṇa* in the Himalayan peaks at age 36]. At best it might lend us a presupposition forced upon a shaky recognition of the utter contingency, even more radically, an-nihilism (noting), of 'something x,' since it was not there really to begin with except as a figment in some fanciful imaginary, or supposed logical necessity, against the grain of that of which no smaller could be conceived. Why is there such a rush to 'save appearances' (Bilimoria 1995; van Fraassen 1980, 4) and to rescue radical contingency from slipping away from perceived reality with no possibility of its return? Here the law of causation (efficient, material, samuttva) and the appeal to sufficiency of reason, which make us press the question of its origination, look like they are breaking apart into 'laws of casualty,' play of *māyā* – in Śaṅkara's words '*tuccha iva*' – 'a trifle husky, as it were' (or in the Sartrean sense of contingency; elsewhere: casual chance, infinitesimal probabilities, or some in-authentic victim of non-originative construction, fictionalism, hence im/probability).

But what, then, is nothing? Is it the mere absence of something whose presence is in doubt as in common understanding, or 'absence' of that as missing in the locus where it should or might have been, as in Nyāya-Prābhākaran epistemology of anupalabdhi (turned into *abhāva*)? '*Abhāva*,' however, to Kumārila (of the Mīmāmsā school) meant the *sui generis pratiyogin* or counter positive mark that each and everything taken to exist comes, as it were, stamped with, i.e., its own absolute negation, *niḥsvabhāva*, which inheres as an indelible signature, a subreptive potentia until actualized, e.g., in *dhvaṃsa*, destruction, or *mṛtyu*, death (Bilimoria 2008a, 55; 2016). My contention here is that the erstwhile Leibnizian question cannot be thought about at the expense of or outside of the challenges and range of possibilities that nothingness opens up or might provide: it is a *sine qua non* of the centrally taken question, as Heidegger rightly pointed out in alerting us to one of the major mistakes of Western civilization: its obsession with the 'metaphysics of presence': the notion that something is always present. To think nothing/ness is then not an indulgence in vain, nor is it really any easier than the thinking about some-thing. Thus, it is a challenge worthy of philosophical consideration. It invites itself, or ought – just as death and the astonishing loss of a loved one – to be engaged or indulged in precisely because it is philosophically challenging, and not easy at that.

Patrick Hutchings (2009) has skillfully and with dexterous wit argued in his review of Leszek Kołakowski that the grand Leibnizian Q: 'Why is there Something rather than Nothing?' may be a trifle over-determined and may have been intended to portend the enquiry in a particular direction: not unlike the submotivation of the so-named Ontological Argument, which Hutchings christens as the tautological argument (480). One might even suspect that it is a throw-away question. So why not begin with the counternegative (*nāstitva-pratiyogin*)?

Well, that is how it would appear from certain other horizons and the multi- perspectives the present disquisition draws upon: not just this particular question or its unique enframement, but rather along with it also the history of ideas and preoccupations with the haunting specter of 'being/Being/self-existence' – what has become fashionable to call 'onto-theology' after Kant, for whom it was the attempted, though in the end flawed, 'way of trying to apprehend God by way of being: as the *highest* being, the *original* being, and the *being* of all being' (Hart 2004: 54). The Enlightenment threw out God (the consequent), but not the antecedent (being) – until Heidegger set to ravage its pretensions, but himself became preoccupied with establishing a metaphysics of *being* as the universal ground of all temporal being (a question I return to later). This of course notwithstanding – though a Kyoto School philosopher may take some solace from it – the occasional nausea that the quizzical second term wondered about in the converse (*subaltern*) question would arouse as the only alternative if radical contingency and im/probable chance work their way to the end (or the beginning, and in between other mortalities), more markedly in non-analytical strains (the anti-logocentric rhetorics of Nietzsche, early Heidegger, Sartre, Derrida; Hegel and Schopenhauer lured by the self-sublating N-factor in Eastern thought) (Bilimoria 2008b, 2010). The alternative attitude that I wish to press for here begins with a subversion of the grand Leibnizian Q. With a little indulgence in and from classical Indian (and *en passant* Chinese thought), I wish to demonstrate that this indeed is the first quiver in their (Eastern) cosmological enquiry. The foregoing in turn set the framing intuition of metaphysics in Indian philosophical thinking and determined the many developments and trajectories that would witness the emergence of, on the otherwise complacent poly-panentheistic[5] Brāhmaṇic altar, a ritual epistemology of negation and absence (Mīmāṃsā); in the forest-ashrams, the disturbing doctrine of māyā: universal illusionism supplemented with *neti neti* 'not this, not that' (*via negativa,* from Upaniṣads to Śaṅkara): And, on the Sylvan side, the Jaina logic of *syādvāda* (seven-step of˙ relativized 'maybe-maybe-nots')' *anekāntavāda* (distributive truth) of naked gymnosophists; in the Nalanda Universities, the Navya-nyāya logico-linguistic doctrine of *nañvāda* (serial negations) (Matilal 1968, 1981, 1998); and last but not least, the damning Buddhist critique of substantial self-existence (*svabhāva*), intrinsicality of essences, denial of the self, deities and deistic god. All that seemed left after the sacrificial smoke whispered into empty space is the two-truths doctrine corresponding to Emptiness (*Śūnyatā*) and 'inter-co-dependent origination of conventional reality': [*samvrti-pratītya-samutpāda* variously interpreted). This in turn is checked by the Four-cornered Logic (*catuṣkoṭi*) that the doyen of Nothingness in Indian philosophy, Nāgārjuna, so devastatingly used in deconstructing pretenses to Absoluteness of any kind, so it would seem, once and for all (Inada 1970; Garfield 1995; Bilimoria 2017). The more Daoist among Chinese thinkers perhaps anticipating the Buddhist alternative led themselves to accept the critical adage 'all being (*you*) is born of non-being (*wu*),' and the advice 'therefore let there always be non-being so we may see their subtlety' added further strings of nothingness to the already extended conjunctive disjunctions: +*being-and-non-being-and-non-being-and-being* + (Lao 1963, Chap. 40). (For all a Daoist would care, as with 11th-dimensional Super-Strings, the additions on both ends could regress as if in Cantorian parallelism *ad infinitum*) (Chen 1969). The huge price, for trading in Buridan's [Mongolian] ass, paid though was a rather grievous one. Daoism survived mostly underground, especially into the modern era; Buddhism was driven out of India and gained its strength elsewhere in Asia, later in Europe too; although comparable post-secular a/theologies with rebounded Heidegerrean anxieties, Sartrean angsts, continue to list strong following in the wohalls of postmodernism, in the likes of Caputo, Hart, and Mark C. Taylor (2007) et al. I shall return to Heidegger and the Postmodern in Part IV.

13.2 Part II

Being *sans* Non-Being of the Classical West over the Rest

From the afore-outlined perspective, a suspicion begins to gnaw at the heart of Western philosophies' preoccupation, at least since Father Parmenides shattered into perplexity the familiar understanding of what 'is' and 'is not,' with the thesis

[5]On Indian Panentheism, and possibilities of Nothingness within that framing theology, see Bilimoria and Stansell (2010), 'Suturing the Body Corporate (Divine and Human) in the Brāhmaṇic Traditions,' Special Issue on Panentheism and Panpsychism, *Sophia*, (Springer) vol 49 No 2, pp. 237–259; see also Levine (1994).

that only being is, that non-being is not, and that there is no becoming and change (Halbfass 1992,1). The question over which the battle is fought is verily the question of *being*: what is; i.e. existent, quiddity and what it means to be something simple, identifiable, and available for objective discovery and control. 'Plato initiated the move toward – what Heidegger called a "productionist metaphysics" – by transforming the question of Being into beingness: a transcendent or permanently present form (*eidos*) that makes things possible' (Hicks 2003). 'Aristotle expanded this productionist attitude by arguing that for something "to be" meant [it] to be the effect of some cause, and "causing" meant to work upon something, to effect it, to make it' (ibid). And so Aristotle invents a science that investigates being as being, and what belongs to it according to its nature. This first philosophy comes to be known as ontology, the science of being in general, and metaphysics, the science of the universal being. 'Aristotle's phrase,' however, '*on hēi on*,' 'being as being,' is as suggestive as it is ambiguous, and his ontology is deeply aporetic' (Heidegger 1929, 1993, 2–3; Doolan 2012; Hart 2004, 55). The concept of being is marked with shakiness, and there is elusiveness of its supposed part-whole 'compositional unity,' universality, differences within, between *per accidens, per se, ens/esse* versus *ousia* (*L. essentia*), and *per potentia*. Since it has no predicables that would encompass all of the above 'properties' and markers, and is neither a concept nor a genus, being qua 'existence' remains indefinable. By the time of Plotinus and neo-platonism, being and nonbeing are transcended in the mystical experience of the One (*to hen*); the theistic philosophies of Judaism, Christianity, and Islam forge a relationship between metaphysics and theology in their quest for the '*highest being*.' Passing through refinements in Latin and Arabic languages, especially in the distinction hedged between essence and existence, the integration is complete with Thomas Aquinas' "*analogia enti*" of divine and dependent beings on the one hand and his twofold correlation of the finite entities with 'universal being' (*esse commune*) and the divine 'subsistent being' (*esse subsistens*) on the other (Heidegger 1996, 4). In other words, as Heidegger notes: 'In medieval times, God became identified with the Being of entities and was depicted – on the Aristotelian principle that beings are inexorably linked with cause – as an all-powerful causal agent who planned, calculated, and produced 'the relatively stable and independent presence' of entities' (ibid). Heidegger continues: 'In *Metaphysics*, Avicenna (ibn Sīnā, 980–1037) sums up the plague of being infecting this period rather perspicuously:

> Existence becomes a problem when the possibility of non-existence is taken seriously. But contingency, or the possibility of non-existence, was not regarded as an ultimate fact by the Greek thinkers…It was in the context of a theistic philosophy, a doctrine of creation, among the Jewish, Christian and Mohammedan thinkers of the Middle Ages, that the question of contingency, and therefore, of existence became acute…The discussion of existence, then, emerges from an earlier condition of thought in which the existence of things is taken for granted and the problem of being is the problem of what really is as opposed to merely apparent, or what is permanent as opposed to what is transitory.' (ibid, 5)

Although a sweeping generalization, the equivocation over existence, in various permutations and pairing of *essentia* with *ens/esse, quidditas* with *actus essentiae*, 'real' and 'apparent,' is patent. In its further development with Wolff, it is noted that *being* ('ens') is defined as what is possible, that is, compatible with existence: *quod possiblile est, ens est.* Existence itself is a mere supplement to the essential possibilities, a 'complementum possibilitatis.' But why would it not occur to these contemplatives in togas and priestly frocks that non-being is the state they identify as '*complementum possibilitatis*' and only that the supplement 'existence' has not yet been added to it; in that sense it is metaphysically *noneist*, a bare *possibilia.*

Nevertheless, being survives and is developed further in Eckhart, Wolff, and Descartes, who at least grounded being as 'what can be presented to the cognizing subject as indubitable': the spiritual substance René deemed to be the *mind* over the entitive body, the super-being, God, over the mechanical world. With Kant, the tight hold on being begins to loosen and lag – consider the elusiveness of thing-in-itself (a limiting concept at best, or perhaps a pointer to the 'unknown') as he shifts focus to the analysis of pure understanding; conditions for the possibility of knowing *sans* Cartesian certitude rather than trying to prove what exists, even as he shatters the spurious predication of existence to essence ('God's essence is to exist'), for 'Being' is obviously not a real predicate; that is, it is not a concept of something that could be added to the concept of a thing (Phillips 2006:154). The Cartesian turn to certainty with Kant's quest for pure knowing spurs phenomenology, which by the time of Husserl calls for *epoché*, bracketing out all ontological assumptions and metaphysical commitments in the more or less intentional and later hermeneutical account of understanding.

Think of the short step from Husserl's phenomenology to Heidegger's ideal of *Dasein* (humanly *be-ing* there) making its own authentic existence as a supplement (*complementum*) out of the remnant *possibilitatis* suggested in Greek philosophy and after. Here being – "to be" – recalls, retrospectively, and portends, prospectively, its own noneist statis in the thrownness-onto-death, the great leveler of all actualizations. So 'what is there?' ("to be") for Heidegger becomes: 'What would its absence (non-abiding presence) be like ("to be not")?'

Quine, on the other end, characteristic of the analytical mood, chose to deal with the question: 'What is there?' differently. It can be answered, he said, in a word, to wit: 'Everything.' (Borges (2000) goes a bit further: 'Everything and Nothing.') But what is existent is ultimately defined as 'the value of a bound variable,' i.e., as an existential commitment in given bodies of discourse that provide by semantic quantification a meaning to what we and others say – *one, some, all.* But the standard Quinean ontology also has us accept the existence of abstract objects – of mathematics (numbers, functions, sets, etc) – hence the Quinean ontological method leads to a form of, at best Platonist nominalism, at worse, fictionalism; indispensable to realism? (Price 2009a, b, 349; D'Amato 2013). To be, for Wittgenstein, on the other hand, appears as a word with 'odd jobs' and deceptive functional analogies with 'full verbs' that have misled philosophers into false depths. There is some relief in contemporary metaphysics where there is an attempt to pin down what *really exists*, as it grounds existence in theorizing on fundamentals, simples, nominals, and compositional nihilism, but by and large turns on cashing out ontological commitments in sentences describing the world; the existents are given in semantics, or in Armstrong's words, 'the real existents are the *truthmakers* for the true sentences of

English' (1997: 2010) (even if there are no great giants in India, and it is the case that except in California giants/Giants are never worshipped – i.e., true just in virtue of counterexamples, false-makers, not existing (Lewis 1999: 204), Bigelow's modification not withstanding). Not too dissimilar was the Nyāya project of developing a semantically saturated theory in which ontology is relegated to a second-order reference, while the semantically relevant elements are given prominence, so that, e.g., properties have pleonastic abstract function (Ganeri 2008: 108) indicated by '*-tva*,' or *–ta* –ness, –hood, which stand in place of simple predication on primitive nominals. Thus, the sentence 'the pot has black handle' is reparsed as 'black-handleness located in the pot' (or 'pot qualified by black-handlehood'); 'the tree exists' might well read as 'existence-hood possessed by the tree;' likewise, 'the dog is missing' as 'absent-ness of the dog;' 'God does not exist' as 'existence-hood [$\Diamond\exists xFx$] is lacking in the concept "God."'

13.3 Part III

The Ancient Indian Existential Quiddity

> Whence this creation has arisen – perhaps it formed itself, or perhaps it did not – the one who looks down on it, in the highest heaven, only he knows – or perhaps he does not know. (Concluding verse in ṚgVeda X.129)

It is not that terms for being/to be and their supplements have been conspicuously absent in Indian thought. We have *as/asti* equivalent to Latin *est* (English *is*, etc.), *and bhū/bhavati, sat, satya, sattva, sattā, sambhava*, and so on, and correlate terms for essence as well, *tattva, guṇa*. But by and large these trump the abstraction over ontological commitment of any serious kind. As in the epics, there was no belief in language being the mirror of nature or reality; the same language could be prevalent in a dream world as well, in numerous possible [modal] worlds, arbitrary conceptual schemes, or in the nebulous world of the gods (indeed Sanskrit was thought be language of the gods), as also in artificial or 'plastic' language, such as in aesthetics. However, in the first-order language, the term that appears most preeminently is the negative contraposition of the above existentials, mainly, *asat*, *abhāva* (non-being, not-to-be, absence). Thus, here I must bring in the time-honored hymnal verse, which I believe is largely responsible for wrecking many a major schism and confusion within the three millennia career of philosophy in India: think of Brāhmaṇism, Śrāmaṇism (Stoics), Ājīvakas (Sophists), Jainism, Buddhism, the various schools of classical Indian philosophy (including Cārvaka, hedonist-materialist), redolent of what Hegel called negativistic-conceptualism (not entirely correct) or nihilism in Nietzschean reading of Buddhism (Bilimoria 2008b, 2017), to the contemporary revivalist interest in paraconsistent logic modeled in part on Buddhist-Jaina-Nyāya logic (Garfield and Priest 2003). We may also make mention of their contributions to mathematics, astronomy, and, more recently, Sanskrit serving as a link-language, especially with its loan digit of zero and null sets, in a variety of computational binary languages used widely in software developments in Silicon Valley and in India.[6]

Going back to around 1500 BC, the ṚgVedic sage ponders: 'In the beginning there was Neither Non-Being (*asat*) Nor Being (*sat*), neither night nor day...what was there, bottomless deep? ' (X.129). As in Manichean thinking, where a certain amount of mythos and poetic license is built into such truth-pondering hymn, 'In the beginning' ("In the Beginning was the beginning... *ever so*": *yuge prathame purvye yuge asataḥ sadajāyata*) makes an oblique reference to whenever it, the unmanifest (*ajāyataikam yathāpūrvamavyakta*), the unmanifest (*avyakta)* and manifest cosmos (*bṛhatividadhat, viśvasṛṣṭi*), might have, or might not have, begun, or worse, even ever have been, for what can possibly come out of the 'bottomless deep,' *ex nihilo* – the infinitesimal continuum of empty space-time? This marks the radicality of contingency at its best. There is no suggestion of the necessity of being, "to be". True to its letter, that would be one insightful rendering of *ex nihilo nihil fit*. Even time (*kāla*) and space (*antarikṣa*/*ākāśa*/*dyaus*), heat (*tejas*, *retas*, *tapaḥ*), and the law, truth (*ṛta, satya, dharma)* governing the order, sun and moon like the gods, the highest witness-bearing God (*asyādhyakṣaḥ sarvajñānadhātā*) in heaven too, (*sūryacandramasau pṛthivī divam jajāna akalpayat)* the highest witness-bearing God (*asyādhyakṣaḥ sākṣisarvajñānadhātā*) in heaven too, came after it all began – again, if at all – the sages are not quite sure, but hope in the heavens – as the rock-group Talking Heads sing, 'the space wherein nothing happens' – that the universe did happen and will continue, otherwise what will ensure their own survival and an hereafter following their impending mortality at the hands of the dark god Yama: the annihilator of all that is being? Total annihilation is though always the threat, as Heidegger's thrownness-into the abyss of death (*mṛtyaveḥ*) also portends.

life of love-death of love-life in death[7]

Why is there this fear of being becoming non-being, rather than it being endlessly, timelessly around or at least moving into becoming (x, y, z..the contingent/transient/chancy world)? (cf. Kakol 2009). Alternatively, why not combine the triadic trinity of being/nothing/becoming in the *highest being*, the transcendent, arguably as in Śaṅkara's Brahman – which Hegel fearfully noticed as being redolent of trifling 'Nature,' or 'God-in-Nothingness,' despite his own idea of *Weltgeist* – and Heidegger's grand vision of *Being*-in-Time? Precisely because the spectre of *asat*, non-being as non-existence (some are happy to render as Nothingness), loomed rather large on the Indic horizon; and note also that logically the hymnal verse begins with a double-marked 'N-factor (bi-negation): Neither/nor' (not, as in Kierkegaard, Either/Or), a logical quiver that the Jaina and Buddhist philosophers

[6] Quite a few of the 'start-ups' were initiated by expatriate Indian trained IT engineers. Could it be that the Indian mind has grown used to thinking in multiple terms of null spaces and multiplications that involve zeros more than any other digit? (Bilimoria 2012b)

[7] See Bilimoria (2011b) 'Grief and Mourning: for Renuka', lecture for Existentialist Society, Melbourne, September 2011, updated pdf at www.pbilimo.com; also under slightly different title in Bilimoria 2012a, p. 172.

developed with great skill into reasoning (*naya*) based on sevenfold-aspect predication (*saptabhaṅgī*) along with *syādvāda* (fuzzily 'maybe-maybe-not-ism') and four-cornered bi-negation dialectics, respectively – a sort of radical negative metaphysics. 'Neither this nor that' into: 'neither is nor is-not': $\neg (p \vee \neg p)$; this, using Nāgārjuna's stock example, translates as 'something, say, self neither is nor is it not;' 'i.e. neither of both disjunctive conjuncts; is there *ever* a self?' in the earlier Mīmāṃsā version with denial of the positive and negative conjunct (*prasajya-pratiṣedha-paryudāsa*) as well, it can be formalized as: $\neg(M \wedge \neg M) \vee \neg (M \vee \neg M)$. Puzzling. Indeed, how can one assert something is not and then disown what you just denied? And there is no retraction either to the originary position; double negation and conjuncts thereto do not collapse disjunctively (a sort of ontological nihilism with the possibility of transcendence as its underbelly; [Matilal 1968; J L Shaw correspondence]). Take his second example: your existing now is caused by itself (p), it is caused by other ($\neg p$); both by itself and other ($p \wedge \neg p$); neither by itself or other ($\neg p \vee \neg \neg p$), nor is it that you are not caused ($p \vee \neg p) \wedge (p \vee \neg \neg p$) does anything where-ever arise? (So none of the above!) (Bilimoria 2016, 2017).

To be sure, debate has raged ever since as to whether the intent here, particularly in the fourth premise, the neither/nor formulation, was to reject the law of non- contradiction (violation of the basic Aristotelian prerequisite for logical thinking) or simply bypassing it and setting aside instead the excluded middle and leaving it fallow as a still-born paradox. It may not worry our Priest either way as it did not worry the Vedic and Buddhist priests for it was their way of acknowledging and recognizing the persistence and work, one might say, of Nothingness in ontological and cosmological realities. The ontological commitments in their truth-making neither supervened on semantic consistency nor on anything given as such in perception or bodily sensations. Such am-bi-valences led European philologists and philosophers, such as Max Müller and Herder and Hegel, closer to our millennium, to adjudge these to be musings or at worse babblings of an infantalizing culture whose sense of logic is no better than that of a desperate robber risking breaking into a house and setting off the alarm by the same stroke, or Nietzsche's madman coming down from the mountains with a lit lantern in broad daylight purportedly looking for God. It also worried Karl Jaspers, who would not go as far as to say, as did Nietzsche, that this is nihilistic but, in so far as all differentiations rather than a decision being taken between opposites as in Parmenides, this negative logic that culminates in Nāgārjuna's deconstructive dialectic 'prepares the way, not for a positive insight developed in logical terms, but, for a silence filled with another source. Here all reasoning annuls itself' (Jaspers 1962, 1969). These were 'illogical times.' Jaspers is wrong as he does not see or appreciate that Nāgārjuna is appealing to the same logic of *reductio ad absurdum* that Indian logicians, the Jainas especially, before him had been using against Brāhmaṇical thinking that moved away from the Ṛgvedic doubts (Bilimoria 2017; Bosley 2003).

Wilheim Halbfass (German-American philologist who taught at Penn in the US until his premature death in 1999) remarks that 'Ṛgveda X.72 and a variety of other sources (e.g. Atharvaveda X.2.28; *BṛhUp* II.1-2) up to and beyond *Chāndogya Upaniṣad* (ChUp III, 19) teach that nonbeing (*asataḥ*, *nāsadīya*), 'was' in the beginning and that *sat* (being) arose from nonbeing. The reference to ChUp is apposite here as the verse in question that Halbfass (1992) invokes a little earlier reads as follows:

> In the beginning, my dear, this world was just Being (*sat*), one only, without a second. To be sure, some people say, 'In the beginning this world was just Nonbeing (*a-sat*), one only, without a second: from that Nonbeing Being was produced' [Ṛgveda X.72]. But verily, my dear, whence could this be? ... How from Nonbeing could Being be produced. On the contrary, my dear, in the beginning this world was just Being, one only, without a second.

This is not representative of Vedic [and Brāhmaṇa] thought; yet it acknowledges there were prior views according to which nonbeing was the origin of 'this world.' This theory not only precedes the Upaniṣadic doctrine, 'but constitutes its indispensable background and counterpart.' As Halbfass goes on to note, 'this elusive and discarded cosmogony from nonbeing is of great significance for the beginnings of Indian thought about being. In a sense, it is more fundamental than the "theory of being"...' (ibid: 26). Nevertheless, it is arguable whether the theory of the origin from *asat* (notably Ṛgveda X.72) should be interpreted as a creation from nothing (*creatio ex nihilo*) and 'that the binary of *sat/asat* should be taken as 'existence' and 'non-existence' in an abstract sense. It might be an anachronism to credit the Vedic authors with an abstract notion of existence (and non-existence). Abstraction is not the point. Cosmogony is a story of how the universe came into existence, or into its present state of being, out of what, what irreducible substrate or remainder thereof. It answers the same sort of question that was asked by the Pre-Socratics, such as Thales, Anaximander, and Anaximenes (ibid, 28).

Moving on, coupling the Vedic insight with the peculiar theory of causality adopted in Indian philosophy, *satkāryavāda,* according to which the effect preexists in the cause, then in a sense the Chāndogya suspicion is right; how can being come out of nonbeing if it is not already in its cause (presuming that there is no interventionist God standing outside of the configuration as in the Biblical cosmogony)? The Chāndogya rejection of Vedic cosmogony from 'nonbeing' as *creatio ex nihilo* would go through, or alternatively the satkāryavāda theory itself would have to be rejected, as it was in some later schools, and the debate was reduced to disagreement concerning the semantics of *sat* and *asat.* Even Śaṅkara, as we noted earlier, entertains the possibility of illusion being, fictionally projected onto 'nonbeing" (*śūnyatā*) in deference to the prevalent Buddhist view (notably the noetic-presentification of Yogacāra-Cittamātra-Vijñānavāda), but then quickly retracts, arguing that it is improbable that such a process of superimposition/transference could go through in the absence of a concrete substrate, and this process (*asadiva*, BSB II.1.17), short of naming it as Brahman, the 'highest being' (that stands at some distance from any involvement with the contingencies of the world hence *akarthṛtva*), he calls inexplicable (*anirvacanīya*), some mystery, not an Absolute primordial given as such; in Upaniṣadic adage:

> *yato vāco nivartante aprāpya manansā saha*: the mind with speech turns back unable to break through [on to the other side].' (In a lesser prosaic tell-tale, one cannot but help recall: 'Hanumān, off to swallow the sun and all that lies beyond that giver of universal light (*agni, tejas, diva, tirohita*), traversing through curving space and what he found to be unending

time, not eternity, reaches a cul-de-sac in his singular-*iti* pursuit; of which he is then not sure whether it is the beginning or the end-point of all that he beholds receding behind him. That *bindu*-blib seemed smaller than the 420th [*chār-soo-bis*] part of the hair-end on Rāvaṇa's balding ten-headed scalps: to keep going in the seemingly infinite abyss of emptiness into which the universe is said to expand (*ekārnavata*), or return back to the securer pristinely best forest by Ayodhyā – that is the question that overcame him. He turned back, alas!' (Dialogue with Ramubhai Gandhi, IICbar, Lodi, Delhi, Feb 2007).)

We have not been able to make much of this curious trope, save to suggest that perhaps there is an acknowledgement of the continuity of nonbeing – in the Chāndogya sense of unevolved, undifferentiated non-being – within the process and the illusion itself: the fictional appearance of the world.

Consider the parallel hymn where the creation of the universe is attributed to a grand sacrificial process (*havih, devānām Puruṣamedha, Ṛg*X.90.16): sacrifice sacrificed sacrifice to itself, and out of this sacrifice arose gods (*astau devāḥ*); the gods in turn sacrificed the great being (*puruṣa*, the would-be progenitor), and out of this arose the four quarters of the universe. Here there is no suggestion of a pre-existent substantial substrate in a simple nominal form; for sacrifice is an abstracted episodic act – at best a verb-form (*kriyā*) 'performing Wittgenstein's 'odd job'" – which it performs upon itself and no other. The gods (*devatās*) emerge effervescently from the mantra-suffused smoke, and they too have to carry out a further sacrificial act for the cosmic progeny to arise. In a much later apocryphal hymn a four-headed god, Brahmā, the cosmic architect or demiurge-to-be, singularly finds himself in what could be described as his first moment of animated breath, seated on a lotus flower, with a certain self-reflexivity, wondering whereforth have 'I,' the strangeness of being, arisen from, by what necessity, for all he beholds around him is a wide, unending open placeless space (*ākāśa/dik*), extending infinitely in all directions, possibly looping into a curve had he a whiff of *qua* GTR (General Theory of Relativity). He thence decides to sink down the lotus stem perchance he could discover the truth-clincher of his own origin, in a 'heard word'(*śruti*) even if authorless; he travels through dark inanimate anti-matter, hollow grids, Ayer's NDE-tunnel, gurgling waters, and ends up being confronted with an idea, a concept, a whispering trope, that emanates from within his inquisitive mind, only to tell him that he, Brahmā, is a figment of the imagination of the mind in which this idea is lodged. Try as much as he would, the intellect (*mahat-buddhi*) he tries to climb up as well recedes into intersecting spiral web of further memes-like ideas, with much chattering logic holding them together, but beyond that he ends up nowhere in particular. He is just an idea, a sublime phantasm. All this, he finally declares, must be the work of nonbeing. One is reminded here of Borges' (2000) ingenious character, tormented by his own emptiness and lack of soul-identity, finally hears God's answer to his Q: 'Neither am I anyone; I have dreamt the world as you dreamt your work, my Shakespeare, and among the forms in my dream are you, who like myself are many and no one.'[8] (Cf. "I'm everything, even as I'm nothing", Sāyana.)

[8] Jorge Luis Borges (2000) *Labyrinths* (Penguin Books), trans. J.E. Irby (I am thankful to Amelia Barili from UC Berkeley for drawing my attention to this forgotten exquisite storyline!)

It is little wonder that the term for being '*sat*' is often nuanced, in derivative combinations, to yield 'truth' as in *satya,* reality (Gandhi's *satyāgraha*: 'truth-force', 'reality-maker'), and truth-marker, *satyavṛtti*, implying that *being* in and of itself has no particular prerogative and that indeed 'being' and 'nonbeing' both presuppose a more fundamental Abgrund, or a comprehensive horizon (Halbfass p32), even when the originary One (*tad ekam*) *per* Ṛgvedic hymn X.129 is said to be beyond *being and nonbeing*. But the transcendence, even if we take this to be the neuter Brahman of the later Upaniṣads, would not be properly described as the disappearance of all distinctions in an undifferentiated primeval substance, or Nature, even the God-in-Nothingness as Hegel took it to be (Bilimoria 2010); rather the transcendence is of a higher abstract conceptual order (which of course the West following Hegel denies to the Hindus).

So much for Vedic thought on non-being. Now let me move slightly to the scholastic interpreters of Vedic praxis based on the aforementioned cosmogony giving way to a cosmology – of the Mīmāṃsakas, and how they applied the insights toward an ontology of non-existence as well as an epistemology of negation and absence.

They posited basically four kinds of non-existence:

1. *prāgabhāva*: prior negation (e.g., the negation of curd in milk, by its theory of *asatkārya*: effect is not prior to its cause); antecedent non-existence
2. *dhvaṃsa*: the negation of milk in the curd; posterior non-existence
3. *anyonyābhāva*: mutual and relational negation: the horse is not a cow, and vice versa; Ram is not Laxman; the horse is not white; Ram is not honest
4. *atyantābhāva*: absolute negation: hare's horn; or the skin below its head is not hard (it can't ever be so), God. (Bilimoria 2008a, 2016)

For each instantiation of being (something x is the case), there are four possible negations and combined multiplication of these ascribable to it.

Crudely, this parallels to or is echoed in the Jaina sevenfold predication (*saptabhaṅgī*), which reads (Matilal 1981, modified):

> A thing *is* existent – from a certain point of view.
> It is *non*-existent – from another point of view.
> It is *both* existent and non-existent *in turn* – from a third point of view.
> It is *indescribable* (that is, both an existent and non-existent simultaneously) – from a fourth point of view.
> It *is* existent and *indescribable* – from a fifth point of view.
> It *is non*-existent and *indescribable* – from a sixth point of view.
> It is *both* existent and *non*-existent and *indescribable* – from a seventh point of view.

What is going on here in terms of logic or the paraconsistent approach? Priest and Routley back in 1983/1989[9] were among the first in the analytical tradition to notice parallels between Jaina logic and modern discursive logic, arguing that the Jaina perspectivism is predicated on the rejection of the law of contradiction (Flügel 2012). Though Ganeri (2001), following Bimal Matilal (our common mentor), dis-

[9] I was in personal correspondence with Richard Routley (later Sylvan) during that seminal period even as he ventured out into non-Western, particularly Jaina logic. Correspondence in Sylvan Archives (Griffin and Priest).

agrees and avers instead that *saptabhaṅgī* is based on an extension of discursive logic via modalized many-valued truth-tables, and hence Jaina logic 'does not involve any radical departure from classical logic. The underlying logic *within* each standpoint is classical, and it is further assumed that each standpoint or participant is internally consistent.' Others have argued that Jaina logic is context-sensitive and a quasi-functional system. I, on the other hand, would like to defend the *dialetheia* (two-way truth) thesis (via Sylvan 2000), inherent in the Jaina logic on historical grounds, not on the formal reconstruction that Ganeri provides, precisely since neither the Mīmāṃsā nor the Buddhist showed any remorse or embarrassment at admitting that some statement can be both true and false in a context where not everything is accepted or some things stand negated. The fuss over the Ṛgvedic verse as we saw and various permutations of *abhāva* as complete absence and negation, the coeval happening of being and non-being in the same context, go toward demonstrating that hunch. I do not wish to be distracted by the question around paraconsistent *vs.* classical logic as such, as I am more interested in tracing the extensive career of negation that gives us some insight into thinking on nothingness.

Various devices are formulated for talking about negation and non-existents in terms of exclusions, prohibitions, mutual negations, and sentential and implicative negations. While largely used in the injunctive ritual and contemplative contexts, they have their logical counterpart also, as well as a robust epistemological theory all their own, and an ontological commitment that the Nyāya theory had bracketed out; since this material is already published I refer the reader to that source (Bilimoria 2008a, b, 2016, 2017).

When neither an existent (*bhāva*) nor a non-existent (*abhāva*) remains before the mind, then since there is no other possibility (having no objects as such), it becomes pacified.

– Śāntideva, *Bodhicaryāvatāra* ('A Guide to the Bodhisattva Way of Life'), IX, 34.

13.4 Part IV

Back to Heidegger

And that brings me back to Heidegger – the last of the metaphysicans, at least in the Continental philosophy tradition. We begin with a quote (that Carnap also used, albeit in a different translation, suggesting this was an example of a 'pseudo-sentence' where logic had been sent on holiday):

> What should be examined are beings only, and besides that – nothing; beings alone, and further – nothing; solely beings, and beyond that – nothing. What about this nothing?…Is the nothing given only because the 'not', i.e., negation, is given? Or is it the other way around? Are negation and the 'not' given only because the nothing is given?…We assert that the nothing is more original than the 'not' and negation… Where shall we seek the

> nothing? Where will we find the nothing?…we do know the nothing…Anxiety reveals the nothing…that in the face of which and for which we were anxious was 'really' – nothing. Indeed: the nothing itself – as such – was there… How is it with the nothing?…The nothing itself nihilates. (Heidegger 1993: 95–6)

In his illuminating short inaugural essay titled '*Was ist Metaphysik*?' in 1929 (2 years later than *Being & Time*, 1927) that appears alongside his essays on Hölderlin, and given to Stefan Schimanski of the 'Manchester Guardian,' who visited the master in his retreat in the Black Forrest in 1946 and 1947 (and the first work to be translated and issued in English[10]), Heidegger complains that science only examines beings, and nothing further; it rejects 'nothing' read as 'not-ing,' 'nullity' (*das Nicht*), as a 'phantasm' (1993: 95–96). In logic, on the other hand, nothing is the occurrence when 'not' or negatedness is given; while Heidegger likes to think the converse: negation (*Verneinung*) and 'not' (*nicht*) are given only because nothing is given (very much as Kumārila we saw earlier, in the Indian tradition, was thinking). So he asserts, 'nothing is more original than the 'not' and negation' (ibid, 97), and a little later: 'Without the original revelation of the nothing, no selfhood and no freedom' (103) (Bilimoria 2016). He then moves straight into an enquiry into nothing or, better, Nothingness; but in this quest for Nothingness, as he puts it, there is similar 'going beyond' what-is, conceived as what-is-in-totality (106). He begins by suggesting that since ancient times the subject of Nothing has been expressed in the highly ambiguous proposition '*ex nihilo nihil fit* – from nothing, nothing comes to be' (107). Even though the proposition never made Nothing the real problem, it brought out from the prevailing notions about Nothing, the overriding fundamental concept of what-is, i.e., beings. Nothing was quickly forgotten and the question of being – Aristotle's study of being of being – or better, in what ways is something *some thing* and what might be its relation to no-thing? – took over the focus. Still it presupposes there was a concept lurking beneath that of Nothing. And what was that? He explains thus: 'classical [ancient] metaphysics conceives Nothing as signifying Not-being (*Nichtseiendes*), that is to say, unformed matter that is powerless to form itself into 'being' and cannot therefore present an appearance. What has 'being' is the self-creating product (*Gebilde*) that presents itself as such an image (*Bild*), i.e., something seen, or being of time: 'being extant.' The origin, law, and limits of this ontological concept are discussed as little as Nothing itself'. (An aside, German Indologists working on the Ṛgvedic verse discussed earlier, rendered '*asat*' in German in exactly the term Heidegger adverts to here for Not-being, No-thing).

Christian dogma, he proceeds to tells us, on the other hand, denies the truth of the proposition *ex nihilo nihil fit* and gives a twist to the meaning of Nothing, so that it

---

[10] 'Was ist Metaphysik?', inaugural lecture to the Freiburg University faculties, July 24, 1929, in the University Auditorium (succeeding his teacher, Husserl). I have used translation in places from the earlier one included by R.F.C. Hull and Alan Crick in *Existence and Being* (Chicago: Henry Regnery, 1949, re- issued 1979), but mainly from D.F. Krell, 'What is Metaphysics?' in *Basic Writings*, revised edn., San Francisco: HarperCollins, 1993. Heidegger meets Stefan Schimanski, June 1946, and again a year later. On their meeting see Schimanski's essay, 'On Meeting a Philosopher,' *Partisan Review* 15, 1948, 506–09. The Sheehan translation (2001) was cited.

now comes to mean the absolute absence of all 'being' outside God: *ex nihilo fit – ens creatum*: the created being is made out of nothing. 'Nothing' is now the conceptual opposite of what truly and authentically 'is;' it becomes the *summum ens*, God as *en in-creatum*. Here, too, the interpretation of Nothing points to the fundamental concept of what-is. In both cases the questions concerning Being (*Sein*) and Nothing as such remain unasked. Hence, we need not be worried by the difficulty that if God creates 'out of nothing' he above all must be able to relate himself to Nothing. But if God is God he cannot know Nothing, assuming that the 'Absolute' excludes itself from all nullity. Not wishing to lose sight of the work of Being, Heidegger's own reformulation of the old proposition '*ex nihilo nihil fit*' runs thus: '*ex nihilo omne ens qua ens fit*: every being, so far as it is a being, is made out of nothing. Only in the Nothingness of *Da-Sein* can what-is-in totality…come to itself.'

Now this particular observation might strike biblical scholars and Christian philosophers of religion as being willfully controversial and unfair. I cannot presume to pronounce on its merits or otherwise, but what I see in Heidegger's excavation is something of significance to my overall argument: that thinking about Nothing has been rather thin, and it is not as easy as Leibniz assumed given the kinds of coding that occur frequently in literary and cultural productions across East and West, and indeed there is more to be got out of Nothing than hitherto supposed. Contrary to general perception, Heidegger's ontology is not one of Nothingness as such; he is not a nihilist, far from it (he distances himself from a 'Philosophy of Nothing' in the Postscript); rather, Being as Da-Sein remains very much the subject and project of metaphysics, and of theology too if you like. There is something sobering in his suggestion that only because 'Nothing is revealed in the very basis of our Dasein is it possible for the utter strangeness' – the dread, the angst, the anxiety, the boredom, the facticity of thrownness in the face of *my* death (it is always *my death*) – 'of what-is' to dawn on us. 'The outermost possibility of death is the way of being of Dasein in which it *is purely and simply thrown back upon itself*' (Kisiel 1995: 336; Heidegger 1996: 235–6). 'Only when the strangeness of what-is forces itself upon us does it awaken and invite our wonder. Only because of wonder, that is to say, the revelation of Nothing, does the 'Why?' spring to our lips. ['Why are there beings at all, why not rather nothing?' (1929 endline)]. Only because this 'Why?' is possible as such can we seek for reasons and proofs in a definite way. Only because we can ask and prove are we fated to become enquirers in this life. The enquiry into Nothing puts us, the enquirers, ourselves in question. It is a metaphysical one' (379).

To be sure, Heidegger never gives up on the quest for the 'ground possibilities of being as a whole' (while Nishitani takes Nothingness as the 'home ground,' Heidegger remains committed to the mereological whole-part discourse: that bit is the Greek in him). For him Nothing is not merely the nugatory that equates with the non-existent (*das Wesenlose*); 'rather,' he preaches, 'we should experience in Nothing the vastness of that which gives every being the warrant to be' (385). Hence, what is instructive is his exhortation that rather than 'a leap of faith' the task of 'letting oneself go into the abyss of Nothing' is more important, that is to say, 'freeing oneself from idols as all have and to which we are wont to go cringing' and lastly, letting this 'suspense' – 'morbid mood, dread' (383) range where it will, so that it may continually swing back again to the ground question of metaphysics, which is wrested from Nothing itself (and he ends with this): 'Why is there any Being at all – why not far rather Nothing?' Wrested from Nothing, Heidegger brings back concepts of sacrifice as gifting and thanking, feeling empathy for the other (*Sorge*/care), disburdening calculative and utilitarian thinking, and all the promises of techno-scientific culture, even obedience to the 'voice of being,' alongside imagination, the work of art, poetical flights into the holy, and so forth.

In this abyss, which is only representationally poised in opposition to Being, Heidegger finds the *Abgrund* of freedom: it is the groundless ground that is indistinguishable from nothing and from which all determinations emerge. Hegel had already explained the peculiar relationship between nothingness and freedom in these words: 'In this highest form of explication nothingness would be freedom. But this highest form is negativity insofar as it inwardly depends itself to its highest intensity; and in this way it is itself affirmation – indeed absolute affirmation' (Taylor 2007: 117). Negativity is affirmative insofar as it is the condition of creative emergence of everything that exists.

It is a theme – this latter – that postmodernist philosophers have taken up and as it were run the full gauntlet on, and I wish to get to this in drawing the essay to a close. 'Perfect nothingness…shadows…neither light nor absence of light: origin of that which has no origin, groundless ground, abyss, freedom, imagination, creativity. For Nietzsche, the plenitude of this void is the nonplace of the birth of tragedy; for Derrida it is *la différance* worked into the non-metaphysical deconstructive theology of *absence*.' Mark C Taylor more recently commenting on these tropes compares Kant's schemata of productive imagination (in the work of poetry, art, etc.) to God creating freely *ex nihilo*. The power of imagination 'reveals' the concealment – the as-yet-unearthed – at the heart of subjectivity. It is precisely in the moments of radical temporality when the subject encounters deep within its own absence that nothingness haunts subjectivity; the *deus absconditus* of Kierkegaard, Luther, Calvin, and possibly Duns Scotus, becomes *subjectus absconditus*; only in the next inspired moment does self-reflexivity arise, and the 'something' presenced to consciousness is given representation or expression. The German Romanticists, such as Schlegel, had identified the springing of this agency within subjectivity variously with the 'breath,' 'Will,' Being, *ousia*, *logos*, *telos*, ideas, even Reason (with Hegel) of Spirit (*Geist*), and the Holy Ghost: 'Every good human being is progressively becoming God.' In short, the premise is that belief in nothing/nothingness in this radical sense of the temporality of subjectivity that is the driving force towards its self-reflexivity is not in-and-of-itself nihilistic; rather, it opens the floodgates of light towards transcendence (even Nietzsche would be cited as conceding to this premise). 'After God – is art; after art – life; Three-in-one–One- in-three' – as Taylor sketches this interloping trinity. But what does 'after' mean in this locution as indeed in the title of his recent, rather controversial book, *After God*[11] (taking a hint from MacIntyre's *After Virtue*)? This is his iteration:

> God is not the ground of being that forms the foundation of all beings but the figure constructed to hide the originary abyss from which everything emerges and to which all returns. While this abyss is no thing, it is not nothing – neither being nor nonbeing [Taylor's exact replication of Ṛgveda and Śāntideva], it is the anticipatory wake of the unfigurable that disfigures every figure as if from within. Far from simply destructive, disfiguring [I read *kronos*] is the condition of the possibility of creative emergence. Even when expected, emergence is surprising – [as the consciousness out of singularity is for Dave Chalmers et al. (2009)] – without surprise, there is no novelty; without novelty, there is no creativity; without creativity, there is no life [animation]'.

For my purposes, what I take away from all this is the preparedness to take the possibility of nothingness as a ground, or the lurking empty space, tunnelling vacuum, or where God intervenes or plays out her Will, energetic Desire (*tejasvikāma, mahimānaḥ*), whatever, which is quite an admission: whether the ultimate cause is traced to an intelligent mind, causeless cause, or an infinite regress of endless internal triggers, disinterested Desire, integers of zeros, old universes, or turtles all the way down…is not the moot point; for all such possibilities seem to have been entertained and dare I say anticipated in the early insights and cosmological developments that occurred in the debates between the Vedic-Upanisadic bards and the śrāmaṇic doubters. 'There is not much that is crudely or naively pre-scientific here; metaphysical it might, even trifle speculative and mythical, but it is also challengingly troubling, or so for any sensitive, worrying philosophical mind' (Bilimoria 2012b).

Radical Nothingness ought not to be feared: it may have therapeutic value in the hallowed Wittgenstenian-Yogacārin sense (an antidote for excessive linguistic conceptualism); it may prove to be the timely yet fairest watchgod on the excesses of the Technoscience culture (to which Heidegger similarly drew attention), as well on fundamentalisms of all varieties, the return of religion to the public sphere (despite

[11] In the discussion that ensues Heidegger has taken the adage '*ex nihilo nihil fit*' rather too literally and hence finds a certain ambiguity in it. As Prof. John Bishop (of Auckland University) pointed out to me (after an APRA plenary presentation of the larger version, 2010, in Melbourne), there are many different and variant interpretations of '*ex nihilo nihil fit,*' and not all scholars or theologians draw the implications that Heidegger does; some may find 'Nothing' here quite compatible with God's nature, and so a positive rather than a negative reading might be apposite. Hence something – at least conceivably capable – *does* come out of nothing. And this may resonate with the Hindu cosmogenic accounts discussed under Part III. I am grateful to John Bishop and Patrick Hutchings for their comments on this section of the discussion. Though it could equally be 'After Gods' in deference to now recognized transcendental pluralism in cross- cultural philosophy of religion, the re-kindled interests in Pantheism (Spinoza; Michael Levine (1994); Forrest), Panpsychism (Schopenhauer; Freya Matthews), Panentheism (Plato[?] via Dirk Baltzly; Hegel; de Chardin; Phil Clayton). More recently, Mark Johnston's (2009) plea for rationally reconsidering some version of poly-heneno-theisms, rather than saving the historically late monotheistic deity of Western origin; and subverting Heidegger's adage: 'Too late for the gods, too early for God': *kasmai devāya haviṣā vidhema* – to which God shall we offer our sacrifice: of West/North or East/South? [echoing Ṛgved a X.82.6]). Some of these alternatives are examined in Special Issue on Panentheism and Panpsychism, *Sophia* Volume 49 Number 2, 24 March 2011.

the Enlightenment's decree), secularism re-seeking the sacred enchantments, as in the hands of Zîzêk, and on other attachments to Absolutes, perhaps also to being/ Being, and an acute partner in inter-faith, intra-deist and inter-faithless conversation of the Four Horsemankind. Meanwhile, on with my frustrated attempt to complete fabricating a machine that creates Nothingness, or work it up at least as the transcendental concept of which no smaller can be conceived. Wouldn't that do?

The Dao (Way) that can be told of is not the eternal Dao;
The name that can be named is not the eternal name...
Therefore let there always be non-being so we may see their subtlety,
And let there always be being so we may see their outcome.
The two are the same,
But after they are produced, they have different names.
They both may be called deep and profound.
Deeper and more profound...
From *Tao-te Ching* by Lao-tzu, trans by Wing-Tsit Chan (Tao = Dao)

Revised in Venus Bay
Dec. 21, 2012 (missed Mayan *pralaya*)

References

Armstrong, D. M. (2010). *Sketch for a systematic metaphysics*. Oxford: Oxford University Press.

Bilimoria, P. (1995). Radhakrishnan – Saving the appearance in Plato's academy. In S. S. Rama Rao Pappu (Ed.), *New essays in the philosophy of Sarvepalli Radhakrishnan* (pp. 327–344). New Delhi: Indian Books Centre.

Bilimoria, P. (1997). On Śaṅkara's attempted reconciliation of 'You' and 'I'. In J. N. Mohanty & P. Bilimoria (Eds.), *Relativism, suffering and beyond essays in memory of Bimal Matilal* (pp. 252–276). New Delhi: Oxford University Press.

Bilimoria, P. (2008a). *Abhāva*: Negation in logic, real non-existent, and a distinctive *pramāṇa* in the Mīmāṃsā. In M. Chakraborti, B. Lowe, M. N. Mitra, & S. Sarukkai (Eds.), *Logic, Navya-Nyāya & applications homage to Bimal Krishna Matilal* (Studies in logic) (Vol. 15, pp. 43–64). London: College Publications.

Bilimoria, P. (2008b). Nietzsche as 'Europe's Buddha' and Asia's superman. Guest issue on continental philosophy of religion. *Sophia, 47*(3), 359–376.

Bilimoria, P. (2010). Hegel's spectre on Indian thought and its God-in-nothingness. *Religions of South Asia, 4*(2), 199–211.

Bilimoria, P. (2011a). War and peace between science and religion: The divine arch after the four horsemen. *Journal of the Indian Council of Philosophical Research (Delhi), 28*(2), 3–30.

Bilimoria, P. (2011b). *Grief and mourning: For Renuka*. Lecture for existentialist society, Melbourne, September 2011. Updated pdf at www.pbilimo.com

Bilimoria, P. (2012a). Of grief and mourning: thinking a feeling, back to Robert Solomon. In K. Higgins & D. Sherman (Eds.), *Passion, death & spirituality: The philosophy of Robert C Solomon* (Sophia Series) (pp. 149–174). Dordrecht: Springer.

Bilimoria, P. (2012b). *All India Radio: The war between science and religion a western import?* Paper presented American academy of religion annual meeting, November.

Bilimoria, P. (2016). Negation *(abhāva)*, non-existents, and a distinctive *pramāṇa* in the Nyāya-Mīmāṃsā. In Purushottama Bilimoria with Michael Hemmingsen (Ed.), *Comparative philosophy & J L Shaw* (Sophia Series) (pp. 183–202). Dordrecht: Springer.

Bilimoria, P. (2017). Thinking negation in early Hinduism and classical Indian philosophy. *Logica Universalis, 11*(1), 13–33.

Bilimoria, P., & Stansell, E. (2010). Suturing the body corporate (divine and human) in the Brāhmaṇic traditions. Special issue on panentheism and panpsychism. *Sophia, 49*(2), 237–259.

Borges, J. L. (2000). *Labyrinths*. (J. E. Irby, Trans.). London: Penguin Classics.

Bosley, R. N. (2003). Jaspers on Lao Tzu, Nagarjuna, and dialectic. In J. W. Koterski & R. J. Langley (Eds.), *Karl Jaspers on philosophy of history and history of philosophy*. Amherst: Humanity Books.

Chalmers, D. M., Manly, D., & Wasserman, R. (Eds.). *Metametaphysics: new essays on the foundations of ontology*. Oxford: Oxford University Press.

Charlesworth, M. J. (1970a). *Summa theologiae, vol 15: The world order (Ia 110–119)* (p. 2006). Cambridge: Cambridge University Press.

Charlesworth, M. J. (1970b). *Philosophy of religion the historic approach*. London: Macmillan.

Chattopadhyaya, D. P. (2006). The magic of zero, gun and gunpowder. In *Religion, philosophy and science: a sketch of a global view*. Shimla: Indian Institute of Advanced Studies.

Chen, E. M. (1969). Nothingness and the mother principle in early Chinese Taoism. *International Philosophical Quarterly, 9*(3), 391–405.

D'Amato, M. (2013). Buddhist fictionalism. *Sophia, 52*(3), 409–424.

Dawkins, R. (1988). *The blind watchmaker*. New York: W. W. Norton.

Doolan, G. T. (Ed.). (2012). *The science of being as being: Metaphysical investigations*. Washington, DC: The Catholic University of America Press.

Flügel, P. (Ed.). (2012). *Studies in Jaina history and culture: Disputes and dialogues*. London: Routledge.

Ganeri, J. (2001). *Philosophy in classical India: The proper work of reason*. London: Routledge.

Ganeri, J. (2008). Towards a formal regimentation of the Navya-Nyāya technical language I & II. In M. Chakraborti, B. Lowe, M. N. Mitra, & S. Sarukkai (Eds.), *Logic, Navya-Nyāya & applications homage to Bimal Krishna Matilal* (Studies in logic) (Vol. 15, pp. 105–138). London: College Publications.

Garfield, J. L. (1995). *The fundamental wisdom of the middle way: Nāgārjuna's Mūlamadhyamakakārikā*. Oxford: Oxford University Press.

Garfield, J., & Priest, G. (2003). Nāgārjuna and the limits of thought. *Philosophy East & West, 53*(1), 1–21.

Halbfass, W. (1992). *On being and what there is: Classical Vaiśeṣika and the history of Indian ontology*. Albany: SUNY Press.

Hart, K. (2004). Religion. In J. Reynolds & J. Roffe (Eds.), *Understanding Derrida (chapter 7)* (p. 2004). London: Continuum.

Heidegger, M. (1929). *Was ist Metaphysik*. Bonn: F. Cohen Verlag.

Heidegger, M. (1993). What is metaphysics? In D. F. Krell (Ed.), *Basic writings* (pp. 89–110). San Francisco: HarperCollins.

Heidegger, M (1996). *Being and time, a translation of Sein und Zeit,* by Joan Staumbaugh. Albany: SUNY Press.

Hicks, S. V. (2003). Nietzsche, Heidegger, and Foucault: Nihilism and beyond. In A. Milchman & A. Rosenberg (Eds.), *Foucault and Heidegger: Critical encounters* (pp. 74–109). Ann Arbor: University of Michigan Press.

Hutchings, P. (2009). Why is there something rather than nothing?' The big question. Review of Leszek Kołakowski, *Why is there something rather than nothing*. *Sophia, 48*(4), 479–489.

Inada, K. K. (1970). *Nāgārjuna: A translation of his Mūlamadhyamakakārikā, with an introductory essay*. Tokyo: Hokuseido Press.

Jaspers, K. (1962, 1966). The operations of thought (chapter on Nāgārjuna). In *The great Philosophers* (2 Vols.). Fort Worth: Harcourt Brace and Company.

Johnston, M. (2009). *Saving God: Religion after idolatry*. Trenton: Princeton University Press.

Kakol, P. (2009). In P. Bilimoria (Ed.), *Emptiness and becoming: Integrating Madhyamika Buddhism and process philosophy*. New Delhi: DKPrintWorld.

Kenny, A. (1969). *The five ways*. New York: Schocken Books.
Kisiel, T. (1995). *The genesis of Heidegger's being and time*. Berkeley: University of California Press.
Kołakowski, L. (2008). *Why is there something rather than nothing? Questions from great Philosophers*. London: Penguin Books.
Lao, T. (1963). *The Way of Lao Tzu Tao-te Ching* (Wing-Tsat Chan, Trans.). Indianapolis: The Bobbs-Merrill Company; also cited in Stanford Encyclopedia of Philosophy http://plato.stanford.edu/ entries/laozi/
Levine, M. P. (1994). *Pantheism: A non-theistic concept of deity*. London: Routledge.
Lewis, D. (1999). *Papers in metaphysics and epistemology*. Cambridge: Cambridge University Press.
Matilal, B. K. (1968). *The Navya-Nyāya doctrine of negation: The semantics and ontology of negative statements in Navya-Nyāya philosophy*. Cambridge, MA: Harvard University Press.
Matilal, B. K. (1981). *The central philosophy of Jainism – Anekāntavāda*. Ahmedabad: L D Institute.
Matilal, B. K. (1998). *The character of logic in India*. Albany: SUNY Press.
Phillips, S. H. (2006). *Philosophy of religion: A global approach*. Fort Worth: Harcourt Brace.
Price, H. (2009a). Metaphysics after Carnap: The ghost who walks? In D. Chalmers, D. Manley, & R. Wasserman (Eds.), *Metametaphysics* (pp. 320–346). Oxford: Oxford University Press.
Price, H. (2009b). Metaphysics after Carnap: The ghost who walks? In D. Chalmers, D. Manley, & R. Wasserman (Eds.), *Metametaphysics: New essays on the foundations of ontology* (pp. 320–346). Oxford: Oxford University Press.
Priest, G. (2005). *Towards non-being: The logic and metaphysics of intentionality*. Oxford: Oxford University Press.
Sylvan, R. (1966). Some things do not exist. *Notre Dame Journal of Formal Logic, 7*, 251–276.
Sylvan, R. (1976). The durability of impossible objects. *Inquiry, 19*, 247–253.
Sylvan, R. (1980). *Exploring Meinong's jungle and beyond: An investigation of noneism and the theory of items*. Canberra: Research School of Social Sciences, Australian National University.
Sylvan, R. (1997). *Transcendental metaphysics: From radical to deep plurallism [sic]*. Cambridge: The White Horse Press.
Sylvan, R. (2000). In D. Hyde & G. Priest (Eds.), *Sociative logic and their applications: Essays by the late Richard Sylvan*. Ashgate Publishers: Aldershot.
Taylor, M. C. (2007). *After God: Religion and postmodernism*. Chicago: University of Chicago Press.
Van Fraassen, B. C. (1980). *The scientific image*. Oxford: Oxford University Press.
Williamson, T. (1998). Bare possibilia. *Erkenntnis 48* (2/3). http://www.jstor.org.ezp.lib.unimelb.edu.au/stable/20012844?seq=3. Accessed 10 Sept 2012.

Purushottama Bilimoria teaches at the Center for Dharma Studies, Graduate Theological Union and University of California, Berkeley, as Chancellor's Scholar, and also Honorary Research Fellow with the University of Melbourne and Deakin University, Australia. He is an Editor-in-Chief of *Sophia* and *Journal of Dharma Studies*.

Part IV
Between Religion and Religions

Chapter 14
Songlines, Sacred Texts and Cultural Code: Between Australia and Early Medieval Ireland

Constant J. Mews

Not the least remarkable attribute of Max Charlesworth as a philosopher was his willingness to explore new directions in the search for wisdom.[1] One illustration of this openness to new forms of thought is evident in the revisions he made to his survey of philosophical attitudes towards religion, originally entitled in 1972 *Philosophy of Religion: Historic Approaches*, but substantially revised in 2002 as *Philosophy and Religion: From Plato to Post-Modernism*. The shift in title signals his growing awareness that religion cannot be studied as a universal in itself, except in relation to specific traditions. In his 2002 introduction, he recognised the explosion that had taken place in the intervening 30 years in awareness of the multiplicity of religious traditions, studied not just through conventional analytic philosophy of religion (whose traditional concerns have been with concepts like God and free will, shaped by Christian tradition), but through history and the social sciences, including anthropology. His sense of the history of philosophy as a continuously evolving process mirrored his own evolution, initially shaped by his own studies at the University of Melbourne under Alexander Boyce Gibson (1900–1972), whose pluralist attitude to philosophy he admired, and then broadened through his studies at the Catholic University at Louvain in the 1950s.[2] Charlesworth's early publications, from *Philosophy and Linguistic Analysis* (1959), to his studies and annotated translations of St Anselm (1965) and St Thomas Aquinas (1970), were marked by

[1] I am indebted to many people in the course of writing this paper, in particular to John Bradley, Deputy Director of the Monash Indigenous Centre, Monash University, and to those who participated in a joint seminar given there on 12 November 2014.

[2] See the account by Max Charlesworth 1996. Douglas Kirsner picks up on this theme in his excellent overview of Charlesworth's career in Kirsner 2012.

C. J. Mews (✉)
Monash University, Melbourne, VIC, Australia
e-mail: constant.mews@monash.edu

P. Wong et al. (eds.), *Considering Religions, Rights and Bioethics: For Max Charlesworth*, Sophia Studies in Cross-cultural Philosophy of Traditions and Cultures 30, https://doi.org/10.1007/978-3-030-18148-2_14

interest in both English and continental philosophical traditions.[3] Moving to Deakin University in 1975 coincided with a broadening of his interests and teaching activity. While his core contribution was as a philosopher, his understanding of religious diversity led him to develop the field of religious studies, in particular through his evolving awareness of aboriginal spiritual traditions, which he argued deserved to be studied alongside other world religions as part of humanity's continuing quest for wisdom. My own specialist background is in the medieval Christian tradition. Nonetheless, I would like to build further on Charlesworth's interest in comparative religious thought, conscious of the difficulty of juxtaposing very different cultural traditions by raising parallels and contrasts between two very different phenomena that Charlesworth called 'religious inventions', namely aboriginal songlines and canonical sacred texts, with specific reference to the Celtic Christian culture of early medieval Ireland. Can the notion of a songline help us to understand the nature of a religious tradition? I suggest that song may provide us with a closer way of accessing the sacred than statements of belief.

Charlesworth's interest in aboriginal religion (a term that he recognised is itself contested) first became evident through his editing with Howard Morphy, Diane Bell and Kenneth Maddock an influential anthology of collection of texts in 1984, under the title *Religion in Aboriginal Australia*, a volume that brought together many of the most distinguished figures in the field.[4] Charlesworth contributed both an introduction to the volume and a reflection on 'Change in Aboriginal Religion', in which he questioned the assumption of T. G. H. Strehlow that aboriginal traditions were essentially static and resistant to change.[5] He followed this up in 1990 with an edited volume on ancestor spirits (Charlesworth et al. 1990). In *Religious Inventions*, published in 1997, he presented four major essays, all relating to the role of creativity and imagination in human attempts to interpret what may be described as revelation, including one on the invention of Australian aboriginal religions.[6] The following year, he edited essays by distinguished specialists, originally delivered as the Charles Strong Memorial Lectures between 1976 and 1994, on the theme of aboriginal spirituality (Charlesworth 1998). In 2005, Charlesworth co-edited another volume of essays on the subject, again with an introduction that demonstrates remarkable capacity to synthesise developments in the field (Charlesworth et al. 2005). Criticising the functionalist tendency of some anthropological approaches, he suggested that aboriginal thought could be called *geosophy* because it concerned a wisdom related to the land, rather than *theosophy*, a wisdom identified with God (Charlesworth 2009). In his personal commitment, Charlesworth situated himself in a catholic Christian tradition. He was nonetheless keenly aware of

[3]Anselm 1965, translated and edited by Max Charlesworth. He also translated and annotated vol. 15 of *Summa Theologiae* (Aquinas 1970).

[4]Charlesworth, M. et al. (eds.), 1984. Charlesworth also edited *The Aboriginal Land Rights Movement* (Charlesworth (ed.), 1984).

[5]Charlesworth, 'Introduction', in Charlesworth, M. et al. (eds.), 1984, pp. 1–20; and 'Introduction: Change in Aboriginal Religion', ibid., pp. 383–87.

[6]Charlesworth 1997; with his essay, 'The invention of Australian Aboriginal religions', pp. 51–79.

how changing philosophical and political perspectives inevitably demanded that any religious tradition be continually reinterpreted in the light of experience, as he argued in one of his last essays, published in 2012 (Charlesworth 2012). The quotation from Bernanos that he used to open *Religious Inventions* articulates a theme that underpins his perspective on different religions, including that of aboriginal spirituality: 'Grace... is everywhere'. At the same time, he insisted that no interpretation of religious experience could be identified with any other, given that human creativity was always shaped by the particular perspectives of its cultural environment.

Building on Charlesworth's sensitivity to the contribution of both historical and anthropological inquiry as complementing that of philosophical analysis, I would like to take further his emphasis on the impossibility of making claims about religion in the abstract, as a universal concept. Rather than focusing on beliefs (as often the case in both philosophy and anthropology of religion), I wish to draw attention to the potential of a particular type of orally transmitted song for articulating core knowledge within a community, mapping a sacred geography that connected the physical world to a universe beyond conventional western notions of space and time. Canonical sacred texts issue from cultures that treasure the written word, in which high authority is given to a scribal class (van der Toorn 2007). Nonetheless, many such sacred texts were originally preserved as oral traditions, firmly evoking a sense of place.[7] Even when recorded in writing, the Hebrew Scriptures are first of all known through recitation, like the Qur'an. As Charlesworth points out, one legacy of the Reformation was increased emphasis in Christianity on the authority of written Scripture as a source of revelation, but only in the last century has there been rediscovery of the awareness of the orally transmitted tradition from which Scripture derives.[8] Post-Reformation Christianity has encouraged emphasis on belief as a core element of religion, as illustrated by widespread use of the word 'faith' (one of three virtues according to St Paul) to refer to religion, even though many spiritual traditions may not directly use such a notion. Obviously there are radical differences between what are sometimes called primal religions or indigenous spiritualities and those religions defined by a received canon, even during the medieval period. Not the least of these is political. Canonical religious traditions tend to be defined by the authority of the written word and its interpreters, colonizing, if not eliminating local religious or ceremonial traditions. In practice, however, even canonical religious traditions tend to be challenged or re-interpreted by those who seek to re-align dominant traditions of interpretation.

Comparative reflection on the vastly different thought worlds of the European Middle Ages and of the first peoples of Australia is inevitably fraught with difficulty.

[7] As has often been observed since the pioneering studies of Ong (1982), oral traditions themselves manifest a kind of literacy; see for example Collins and Blot (2003). On the vitality of place in reinterpreting our awareness of sacred texts, see John D'Arcy May's article (May 2006). He takes his departure from a comment by Eugene Stockton, 'For an Aboriginal, surveying the landscape is like reading the Bible', quoted in Eugene Stockton's piece, 'The Mindful Land' (Stockton 2003).

[8] Charlesworth, 'Universal and Local Elements in Religion', in Charlesworth 1997, pp. 93–94.

Without knowledge of all those languages, how does someone raised in a Western tradition avoid the charge that one is simply imposing ideas onto a world view that has nothing comparable to the modern notion of 'religion' as a universal (itself a mythic construct, shaped by political concerns, as Talal Asad and Masuzawa remind us)?[9] The term *religio* is itself a concept that has undergone many transformations in its history.[10] The particular suggestion I would like to pursue here is that appreciating the role of song in a religious or spiritual tradition may provide a way to understand what western commentators identify as beliefs. Christian theology only makes sense, not as the study of abstract beliefs, but as commentary on the scriptural traditions that encapsulate a perception of wisdom and law inherited across time. The establishment of a canon of sacred texts is invariably a political process, as dominant forces in a community decide which oral traditions should be preserved. In the case of medieval Christianity, however, shared orthodoxy was always supplemented by local traditions, often shaped by the memory of saints and teachers who re-interpreted the Scriptures in the light of their local community. Indigenous sacred songs about spirit ancestors creating the land cannot be identified with creation stories in other religions. Yet it can be helpful to appreciate differences between forms of cultural code that shape the evolution of particular communities, through interaction with their environment. Indigenous Australia and medieval Ireland have been marked by an experience of dispossession. While medieval Ireland was shaped by Latin catholic Christianity, its sacred traditions were in practice highly variegated, reflecting the multiplicity of kingdoms and tribal identities by which it was constituted. Pre-colonial Australia was vastly different, in not being shaped by a religion with universalising claims. Nonetheless, it was a continent, on a much larger scale, with over two hundred separate languages (and many more dialects), each with song traditions in continuous evolution, only a fraction of which have ever been recorded. In Ireland, stories and songs about saints played a key role in shaping identity and providing a map that could orient a community to a wider universe, just as stories and songs about spirit ancestors mapped out the land, sea and sky of the Australian continent and its islands, signalling a law never put into writing.

14.1 Songlines and the Dreaming

For philosophers, the study of religion is often considered to be pre-eminently about belief, with non-religion associated with the absence of belief. This credal bias of post-Reformation Christianity certainly affected the way anthropologists in late nineteenth-century Australia, shaped by missionary experience, focused on what quickly came to be considered a core belief, namely what is variously translated as 'the Dreaming' or 'The Dreamtime' (derived from the Arunta notion of Alcheringa

[9] Talal Asad, 'Religion as an Anthropological Category', in Asad 1993, pp. 27–54; Masuzawa 1993.

[10] See for example Nongbri 2013, and Barton and Boyarin 2016.

or Altyerre), as meaning a sacred time or place, beyond immediate reality, but connected to the present through performance of dance and ceremonial song. There has been much debate on whether the concept is a colonial construction imposed on aboriginal culture by Frank Gillen and Baldwin Spencer in the late nineteenth century, and elaborated upon by the missionary, Carl Strehlow, to evoke an idealised 'primitive' core identity, or whether it represents a genuine attempt at cross-cultural linguistic analysis.[11] Unfortunately, so many of the narrative traditions in which such concepts might have been invoked, have been lost over the last hundred years, that it is not easy to assess the question. Both missionaries and anthropologists tended to focus on asking questions about beliefs rather than engage in the much slower process of listening to and learning what they tended to call ritual, a term that itself evokes lack of interest in the conceptual structure of chant. In a continent in which there were, prior to colonial settlement, over two hundred distinct languages, each with their own narrative traditions. It is evidently extremely dangerous to generalise about what might constitute a core belief. In terms of practical experience, what matters within any community are the specific ceremonial chants that relate very specifically to particular places, to which the community is connected. While these chants were never written down, they were transmitted orally, just as happened in the Christian Church for the first thousand years of its existence (although plainchant would become increasingly structured according to theoretical canons.) Whereas indigenous chants are so much to do with the land, Jewish, Christian and Islamic chants tended to create a map of an interior universe, interpreting places like Jerusalem as a metaphor for an idealised future world. In this respect the Psalms provided a foundational body of chant in Jewish and Christian tradition, learned by heart. The word *Qur'an* itself means recitation, to be listened to rather than to be read. Thinking about a sacred text as in part generated from including within their core equivalents to 'songlines' may highlight the particular kind of map that they offer that serve very specific moral and political purposes, associations are not so much with a specific place in the immediate vicinity, as to a location, like Jerusalem, Rome or Mecca to which the community is spiritually connected.

The notion of a 'songline' as an orally transmitted sacred song that recounts the migration of spirit ancestors (often a specific creature) along a particular line or track, connected to a specific community, does not have a long pedigree in anthropological literature. The Oxford English Dictionary records its earliest known use within a single entry in a handlist of surviving chants, produced in 1966 by the pioneering ethnomusicologist, Alice Marshall Moyle (1908–2005). She documented surviving recordings of aboriginal chants from across the continent, some of which go back to the early twentieth century.[12] Ronald H. Berndt used the term song

[11] Patrick Wolfe argues the case for colonial invention of the concept of Dreamtime(Wolfe 1991).A nuanced criticism of the linguistic issues involved is offered by Jennifer Green (Green 2012).The role of ceremony within the concept is emphasized by Lynne Hume (Hume 2004).

[12] Moyle: 'Njuṇgunj/Miḷgu songline and ceremonials, relating to the travels of Maḷu (kangaroo) and associated ancestors' (Moyle 1996, p. 165). In the *Oxford English Dictionary*, this brief reference is recorded as the first known use of the word to mean a type of song.

cycles (borrowing a term from European literature) to refer to these chants, and was very aware of how they related to particular places.[13] The word songline was first given limited treatment in print in 1978 by Robert Tonkinson in a relatively brief discussion of myth, ritual and songlines in relation to the Mardujara aborigines of the western desert. He observed that songlines 'trace ancestral tracks and illustrate Dreamtime happenings in abbreviated, rhythmic, and exciting fashion' (Tonkinson 1978, p. 105). The author who seized on this idea in a major way was the novelist and travel writer, Bruce Chatwin who used it as the title of an ethnographic novel, *The Songlines* (1987), to describe what he saw as a lost nomadic culture, held together by a web of sacred song across the continent (Chatwin 1987). He saw songlines as a metaphor of the human condition. Chatwin was himself powerfully influenced by *Songs of Central Australia* (1971), by T. G. H. Strehlow, son of Carl Strehlow, who had himself been fascinated by the notion of the Dreamtime in the early twentieth century. Chatwin's actual experience of Central Australia was limited to two visits in 1983 and 1984. Although T. G. H. Strehlow never used the specific term 'songline' in his massive reflection – on aboriginal poetry (informed by awareness of Old Norse and Old English traditions), he did speak about tracks made by spirit creatures, recorded by *tjurunga* or other symbols and signs, remembered through song (Strehlow 1971).[14] Chatwin's globalising generalisations about these *tjurunga* lines or 'dreaming tracks', gleaned from a limited range of sources (without necessarily gaining permission to do so) inevitably raised caution in both the indigenous and academic community.[15] While he was fascinated by the image of the nomad as someone always engaged on a journey, he never learned the language of any particular community. The songline was not a notion that attracted attention in any of the volumes relating to aboriginal religion edited by Charlesworth between 1984 and 2005.

The term was used, however, in the title of a brilliantly original and highly personal account by John Bradley, published in 2010, *Singing the Saltwater Country: Journey to the Songlines of Carpentaria* (Bradley 2010). Bradley describes how, over a period of over three decades, he came to learn the songlines or *kujika* from the elders of the Yanyuwa people in Carpentaria. Whereas classical ethnographic studies often underplay the role of the ethnographer in eliciting information, Bradley does not shy away from the drama and sheer humanity of his interaction with the people whose culture he is learning. What matters is not just the words, but the process of singing and dancing: 'It is breath being purposefully used that creates the matrix of sound which is the *kujika*, and represents the unity of Law.' (Bradley 2010, p. 245)

[13] Berndt 1951, pp. xxvi, xxviii, xxix, 7, 9, 10, 17, 18, 39, 40, 85, 113, 115, 135.

[14] See also *Central Australian Religion*, 1978, p. 729, discussed by W. E. H. Stanner, 'Some Aspects of Aboriginal Religion', in Charlesworth 1998, p. 5.

[15] Nicholas Shakespeare records his presence in Australia in *Bruce Chatwin: A Biography* (Shakespeare 2001, pp. 426–46, and pp. 511–17) on the publication of *The Songlines* (Chatwin 1987) as Chatwin's Testament. Shakespeare comments on Chatwin's debt to Strehlow (p. 433), his modelling the figure of Arkady Volchok on Toly Sawenko, engaged in mapping sites for the Aboriginal Land Council (pp. 436–49) and of Father Flynn on Pat Dodson, then a Catholic priest of Aboriginal and Irish descent (pp. 440–42).

Bradley's focus on Law as a foundational concept in these chants, well-summarised in his conclusion, provides not just a focus for indigenous understanding of the sacred, but a potential point of intersection with other religious traditions. Not only has he written a first-hand account of his journey with these people, but he has worked with the Yanyuwa community in recording these *kujika*, enriching their narrative by subtitled digital animation of their stories about spirit ancestors, whether the groper fish or the tiger shark. Bradley argues that these *kujika* do much more than simply map the land. They connect those who perform and listen to them to an unwritten Law of the land, establishing the basis for kin groups, and the balance of power between various different groups, both human and non-human who share the land and sea (Bradley 2010, pp. 250–51). While these lines are at one level geographical, they also connect people across time, providing a map that is also cosmic, in that they re-connect individuals and peoples to a deeper level of reality, regenerating the world. Needless to say, loss of knowledge of these *kujika* is a cause of grief, as also of the various species that they celebrate. In a sense, the *kujika* that he has recorded, some of which take many days, if not weeks to perform, constitute the oldest sacred texts of humanity, animating a community in the same way as DNA provides a core genetic code of material, from which living cells take their being. Whatever we call them, these sacred songs provide a map not just of the land, but of a sacred geography that reminds people of the moral and spiritual place to which they belong.

Bradley's focus on their relationship to Law makes them more than simply a device for tracking the land. As he observes, transcribing the text of these *kujika* on paper and translating them into English inevitably strips them of life, independent of the ceremony of which they are part. Yet enough survives through his translation of these texts to evoke poetic recreation of all the living creatures they document.[16] These songlines preserve generations of collective knowledge about the land and the life that it supports. The complexity of the tradition of what the Yanyuwa call *kujika* demands specialist knowledge, like that of any ceremonial tradition. The translated words may not look like any form of philosophical inquiry, in that they are concerned above all with the actions and places of spirit ancestors, who connect the physical world to another realm of reality. Yet in their way, these songs are concerned not just with the generation of life, but with suffering and death and thus the cycle of existence. The performance of such chant, like that of liturgical plainchant in the medieval West, serves to move the participant from the constraints and pressures of the world into a more enduring reality that transcends time. The knowledge it communicates may be collective rather than belonging to any particular individual, but it relates to a broader body of wisdom and law underpinning the world. In practice, however, knowledge of a vast number of songlines has been lost in many parts of Australia, as a consequence of colonisation. Stories about the past may be preserved by elders and passed on to oral historians recording them in English, but no longer in the context of ceremony by which true songlines were traditionally recreated.[17]

---

[16] See, for example, the excerpts included in Bradley 2010, pp. 261–82.

[17] This is the case with Margaret Somerville and Tony Perkins writing about the Gumbaynggirr culture of coastal Australia (Somerville and Perkins 2010).

14.2 The Songlines of Celtic Tradition

Both in twentieth-century Australia and in early medieval Europe, indigenous traditions suffered from missionaries who equated the Christian religion with the values of a colonizing culture. Yet while some Christian missionaries in the early medieval period (like St Boniface in the eighth century) made a point of deliberately cutting down sacred trees and erecting their churches over the location of sites of pagan worship, in practice medieval Christianity often came to accommodation with local pagan traditions, even if this sometimes flouted official precept. One example of this might be the establishment in the fourth century of the feast of Christmas on 25 December, calculated by early liturgists to take over an ancient seasonal celebration of the passage of the winter solstice and thus the victory of the sun so as to celebrate the incarnation (Nothaft 2012). Few of the traditions of the Celtic world that once crossed so much of Europe prior to Roman colonisation have survived. The dominant pagan traditions that have survived from southern Europe are those of Greece and Rome, as preserved in classical literature. The Christian religion offered an alternative set of songlines, drawn from Hebrew tradition and re-interpreted in the light of the teaching of Jesus, whose teachings were themselves transmitted orally for several decades, before being recorded in writing. The Hebrew Scriptures themselves contained many stories about place, above all about the promised land. The Christian Church moved towards a more interior interpretation of these songlines, focused around the persona and teaching of Jesus about the message of these traditions. In the process, songs about sacred places were absorbed into a Christian framework.

Inevitably the early centuries of the Christian movement were marked by sharp competition between its own teachers and the philosophers of the ancient world, each competing to offer individuals escape from the constraints of a world, in which civilisation was defined by urban life and rejection of what was barbarian. Charlesworth's analysis of this period as marked by a vision of philosophy as itself a religion defines a perspective that still has its adherents (Charlesworth 2002, pp. 11–29). He sets up the conceptual framework by which orthodox Christianity defined itself against gnosticism, in the sense of a dominant narrative and intellectual doctrine, that excluded those traditions that it perceived as too marginal. The contested evolution of Christian orthodoxy was about the establishment of a creed that could be chanted by the entire Christian community (Wilhite 2015). The opening verses of John's Gospel, for example, similarly function not just as a statement of belief in the incarnation, but as a didactic hymn that would be chanted by the community, in this case recounting a story of how the universal *Logos* became manifest in human form, through imagery of light – itself drawing on Jewish hymnic tradition (Gordley 2009). While the Gospels do not constitute a *kujika* in the sense of being about a specific place, they offer a metaphorical map of the spiritual life, defined by the journey of Jesus from Galilee to his death and resurrection in Jerusalem. In order to limit the inevitable fragmentation involved in allowing too many such 'songlines', episcopal and imperial authority combined to identify four different versions of the Gospels as canonical, as defined in the form of a book, rather than of a scroll (Grafton and Williams 2006). In practice, many more Gospels remained in circulation, as well as lives of saints, which each interpreted those Scriptures in particular ways. Ambrose's hymns played a key role in defining orthodoxy (Dunkle 2016). In the early fifth century, St Augustine of Hippo argued against the emphasis of Pelagius on reading the Scriptures as a call to moral reform, on the grounds that it minimized the role of divine grace in freeing humanity from the stain of original sin. This produced continuing debate in subsequent centuries (Hwang et al. 2016). While his perspectives became influential in the definition of orthodoxy, there remained an important current of thought that did not absorb his pessimism about the corruption of the will, as the consequence of Adam's sin (Tatha 2002). The survival of many letters of Pelagius (1991) under the name of Jerome itself testifies to the fluidity of orthodox tradition.

Ascetic Christianity, often criticised as being unfriendly to the human body, interpreted the Hebrew and Christian Scriptures as a call to watchfulness and spiritual effort rather than as about total dependence on divine grace, as Augustine tended to argue in later life. Pelagius, a British monk, was just one exponent among many of this ascetic tradition, which had a powerful influence in the British Isles in the early middle ages and was critical of misuse of episcopal authority.[18] Ascetics of this kind, often suspicious of extravagantly dressed bishops, saw themselves as more able than the philosophers of antiquity to effect moral reform by drawing on the imagery of Scripture rather than the abstract reflection of a philosophical elite. In the Latin West during these centuries, only a few committed intellectuals, most famously Boethius in the early sixth century, preserved the tradition of classical philosophy, synthesised with great elegance in *The Consolation of Philosophy*, a fusion of prose and poetry in praise of *Sophia*, Wisdom (Marenbon 2003). Unlike Augustine, Boethius did not believe that pagan wisdom had to be subordinated to Scripture. While Boethius was a Christian, who offered rational rather than Scriptural arguments to defend orthodox understanding of the Trinity and the nature of Christ, as well as formulating axioms of theological argument, he considered the pursuit of *philosophia* to be the exercise of a rational mind rather than the fruit of grace. If there is any limitation to Charlesworth's presentation of the relationship between philosophy as the handmaiden of religion in the medieval period, is that he underplays the tension between such core thinkers as Augustine and Boethius who came to differ quite radically in the role they assigned to philosophical inquiry.[19] To put the contrast between them rather crudely, Augustine always understood *theologia* to be a pagan concept, and saw philosophy as always subordinate to Scripture (Augustine 1972, (trans. Bettenson), VI.5, p. 234). Boethius, by contrast, considered theological reflection (on that which was abstract and without motion) to belong to the highest sphere of philosophy (Boethius, *De Trinitate* I, 1973). While

[18] The influence of Pelagius in the British Isles is emphasised by Michael W. Herren and Shirley Ann Brown in *Christ in Celtic Christianity* (Herren and Brown 2002); possibly, Pelagius is only one representative of a broader ascetic tradition.

[19] Charlesworth tends to downplay the contrast between Boethius and Augustine (Charlesworth 2002, p. 55).

Boethius did acknowledge his awareness of Augustine's resolution of these issues, he adopted a very different perspective, turning not to Scripture, but to the tools of philosophy to resolve questions about God and Christ. As an educated philosopher, Boethius had no particular interest in the wisdom of the land. His ideal of Wisdom was one of transcendent abstraction, although able to be accessed through philosophical study as well as through the person of Christ. In the twelfth and thirteenth centuries, scholastic ways of doing theology would emerge that drew in varying ways on the perspectives of both Augustine and Boethius, but tending (with only notable exceptions, as in the case of Hildegard of Bingen) to ignore the embodied wisdom of the natural world.

These traditions of wisdom through and about the natural world, what Charlesworth had suggested might be called *geosophy*, have often been preserved in Europe in more physically remote regions, away from settlement of the land, as in Australia. One good example of this is given by the book of Kells, belonging to the abbey of Iona from soon after its composition, c. 800 CE. On every page we find birds, fish, and animals depicted alongside the sacred text, clearly signalling the profound connection between the sacred text and the natural world, such as we find in so much Celtic tradition.[20] The four evangelists are presented as embodying four elements in creation (Matthew a winged man, Mark a winged lion, Luke a winged calf, John a winged eagle), all imagined as spirit messengers passing on the Gospel. Only occasionally do records survive of the oral traditions of the Celtic world of the early medieval period, with texts like the *Tain* (The Cattle Raid of Cooley), which relates how the hero of Ulster, Cú Chulainn, resists the ambitions of Queen Medb of Connaught to control a powerful bull, who travels around Ireland as a mythic beast (*The Táin* 2007). Early medieval Celtic culture drew extensively on the natural world to interpret the Scriptures, which provided only one strand of its oral traditions.

Early medieval Ireland is not normally remembered as a period of great philosophical activity, with the exception of John Scotus Eriugena, the remarkably educated Irish monk in the ninth century who used his knowledge of Greek to distance himself from Augustine and absorb instead the Platonism of the Greek Fathers of the Church, and to create a philosophical system in his *Periphyseon* (*De divisone naturae*) based around the notion that *Natura* combines both God and creation, which unfolds from God's being. Histories of philosophy (and that of Charlesworth is no exception here in *Philosophy and Religion*) tend to privilege the scholastic period as the great age of philosophical enquiry, because this was when the Latin writings of Aristotle became widely accessible. Yet there were important centres of learning in early medieval Ireland even in the seventh century, notably the abbey of Bangor in the north-east (from where Columbanus set out to evangelise Europe in the late sixth century) and Lismore in the south-east. One of the earliest known discussions about the wonders of creation from Ireland survives in a treatise *On the Marvels of Holy Scripture*, datable from internal references to 655 and dedicated in particular to 'the Carthaginians', an allusion to the Church established by St

[20] For a measured account of an often popularised theme, see Mary Low 1996.

Carthage or Carthach (c. 560–c. 639), popularly known in Irish as Mochuda. This treatise is not just a compilation of patristic learning, but incorporates naturalistic traditions that seem likely to have been absorbed from pre-Christian Irish scientific learning. It explains miracles as a manifestation of God's working through creation (such as Elijah, seen by the apostles with the transfigured Christ, as a likeness of the resurrection).[21] Only through such texts can we glimpse how Christian narratives may have been shaped by local pre-Christian traditions, as well as by patristic learning.

While nothing is known of any writings by St Carthage, the account of his career recorded in more detailed fashion in a Latin Life and in a more vivid vernacular narrative provides an unusual twist on the familiar theme of the holy man of humble origins, who travels far for his education, and survives adversity to become a famed teacher.[22] It tells how Carthage was himself inspired to a monastic career in his native Kerry by hearing the singing of the disciples of his spiritual mentor, Carthage the Elder. He subsequently travelled across Ireland to study at the famous school at Bangor in the late sixth century, before establishing a major community at Rahan, near the centre of Ireland, for some 40 years. There he develops a special reputation for looking after lepers, who reportedly flocked to Rahan from all over Ireland, until hostility with local abbots and bishops, working in tandem with ambitious secular rulers, forces Carthage to move with his monks and lepers to find refuge at Lismore, in Munster, in south-east Ireland. In both accounts, the spiritual model of St Carthage is invoked as Colum Cille (Columba) rather than St Patrick, who is associated with the Church of Armagh. Whereas Patrick is remembered for his debates with pagan Druids and driving snakes out of Ireland, Carthage was revered not just for attracting lepers, but for surviving the hostility of his peers, and establishing a new foundation at Lismore. Separate evidence leads us to consider that Lismore became a centre of learning, comparable to Bangor and Iona, even by the mid seventh century. While nothing written by Carthage survives, it does seem that he attached great value to the written word and the cause of education. Such is the power of local tradition that the name of this saint is still only widely known around the region of Lismore in Ireland, and that most of the known churches of St Carthage in Australia (including that of St Carthage's cathedral in Lismore, New South Wales, and of St Carthage's Parkville, Melbourne, where Max Charlesworth was a regular parishioner), were established

[21] *De mirabilibus Sanctae Scripturae,* falsely printed among the works of Augustine by Jacques-Paul Migne, *Patrologia Latina* 35 (Paris, 1860), cols 2149–2200; see Marina Smith, 'The Body, Death and Resurrection: Perspectives of an Early Irish Theologian' (Smith 2008).

[22] On St Carthage, see my study, 'The flight of Carthach (Mochuda) from Rahan to Lismore: lineage and identity in early medieval Ireland' (Mews 2013). The Latin text was published as the *Vita Sancti Carthagi* (1997); an English translation of an early modern Irish version of this text was produced by P. Power, *Life of St Declan of Ardmore (ed. from Ms in the Bibliothèque royale, Brussels), and Life of St Mochuda of Lismore (ed. from Ms in the Library of the Royal Irish Academy)* [*LM*], Irish Texts Society 16 (London, 1914; repr. Dublin, 1995), pp. 74–147. The Irish account of his expulsion from Rahan and various songs about Mochuda were edited and translated by C. Plummer, *Bethada náem nÉrenn: Lives of Irish Saints* (Plummer 1922, 1, pp. 300–16, and 2, pp. 291–302).

by clergy connected to Lismore in Ireland.[23] In churches connected to this saint, Carthage's name was included within the litany of the saints chanted at Easter Saturday over the blessing of the font. The particular combination of saints names in Irish litanies reflects the lineage and the places to which a particular community was connected.[24]

In such stories, the spirit ancestor has become the saint, whose physical journeys are presented as extending the journeys of the heroes of Scripture, in the process marking out the sphere of influence of a particular religious community. While they cannot be considered as philosophical texts, in the strict sense of the word, they offer an account of the spiritual journey of a holy man or woman, in the process picking out a Scriptural theme. Thus while accounts of Patrick emphasize confrontation with the authority of pagan priests, the Life of Carthage is very concerned with the places to which the saint travelled, in turn evoking the travels of Moses to the promised land. Near its conclusion, it tells a story about how an old man impatiently asked Carthage for both milk and beer, to which the saint responds by blessing a particular spring at Lismore that produced first milk, then beer, then wine, and telling him that he could take as much as he wanted (*Vita Sancti Carthagi* 57, p. 198). The story expands on one told about Brigit that she turned water into beer for a leper, in turn connecting to the story told about Jesus in John 4: 1–27 speaking to the Samaritan woman (who did not worship at Jerusalem) at Jacob's well, telling her that she could have life abundantly. The transformation of the water into milk, beer and wine offers an image of the trinitarian nature of God, evoking an image of divine attributes of living water. The saint's life, recited on the anniversary of his feast (14 May) functions as a songline through its connecting Lismore to various other places in Ireland, all known to the saint. The Irish songs attributed to Mochuda attest to the enduring power of his reputation, including one about how he threw down a powerful ruler, Blathmac (Plummer 1922, vol. 2, p. 298). These accounts cannot be described as philosophy, but they do provide a kind of map, in which the saint is the exemplar of the pilgrim, leading his flock to their heavenly home. Christian narratives tend to be about saints and the need for human reform, rather than about our need to reconnect to natural ancestors. They are clearly not in the same category as an indigenous songline in that they tend not to be about creatures in the natural world, but about personal heroes. Nonetheless, they function as a way of giving a specific local spin to stories otherwise transmitted through canonical religious texts and institutions. Only through concerted critical effort can these memories, largely forgotten in the historical record, be retrieved, in the same ways as John Bradley has done with the *kujika* of the Yanyuwa people.

[23] See Chris Watson, 'St Carthage in Australasia' (Watson 2013).

[24] On the genre of the litany, see a study of an Irish prayerbook (in which *Mochuda* is named alongside other Irish saints), copied in the Cork region in the early nineteenth century, but given to the State Library of Victoria, Melbourne, studied by Constant Mews, Julia Kuhns and Chris Watson, 'Remembering the Saints of Munster: An Irish Prayer Book copied by Dáibhí de Barra' (Mews et al. 2014).

14.3 Conclusion

Max Charlesworth never included any discussion of aboriginal culture in his 1972 historical survey, *The Philosophy of Religion*, or in its revised format, *Philosophy and Religion from Plato to Postmodernism*. The dominant songline, as it were, of the Western cultural tradition still tends to see philosophy as starting with the Greeks and as moving forward to modernity and beyond, rather than as a constant of human culture. It is a perspective that privileges progress, and ideals of emancipation through reason and dispute. Yet Charlesworth was aware that the pursuit of wisdom could be achieved not just through rational enquiry, but through human creativity at any point of time and any cultural condition. During the 1960s, when he was actively writing about the great medieval Christian scholastics, St Anselm and St Thomas Aquinas, his fascination was with how they sought to identify through reason the core themes of Scripture. Their core conceptual framework was provided by daily singing of the psalms, themselves ancient reflections on the human condition. The result of that interaction between Scripture and reason is what Latin Christians in the twelfth century came to call theology. While theologians might focus on issues of belief, perhaps the most powerful way medieval Christianity exerted an influence on society was through plainchant, which retold the great themes of Scripture through the medium of song rather than the written word.

Charlesworth never succumbed to the temptation to elevate the medieval version of the Christian songline into a fixed icon of philosophical and religious truth like some of his contemporaries. His respect for both Anselm and Aquinas was framed by awareness that they were tackling serious philosophical questions, within the framework of the scientific and philosophical tools becoming available to them in the world in which they lived, without assuming that their interpretations of Scripture and Christian doctrine should remain canonical for subsequent generations. Always attentive to the insights of new philosophical movements, even if they were completely outside the confines of received religious traditions, he saw philosophy as a quest that could never be colonised by anyone school of thought, pursued in many different cultural environments. This was the frame of mind that led to the establishment of the journal *Sophia* in 1962, breaking a mould in its recognition that philosophy and religious studies could both be concerned with the ideal of wisdom, both within and outside western traditions of philosophical discourse (Garfield 2012).

Charlesworth's discovery of aboriginal culture and spirituality in the 1980s can be understood as participating in a broader shift within Australian culture towards greater recognition of indigenous culture. In a sense, he was preparing the ground for discussion that did not fit into the framework of *Philosophy and Religion from Plato to Postmodernism*, the 2002 revision of his early monograph. The suggestion offered here is that the notion of a songline, a sacred chant closely associated with a particular journey of a spirit ancestor, given particular attention by John Bradley in his account of learning the *kujika* of the Yanyuwa people, might provide a way of thinking about elements within other sacred texts, concerned with the notion of the journey. In both cases, we are dealing with cultural code that needs to be interpreted.

Indigenous songlines relate much more to the living dynamism of the land. By contrast, canonical sacred texts tend to be more concerned with social relationship and ethical principles, although always situated within the context of place. Bradley's awareness of the relationship between these songlines and an unwritten law of the land speaks to a sense of sacred, not unconnected to the awareness of other religious traditions which communicate a sense of cosmic law. In many of the major world religions, celebration of the natural world (at least in the eyes of many of its dominant interpreters) has often been subordinated to concern about ethics and authority. Indigenous traditions, by contrast, are first of all about the sacredness of the land.

The example of narratives about the lives of the saints in early medieval Ireland provides an analogue to traditional songlines, although their heroes are individuals rather than spirit ancestors from the natural world. In their way, stories about the saints (preserved through song as well as prose narratives) provide maps of the known universe, often relating specific places to a spirit world of mythical ancestors. Vernacular Irish tradition preserved an acute sense of the natural world that crept into the narrative structure of stories told about saints and their command over the forces of nature. Such stories may provide an equivalent to the songline, in delineating the journey of a saint, through imagery shaped by Scripture. Max Charlesworth made an important step in reminding his readers of the significance of indigenous traditions, even if they seemed far removed from the classical philosophical concerns of Western civilisation. Indigenous Australian traditions demonstrate an awareness of connection to the natural world more specific than any of those 'world religions', concerned with the fate of the human soul. It is as if the process of reflecting on the destiny of the individual soul has disconnected individuals from the land into which they have been born. The curse of being a migrant nation is that most of us remain visitors to a land, of which we do not know its most sacred songs.

There is a vast distance between chants that are orally transmitted and those that have been recorded and standardized in writing. Yet whether we speak about *kujika* in Carpentaria, songs about saints in Ireland, or sacred stories of the Hebrews, Christians, Muslims or followers of the Buddha, we have texts that are part of a community's cultural code, defining its values in a similar way to genetic code. In different situations, that code will be interpreted in different ways, depending on the needs of the situation. Song has always played a key role in sacred traditions, whether transmitted orally in indigenous communities, or in religions defined by a canonical written text. My suggestion is that in their very different ways, indigenous songlines and sacred texts may function as cultural codes, needing to be re-interpreted and re-translated if they are to help a culture survive difficult situations. To expand on a phrase used by Max Charlesworth in *Religious Inventions* (Charlesworth 2012), songlines are like sacred texts in being religious inventions, belonging to the cultural treasury of humanity.

References

Anselm. (1965 [1078]). *St. Anselm's Proslogion; A reply on behalf of the fool, by Gaunilo; The author's reply to Gaunilo* (Translated with an introduction and philosophical commentary by Max Charlesworth). Oxford: Clarendon Press.

Aquinas. (1970). *Summa theologiae: [The world order] 1a.110-19, volume 15* (Volume translated and annotated by Max Charlesworth). London: Blackfriars: Eyre & Spottiswoode.

Asad, T. (1993). *Genealogies of religion: Discipline and reasons of power in Christianity and Islam*. Baltimore: Johns Hopkins Press.

Augustine. (1972). *The city of god* (H. Bettenson, Trans.). Harmondsworth: Penguin.

Barton, C. A., & Boyarin, D. (2016). *Imagine no religion: How modern abstractions hide ancient realities*. New York: Fordham University Press.

Berndt, R. H. (1951). *Kunapipi: A study of an Australian aboriginal religious cult*. New York: International Universities Press.

Boethius. (1973). *De Trinitate* (H. F. Stewart & E. K. Rand, Ed., & Trans.). Cambridge, MA: Harvard University Press.

Bradley, J. (2010). *Singing saltwater country: Journey to the songlines of Carpentaria*. Crows Nest: Allen & Unwin.

Central Australian religion: personal monototemism in polytotemic community. (1978). Adelaide: Australian Association for the Study of Religions.

Charlesworth, M. (1984). *The Aboriginal land rights movement* (2nd ed.). Richmond: Hodja Educational Resources Cooperative. [First published by Deakin University in 1983].

Charlesworth, M. (1996). Gibson, Alexander Boyce (Sandy) (1900–1972). In Australian dictionary of biography. Canberra: National Centre of Biography, Australian National University. http://adb.anu.edu.au/biography/gibson-alexander-boyce-sandy-10295/text18215. Accessed 17 Nov 2014.

Charlesworth, M. (1997). *Religious inventions: Four essays*. Cambridge: Cambridge University Press.

Charlesworth, M. (1998). *Religious business: Essays on Australian aboriginal spirituality*. Cambridge: Cambridge University Press.

Charlesworth, M. (2002). *Philosophy and religion: From Plato to postmodernism*. Oxford: Oneworld.

Charlesworth, M. (2009). Anthropological approaches to 'primitive' religions. *Sophia, 48*(2), 119–125.

Charlesworth, M. (2012). Translating religious texts: 'When we learn to speak, we are learning to translate' Octavio Paz. *Sophia, 51*(4), 423–448.

Charlesworth, M., Morphy, H., Bell, D., & Maddock, K. (Eds.). (1984). *Religion in aboriginal Australia: An anthology*. St. Lucia: University of Queensland Press.

Charlesworth, M., Kimber, R., & Wallace, N. (Eds.). (1990). *Ancestor spirits: Aspects of Australian Aboriginal life and spirituality*. Geelong: Deakin University Press.

Charlesworth, M., Dussart, F., & Morphy, H. (Eds.). (2005). *Aboriginal religions in Australia. An anthology of recent writings*. Aldershot/Hants: Ashgate.

Chatwin, B. (1987). *The Songlines*. London: Jonathan Cape.

Collins, J., & Blot, R. K. (2003). *Literacy and literacies: Texts, power and identity*. Cambridge: Cambridge University Press.

Dunkle, B. P. (2016). *Enchantment and creed in the hymns of Ambrose of Milan*. Oxford: Oxford University Press.

Garfield, J. (2012). Max Charlesworth's Sophia: The first half-century and the next. *Sophia, 51*(4), 419–421.

Gordley, M. (2009). The Johannine prologue and Jewish didactic hymn traditions: A new case for reading the prologue as a hymn. *Journal of Biblical Literature, 128*(4), 781–802.

Grafton, A., & Williams, M. (2006). *Christianity and the transformation of the book: Origen, Eusebius and the library of Caesarea*. Cambridge, MA: Harvard University Press.

Green, J. (2012). The Altyerre story: 'Suffering badly by translation'. *The Australian Journal of Anthropology, 23*(2), 158–178.

Herren, M. W., & Brown, S. A. (2002). *Christ in Celtic Christianity: Britain and Ireland from the fifth to the tenth century*. Woodbridge: Boydell.

Hume, L. (2004). Accessing the eternal: Dreaming 'the dreaming' and ceremonial performance. *Zygon, 39*(1), 237–258.

Hwang, A. Y. B., Matz, J., & Casiday, A. (Eds.). (2016). *Grace for grace: The debates after Augustine and Pelagius*. Washington, DC: Catholic University of America.

Kirsner, D. (2012). Max Charlesworth: A philosopher in the world. *Sophia, 51*(4), 561–569.

Low, M. (1996). *Celtic Christianity and nature: Early Irish and Hebridean traditions*. Edinburgh: Edinburgh University Press.

Marenbon, J. (2003). *Boethius*. Oxford: Oxford University Press.

Masuzawa. (1993). *In search of dreamtime: The quest for the origin of religion*. Chicago: University of Chicago Press.

May, J. D. (2006). Rootedness: Reflections on land and belonging. In W. G. Jeanrond & A. D. Mayes (Eds.), *Recognising the margins: Developments in biblical and theological studies: Essays in honour of Sean Freyne* (pp. 146–159). Dublin: Columba Press.

Mews, C. (2013). The flight of Carthach (Mochuda) from Rahan to Lismore: Lineage and identity in early medieval Ireland. *Early Medieval Europe, 21*(1), 1–26.

Mews, C., Kuhns, J., & Watson, C. (2014). Remembering the saints of Munster: An Irish prayer book copied by Dáibhí de Barra. *Australian Journal of Irish Studies, 14*, 111–129.

Moyle, A. M. (1996). *Handlist of field collections of recorded music in Australia and the Torres Strait*. Canberra: Australian Institute of Aboriginal Studies.

Nongbri, B. (2013). *Before religion: History of a modern concept*. New Haven: Yale University Press.

Nothaft, C. P. E. (2012). The origins of the Christmas date: Some recent trends in historical research. *Church History, 81*(4), 903–911.

Ong, W. J. (1982). *Orality and literacy: The technologizing of the word*. London: Routledge.

Pelagius. (1991). *The letters of Pelagius and his followers* (B. R. Rees, Ed., & Trans.). Woodbridge: Boydell Press.

Plummer, C. (1922). *Bethada náem nÉrenn: :Lives of Irish saints* (Vol. 2). Oxford: Clarendon Press.

Power, P. (1995). *Life of St Declan of Ardmore,* and *Life of St Mochuda of Lismore* [LM]. Irish Texts Society 16, 74–147. Dublin (reprint) (originally London, 1914).

Shakespeare, N. (2001). *Bruce Chatwin: A biography*. New York: Anchor Books.

Smith, M. (2008). The body, death and resurrection: Perspectives of an early Irish theologian. *Speculum, 83*, 531–571.

Somerville, M., & Perkins, T. (2010). *Singing the coast*. Canberra: Aboriginal Studies Press.

Stockton, E. (2003). The mindful land. In J. Cameron (Ed.), *Changing places: Re-imagining Australia* (pp. 234–242). Double Bay: Longueville Books.

Strehlow, T. G. H. (1971). *Songs of Central Australia*. Sydney: Angus and Robertson.

Tatha, W. (2002). *Original sin: Origins, developments, contemporary meaning* (p. 2002). New York: Paulist Press.

The Táin: A new translation of the Táin bó cúailnge (Ciaran Carson, Trans.). London: Penguin, 2007.

Tonkinson, R. (1978). *The Mardudjara aborigines: Living the dream in Australia's desert*. New York: Holt, Rinehart and Winston.

van der Toorn, K. (2007). *Scribal culture and the making of the Hebrew Bible*. Cambridge, MA: Harvard University Press.

Vita Sancti Carthagi. (1997). In *Vitae sanctorum Hiberniae*, I, pp. 52–99. Edited by C. Plummer. 2 Vols. Dublin (reprint) (originally Oxford, 1910).

Watson, C. (2013). St Carthage in Australasia. In A. Ahlqvist & P. O'Neill (Eds.), *Celts at home and abroad: A festschrift for Malcolm Broun* (Sydney Series in Celtic Studies, 15) (pp. 367–380). Sydney: Celtic Studies Foundation.
Wilhite, D. E. (2015). *The gospel according to heretics: Discovering orthodoxy through early christological conflicts*. Grand Rapids: Baker Academic.
Wolfe, P. (1991). On being woken up: The dreamtime in anthropology and in Australian settler culture. *Comparative Studies in Society and History, 33*, 197–224.

Constant J. Mews gained his BA and MA from the University of Auckland, New Zealand, and his DPhil from Oxford University. He is Professor within the School of Philosophical, Historical and International Studies, Monash University, where he is also Director of the Centre for Religious Studies. He has published widely on medieval thought, ethics and religious culture, with particular reference to the writings of Abelard, Heloise, Hildegard of Bingen and their contemporaries, including *Abelard and Heloise* (New York: Oxford University Press, 2005) and *The Lost Love Letters of Heloise and Abelard. Perceptions of Dialogue in Twelfth-Century France*, 2nd edn (New York: McMillan Palgrave, 2008). His research interests range from the early Middle Ages to late medieval religious and intellectual culture, as well as the interface between various religious and ethical traditions.

Chapter 15
Charlesworth on Philosophy and Religion

Graham Oppy

Charlesworth (2002) is a substantial reworking of Charlesworth (1972), occasioned by 'an extraordinary revolution … in philosophy of religion' in the intervening period. According to Charlesworth, the scope of philosophy of religion had been vastly enlarged on the back of: (a) the long overdue recognition of the radical diversity of religions; (b) the invasion of the social sciences into the study of religious systems; and (c) the emergence of new – 'postmodernist' – ways of doing philosophy of religion (1). (This page number – and all subsequent page numbers – refer to Charlesworth (2002).)

The main thesis of Charlesworth (2002) is that there are five approaches to philosophy of religion that constitute a grid on which most philosophies of religion can be located: (1) philosophy as religion; (2) philosophy as handmaid of religion; (3) philosophy as making room for faith; (4) philosophy as analysis of religious language; and (5) philosophy as postmodernist critique of the religious domain. Although the book ends with a brief discussion of the kinds of criteria to be invoked in an attempt to adjudicate between these five approaches, the chief aim of the book is to describe and analyse 'the main ways in which philosophy and religion have wrestled with each other in the … two thousand years of Western thought' (176).

I begin with a brief summary of what Charlesworth has to say about the five approaches that he identifies, including his account of the strengths and weaknesses of each. I shall then turn to consider the merits of his 'grid' and his account of the nature and scope of philosophy, religion, and philosophy of religion.

G. Oppy (✉)
Monash University, Clayton, VIC, Australia
e-mail: graham.oppy@monash.edu

P. Wong et al. (eds.), *Considering Religions, Rights and Bioethics: For Max Charlesworth*, Sophia Studies in Cross-cultural Philosophy of Traditions and Cultures 30, https://doi.org/10.1007/978-3-030-18148-2_15

15.1 Philosophy as Religion

According to Charlesworth, those who take the 'philosophy as religion' approach take the task of philosophy to be to lead sages to supra-mundane vision and illumination: religion is the culmination of philosophy (12). For Charlesworth, 'philosophy as religion' is an austerely contemplative approach to religion which is radically ahistorical, esoteric, abstract, theoretical, and committed to denial of any distinction between natural reason and supernatural truth (39). Charlesworth cites Plato, Aristotle, Plotinus, Pseudo-Dionysius, Al Razi, Al Farabi, Avicenna, Averroes, Leibniz, Spinoza, Hegel, Whitehead and de Chardin as exponents of this approach.

In Charlesworth's estimation, the primary complaint against the 'philosophy as religion' approach is the conception of the nature and scope of philosophy that goes along with it. While this approach has the advantage that it makes religion a rational enterprise that is worthy of human beings at their best and most human, it has the disadvantage that it presupposes a high metaphysical conception of philosophy that is open to various kinds of philosophical objections. But – according to Charlesworth – while philosophical positions are always tentative and revocable, religious assent typically implies absolute and irrevocable commitment (43).

15.2 Philosophy as Handmaid of Religion

For Charlesworth, the 'philosophy as handmaid of religion' approach restricts philosophy to the twin tasks of (a) showing the 'non-impossibility' of the articles of faith; and (b) proving the 'preambles or presuppositions' of faith: roughly, that God exists and has some attributes that are accessible to our reason and understanding (79). On this approach, there are truths of revelation that cannot be established or grasped by merely philosophical inquiry but, nonetheless, religious faith depends upon philosophy for its 'defence' and for the 'justification of its preambles and presuppositions'. In contrast to the 'philosophy as religion' approach, the 'philosophy as handmaid of religion' approach allows room for an order of revelation and faith that transcends the order of philosophy and pure reason. Charlesworth cites Philo, Justin Martyr, Clement of Alexandria, Origen, Augustine, Abelard, Anselm, Bonaventure, Albertus Magnus, Alexander of Hales, Maimonides, Aquinas, Cajetan, John of St. Thomas, Garrigou-Lagrange, Gilson, Maritain, Mascall, and Farrer as proponents of the 'philosophy as handmaid of religion' approach.

In Charlesworth's estimation, while this approach is not quite so directly vulnerable to charges of 'religious intellectualism', it still involves a predominantly intellectualist or speculative view of religion. Moreover, since the understanding of the mysteries of faith involves at least the 'negative' employment of philosophical reason, the 'philosophy as handmaid of religion' approach is also open to charges of 'esotericism', 'ahistoricity', and 'impersonalism'. But, in Charlesworth's view, the most important objection to the 'philosophy as handmaid of religion' approach is that it makes religious belief dependent upon the viability of a specific conception of philosophy and upon the success of particular arguments that issue from that conception of philosophy: if philosophy cannot do the work of 'justifying the preambles and presuppositions of faith', then religious belief is embroiled in philosophical disputation (81).

15.3 Philosophy as Making Room for Faith

On Charlesworth's telling, the 'philosophy as making room for faith' approach meets the primary difficulties that face the 'philosophy as religion' and 'philosophy as handmaid of religion' approaches. In his view, the 'philosophy as making room for faith' approach: (a) makes religious faith independent of any direct reliance upon disputable philosophical premises; (b) guarantees the transcendence of the religious order; and (c) gives primacy to the practical mode of religious faith and its personal and 'inward' character (128). Charlesworth cites Tertullian, Peter Damian, Bernard of Clairvaux, Al Ghazali, Ockham, Nicholas of Autrecourt, Luther, Calvin, Pascal, Rousseau, [Hume], Kant, Kierkegaard, Mansell, Otto, Tillich, Barth, Kaufmann, and Cupitt as proponents of the 'philosophy as making room for faith' approach.

For Charlesworth, the primary difficulties that confront the 'philosophy as making room for faith' approach are (a) that we need to rely upon philosophical argument in order to draw the limits to reason that would make room for faith; (b) that it is hard to make sense of the idea that reason can be used to establish the bounds of reason; and (c) that the separation of the practical realm and the realm of faith from the speculative realm makes it impossible to give any account of the object of faith. In the end, the 'philosophy as making room for faith' approach effectively denies the autonomy and transcendence of faith (130).

15.4 Philosophy as Analysis of Religious Language

According to Charlesworth, the 'philosophy as analysis of religious language' approach is an attempt to elaborate a philosophy of religion without appeal to traditional metaphysics (133). Charlesworth's discussion takes in logical positivism, ordinary language philosophy, and broadly Wittgensteinian approaches to philosophy, citing Ayer, Braithwaite, Hare, Malcolm, Wittgenstein and Phillips.

Charlesworth makes piecemeal criticisms of the various 'philosophy as analysis of religious language' approaches. If he thinks that there is a more general critique to be made, perhaps it lies in his (implicit) suggestion that any view of philosophy of religion that takes it to be an essentially descriptive and non-explanatory inquiry will be severely compromised. If philosophy can have no transcendent function over and above the analysis of particular language games and forms of life, then philosophy can have nothing to say about the transcendent realm of the divine (148). In Charlesworth's eyes, those who suppose that there is a transcendent realm are bound to think that the 'philosophy as analysis of religious language' approach is hopelessly compromised by its minimalism and reductionism (153).

15.5 Philosophy as Postmodernist Critique of the Religious Domain

According to Charlesworth, the 'philosophy as postmodernist critique of the religious domain' is another attempt to elaborate a philosophy of religion without appeal to traditional metaphysics (155). On Charlesworth's account, postmodernism is an anti-foundationalist approach to philosophy which takes interpretative communities to be final points of reference in interpretative exercises, and claims that everything must be understood and interpreted within specific – and specified – contexts. In particular, for Charlesworth, postmodernists deny that there is – or can be – a meta-contextual, God-like vantage point from which epistemological, ontological and metaphysical standpoints may be judged and justified. Charlesworth's discussion of postmodernism takes in a wide range of thinkers and writers: Nietzsche, Heidegger, Gadamer, Derrida, Foucault, Habermas, Rorty, Fish, Marion, Taylor, Guarino and Hart, among others.

Charlesworth is sceptical that there could be a postmodernist philosophy of religion, on analogy with the 'philosophy as religion', 'philosophy as handmaid of religion', and 'philosophy as making room for faith' approaches. Moreover, Charlesworth suspects that postmodernist critiques of metaphysically based religion and theology may be caught in 'fatal paradoxes'. While postmodernists object to 'totalising' claims about facts, truth, correctness, validity, and clarity, they make 'totalising' claims about contexts, situations, interpretations, justifications, hybridity, plurality, difference, and so forth. In Charlesworth's view, while postmodernism may have a valuable therapeutic effect, it is hard to see how it could lead to anything that deserved to be called a 'philosophy of religion' (172).

15.6 Criteria for Judgment

According to Charlesworth, any comparative assessment of the five approaches to philosophy of religion must make reference to two distinct sets of criteria. On the one hand, there are purely philosophical considerations arising from the conception of philosophy's nature and role on each of the five approaches to philosophy of religion. On the other hand, any philosophical account of religion that leads to systematic theological 'reductionism' is – in Charlesworth's eyes – clearly inadequate: a philosophy of religion that evacuates religion of any specific meaning of its own by reducing it to that which is not religion is inadequate as philosophy of religion (176).

On the first hand, Charlesworth suggests that (a) 'philosophy as religion' is viable only if some kind of transcendental metaphysics is possible; (b) 'philosophy as handmaid of religion' is viable only if philosophy can have a transcendental metaphysical role; (c) 'philosophy as making room for faith' is viable only if 'critical' philosophy is viable; (d) 'philosophy as analysis of religious language' is viable only if philosophy must have an 'analytic' or 'therapeutic' or 'anti-metaphysical' role; and (e) 'philosophy as postmodernist critique of the religious domain' is viable only if philosophy cannot have a metaphysical or foundationalist role (175).

On the second hand, Charlesworth admits that it is very difficult to say what 'reductionism' amounts to – though he does suggest that, perhaps, Hegel, Arnold, and Santayana may be taken as exemplary proponents of 'reductive' accounts of religion. But, even if there are clear cases, there are also hard cases: Charlesworth himself admits that it is hard to determine whether Kant, Plato, Plotinus, Spinoza, and Tillich are 'reductionists'. Recent discussions of 'reduction', 'supervenience', 'emergence' and the like strongly suggest that it is no easy task to achieve philosophical consensus about the proper understanding of these terms.

15.7 Qualifications

Before we turn to a critical assessment of Charlesworth's account of philosophy of religion, we need to note two disclaimers that Charlesworth introduces.

First, he observes that, 'for the purposes of this book', the religious domain is identified with 'the great monotheistic religions': Judaism, Christianity and Islam. To justify, or excuse, the lack of any attention paid to Hinduism, Buddhism, Jainism, Sikhism, Shintoism, Taoism, and so forth, Charlesworth merely observes that the philosophy of religion is very much a creation of Western philosophical and theological traditions: while there are analogous developments in Hinduism and Buddhism, philosophy has never had for them the autonomous status that it has enjoyed in the West (5).

Second, Charlesworth notes that he makes no detailed reference to feminist views on philosophy of religion. While he allows that there is a valuable feminist *perspective* on philosophy and theology, he denies that there can be either a feminist form of rationality or a feminist mode of doing philosophy and theology. In particular, he says that, in order to show to both women and men that there is a *sui generis* feminist mode of philosophical rationality, feminists would have to explain themselves in terms of commonly acknowledged canons of philosophical rationality which transcend gender differences (6). While Charlesworth does not explicitly address the broader issue, it seems plausible to suppose that he intends what he says about feminist views on philosophy of religion to extend to any other 'sub-group' views on philosophy of religion, ordered according to race, or ethnicity, or sexual orientation, or social class, or political orientation, or the like.

15.8 Diversity of Religions

It is curious that Charlesworth claims that long overdue recognition of the radical diversity of religions has contributed to the vast enlargement of scope of philosophy of religion, yet then – for the purposes of his book – goes on to identify 'the religious domain' with the Abrahamic religions. There is not the slightest shred of plausibility in the claim that recognition of the radical diversity of religions contributes significantly to the differences between Charlesworth (1972) and Charlesworth (2002). Of course, in making this observation, I do not mean to deny the correctness of the suggestion that western philosophy *may* be witnessing a long overdue move towards recognition of the radical diversity of religions. However, I would certainly want to add that, more than a decade after the publication of Charlesworth (2002), western philosophy is still broadly failing to make sufficiently serious engagement with the radical diversity of religions. One has only to consider – for example – the contents of handbooks and anthologies of philosophy of religion published by the major western presses to recognise that there has been little more than token engagement with the radical diversity of religions in the past decade.

Perhaps it is also worth noting that Charlesworth (2002) contains no references to the work of either John Hick or Ninian Smart. Hick's religious pluralism was explicitly and self-consciously framed as the outcome of serious [Christian] engagement with the radical diversity of religions; but it is not at all clear where Hick's religious pluralism should be located on Charlesworth's 'grid'. It may not be entirely outrageous to suggest that there are elements of each of 'philosophy as religion', 'philosophy as handmaid of religion', and 'philosophy as making room for faith' in Hick's interpretation of religion. Moreover, the field of religious studies – which received serious early support from both Hick and Smart – makes no contribution at all to the investigation that Charlesworth undertakes.

15.9 Invasion of the Social Sciences

It is hardly any less curious that Charlesworth claims that the 'invasion of the social sciences' – anthropology, sociology, psychology and history – has contributed to the vast enlargement of scope of philosophy of religion, yet (a) fails to make substantial use of any materials from anthropology, sociology, psychology and history; and (b) more or less makes no mention of works in these fields, except in footnotes to the paragraph in which he claims that there has been an invasion of the social sciences in the study of religion. There is no plausibility in the claim that recognition of 'the invasion of the social sciences' contributes significantly to the differences between Charlesworth (1972) and Charlesworth (2002). Nonetheless, in this case, it seems to me to be clearly true (a) that the social sciences – including the cognitive sciences – are having a steadily increasing degree of influence in philosophy of religion; and

(b) that experimental philosophy, in its application to philosophy of religion, has introduced some of the methods of the social sciences into the practice of philosophy of religion.

On my reckoning, there are only six people who might plausibly be classified as social scientists who are mentioned by Charlesworth. None of the six – Durkheim, Evans-Pritchard, Freud, Geertz, Levi-Strauss and Weber – is mentioned more than once, and none of them is paid substantive attention. Moreover, fundamental questions that have caused serious concern for social scientists – e.g. whether the idea that there is such a thing as religion is merely a Western conceit – are not taken up in Charlesworth's investigation.

15.10 Charlesworth's Project

Although Charlesworth claims that his study attempts to display the various basic ways in which philosophy has come to terms with the religious domain as defined by the great monotheistic traditions in the West and the Middle East (4), it is clear that this is not an accurate characterisation of what his study actually does. While – as I shall argue later – this is also not right, it seems to me that it would at least be closer to the truth to say that what his study attempts to display is the basic ways in which philosophers who view themselves as participants in – or fellow travellers with – monotheistic religions have conceived of the relationship between their philosophical beliefs and their religious beliefs. In particular, it seems at least initially plausible to say that 'philosophy as religion', 'philosophy as handmaid of religion', and 'philosophy as making room for faith' are all families of ways in which philosophers who view themselves as participants in – or fellow travellers with – monotheistic religions have conceived of the relationship between their philosophical beliefs and their religious beliefs.

'Philosophy as religion' is clearly a minority view – if represented at all – among Christians, Muslims and Jews who are serious practitioners of their religions. Many of the monotheists whom Charlesworth mentions under this head – Plato, Aristotle, Plotinus – were not members of an Abrahamic faith; and many of those who were nominally members of Abrahamic faiths – Leibniz, Spinoza, Hegel – had marginal standing within their faiths, and were widely regarded as heretics, or worse. On even the most casual consideration, there is evident difficulty for 'people of the book' in accepting 'philosophy as religion'.

If we set aside 'philosophy as religion', then the serious options that Charlesworth provides for Abrahamic philosophers of religion are 'philosophy as handmaid of religion' and 'philosophy as making room for faith'. Charlesworth's standard bearer for 'philosophy as handmaid of religion' is Aquinas; and his standard bearers for 'philosophy as making room for faith' are Kant and Kierkegaard. Interestingly, Charlesworth classifies Plantinga as a 'neo-Thomist' (5), but also acknowledges that Plantinga delineates a theory of knowledge and methodology sympathetic to [the 'philosophy making room for faith' approach of] Lutheran and Calvinist theology (149). The lesson that I am inclined to draw at this point is that Charlesworth's 'philosophy as handmaid of religion'/'philosophy as making room for faith' dichotomy does not provide a very useful grid for classifying ways in which Abrahamic philosophers of religion think about the relationship between philosophy and religion.

I am inclined to think that 'philosophy as analysis of religious language' and 'philosophy as postmodernist critique of the religious domain' are unlikely to be attractive ways for Abrahamic philosophers of religion to think about the relationship between philosophy and religion. This is particularly clear in the case of 'philosophy as analysis of religious language': it is plainly worth noting that the philosophers that Charlesworth cites under this label are almost all atheists or irreligionists. Moreover, while it is clearly true that many Abrahamic philosophers of religion self-identify as postmodernists, it is far from clear that those Abrahamic philosophers of religion are not also appropriately classified using one or both of the 'philosophy as handmaid of religion' and 'philosophy as making room for faith' labels. Philosophy, as religion, is given to many kinds of syncretism.

15.11 Philosophy, Religion, and Worldview

If we think that Charlesworth's 'philosophy as handmaid of religion'/'philosophy as making room for faith' dichotomy does not provide a sufficiently fine-grained grid for classifying ways in which Abrahamic philosophers of religion think about the relationship between philosophy and religion, we might suppose that there is a more useful grid that we could put in its place. Furthermore, we may suppose that it remains a question to be answered whether Charlesworth's preliminary investigations provide a useful resource for such an undertaking.

Of course, not all philosophers of religion are Abrahamic philosophers of religion. Before we turn to consider the ways in which Abrahamic philosophers of religion think about the relationship between philosophy and religion, it will be profitable to think about the ways in which philosophers of religion think about the relationship between philosophy and religion. And, in order to approach that topic, we first need to consider the ways in which philosophers of religion think about philosophy, and the ways in which philosophers of religion think about religion.

There are many different ways of thinking about philosophy. Some philosophers think of philosophy primarily as an *activity*; some philosophers think of philosophy primarily as a *way of life*; some philosophers think of philosophy primarily as a *systematic body of doctrines*. I think that philosophy is primarily a *domain of inquiry*: philosophy is the discipline that addresses questions for which we do not yet know how to produce – and perhaps cannot even imagine how to produce – agreed answers using the methods of other disciplines. A consequence of my way of thinking about philosophy is that, for almost all other disciplines, there are borderline questions for which it is not currently clear whether those questions will, in time, be given agreed answers using what will then be established methods of those disciplines: for almost all disciplines, there is the sub-field of philosophy that is the *philosophy of* that discipline. Where a subject matter is taken up in a range of disciplines, the philosophy of that subject matter may well take in borderline questions from a range of disciplines. I say that this is how it is with philosophy of religion; there are no agreed answers to the questions addressed in philosophy of religion, and no agreed methods for resolving disagreements about the answers to these questions in relevant related disciplines: history, sociology, religious studies, and so forth. (I subscribe to the view that Chalmers (2015) calls 'disciplinary speciation'. I explain the view in a bit more detail in Oppy (2018: 38-40).)

There are many different ways of thinking about religion. Some philosophers have supposed that there is no such thing as religion: the concept of 'religion' is a Western construct whose employment serves only to advance and protect Western economic and political interests. (See, for example, Boyarin (2016), Nongbri (2013), and Smith (1963).) Some philosophers have supposed that there are no interesting generalisations that can be made about religion: the concept of 'religion' is a family resemblance concept that resists informative analysis or definition. Some philosophers have supposed that their own religion is the one true religion, and that 'religion' can be satisfactorily defined in terms of that one true religion. I think that religions are, very roughly, forms of social organisation that regulate passionate, communal displays of costly commitments to non-natural agents and/or costly attempts to overcome non-natural superstructures of reality, thereby providing mastery of people's existential anxieties about death, deception, disease, catastrophe, pain, loneliness, injustice, want, loss, and the like. Religions have many dimensions: symbols, creeds, scriptures, sacraments, rituals, sharia, music, sacred buildings, sacred places, institutions, populations, histories, theoretical interpretations, and so forth. However, one thing that is central to religions is the provision of *worldviews*: accounts of the world and our place within it that aspire to a certain kind of comprehensiveness and fundamentality. (Elsewhere, I use the term 'big picture' rather than the term 'worldview'. What I have in mind is closer to 'theory of everything' than it is to what many others who use the word 'worldview' have in mind. For further elucidation, see Oppy (2018: 151-3).)

Given my characterization of philosophy and religion, it should come as no surprise to be told that I think that one of the central questions for philosophy of religion is the articulation, evaluation, and comparative assessment of worldviews. Since not all worldviews are *religious* worldviews, this central question is not merely a question for philosophy of religion. However, because religious worldviews are *worldviews*, the question is one of central significance for philosophy of religion.

There are various conceivable outcomes for philosophical investigation of worldviews. Philosophical investigation might suggest that the best worldviews that we have are religious worldviews. Philosophical investigation might suggest that the best worldviews that we have all belong to a particular religion. Philosophical investigation might suggest that the best worldviews that we have are non-religious – naturalistic, humanistic – worldviews. Philosophical investigation might make no suggestions about which are the best among currently accepted worldviews. Philosophical investigation might suggest only that there are many kinds of best worldviews, including some that are religious and some that are non-religious. Philosophical investigation of worldviews might turn out to be utterly intractable or otherwise entirely unable to secure any kind of expert agreement on the ranking of worldviews.

15.12 An Alternative Grid

There are many views that Abrahamic philosophers of religion take on the outcome of philosophical investigation of worldviews. Some think that philosophical investigation demonstrates the *superiority* of particular Abrahamic worldviews to all other worldviews. Some think that philosophical investigation demonstrates the *non-inferiority* of particular Abrahamic worldviews to all other worldviews. Some think that philosophical investigation is *inconclusive*: given merely philosophical investigation, we are left in the dark about the relative merits of best worldviews. Some think that philosophical investigation *appears* to demonstrate the *non-superiority* of any Abrahamic worldviews to all competing – naturalistic, humanistic – worldviews. Some think that philosophical investigation *appears* to demonstrate the *inferiority* of all Abrahamic worldviews to competing – naturalistic, humanistic – worldviews.

Philosophical investigation of worldviews recognises many dimensions for assessment: etiological, methodological, ontological, epistemological, axiological, normative, explanatory, descriptive, and so forth. Since it is unclear how to weigh these dimensions, it seems plausible to suppose (a) that those who think that the superiority of some worldviews can be demonstrated maintain that it can be demonstrated that some worldviews are superior to all other worldviews on every one of the dimensions of assessment; and (b) that those who think that the non-inferiority of some worldviews can be demonstrated maintain that it can be demonstrated that some worldviews at least break even with all other worldviews on every one of the dimensions of assessment.

Those who think that philosophical investigation demonstrates the *superiority* of particular Abrahamic worldviews to all other worldviews appear not to leave any crucial role for faith when it comes to acceptance of worldview. After all, if a particular Abrahamic worldview is demonstrably superior to all other worldviews, then any competent person will adopt that worldview upon being provided with a suitable demonstration. While it might be true that one could accept the Abrahamic worldview in question merely on the basis of faith, it is not clear that this could be doxastically virtuous in circumstances in which a demonstration of that worldview is available to you.

Those who think that philosophical investigation demonstrates the *non-inferiority* of particular Abrahamic worldviews to all other worldviews and those who think that – given merely philosophical investigation – we are left in the dark about the relative merits of best worldviews may appear to leave a crucial role for faith when it comes to acceptance of worldview. For, given that philosophy does not provide decisive reasons to favour one worldview over all others, it may appear that the only consideration that can then justify the acceptance of one worldview rather than some other must be something like faith. However, there is at least room for suspicion that what is required here bears only a very loose resemblance to religious faith; after all, for example, 'methodological conservatism' is not typically regarded as being very much like *religious* faith.

Those who think that philosophical investigation *appears* to demonstrate the *inferiority* of all Abrahamic worldviews to competing – naturalistic, humanistic – worldviews may also appear to leave a crucial role for faith when it comes to acceptance of worldview. However, on the one hand, if you are presented with a demonstration of the inferiority of all Abrahamic worldviews to competing worldviews, and if you recognise that you have indeed been presented with such a demonstration, then it cannot be doxastically virtuous for you to continue to accept an Abrahamic worldview. And if, when presented with a demonstration of the inferiority of all Abrahamic worldviews to competing – naturalistic, humanistic – worldviews, you merely fail to recognise that it is a demonstration of the inferiority of all Abrahamic worldviews to competing worldviews, then – setting aside questions about the culpability of your failure to recognise that you have been presented with a demonstration of the inferiority of all Abrahamic worldviews to competing worldviews – there is no further role for faith to play in your continuing to espouse an Abrahamic worldview. Moreover, on the other hand, if you are presented with what merely purports to be a demonstration of the inferiority of all Abrahamic worldviews to competing worldviews, but you mistakenly suppose that it is indeed a demonstration of the inferiority of all Abrahamic worldviews to competing worldviews, then it cannot be doxastically virtuous for you to continue to accept an Abrahamic worldview, quite apart from any considerations about the virtues of faith. And if, when presented with what merely purports to be a demonstration of the inferiority of all Abrahamic worldviews to competing worldviews, you correctly identify that it is not a demonstration of the inferiority of all Abrahamic worldviews to competing worldviews, then there is no role left for faith to play in the maintenance of your Abrahamic worldview.

If we take seriously the diversity of religions and the evidence from the social sciences, then, I think, we must take seriously the idea that it is part of the project of philosophy of religion to articulate, compare, and assess religious and non-religious worldviews. But, if we do take seriously the idea that it is part of the project of philosophy of religion to articulate, compare, and assess religious and non-religious worldviews, then we cannot suppose that Charlesworth's investigations shed much light on the relationships that hold between philosophy, religion and philosophy of religion. 'Philosophy as religion', 'philosophy as handmaid of religion', and 'philosophy as making room for faith', are simply not appropriate ways of thinking about the project of articulating, comparing and assessing religious and non-religious worldviews.

15.13 Residual Questions

The discussion to this point leaves many questions unanswered. In particular, it might be suggested that, even if I am right in claiming that Charlesworth's investigations do not shed much light on the relationships that hold between philosophy, religion and philosophy of religion, it may still be the case that Charlesworth's investigations illuminate the basic ways in which philosophers who view themselves as participants in – or fellow travellers with – monotheistic religions have conceived of the relationship between their philosophical beliefs and their religious beliefs. However, as I foreshadowed some pages back, I do not think that it is correct to claim that Charlesworth's investigations do illuminate the basic ways in which philosophers who view themselves as participants in – or fellow travellers with – monotheistic religions have conceived of the relationship between their philosophical beliefs and their religious beliefs.

I am happy enough to accept that Charlesworth's investigations do illuminate the basic ways in which philosophers who view themselves as participants in – or fellow travellers with – monotheistic religions have conceived of the relationship between what they took to be their philosophical beliefs and their religious beliefs, given their understanding of the nature and source of their philosophical beliefs and religious beliefs. However, it is one question what people take to be their philosophical and religious beliefs, given *their* understanding of the nature and source of philosophical and religious beliefs; it is quite a different question what are the philosophical and religious beliefs of those people, given *our* understanding of the nature and source of philosophical and religious beliefs.

Consider Aquinas. He thinks that some of his beliefs – his 'religious beliefs' – are revealed to him by God, via scripture, or religious experience, or the like; and he thinks that some of his beliefs – his 'philosophical beliefs' – are such that he arrived at them through the use of human reason, without any further divine assistance. For Aquinas, unaided reason does not deliver the belief that the world is only finitely old; so, he thinks, his belief that the world is only finitely old is a 'religious' belief but not a 'philosophical' belief. On the other hand, for Aquinas, unaided reason delivers the belief – confirmed by scripture – that there is an unmoved mover; so, he thinks, his belief that there is an unmoved mover is both a 'religious' belief and a 'philosophical' belief. By his own lights – given his further belief that reason cannot contradict revelation – Aquinas could see himself as a poster boy for 'philosophy as handmaid of religion'. But, by our lights, given how little effort Aquinas puts into systematically articulating, evaluating and comparing non-religious alternatives to his own worldview, we are in no position to judge what he would have said had he undertaken a systematic evaluation of a wide compass of worldviews.

The critical observation that we have just made about Aquinas – that he does not pay sufficiently serious attention to non-religious worldviews – applies in even greater measure to Charlesworth himself. Ancient atomism, modern materialism, and contemporary naturalism have all thrown up non-religious worldviews that must be taken into account in any serious reckoning of religious worldviews. To suppose that the views of the relationship between philosophy and religion of proponents of ancient atomism, modern materialism, or contemporary naturalism might be captured by one of 'philosophy as religion', 'philosophy as handmaid of religion', and 'philosophy as making room for faith' is transparently implausible. Sensitivity to the radical diversity of religions should go hand in hand with sensitivity to the radical diversity of religious and non-religious worldviews; but no one with the latter sensitivity can suppose that Charlesworth's 'grid' is fit for its self-professed intended purpose.

While I don't have space left to do full justice to this issue, I should also say something concerning Charlesworth's remarks about feminist perspectives on philosophy of religion. Given that worldviews are accounts of the world and our place within it that aspire to a certain kind of comprehensiveness and fundamentality, it seems to me that it makes perfect sense to identify a sub-class of feminist worldviews: a sub-class of worldviews whose *ideology* draws upon various kinds of feminist analyses. Moreover, I think, the same can be said about worldviews whose *ideology* draws upon analyses ordered according to race, or ethnicity, or sexual orientation, or social class, or political orientation, or the like. But, if there can be feminist worldviews – both religious and non-religious – then those worldviews cannot be ignored in a philosophy of religion that aspires to give a comprehensive comparative assessment of worldviews.

15.14 Concluding Remarks

Charlesworth (2002) is a work of impressive scholarship and erudition. It demonstrates intimate acquaintance with many who might reasonably be pigeon-holed under the 'philosophy as religion', 'philosophy as handmaid of religion', 'philosophy as making room for faith banners', 'philosophy as the analysis of religious language' or 'philosophy as postmodernist critique of the religious domain'. However, in my view, the work has serious shortcomings, due in much larger part to what it overlooks than to what it includes. When we consider the truly radical diversity of religious and non-religious worldviews – as well as the truly radical diversity of conceptions of philosophy and religion – it ceases to be plausible to suppose that the 'grid' that Charlesworth provides is useful for neophytes, established scholars, or anyone in between.

References

Boyarin, D. (2016). *Imagine no religion*. New York: Fordham University Press.
Chalmers, D. (2015). Why isn't there more progress in philosophy? *Philosophy, 90*, 3–24.
Charlesworth, M. (1972). *Philosophy of religion: The historic approaches*. New York: Herder and Herder.
Charlesworth, M. (2002). *Philosophy and religion: From Plato to postmodernism*. Oxford: One World.
Nongbri, B. (2013). *Before religion*. New Haven: Yale University Press.
Oppy, G. (2018). *Naturalism and religion*. London: Routledge.
Smith, W. (1963). *The meaning and end of religion*. Minneapolis: Fortress Press.

Graham Oppy is Professor of Philosophy at Monash University, Fellow of the Australian Academy of Humanities and Chief Executive Officer of the Australasian Association of Philosophy. His authored books include *Ontological Arguments and Belief in God* (CUP, 1996); *Arguing About Gods* (CUP, 2006); *Describing Gods* (CUP, 2014); *The Best Argument Against God* (Palgrave, 2013); *Reinventing Philosophy of Religion: An Opinionated Introduction* (Palgrave, 2014); *Naturalism and Religion* (2018, Routledge); *Atheism: The Basics* (Routledge, 2018); and *Atheism and Agnosticism* (CUP, 2018). His edited books include *The History of Western Philosophy of Religion* (Acumen and OUP, 2009, with Nick Trakakis), *Interreligious Philosophical Dialogues* (Routledge, 2018, with Nick Trakakis), *Ontological Arguments* (CUP, 2018) and *Companion to Atheism and Philosophy* (Blackwell, 2018).

Chapter 16
Religion and Religions

Paul Rule

In a long enormously productive life Max Charlesworth contributed to a variety of areas, not just sub-fields of philosophy such as bio-ethics and political philosophy nor even the critical study of general theories and methodologies such as existentialism and linguistic analysis, but in an inter-disciplinary – or perhaps better, multi-disciplinary – way to key areas of human living. Not the least important both in itself and to Max personally was religion.

In the late 1990s Max wrote several essays on religion and religions which I, as a religious studies specialist, have found challenging as well as provoking fruitful reflection. Here I want to take up some of those challenges and to consider where they lead.

I reluctantly put aside his contributions both as an editor and a commentator to the study of Australian Aboriginal religions. I have seen little evidence that his remarkable essay on 'The invention of Australian Aboriginal religion' has had the impact it should have had on Aboriginal Studies.[1] Methodological reductionism, especially as practised in anthropology, still resists the 'issues of a theological-philosophical kind' the neglect of which Charlesworth deplored (Charlesworth 1997, p. 79). Even many Aborigines themselves refuse to speak of their religion except in terms such as 'spirituality' and 'ceremonies' which may represent their own mainstream modern Australian self-perception but scarcely does justice to their rich cultural and religious inheritance.

Such Aborigines share that reluctance to speak of 'religion' which I, and I am sure Max Charlesworth too, found increasingly in his students, even those who came in large numbers to the few courses that governments and university administrators in Australia now permit. Presumably this comes from identification of 'religion' with 'religions', institutions which impose beliefs and behaviours which they

[1] See 'Essay 2: The invention of Australian Aboriginal religions', in Charlesworth 1997, pp. 51–80.

P. Rule (✉)
Latrobe University, Bundoora, VIC, Australia

P. Wong et al. (eds.), *Considering Religions, Rights and Bioethics: For Max Charlesworth*, Sophia Studies in Cross-cultural Philosophy of Traditions and Cultures 30, https://doi.org/10.1007/978-3-030-18148-2_16

seem not to live up to in practice and hence are rightly in bad odour; or which are simply thought irrelevant to contemporary lifestyles. And yet so many are 'seekers' or simply curious about something that does not fit into the world in which they have been socialized. Others, however, are bewildered by what Charlesworth called in a 1995 essay 'the scandal of religious diversity'. So let us turn first to this formulation of his thoughts on religion and religions.

16.1 The Scandal of Religious Diversity

In an article entitled 'Ecumenism between the world religions', published in 1995 in the 100th issue of *Sophia* (Charlesworth 1995), the journal he edited for so many years, Max Charlesworth began by outlining why the diversity of world religions in the world was scandalous. The problem – and here I use my language not his – could not be resolved by simple formulae such as 'all religions are ultimately the same' or 'religions are all equally wrong (or worse, harmful)'. Religions, he rightly pointed out, make truth claims which no amount of fiddling, selecting, rationalizing can make compatible with those of other religions and certainly not of those opposed to religion per se.

In presenting the problematic of the plurality of religions he makes two valid and central points. Firstly, that pluralism is part of the modern human condition: 'the problem of religious diversity is paralleled by the problem of cultural and ethical diversity' (Charlesworth 1995, p. 142). Secondly, and here as an historian of religion I can only approve, Charlesworth the philosopher stresses the historical and cultural mediation of religious traditions, even or perhaps especially those that claim to derive from some sort of revelation.

This is, however, not developed, and might have been.[2] All revelations, even the very personal Buddhist-style 'enlightenment' experiences, if they are to be universalized must be passed on, become 'traditions'. They are received and transmitted through language; language is the product of culture and historical experience. In all transmissions static occurs: messages are scrambled, the peripheral becomes the main point, parts rendered unintelligible by time are quietly omitted. Is the scandal of religious diversity fundamentally the scandal of human linguistic diversity?[3]

[2] Two pages (pp. 8–10) are devoted to it in the Introduction to *Religious Inventions: Four Essays* (Charlesworth 1997), a brief but masterly summary of the debate about 'the reception of revelation' in modern Christian theology. The theological and philosophical problems inherent in revelations is a universal problem in the study of religions and one often underestimated. I have argued that it was the unrecognized central issue in the controversy over Salman Rushdie's *Satanic Verses*. See Rule 1995.

[3] Another tantalizingly brief section (pp. 12–13) in the Introduction to *Religious Inventions* under the heading 'The Interpretive-Inventive Perspective' ends with an appeal that satisfies a pragmatic historian like me but, I fear, would not satisfy many philosophers: 'Nevertheless, despite all opportunities for mistakes and misunderstandings and misrepresentations, and the lack of any court of appeal, languages work successfully most of the time and we do not in fact end in subjectivism or linguistic anarchy'.

It is not only Western religion which displays such diversity. A common language has not prevented religious diversity in, for example, China, where two major indigenous traditions, Confucianism and Daoism dispute priority in pointing the Way (*Dao*) with imported religions that have taken on distinctive Chinese forms (the major one being Buddhism) and those that have not – 'the religions of the Book' – Judaism, Christianity, Islam. The last mentioned, however, all have had serious internal disputes over the terms used in Chinese for their monotheistic concepts and have, with time, been sinified in many ways.

The central problem, the 'pluralism of autonomous and incommensurable revelations' as Charlesworth nicely labels it, resists rationalization either of the flat denial type ('exclusivism'), or the superficial resolution type ('syncretism'). In recent decades, he goes on to say, a variety of 'inclusivist' solutions have been proposed such as Karl Rahner's 'anonymous Christians' and the 'Geluk' Buddhist theory of partial and final truth but, he argues, they imply 'multiple revelations' and themselves depend on very specific philosophical assumptions not shared outside their own traditions.

The upshot of all this, concludes Charlesworth, is that the problem of religious diversity remains unsolved on both religious and philosophical grounds but that 'it does provide a basis for genuine ecumenical dialogue between the world religions'. Further that 'by recognizing that a religious believer can hold that genuine developments of religious values may take place in other religions, it makes such dialogue absolutely necessary' (Charlesworth 1995, p. 159).

One can but agree. But what is 'dialogue'? Between whom, and what are the ground rules and perhaps even more importantly the criteria for success of such dialogue? Conversion on one side or on both to a third position? Should it be a dialogue of leaders, of accepted teachers, of ordinary believers in the traditions? A dialogue of faiths or of beliefs? A dialogue of words or of practice, formulations or experiences? A dialogue of silence or silences, of presence rather than action? Can there be multiple allegiances to the point of multiple participation? What of multi-faith communities? Some of these possibilities had not been systematically explored in 1995 except perhaps in the lives of a few pioneers like Charles de Foucauld, Bede Griffiths, Raimundo Panikkar and Thomas Merton. But they have received much more attention in recent decades and they are foreshadowed in other of Charlesworth's works.

16.2 Religious Inventions

In *Religious Inventions: Four Essays,* he raises some fundamental questions about religion and religions.[4] He points in the Introduction to some features of the current religious situation which are, I believe, as true two decades later as then. Despite a dominant scientism and the decline of many organized religions, religion is not in

[4] See Rule 1999.

decline. In 1997 the influence of Evangelical Christianity and fundamentalism on American society was the most prominent signifier. I am sure if he had been writing two decades later the rise of militant Islamism would have figured in his analysis. 'The persistence of religion' is a world phenomenon and a continuing one.

Another issue raised in the introduction in a brilliant but undeveloped fashion is what Charlesworth calls 'the gratuitousness of authentic religion' (Charlesworth 1997, pp. 10–12). The dialogue or failure of such which characterizes much of the current debate about atheism is certainly partly due to sheer ignorance about religious phenomena but also to something akin to tone deafness in reception of music. Many of Richard Dawkins' critics have pointed to their complete failure to recognize themselves in his works: how they actually think and feel, even what they say and do. Surely religion if it is to be criticized needs to be presented as it is. Why is ignorance of world religions not considered as serious a defect in the education of an Australian citizen as, say, ignorance of our political system? I note that none of the proposals for testing suitability for citizenship of our multi-cultural society include knowledge of the religions of Australians and, judging by public pronouncements, few of the proposers could pass such a test.

The first essay in *Religious Inventions*, 'The diversity of revelations', reopens the issue of 'the brute fact' or 'prima facie scandal' of religious diversity. My first reaction to these terms was and remains that the diversity of religion to me is no 'scandal', not even really a challenge, but an invitation to explore, compare, borrow and develop. Perhaps again this is what distinguishes an historian of religion from a philosopher of religion. However, Max Charlesworth was no absolutist and he rightly dismissed all approaches to the fact of religious diversity that sought to deny or eliminate such diversity. The world of the Hebrew and Christian scriptures was a world of religious diversity; the romantic view of a unitary medieval Christendom was never a reality. As Charlesworth emphasizes, religious diversity only became a problem, a scandal, when from the Seventeenth Century on philosophers proclaimed religion to be one. One might add that it was only when confidence in the notion of one universal truth developed in Europe: it has never really taken hold in the non-Western world, even in the form of variants of Marxism.

Still, once raised, the ghost needs to be exorcized. How can this problem be characterized? Here is Charlesworth's formulation:

> What modifications in one's religious position as a Buddhist or a Christian or a Hindu has one to make in order to accommodate this fact so that a person might say, 'I am a Christian or a Hindu or a Muslim or a member of the Australian Pitjantjatjara people and I believe that the teachings of my religion are true, but at the same time I recognise and accept the fact that there are other religious systems and that other people believe that the teachings of their religion are true? (Charlesworth 1997, pp. 26–27).

At first sight, this seems a reasonable proposition. But, on reflection, I wonder whether it is psychologically sound. The most extreme religious bigot may still accept the sincerity – but not, of course, the truth – of the other's belief system. And the most extreme libertarian may without self-contradiction not agree with the consequences of certain kinds of free speech.

Nor, I think, does it really help us to evolve a coherent position vis a vis the religious other. The issue is not acknowledging the nature of their religious convictions but the truth of their beliefs. And this is precisely the reason for all the contortions of the meta-theorists like John Hicks whose formulae for reconciliation of the world's religions end up appearing vacuous and bloodless as well as, in the end, leaving out in the cold many flourishing religions or systems acknowledged as such.

I would add a further problem, particularly for the religious true believer. The theologies of many world religions are extremely sceptical about human ability to read the mind of God. Theoretical physicists like Paul Davies may be able to[5]; or Shirley Maclaine who told us in 1987 that she herself was God.[6] But I would think it was precisely those of deep religious belief and experience – I am thinking especially of some of the great mystics – who question our ability to know how God works in the world. Could it be that God wills religious diversity and that this is quite compatible with a unique saving action enshrined in one or more religious tradition?

Mention of the mystics brings us to another theme in Charlesworth's discussion of religious diversity: his denial that 'religious experience', especially mystical experience, can somehow find a way out of our dilemma. In a section entitled 'Parenthesis on the unity of religious experience' in the first essay in *Religious Inventions*, Max demonstrates that such attempts – that of W.T. Stace is perhaps the best known – suffer from the same defects as naïve empiricism in philosophy of science, a belief that experience is 'theory independent'. I would add that neither can it survive a serious examination of the sources, the self-contradictory but apparently irresistible attempts of mystics to utter the unutterable or, as Samuel Beckett says, 'eff the ineffable'.[7] Their descriptions of their ineffable experiences always echo the language of their religious traditions. There is 'no exit' here.

After his review of the main positions of contemporary thinkers on reconciling religious diversity Charlesworth settles on the view that 'other religious systems can have a positive value of their own and that the fact of religious diversity has a positive meaning' (Charlesworth 1997, pp. 40–41). He devotes the remainder of the essay to somewhat undercutting it by pointing to the internal contradictions and difficulties in the work of all the major proponents of such a position which he calls 'a pluralism of autonomous and incommensurable revelations'. There is no contradiction in this. He argues that philosophical treatments of the question must inevitably fall away at some point and that the theological 'answer' which locates it in the 'mystery' of God although not an intellectual reconciliation may be a very satisfactory personal one.

---

[5] See Davies 1992.

[6] In a TV mini-series called 'Out on a limb'.

[7] Not, as one might think, in *Waiting for Godot*, but in *Watt*. Beckett, apart from his usual provocativeness, is also invoking the Greek roots of the English 'ineffable'.

16.3 A Credo for the Religious Believer

Max Charlesworth concluded his essay in *Religious Inventions* with a seven point 'credo for the religious believer', repeated in what I think was his last contribution on the subject, 'Religion and religions' in a symposium *Managing religious diversity* (Charlesworth 1999).

I think this was an admirable and useful exercise but that it is as much an illustration of the intractability of the problem of religious diversity as a solution to it. My analysis is not in the least meant to be a reflection on Max Charlesworth's integrity or lucidity but is presented as an illustration of how far we still have to go.

The first article of the "credo' reads:

1. I believe that 'God' wills that all should be saved or achieve enlightenment and that all human beings have access to the means of salvation or enlightenment through some mode of revelation.

The very awkwardness of expression: the apparent embarrasment of 'salvation or enlightenment', 'some mode of revelation', the quotation marks round 'God' and an accompanying footnote[8] point to the great problem of Buddhist theism/atheism/non-theism; the conceptual incompatibility of 'salvation' and 'enlightenment'; and of revelation with Buddhist 'enlightenment'. It could be argued that there are functional if not conceptual equivalents[9] and nobody could object to the exercise of empathy, of personal reaching out. But is it a precondition for serious dialogue to 'believe' that one's 'God' has such a will? And does it apply equally to the Buddhist believers who participate in the dialogue: what or who is their 'God' and does he/she/it have a 'will'?

The second item in the 'credo' of the modern religious believer according to Charlesworth, is an acknowledgment of the priority of one's own tradition:

2. I believe (as a Christian, or a Jew, or a Muslim, or a Hindu or Buddhist etc.) that my religious tradition has a privileged and paradigmatic status and that 'God' has revealed himself most completely in that tradition.

This is nicely phrased – 'privileged and paradigmatic', 'most completely' – but the spirit of Gautama Budddha hovers over that 'revelation' as well as 'God' in quotation marks.

Perhaps the most original and interesting of the author's ideas is the following:

3. I believe that certain authentic religious values which are implicit or latent within my traditiion, but which have not actually been developed within that tradition may be manifested or expressed in other religious traditions.

[8] The note in the original reads: '"God" is taken here to mean any source of revelation or disclosure of "the divine".'

[9] It should be noted that Charlesworth begins his list with the term 'operationally' which may be the equivalent of my 'functional'.

I presume Max was thinking amongst other things of the popularity among many especially younger Christians of yoga, Zen meditation, Kabbalah, Sufism and so on. In a long teaching career I was constantly surprised at students telling me that Christianity had no tradition of meditation, or religious chant or monasticism or whatever and that the student had discovered it elsewhere: a reflection no doubt on religious education and religious practice in Australia. Thomas Merton's late religious quest took him not only to Eastern monasteries but to artists, writers, physicists and political activists. 'Where the Spirit moves'?

The next clause touches on more sensitive territory, especially for modern Christians:

4. I believe that there is also the possibility of authentic religious revelations, complementary to the paradigmatic revelation of my tradition but 'outside' my own tradition.

Nothing here would have surprised the Fathers of the Church or a medieval Christian like Dante. It was generally believed that Virgil had foreshadowed the coming of Christ, that Zoroaster and Hermes Trismegistus were inspired prophets and so on. But, especially since the Reformation, the parameters of 'revelation' were narrowed by theologians of the Catholic as well as the Reformed traditions. How that certainty about one and one only definitive and unique revelation squares with the gratuitousness of God is hard to see, at least to this naïve historian.

The fifth in the original formulation, whether deliberately or accidentally omitted in the later list of six, is, however, extremely interesting.[10] It is a vision of an ultimate reconciliation, The problem, and this may have been why it was omitted in the later listing, is that its implicit eschatology seems too Christian for it to be accepted by some other faiths. On the other hand it gives some insight into Max's personal religious inspiration. The discussion of the diversity of religions was, it would seem, far from being a mere academic exercise. It reads:

5. I believe that 'God's revelation' will only be known in its fullness when, as an ideal limit, all the 'revelations' and their 'developments' are brought together in some way.

The sixth belief in this credo is similarly visionary but, I believe, eminently defensible theologically and in terms of the current situation:

6. I believe that religious diversity is in some sense willed by 'God' and has its own intrinsic meaning and purpose and is not merely the result of sin and ignorance.

Of course, here again we are trying to read the mind of God but this is a belief, something going beyond knowledge to the realm of commitment, dare one say of 'faith'.

The culminating item in the Charlesworth credo is in some ways the nub of it:

---

[10] It would be useful to discover whether Max himself or the editor omitted it from the symposium volume. Perhaps he thought it too personal, too 'mystical' even, for a philosophico-theological discussion.

7. I believe that respect for openness and dialogue with other religious traditions, must be part of any authentic religious tradition.

One can only speculate how many religious traditions would pass such a test of authenticity; and how many believers would be excluded or exclude themselves from dialogue under these conditions, but the message is clear. We live in a world where 'openness and dialogue' between religions or better religious believers is no longer, if it ever was, an optional extra.

16.4 Conclusion: Max Charlesworth's Legacy in the Study of Religious Diversity

The works we have examined are a remarkable legacy. They provide a sane and comprehensive agenda for not just the study but the practice of inter-religious dialogue. Certainly the machinery and ground rules for such dialogue need much more work and experiment. Parliaments of Religion and such like, at least in my limited experience, suffer from the faults of our political parliaments as participants speak across each other, score points and aim at victories rather than change on both sides. Small group even individual face to face exchanges have been far more fruitful but they often fizzle out for lack of structure. The Charlesworth Credo could, if more widely known, provide such a structure.

References

Charlesworth, M. (1995). Ecumenism between the world religions. *Sophia, 34*(1), 140–159.

Charlesworth, M. (1997). *Religious inventions: Four essays*. New York: Cambridge University Press.

Charlesworth, M. (1999). Religion and religions. In G. Bouma (Ed.), *Managing religious diversity: From threat to promise* (pp. 28–46). Sydney: Australian Association for the Study of Religions. Also published in *Australian Religion Studies Review, 12*(2) (Spring 1999), 28–48.

Davies, P. (1992). *The mind of God: The scientific basis for a rational world*. New York: Simon & Schuster.

Rule, P. (1995). The Rushdie affair: Tolerance, pluralism or secularism? *Sophia, 34*(1), 226–232.

Rule, P. (1999). (Review of) Max Charlesworth, religious inventions: Four essays. *Sophia, 38*(1), 122–126.

Paul Rule has an honours degree in History from the University of Melbourne and a doctorate in Asian Studies from the Australian National University and taught History and Religious Studies from 1974 to 2002 at La Trobe University where he is currently a research associate in the China Studies Research Centre. He has been President of the Australian Association for the Study of Religions and has published articles and books mainly on Chinese and Aboriginal religion and on theology of religions. He is working on a history of the Chinese Rites controversy and editing a four-volume translation of the *Acta Pekinensia* on the papal legation of Maillard de Tournon to China (1705–1710) for the Ricci Institute for Chinese-Western Cultural History at the University of San Francisco and the Macau Ricci Institute.

Chapter 17
A Perspective on Religious Diversity

Peter Wong

17.1 Ecumenism Among the Religions of the World

In celebrating the one hundredth issue of *Sophia*, and as its founding Editor, Max Charlesworth contributed an article entitled, "Ecumenism between the World Religions" (Charlesworth 1995). The article explores possible responses to the problem of religious diversity: How can the different and varied claims of the religions be reconciled when they are often incompatible with each other?[1]

Using as the template Christianity's ecumenical approach, Charlesworth outlines four possible positions when applying the so-called "ecumenical" to different religions of the world. Apart from exclusivism (i.e., Position 1: there is nothing of religious significance in other traditions) and syncretism (i.e., Position 2: all traditions are equally good and true), which Charlesworth takes to be extremes and to be rejected, the remaining two positions are concerned with accepting values in religions other than one's own. At first glance, these two positions appear to be closely related but differ in the degree of valuation of other religions: Position 3 takes what is valuable in other religions as a paler reflection of one's own; whereas Position 4 accepts that other religions might have certain values more developed than those of one's own. For Charlesworth, this last position does not require one to give up the

[1] "How can all these religious systems be true since their truth claims very often appear to be incompatible with each other?" (Charlesworth 1995, p. 140)

But as Charlesworth has pointed out in the Ecumenism article, he is not specifically concerned about "religious diversity" as a philosophical problem *per se* (Charlesworth 1995, p. 142). Rather, he is more interested in exploring religious diversity "from within the religious sphere." Be that as it may, there is much in Charlesworth's article that contributes to understanding religious diversity from a philosophical point of view.

P. Wong (✉)
China Studies Research Centre, Latrobe University, Melbourne, VIC, Australia
e-mail: P.Wong@Latrobe.edu.au

P. Wong et al. (eds.), *Considering Religions, Rights and Bioethics: For Max Charlesworth*, Sophia Studies in Cross-cultural Philosophy of Traditions and Cultures 30, https://doi.org/10.1007/978-3-030-18148-2_17

claim of preeminence regarding the religion to which one owes allegiance – it is a feature that he seems to take to be the indelible mark of a believer. According to Charlesworth:

> The fourth view attempts to acknowledge that other religious systems can have a positive value of their own. Thus, a Christian will hold that the Christian tradition has a privileged or paradigmatic status in that it is in the person of Jesus Christ that God has revealed him most fully (but not exclusively) to us. (Charlesworth 1995, p. 153)

To say that a tradition has a paradigmatic status would seem to involve a claim of superiority: "Despite the fact that there are things we can learn from other religions, my religion is still the best."[2] In that case, what is the difference between Position 4 and Position 3? Is Position 4 merely the recognition that there is value in other religions to a greater degree than Position 3? That would seem to be the case if not for one crucial difference: Position 4 also allows for a similar claim of paradigmatic status to be made by someone else from a different religion regarding their own. The following questions formulated by Charlesworth might help to elucidate this position:

> How can a Christian or a Buddhist or a Hindu [or a Muslim], or for that matter a member of an Australian Aboriginal people, come to terms with the fact that there are other and different and incompatible religious systems in the world? What modifications in one's religious position as a Buddhist or a Christian or a Hindu [or a Muslim] has one to make in order to accommodate this fact so that a person might say, "I am [a Buddhist or] a Christian or a Hindu or a Muslim or a member of the Australia Pitjantjatjara people and I believe that the teachings of my religion are true but at the same time I recognise and accept the fact that there are other religious systems and that other people believe that the teachings of their religions are true"? (Charlesworth 1995, p. 143)

Position 4 has to do with extending the recognition of the truth of religious teachings to religions other than one's own. Thus, what is taken to be paradigmatic is not restricted to one's religion. This raises the question about the coherence of such a position. How can there be more than one religion that is paradigmatic? And if it were to be possible, then how could one response to Charlesworth's question: "What modifications in one's religious position… has one to make in order to accommodate this fact"?

In a later iteration of the 1995 article, Charlesworth discusses Karl Rahner's notion of "anonymous Christians" in which he writes: "Rahner refers to believers of good will in other religions as 'anonymous Christians', a description which has given great offence."(Charlesworth 1997, p. 42).[3] The conferring of "anonymous" membership to an individual who does not belong to one's own religion, could indeed be offensive – particularly when that person is unaware of such a dubious honour. However, the allowance and expectation of that particular individual or

[2] Charlesworth anticipates this critique. See Charlesworth 1995, p. 159.

[3] Charlesworth goes on to cite Joseph Wong, "Rahner proposed the theory of anonymous Christianity not for proclamation to outsiders but solely for Christian consumption… to convince Christians that God's saving presence is greater than humans and the Church" (Charlesworth 1997, p. 42).

others from the other religion to do likewise to oneself seems to ameliorate the tone of an apparent insult somewhat. Charlesworth writes:

> Rahner relates that he was once asked by the Japanese philosopher Nishitani, "What would you say if I were to treat you as an anonymous Zen Buddhist?" Rahner's response was that Nishitani should in fact treat him in exactly this way. (Charlesworth 1997, p. 42)

One might raise the objection that such an expectation of a mutual claim to, and acceptance of, the preeminence of each other's religion is in fact *not* an acceptance of the truth of each other's beliefs and doctrines; rather, it is only an agreement about a religious sentiment (i.e. that this is *my religion*). One could call this the subjective or the psychological aspect of belonging to a religion (the psychological aspect of the "paradigmatic").[4]

Yet the psychological interpretation is insufficient to satisfy Charlesworth's construal of Position 4; he expects a recognition and acceptance of "authentic religious values."[5] This, I suggest, is needed in order for Position 4 not to fall into relativism or syncretism of the kind Charlesworth finds objectionable, such as the view that "all religions are good." Moreover, the syncretic approach is too simplistic; for genuine recognition of religious diversity, each party must be able to recognise specific religious values in the other and acknowledge each other's claim to truth and uniqueness.

However, this leap from ecumenical considerations within the Christian world to resolving the quandary of religious diversity might prove to be too wide a gulf. Among the various Christian churches and sects, there is the sharing of a common story or a common figure that provides a platform upon which values and truths can be shared across sectarian boundaries. But could religious values be recognised across different religions, with different central figures, founding myths, and philosophical assumptions?

Related to the foregoing question is another aspect of the "paradigmatic" which involves a more "objective" or non-psychological sense: religious views are paradigmatic in the sense that religious views and their myths constitute and shape the framework within which values and truths are understood, appreciated and

---

[4] Nevertheless, it is a crucial aspect of religious life – to commit oneself fully to a particular tradition is the prerequisite in bringing about the kind of personal transformation so desirable to the religious seeker. (This feature is also prominent in the Confucian tradition, despite its apparent humanistic tendencies (C.f. the notions of "*cheng* 誠" in *Zhongyong*, and "*jinxin* 盡心" in *Mencius*).) The question is, does the Confucian approach require its followers to assent to the claim that their beliefs are true? It appears not. (Neither does this appear to be an important aspect in most sects of Buddhism.)

[5] "We saw in the discussion of ecumenism between the Christian Churches that certain values may be developed in one form of Christianity and not in others. So also in the wider sphere of the world religions, certain *authentic religious values* that are implicitly in the Christian revelation, but which have not been actually developed or actualised within the historical forms of Christianity, may be manifested or expressed in Hinduism or Buddhism or Islam etc. And of course, the same is true of the other religions vis-à-vis Christianity and the other 'world religions'" (Charlesworth 1995, p. 155, Italics added).

articulated.[6] This sense of the paradigmatic raises the problem of whether understanding across religions can be possible. If frameworks significantly differ between different religions, cultures, and languages, then can the claims made within one framework be translatable to another? This especially when no universal, or mutually acceptable, reference framework can be found.[7] It appears Charlesworth is cognisant of this point; in his discussion of relativism and syncretism (Position 2), he writes:

> The meaning of any religious proposition can only be determined by reference to a particular context or system and it is not at all clear how one can compare, at least directly, religious systems and the 'truth' of one system as against another. (The situation is all the more complex in that those systems usually have philosophical theories of one kind or another bound up with them…) (Charlesworth 1995, p. 150)

Charlesworth makes the point as a way of arguing against those who claim that all religions are essentially the same; i.e. to make such a claim amounts to saying that there is a "truth" to which all religions conform, a position which is ultimately untenable.[8]

It is interesting that, given the above, Charlesworth does not come to the conclusion that recognition of religious values is impossible across the divides of religious traditions. For him, Position 4 remains the best response there is to the problem (or, phenomenon) of religious diversity. While I am sympathetic to Charlesworth's position – that addressing the problem of religious diversity requires both the acceptance of religion as paradigmatic to its adherents and that there must be an admission of genuine incompleteness within one's own tradition,[9] there remain unresolved difficulties. First, as has been mentioned, it has to do with the question of understanding across different frameworks. Second, Charlesworth's approach is largely based on the Christian perspective; his articulation of religious diversity is strongly monotheistic, and relies upon the centrality of revelation as key to understanding the religious life. This is too narrow in scope when attempting to encompass pantheistic and non-theistic traditions, the former such as Advaita Vendanta and the latter such

[6] C.f. Morny Joy's article, "Philosophy and Religion" (Joy 2004), in which she explores, with great nuance, how truths are mediated by culture and language.

[7] See Charlesworth's discussion in the sections entitled "A pluralism of autonomous and incommensurable revelations" (Charlesworth 1995, pp. 155–157), and "Multiple revelations: difficulties" (Ibid., pp. 157–158). Charlesworth examines the strategies of Hicks, Pannikar and Henry Corbin in resolving the difficulty. He points out the limitation of Pannikar's and Corbin's using a neo-Platonic framework to resolve the problem of diversity: it would never work for religions such as Buddhism or Australian Aboriginal religions.

[8] In another place, Charlesworth makes a similar point about mystical experiences which cannot be described independent of context. He writes, "But our basic experiences of the world are not, in fact, 'theory independent', since we can experience the world only within a context of non-observational or theoretical factors" (Charlesworth 1997, p. 38).

[9] The notion of "incompleteness" might be going too far for Charlesworth, who prefers the view that the Christian Revelation is full but not exhaustive. C.f. Charlesworth's view, following John Hicks, regarding the non-exhaustive nature of God's revelation: "Christians can say that God is truly to be encountered in Jesus but not only in Jesus" (Charlesworth 1995, p. 153).

as Buddhism and Confucianism, within the notion of religious diversity. It might be fair to say that this monotheistic stance weakens Charlesworth's articulation of Position 4. On the other hand, in Charlesworth's defence, one needs to bear in mind that he is not attempting to create an understanding of religiousness that is universally acceptable. Rather, being true to his defence of Position 4, he is working from the perspective of his own religious affiliation: his question is, "How can a Christian come to terms with the fact that there are other and different and incompatible religious systems in the world?" And he would expect others similarly to work within their own religious traditions in addressing this question.

Following Charlesworth's approach, it seems that we need to learn the meaning of religiousness for a different tradition on a case by case basis. The recognition of values that are not available in one's own tradition can only be achieved painstakingly – through paying close attention and through being open about the possible gaps in one's own religious understandings. Just how wide the gap might be is somewhat unclear. For Charlesworth, his approach is to maintain the claim to eminence regarding one's own tradition while being open to extending the tradition. The difficulty is that what one party sees in the other is still through one's own lens: e.g. Christians might tend to value Confucianism according to the Christian yardstick – James Legge's translations and commentary on the classical Confucian texts come to mind. Furthermore, it is not clear if that which Christians find valuable in Confucianism might be what Confucians themselves value. For genuine learning and engagement, wouldn't one need to step out of the familiar comfort of one's shoes? It seems that this is necessary for there to be mutual recognition and acceptance of values across religions. Importantly, so that this is not a narcissistic self-affirming exercise, it entails an openness to change. And traditions are capable, and do, change – something that Charlesworth recognises.[10] This can occur through the sharing of different forms of religious living and open dialogue, and hopefully, not through coercion but through mutual appreciation.

17.2 Another Way of Being Religious

Given the problem of understanding different philosophical frameworks, cultures, and languages, especially when informed by religious differences, how then can we come to appreciate another religion? A Daoist story might suggest a way:

> Zhaungzi and Hui Shi were strolling across the bridge over the Hao River. Zhuangzi observed, "The minnows swim out and about as they please – this is the way they enjoy themselves."
>
> Master Hui replied, "You are not a fish – how do you know what they enjoy?"

[10] C.f. Charlesworth's 1995 article, in which he discusses the dynamic nature of Christian self-understanding: "The so-called 'deposit of faith' is not fixed and static (as the various forms of fundamentalism claim), but dynamic and open to change in the sense that virtualities and possibilities in the original 'revelation' are continually being disclosed" (Charlesworth 1995, p. 144).

> Zhuangzi retorted, "You are not me – how do you know that I don't know what is enjoyable for the fish?"
>
> Master Hui said, "I am not you, so I certainly don't know what you know, but it follows that, since you are certainly not the fish, you don't know what is enjoyment for the fish either."
>
> Zhuangzi said, "Let's get back to your basic question. When you asked '*How* do you know what the fish enjoy?' you already knew that I know what the fish enjoy, or you wouldn't have asked me. I know *from here* above the Hao River."[11]

The final move in Zhuangzi's repartee with Hui Shi has to do with the reasonableness of the question regarding the fish's enjoyment. We assume that fish have some kind of an emotional life because we share with them some similarities: fright or flight response, appetite, sexual reproduction, mortality, and so forth. That the fish is a sentient form of life and that they are possibly capable of an emotional life, no matter how rudimentary, seems reasonable. Even if we are doubtful, at least it makes sense to speak of the enjoyment of the fish. Yet, this still leave unaddressed Zhuangzi's knowledge about what the minnows enjoy.

It would seem that the normal ways in which we know a fellow human being is enjoying themself is unavailable to us: fish neither smile nor laugh, sing nor speak. Yet, can't we tell if someone we know very well is enjoying themself even when such clues are unavailable? I think of my mother humming tunelessly as she walked passed me; I think of sitting under the moonlight with a friend still and silent; I think of my cat slumped over my lap.

While I have little knowledge about fish, I can imagine that given the opportunity to know them better, especially a particular group of fish in a particular place, I can come to know what they might enjoy, or that perhaps they do not enjoy doing anything at all. How they race towards a food source, how they speed away from a predator, how they wiggle sluggish in the cold of winter, how they might prefer a particular patch of weed, how they like to sun themselves on a chilly morning, and so forth. And I believe I can tell the difference between enjoyment and non-enjoyment of particular kinds of fish. What seems to be required is a sympathetic imagination and the willingness to pay close attention.

Nevertheless, there is quite a distance between knowing the fish's enjoyment and appreciating the religious sentiments of another person. The recognition of religious value requires a level of understanding way beyond the simple joys of an embodied sentient being. It requires intimate understanding of hope, fear, despair, and trust, experienced within a complex social and cultural context. The level of understanding required in the case of human persons presumes much more. Understanding the mere act of stopping to say a short prayer at a roadside shrine as a religious act is no simple matter. (However, this is not to say that enjoyment cannot be a form of religious experience. We will return to the topic of enjoyment towards the end of this section.)

---

[11] From *Zhuangzi*, the Chapter, "Autumn Floods" ("Quishui" 秋水), Trans. Roger Ames, in Ames 1998, p. 219.

What do we say in response to the question, "What is the basis of your claim that you've recognised another culture's religiosity or religious values?" For a start, we might respond by appealing to Zhuangzi's reply: the question presupposes that it is reasonable to speak of someone's religiousness from another culture or practice, in fact, we do not dismiss the question as nonsensical. This certainly involves a charitable attitude, but it also requires an awareness that what may initially look similar might be due to our own expectations and values, and our understanding of another culture is in need of careful observation and continual adjustment. And isn't that sufficient basis to begin our investigation?

What follows is an attempt at articulating a sense of religiousness on the terms of Confucianism.

Let me begin with the bound compound that is used in modern Chinese to render "religion", "*zongjiao* 宗教", which is borrowed from the Japanese "*shūkyō*", a bound term coined to convey the Western understanding of the term.[12] "Religion", as such, is not a concept familiar to the Chinese, and together with other neologism such as, "*kexue* 科學" for "science" and "*zhexue* 哲學"for "philosophy," they were introduced into the language in order to facilitate China's understanding of the West. Nevertheless, the term "*zongjiao*" itself is not completely novel; though mined by the Japanese for the modern use, it has deep roots in the Buddhist world. Originally it meant "the teachings of the Buddha and those of his followers or sects".[13] In some circumstances, it could also mean "teachings of a (Buddhist) sect".[14] It is not difficult to see why "*zongjiao*" was chosen to convey the sense of teachings that applies to traditions beyond Buddhist sects. Also, it is interesting to note that in current Japanese usage, the term can connote the sense of a sectarian or dogmatic teaching that involves a hint of exclusiveness.[15] While it is not clear if the sense of "religion"

[12] See Anna Sun's sociological study on Confucianism, especially Sun 2013, p. 23ff.

[13] According to the dictionary, *Ciyuan* 《辭源》, the term "*zongjiao*" first appeared in Buddhist writings to differentiate the teachings of the Buddha (*jiao*) from those of his followers (*zong*). When appearing together, "*zongjiao*" means "the teachings of the Buddha and those of his followers or sects"; i.e. the sum total of Buddhist teachings. On the other hand, the Buddhist scholar, Wu Rujun 吳汝鈞 also mentions other usages of "*zongjiao*" in the Buddhist world. He locates the term in other writings of Chinese Buddhism, in which *zong* refers to the schools or sects of Buddhism, and *jiao* to the dissemination of their teachings. Furthermore, Wu also identifies other usages, in which *zong* refers to that which cannot be spoken of (*prasiddhi*); and *jiao* as the attempts at communicating the unsayable. In view of this, it seems that we need to be careful about the more intuitive reading of *zongjiao* as "sectarian teachings".

[14] According to the *Encyclopedia of Chinese Buddhism* (*Zhonghua fojiao baikequanshu* 中華佛教百科全書): "或指一宗之教為宗教, 如《佛祖統紀》卷二十九有「賢首宗教、慈恩宗教」之說."

[15] "To use *kyō* [教] in *shūkyō* [宗教] suggests a Japanese impression that the Western concept of 'religion' is more about doctrine or creed than practice… The term '*shū*' suggests a discrete religious community with common practices and teachings. In fact, the term '*shūkyō*' was not truly a neologism. There was a rather arcane Buddhist use of the term to mean specifically the doctrines of any particular Buddhist sect or school. Given this etymological context, to inquire in Japanese whether someone is 'religious' (*shūkyōteki*) may seem a little like asking them if they are 'sectarian' or 'dogmatic.' In choosing such a word to designate 'religion,' the scholars who created the neologism might have been thinking of the evangelical and exclusivist aspects of the Western religions they have encountered…" – Kasulis 2004, pp. 30–31.

being sectarian in nature dominates modern Chinese usage of the term, the contemporary debate in China on whether Confucianism could be classified as a "*zongjiao*"[16] seems to suggest that the Chinese too tends toward a sectarian interpretation of the term. In any case, the use of "teaching (*jiao* 教)" as one part of the term, *zongjiao*, to translate "religion" ensures that it is not necessarily understood in terms of belief or faith. If the following understanding of religiousness in Confucianism gains acceptance, then not only the Western usage of "religion" but the modern Chinese usage of *zongjiao* would also require revision.

Another issue concerns the status of Confucianism as a "religion". In Anna Sun's work, *Confucianism as a World Religion,* she distinguishes various aspects of Confucianism: as philosophy or a School (*Ruxue* 儒學, *Rujia* 儒家), as a religion (*Rujiao* 儒教). I will not be making such a distinction in this essay. Rather, I am treating Confucianism as a religious tradition. This is partly because it is misleading to speak of Confucianism as a self-consciously organised religion in the modern sense: while there might be a part of Confucianism that fitted the term, it was only one recent moment in its long history.[17]

In anticipation of the discussion that follows, I seek to show that central to Confucianism is something other than a concern with belief. In contrast to Christianity, which – as we have seen in Charlesworth's paper – tends to be expressed in terms of belief and faith in God and Revelation, I suggest that Confucian religiousness ought to be understood differently. It has more to do with human attainment understood in the context of ritual and cultural forms: becoming human, and creating the community that enables such an attainment is the main religious project. Furthermore, it is accompanied by a set of attitudes and values which could be generally described as spiritual or religious: namely, a more expansive sense of self, gratitude for life, and the centrality of the ordinary.

In *Analects* 12.1, Confucius' most loved student enquired about the way to become human:

> Yan Hui asked about becoming human (*ren* 仁).[18] The Master replied, "Through disciplining oneself and returning to ritual propriety (*li* 禮) is the way of becoming human. If for the

---

[16] See Anna Sun, "The Confucianism as a religion controversy in contemporary China", in Sun 2013, pp. 77–93.

[17] The idea of a Confucian religion, in the Western sense of the term, began as a movement or a series of movements in the early twentieth century China. One of the earliest attempt was Kang Youwei's formation of Kongjiaohui 孔教會 (The Confucian Church) (my translation), and his attempt at enshrining Confucianism as China's state religion in the constitution of the newly formed Republic. (See Sun 2013, pp. 42–43.)

[18] There is a variety of possible rendering for *ren* 仁: "perfect virtue" (James Legge), "humanity" (Tu Wei-ming), "benevolence" (D. C. Lau), "noble" (A. C. Graham), "authoritative conduct" (David Hall and Roger Ames), "total virtue" (Robert Eno), and so forth. Rather than adopting one of the foregoing, I propose that *ren* necessarily involves a certain conceptual vagueness. Moreover, the term is mainly used evocatively in the *Analects*, and therefore analytical strategies which typically seek to obtain a precise, unequivocal, universally applicable description of the term would be, at best, limited, or at worse, misleading. Instead, I propose that the translation of the term ought to retain an imagistic quality, which in this case is that of the human. This I hope to elaborate in a forthcoming work.

space of one day you can do this, then the whole world will be moved by your having become human. Becoming human begins with oneself, how can it originate from others?"

On the one hand, this passage could be taken as a superb expression of a particular brand of humanism, and is therefore non-religious insofar as it does not mention God or any plane of existence that is specifically other-worldly. On the other hand, if one follows the argument of Herbert Fingarette (1972), then Confucius' instruction on the importance of adhering to ritual propriety could be understood to be of great religious significance.

Fingarette's argument is twofold. First, it is a reflection from the power of ceremony or ritual, which he describes as "magical". Fingarette's understanding of the "magical" is related to how ceremony can be effective in the ordinary and everyday; it is a power that is derived from the performative aspect of ceremonies. (Although Fingarette references J. L. Austin (Fingarette 1972, p. 11), their respective points on the performative are related but distinct.) This is most clearly brought out in his consideration of everyday rituals.

Even in day to day rituals, with the appropriate words and gestures, people can be moved to return a greeting, or carry out a request or suggestion without the need for coercion. For Fingarette, such are the "magic" of ritualised interactions within a civilised community. And I would add, for the Confucians, such everyday rites form a continuum with the more solemn rites, such as marriage, funeral, state sacrifices and so forth. For them, rites and ceremonies are the mark of a civilised community.[19] It is also true to say that the power of ritual is well understood by the Confucians[20] who were experts in ceremonies and rites. Significantly, it is with Confucius and his followers that the term *li* 禮 has expanded in usage, from the original sense of solemn ceremonies and rites to encompass those ritualised interactions of the everyday variety we've just noted, and further to include a more abstract notion of ritual propriety. As such, Confucius' philosophy of *ren*, understood as the teaching on how to become human, is best understood within the context of ritual performance. Furthermore, according to Fingarette:

> In general, what Confucius brings out in connection with the workings of ceremony is not only its distinctively human character, its linguistic and magical character, but also its moral and religious character.[21]

---

[19] There is a question regarding how ethnocentric is the Confucian understanding. How accepting is the Confucian of other cultures? C.f. *Analects* 14.17: Confucius was reported to have praised Guan Zhong for his work in ensuring that the Chinese culture is intact.

[20] The proper Chinese term for the Confucians is "Ru 儒".

[21] Fingarette goes on further to say, "…to act by ceremony is to be completely open to the other; for ceremony is public, shared, transparent…. It is in this beautiful and dignified, shared and open participation with others who are ultimately like oneself… that man realizes himself." (Fingarette 1972, p. 16)

However, the "magical" effects of ritual alone does not necessarily entail a religious attitude.[22] For that matter, neither is ritual, strictly speaking, "unique to religious institutions or traditions" (Bell 1997, p. 164.)

The mention of "religious character" in the foregoing quotation brings us to the second part of Fingarette's argument. In Confucianism, through ritual cultivation, a person can become so thoroughly imbued by ritual propriety that their life can serve as, metaphorically speaking, a ritual vessel; that is to say, they can become an essential ingredient in the performance of community, itself understood as the enactment of a holy ritual. Viewed this way, the life of a civilised, human community could be understood as a religious event. In Fingarette's words, "Human life in its entirety finally appears as one vast, spontaneous and holy Rite: the community of man. This, for Confucius was indeed an 'ultimate concern'; it was, he said, again and again, the only thing that mattered, more than the individual's life itself"[23] (Fingarette 1972, p. 17). Understood so, one can make better sense of the words from *Analects* 12.1 quoted previously: "If for the space of one day you can do this, then the whole world will be moved by your *having become human*" (emphasis added). Put another way, it is only from a religious perspective that one can truly make sense of *Analects* 12.1.

Moreover, it's important to note that the notion of "human" here is not ontologically fixed – i.e. it is not the case that the human be ontologically dependent upon a transcendent reality or deity; there is no divinely ordained hierarchy of existence. Yet, neither is the human necessarily divine. Humanity is experienced as a historicised, socialised, embodied event, and it is therefore conditioned. But the human's potential for self-creativity and for affecting their circumstances is unbounded. Theistic religions tend to emphasise the limited nature of human existence, and therefore religiousness is experienced as a transcendence through connection with a reality that is greater than s/he is. Humanistic religious traditions such as Confucianism emphasises human possibilities. Therefore, their sense of religiosity is developed through expanding one's humanity that becomes increasingly inclusive of other people and the world, with whom they are in ever greater and deeper relationships, resulting in a greater capacity to create and nurture. We see this in the

[22] There is a relevant discussion in Catherine Bell's "Characteristics of Ritual-like Activities", Chapter 5 of *Ritual: Perspectives and Dimensions* (Bell 1997, pp. 138–169). Important to this discussion that surveys different ritual activities across cultures is Bell's conclusion, which states "However, the examples of ritual-like activity suggest that what goes on in ritual is not unique to religious institutions or traditions…" (p. 164).

While one accepts Bell's view that the scope of ritual covers a broad spectrum, from religious to the secular, and that it is multi-faceted, complex and context dependent, it remains the case that what is most distinctively religious in Confucianism is best considered within the context of ritual performance. Moreover, a narrow construal of "religion" in Western theistic understanding is an obstacle to proper understanding of Confucian values.

[23] The notion of "ultimate concern" is normally associated with the work of Paul Tillich. In his book, Fingarette simply mentions this notion without attribution. My thanks to an anonymous reviewer for pointing this out.

Chinese practice of divinising cultural heroes, as well as their vision of the human in partnership with the natural creative and nurturing forces of the cosmos.[24]

Yet, one cannot become human without reference to other people. In fact, for there to be rites at all, an entire community is implicated: the life of a person dedicated to ritual propriety can only make sense within the context of lives in community. In connection with this, the Confucian Xunzi, who lived some two hundred years after Confucius, sees the very founding of a community, and the establishing of social order and its maintenance, to be a project of utmost importance. Xunzi, in keeping with the teachings of Confucianism, seeks to establish a social order that is based on the model of ritual performance. It is an aspect of cultivation that is often referred to as "outer kingship".[25] In other words, it is the world-engendering and world-ordering work that was begun by the sage kings which is to be continued and maintained by those who would follow the Confucian way. Perhaps this could be viewed as a missionary aspect in Confucianism. It is not, however, the sense of mission construed narrowly as the proselytising activities of zealous adherents; rather, it is a mission that involves the realisation of a civilised world that makes possible and facilitates the emergence of sagely persons.

Moreover, Xunzi's philosophy is motivated by a concern to achieve harmony among the various participants of the world, human and non-human, through the establishment of a ritual order. Such a project culminates in the inclusion of the natural world, expressed by the vision of the human forming a triad with the heavens and the earth (*yutian di san* 與天地參).[26] Through such a vision, the function of the rites become more lofty: it is the way that allows humans to create for themselves a niche within the world, framed by the heavens and the earth. In other words, the ritual order is the condition that would enable humanity to realise our destiny (*ming* 命) as the ritual regulator of the world, a destiny not preordained but one that we humans have created and need to continue to realise for ourselves.

Apart from this grand vision, there is also a personal dimension to cultivation, which further enhances the understanding of religiousness in this tradition. Briefly, there are three important themes:

1. A more expansive sense of self

An important religious value found in many religious traditions is the shifting of perspective, sometimes called "conversion" or "repentance", from that of a

---

[24] "Being capable of aiding the transformation and nurturing of the natural world, then they are able to form a triad with *tian* (the heavens) and the earth." – *Zhongyong* 22.

[25] The chapter "Below in the Empire" in the *Zhuangzi* contains a well known four-character phrase that describes the way of the ancients, reckoned by many as an apt summary of the philosophical theme of early Chinese thought – namely, "*neishengwaiwang* 內聖外王", which is rendered by A. C. Graham as "inwardly a sage and outwardly a king." So widely accepted is the phrase that it has become a common parlance, and Confucians of later periods saw no problem in adopting it as a general characterisation of Confucian cultivation.

[26] The term "*san* 參" translated as "triad," literally means "three." Thus, the expression "*yutian di san* 與天地參" is understood to mean forming a party (or partnership) of three with *tian* and the earth.

self-interested, narrow minded existence to that of a more expansive way of being such that one's concern becomes transformed and elevated.

Such an understanding is particularly pronounced in the teachings of Mencius, for whom the project of becoming human is understood as an attempt to lead one's inchoate self to becoming the great self, accomplished through heartfelt commitment in one's primary relationships. The process begins with seeking one's heart that has strayed (*qiufangxin* 求放心), followed by maintaining (*cunxin* 存心) and nurturing it (*yangxin* 養心), and finally, it is given full expression in being utterly engaged (*jinxin* 盡心).

For Mencius, the four interpersonal affective responses (sympathy, shame, deference, and discrimination) are key to achieving the great self of the Confucian sagehood, which is characterised by benevolence, integrity, propriety, and wisdom. It is Mencius' understanding that those simple, emergent, affective responses correspond to, and are continuous with, the sagely qualities. Thus, cultivation is understood as a non-coercive tending of those "four emergent shoots" to becoming the qualities of the sagely person by informing and transforming the nature of their interactions and relationships.

The Chinese philosopher, Xiong Shili, when commenting on another key Confucian text, the *Great Learning* (*Daxue*大学), states:

> …the cultivating of the person is the root.[27] Those who are noble honour their persons and cultivate themselves by blending together the inner and outer.… The family, state, and world are my person.… Petty persons do not know that the scope of their personhood is so vast that nothing is beyond it, but selfishly take their body to be themselves.[28]

2. Gratitude for life

Confucian spirituality is realised in a profound sense of gratitude, especially with regard to the gift of life. Concretely, this finds expression in filial conduct towards one's living parents and the offering of sacrifices to one's deceased forebears. From the Confucian perspective, the practice of sacrificing to the ancestors is not precisely based upon a belief in the supernatural existence of ancestors with powers to affect the living. Neither is it precisely to do with a sense of commemorating their great deeds. Certainly, if one's ancestors had been important personages in the past, it would certainly contribute to the reason for honouring one's ancestors, but far more important is the expression of gratitude to one's roots, no matter who they

[27] Xiong Shili is referring to an explicit statement in the *Great Learning* (*Daxue*大学) regarding cultivating the person: "From the Son of *Tian* to the common person, all accept the cultivation of the person as the root. It is not the case that the tips can be in order when the root is in chaos. There has never been the case in which those who are more intimate suffer neglect while those further away enjoy favour. This is called 'understanding the root'; this is called 'the arrival of understanding.'" (「自天子以至於庶人, 壹是以脩身為本, 其本亂而末治之者否矣。其所厚者薄, 而其所薄者厚, 未之有也。此之謂知本, 此謂知之至也。」)

[28] 「(八條目雖似平說。其實,) 以脩身為本。君子尊其身, 而內外交脩。…家國天下, 皆吾一身。…小人不知其身之大而無外也。則私其七尺以為身。」 – From Xiong Shili熊十力,《讀經示要(上冊)》, 2nd ed. (台北: 明文書局, 1999 (1945)), 頁199–200.

were, great or small. Wei Zhengtong 韋政通 in expounding on "ancestor worship", offers the following explanation:

> …the reason for sacrificing to the ancestors is because they are the source of our lives. Because the ancestors are the source of our lives, we must requite our roots, and we must recall our beginnings. To recall our beginnings is to not forget the origin of life; to requite our roots is to not forget the beneficent gift of life.[29]

This practice of honouring the ancestors are then extended by the Confucians to include one's living parents. It involves a kind of gratitude that is not conceived as a response to benefits received, either from one's ancestors or parents, living or deceased. Such a kind of gratitude needs to be understood as a religious attitude.

Rush Rhees, in an article entitled "Gratitude and ingratitude for existence" (Rhees 1997, p. 159), seeks to contrast moral considerations with religious considerations in certain situations, such as in response to the question, "Is life worth living?" (Rhees 1997, p. 160) And examples of possible approaches of answering that question through moral considerations are: "by considering the amount of good and the amount of evil in our lives and around us; by considering what we can expect; by considering the value of endurance and courage even in defeat; by examining the judgement that everything is futile; and so on" (Rhees 1997, p. 162). In contrast, there is another kind of answer for which the foregoing considerations are irrelevant. Answers of the latter kind, whether in the affirmative or negative, are best understood as expressions of gratitude or ingratitude to existence, and Rhees thinks that they are religious in tone. This is because such expressions cannot be derived from moral considerations.

3. The centrality of the everyday

The work *Zhongyong* 中庸, first collected in the *Book of Rites* (*Liji* 禮記) and later singled out to form one of the Four Books by the neo-Confucians, identifies a term that expresses another main theme of Confucian religiousness – "*zhongyong* 中庸", which could be rendered as "centering oneself in the ordinary." The conventional rendering of "Doctrine of the Mean"[30] does not do the term justice. In the work, "*zhongyong*" is then further complemented and elaborated by the term "*cheng* 誠", though the meaning of "*cheng*" is so broadly construed that it is difficult to be rendered in a unique translation except to say that it spans the spectrum that covers the following senses: being true to one's commitment and circumstances, reflecting transparently and candidly one's feelings and thoughts, and being wholehearted in one's engagement with people and the world.

Moreover, it seems that the teachings on *cheng* 誠 in the *Zhongyong* might be helpful in understanding the process by which a person can attain the great self of the noble person. In fact, the *Zhongyong* explicitly suggests that *cheng* is the very

[29] 「…人所以要祭祖, 是因為祖為我們生命的來源。因為祖為我們生命的來源, 所以必須報本, 必須復始。復始者, 不忘生命之原始; 報本者, 不忘其給予生命之恩。」 – Wei Zhengtong 1993, p. 547.

[30] C.f. James Legge's translation, "The Doctrine of the Mean", in his *The four books*.

process by which one achieves profundity in cultivation. As a religiousness that is not conceived in terms of relationship with the divine, *cheng* appears to be the process that replaces the role played by divine guidance and grace in the pursuit of becoming human.

A person can become great by working on what is originally ordinary and everyday. A truly evocative description about this process is found in the following passage:

> Now the heavens (*tian* 天) begin with the accumulation of limited lights and culminate in being inexhaustible, enabling the suspension of the sun, moon and stars, and the sheltering of the myriad things. As for the earth, it is the accumulation of pinches of soil and culminates in breadth and depth; it supports Mount Hua and feels not its weight, accommodates the Yellow River and the sea without losing a drop, and carries the myriad things. The mountain is the accumulation of fist-sized stones and culminates in being wide and large for the growth of grasses and trees; it is the home of animals and the storehouse of precious minerals. It is the accumulation of water, ladle by ladle, which culminates in the unfathomable depths; it is the dwelling place of giant turtles and lizards, sea leviathans and dragons, fish and turtles, and it enables the increase of goods and wealth. (*Zhongyong* 26)

And "*cheng* 誠"is identified as the way that enables such a successful progression from ordinary to profound as described in the following passage:

> *Cheng* 誠 is the way of the heavens; realizing *cheng* is the way of the humans. As for *cheng*, it is to be effortlessly centered, it is attained without deliberation, and it is to be freely centered in the way. It is the sage. As for those who seek to realize *cheng*, they choose the felicitous and grasp it firmly. (*Zhongyong* 20)

And this quality of *cheng* is further elaborated as follows:

> Therefore, utmost *cheng* 誠 is ceaseless: Ceaseless then enduring, enduring then potent, potent then pervasive, pervasive then broad and thick, broad and thick then limpid and luminous. Being broad and thick, the myriad things are borne up; being limpid and luminous, the myriad things are sheltered; and being pervasive and enduring, things are brought to accomplishment. Broad and deep, it complements the earth; limpid and luminous, it complements *tian*; (and thus) it is pervasive, enduring, and without boundary. For those that are thus, they are not seen yet are manifest, they do not move yet changes occur, they do nothing yet works are accomplished. (*Zhongyong* 26, translation adapted from Ames and Hall 2001, p. 107)

This vision of becoming great through working on the ordinary is profound indeed.

Finally, working on the ordinary does not mean that following the way is a teeth-gritting, fist-clenching exercise in sheer determination. On the contrary, it is ultimately pleasurable. Hence, Mencius says, "There is no greater joy than discovering *cheng* upon self-examination." And we might add, perhaps it is not only the reflexive discovery of *cheng* that gives one great pleasure, but also that the very act of giving oneself over wholeheartedly to one's commitment that one is relieved of the kind of anxieties that plague the petty person, and thereby rendering oneself available to enjoyment.

Enjoyment has always been allied with music in the Chinese culture.[31] And music, in turn, is the counterpart of rites and ceremonies; for it accompanies and

[31] The *Book of Music* (Yueji 樂記) states: "Music (*yue* 樂) is enjoyment (*le* 樂)." The sense of this

enlivens their performance. More profoundly, Robert Neville notes: music is an outpouring of a way of life that is imbued with ritual sensibility (Neville 2009, p. 36).[32] Enjoyment is the proof of music well played and ritual well performed. It is also the fruit of a religious life well lived.

17.3 Acceptance of Other Traditions from a Confucian Perspective: What Happens When the Shoe Is on the Other Foot?

In keeping with Charlesworth's aspiration and invitation, I would like to end by considering briefly what Confucianism might do when encountering a religious tradition very different from its own; how might it respond to Charlesworth's questions: "How can a Confucian come to terms with the fact that there are other and different and incompatible religious systems in the world? What modifications in one's religious position as a Confucian has one to make in order to accommodate this fact?"

Historically, ever since the time of Confucius, the tradition that evolved from his and his students' teachings has always encountered other competing and incompatible traditions. First, there were Mohism and philosophical Daoism; and then later, Buddhism and popular Daoism. And there had been much interaction among them, often in contention as they vied for the hearts and minds of the people. At the same time, although each tradition has their own central concerns and key texts, and each contains a web of schools, movements and sects, the boundaries between them are not always distinct. This is especially the case with regard to membership of those traditions. Chinese persons often espouse multiple traditions. In part, this has to do with the lack of emphasis on belief and the lack of pursuit of clear articulation of teachings to the exclusion of others. More often than not, one could adopt different traditions according to one's life circumstances. It's not surprising that there is a tendency towards syncretism with regard to the three traditions. However, it is worth noting that such syncretic tendencies are not a necessary feature of the Chinese traditions. Rather, one might think of them as having to do so either out of political expediency or the demands of society. For the Chinese traditions, syncretism in part arose from the need of scholar-officials to get the emperor's ear – the composition of *Lüshi chunqiu* 吕氏春秋 as a syncretic Daoist work that unbashfully incorporates

statement on one level is a play on the character "樂", which, depending on how it is pronounced, could mean "music" or "enjoyment". On another level, the connection between music and the aesthetic enjoyment that is derived from the playing or listening of it is obvious.

[32] I would suggest that the significance of music goes even further. One could speak of a musicality in ritual performance that provides us with a nuanced way of articulating the quality of performances. In fact, the Confucian *ren* 仁 (being and becoming human) could be understood as the music of the great self. (See Wong 2012).

the thoughts of various schools, Confucianism included, is a case in point.[33] We see this also in the time of Jin 晉 and Song 宋 China, during which there was an increased tendency to emphasise the harmony of the traditions. This is represented by views such as "the three teachings are of the one family" (*sanjiaoyijia* 三教一家) or that "the three teachings are of the one source" (*sanjiaoyiyuan* 三教一源.)[34]

Obviously, the syncretic tendency in the history of Chinese traditions does not exemplify Charlesworth's understanding of "ecumenism" as articulated in Position 4. While people might have the capacity to recognise other traditions to be of the same family or source, Confucianism remains paradigmatic for the erstwhile Confucian; what does it have to say about the fact of there being other traditions?[35] This, I think, is a question to which Confucianism needs to respond. Furthermore, there is the question of how well the syncretic strategy will work for the more doctrine driven, and faith based traditions. It would seem that genuine acceptance of diversity is a notion that still awaits discussion and development.

Possible arguments for recognition and accommodation of other traditions as conceived in Position 4 could be found in teachings to do with two of Confucianism's most important terms: *li* 禮 and *ren* 仁. That is to say, one must accord whomever one comes into contact with every necessary courtesy and respect as required by the demands of ritual propriety and dedication to the project of becoming human – and more. This is clearly expressed in the following passage from the *Analects*:

> Zhonggong 仲弓 enquired about *ren* 仁. The Master said, "When away from home, treat others as if you are at home receiving honoured guests; when requiring service from commoners, treat it as seriously as if partaking the great rites. Do not apply to others what you would not want for yourself, then you will not incur resentment when in public office or at home." (*Analects* 12.2)

The foregoing passage situates the attainment of *ren* within the context of ritual propriety. It does so by taking the propriety of receiving honoured guests and participating in the great rites, and extending them to those who are not the usual recipients of those ritual practices. However, this is not so much the universalising of a ritual response to include everyone, but a requirement to continue to expand the circle of relatedness.

The expanding circle, given expression by the motif of family, finds its most expansive scope in the words of the neo-Confucian, Zhang Zai 張載:

> Creative Qian 乾 is my father and receptive Kun 坤 is my mother, and even such a small creature as I finds an intimate place in their midst. Therefore that which fills heaven and

---

[33] I am grateful to Karyn Lai for her pointing out that syncretism is not inherent to the Chinese traditions.

[34] The phrase, "sanjiaoyijia 三教一家", comes from the Daoist, Tan Chuduan 譚處端, 三教詩. And the phrase "sanjiaoyiyuan 三教一源" comes from the Qing emperor, Yongzheng 雍正. C.f. 「三教合一」 in Wei Zhengtong 1993, p. 82.

[35] Take for example, *Analects* 15.40, "People who have chosen different ways (*dao* 道) cannot make plans together" (道不同, 不相為謀). Trans. Ames and Rosemont. Here I understand "ways" to be the different religious or philosophical traditions.

> earth I regard as my body and that which directs heaven and earth I consider as my nature. The people are my brothers and sisters, and things are my companions. (Zhang Zai, *Ximing* 西銘, trans. Wing-Tsit Chan, p. 497, translation adapted.)

Yet, as grand and inclusive this vision of the cosmic family might be, one wonders if this is enough to accommodate religious diversity. It seems that this vision would face the same kind of objections raised against Rahner's "anonymous Christians". Would the Christian appreciate being considered a member of the Confucian family? We know that Rahner (and Charlesworth) would. But as we have pointed out previously, such visions do not preserve the values of other traditions. What does it say about the place of the ways and traditions of those who do not share the Confucian way?

Does the notion of religious diversity suggest for the Confucian that there could be more than one family? In which case, how would each family relate to one another (without an appeal to a higher order family that unites all)? Can the Confucians accept a world in which the ritual order admits of multiple centres? And what about religious traditions that are not concerned about ritual or propriety (or that becoming human is not the central concern)? Does Confucianism have the resources to recognise religious values in other religions on their own terms? How would Confucianism accommodate monotheistic faith? And what happens to authoritativeness of the Confucian way when it admits to a plurality of ways?

As Charlesworth has pointed out in his discussion of Position 4, in order for there to be recognition of other traditions, there needs be a willingness to change, to modify one's view about the world, to include what is valuable in other traditions within one's own. I think we now recognise that most religious traditions in the world are dynamic and changing. In fact, a number are adept at incorporating their oppositions' strong points into their own – something that the various Chinese traditions have also done in the course of their long history. For example, the development of the notion of *li* 理 (pattern, coherence) in neo-Confucianism is a result of assimilating Buddhist metaphysics; the development of Zen Buddhism stems from incorporating Daoist and Confucian philosophies – such as the Daoist notion of spontaneity, and the Confucian emphasis on the significance of the everyday; and popular Daoism's promotion of morality, such as filial piety, that is a direct result of absorbing Confucian values.

However, this doesn't necessarily translate into amicable acceptance or tolerance of each other, nor admission of mutual influence. While on the level of the individual, it might be possible to espouse more than one religious tradition, it does not mean that the traditions themselves are accepting of other traditions. It is important to note, by acceptance, we do not mean wholesale agreement with other traditions. Rather, it is to take other traditions seriously and to take them as dialogue partners with whom insights might be found. For this to happen, it also must be possible to disagree with one another. In this sense, one wonders about the mutual critique and rivalry that existed over the centuries among Confucianism, Daoism, and Buddhism. At what point are they disagreeing meaningfully, and when are they deliberately misconstruing each other's teachings? I think it would require a close study of specific cases for there to be clarity.

Let me end with a passage from the *Analects* that speaks of the importance of enquiring about the ways of conducting onself in a place, even if one is fully familiar with them. Respect is a requirement of ritual propriety:

> When Confucius visited the grand ancestral temple, he would enquire about every matter. Someone said, "Didn't they say that the son of the man from Zou village knows ritual propriety? Yet when he visited the ancestral temple, he enquired about every matter." When the Master heard about it, he said, "It is ritual propriety." (*Analects* 3.15, adapted from Ames and Rosemont).

The respect of ritual propriety goes beyond respect for the individual; it includes the details of the customs of their place. And I would argue that such a sense of respect needs to be accorded to those from a different tradition. This too is ritual propriety.

The requirement for respect finds corroboration in the final item of Charlesworth's Credo for the believer when faced with religious diversity; respect is the ground upon which understanding among religious traditions can be built:

> I believe that respect for, openness to, and dialogue with, other religious traditions, must be part of any authentic religious tradition. (Charlesworth 1997, p. 50)[36]

References

Ames, R. T. (1998). Knowing in the Zhuangzi: "From here, on the bridge, over the River Hao". In R. Ames (Ed.), *Wandering at ease in the Zhuangzi* (pp. 219–230). Ithaca: SUNY.

Ames, R. T., & Hall, D. L. (2001). *Focusing the familiar: a translation and philosophical interpretation of the Zhongyong*. Honolulu: University of Hawaii Press.

Bell, C. (1997). *Ritual: Perspectives and dimensions*. New York: Oxford University Press.

Chan, W-T. Translator and Compiler. (1963). *A source book in Chinese philosophy.* Princeton: Princeton University press.

Charlesworth, M. (1995). Ecumenism between the world religions. *Sophia, 34*(1), 140–160.

Charlesworth, M. (1997). The diversity of revelations. In *Religious inventions: Four essays* (pp. 23–50). Cambridge: Cambridge University Press.

Fingarette, H. (1972). *Confucius: The secular as sacred.* New York/Hagerstown/San Francisco/London: Harper & Row.

Joy, M. (2004). Philosophy and religion. In P. Antes, A. W. Geertz, & R. R. Warne (Eds.), *New approaches to the study of religion (Volume 1): Regional, critical, and historical approaches* (pp. 185–217). Berlin/New York: Walter de Gruyter.

Kasulis, T. (2004). *Shinto: The way home*. Honolulu: University of Hawaii Press.

Legge, J. (?). *The four books*. Shanghai: The Chinese Book Company.

Neville, R. (2009). *Ritual and deference: Extending Chinese philosophyin a comparative context.* Albany: SUNY.

[36] See also the end of the chapter, "Religion and Religions", by Paul Rule in this volume.

Rhees, R. (1997 (1955)). Gratitude and ingratitude for existence. In D. Z. Phillips (Ed.), *Rush Rhees on religion and philosophy* (pp. 159–165). Cambridge: Cambridge University Press.
Sun, A. (2013). *Confucianism as a world religion: Contested histories and contemporary realities*. Princeton/Oxford: Princeton University Press.
Wong, P. Y. J. (2012). The music of ritual practice – An interpretation. *Sophia, 51*(2), 243–255.

References in Chinese

Xiong, Shili 熊十力. (1999 (1945)). *Dujingshiyao*《讀經示要》. 2nd ed. Volume 1. Taipei 台北: Mingwen Bookshop 明文書局.
Wei, Zhengtong 韋政通. (1993). *Zhongguozhexueqidian*《中國哲學辭典》. Beijing 北京: Shuiniuchubanshe水牛出版社.

Peter Wong has a long association with *Sophia* as a book reviews editor among other roles. He is a graduate of the Philosophy Department at the University of Hawai'i. His research interests include the religiousness of pre-Qin Confucianism, ritual studies, and the philosophy of religion. He currently works at the Chinese Studies Research Centre at Latrobe University.

MIX
Papier aus verantwortungsvollen Quellen
Paper from responsible sources
FSC® C105338

If you have any concerns about our products,
you can contact us on
ProductSafety@springernature.com

In case Publisher is established outside the EU,
the EU authorized representative is:
Springer Nature Customer Service Center GmbH
Europaplatz 3, 69115 Heidelberg, Germany

Printed by Libri Plureos GmbH
in Hamburg, Germany